CLERGY
DESK
BOOK

6/90

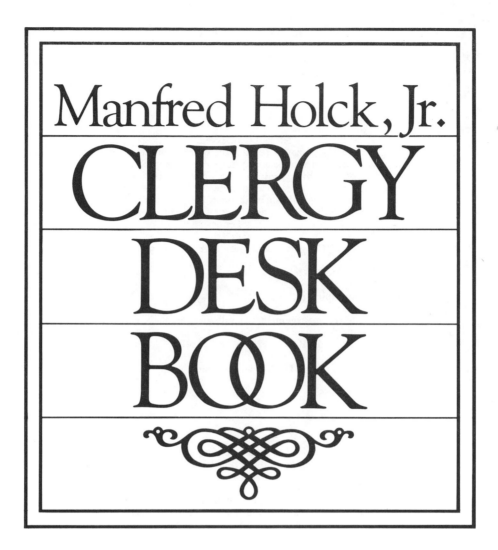

Manfred Holck, Jr.

CLERGY DESK BOOK

Second Edition

ABINGDON PRESS
NASHVILLE

CLERGY DESK BOOK

Second Edition

Copyright © 1990 by Abingdon Press

Copyright © 1985 by Abingdon Press

Library of Congress Cataloging in Publication Data

HOLCK, MANFRED.
  Clergy desk book.
  Bibliography: p.
  Includes index.
  1. Church management—Handbooks, manuals, etc.
  I. Title.
  BV652.H56   1985   254   83-24540

ISBN 0-687-08658-2

MANUFACTURED BY THE PARTHENON PRESS AT
NASHVILLE, TENNESSEE, UNITED STATES OF AMERICA

To
my wife,
Lois—
A Partner
in Ministry

CONTENTS

THIS IS A book for parish pastors—busy, active, aggressive clergy who are looking for new ways to provide effective leadership for their congregations.

It is a book about managing the church, about clergy managing their congregations. It comes out of my experience as both pastor and parishioner. It is the result of more than twenty-five years in ministry in a variety of roles—parish pastor, college administrator, church pension plan executive, magazine publisher, writer, and lecturer. It is the way I think a congregation should be and can be handled by the clergy leader.

This is a book of ideas, many ideas, varied ideas. Some are better than others, of course, but I have tried to share with readers those plans, programs, ideas, worksheets, guidelines, outlines, and thought stimulators that I believe to be significant for ministry. Here's a brief synopsis of the thirteen chapters in this book:

A considerable wealth of information is offered here beginning in chapters 1 and 2 with a discussion of the concept of the pastor as manager and leader of the congregation. In chapter 3 staff relationships, staff support, staff effectiveness are seen as what makes the difference in how well that management is achieved. Without staff support the mission will be encumbered; with staff support a lot can be done.

Volunteers are the very crux of the life of any congregation. In chapter 4, I describe how volunteers can be catered to in such ways that all those people will make a big difference in how effective the ministry of the congregation will be. Well-motivated and organized volunteer leaders will do wonders for the life of the church.

Chapter 5 offers a variety of exciting and creative ideas for developing all kinds of useful programs within your congregation. Property, equipment, and groups must be maintained, not by the pastor, but by responsible committee persons. I explain why and how in chapter 6. Communications between pastor and members and between members (discussed in chapter 7) is crucial to effective fulfillment of mission.

Without adequate compensation, the paid staff cannot function. That's the point of chapter 8. And church finance and recordkeeping are essentials for the well-managed church program, as described in chapter 9.

My hearty thanks to Ashley Hale, managing partner of the Church Development Center in San Jacinto, California, for preparing chapter 10 on fund raising and stewardship. Hale is a regular contributor to *The Clergy Journal* magazine and a successful counsellor and fund-raiser for churches.

More and more churches are going to do their work with computers. A beginning knowledge of what's involved and how to organize the church to consider getting a computer are described in chapter 11.

Without members there is no church. See chapter 12. Cultivating, nurturing, and caring for the membership is a top priority item for the parish pastor.

Finally, churches pay taxes. Chapter 13 describes which taxes churches pay and how.

It is impossible to express adequate thanks to all those people who have contributed to this volume. Many are the members of my congregations over the years whose ideas have found their way into this book. Church leaders and fellow parish pastors from all over the country have exerted an influence on what I have written. To them all I offer my thanks and appreciation.

Special help has come from the Reverend Delmar Dolton, pastor emeritus of Holy Cross Lutheran Church, Yoakum, Texas; the Reverend Dale Peterson, pastor of St. Paul Lutheran Church in Farmers Branch, Texas; the Reverend Richard Jessen, pastor of First Lutheran Church in Cedar Rapids, Iowa; and the Reverend Ross W. Marrs, pastor of First United Methodist Church in Bloomington, Indiana.

I especially want to thank Dr. Lowell R. Ditzen, Emeritus Director of the National Presbyterian Center in Washington, D.C., for his influence on my professional career. His books, his friendship, and his meticulous concern for the details of church administration have been especially inspiring. I am deeply indebted to him for his leadership and assistance.

But mostly, I am grateful to my wife for her patience—often sorely tried—whenever I have been with a book. This one is no exception. The time spent in research, writing, typing, editing, and typing again (all on computer!) is precious time spent away from family. I regret that time lost but am grateful for the opportunity to be able to share with others this ministry. That ministry will now go on in the printed pages, while my time is devoted more resolutely to my first love.

Manfred Holck, Jr.
Winter 1985

CHAPTER 1

THE MINISTER
AS MANAGER, LEADER,
ADMINISTRATOR

W HO RUNS THIS church, anyway?" It was an offhand remark made in a passing comment by church council member Lew Harris. The pastor of St. Timothy's had decided a pilot project was needed to minister to the low-income neighborhood kids. With seed money from interested members, the pastor had already hired a young woman, fresh out of college with a degree in sociology. But the first Lew Harris knew anything about the program was when the new staff member reported to the church council.

"Doesn't anyone make decisions around here except the pastor?" That was Sally Simpson speaking up. Lew was not alone in his bewilderment at this independent staffing decision by the pastor. Sally and Lew both thought the pastor should have consulted the council, laid out the job responsibilities and program objectives, interviewed other prospective applicants, and sought advice from the lay leaders about this whole thing.

"What we need," mused Sally, "is a personnel committee, to hire and evaluate. But even before that, someone needs to decide where this congregation ought to be going and who's going to run the show."

Over at St. John's, down the block, no one cared about the neighborhood. So many members lived out in the suburbs now that the neighborhood was unknown to them, feared for its potential crime possibilities more than sympathized with for the plight of its people. Sunday worship was the only activity for most members, with the pastor spending endless hours over commentaries and lexicons in his study at home in order to write the perfect sermon for these people. No one seemed to care about anyone else or really even about what the pastor did or did not do.

At least at St. Timothy's someone (the pastor) cared and someone (the pastor) took action. At St. John's nothing happened. Yet both were being managed because both were in existence, both were still there, both had members, money, and buildings, a heritage, a location, and a pastor.

No matter the program or lack of program in a church, no matter the channels followed or ignored, no matter who takes notice, asks questions or doesn't, all churches are managed. All congregations have a manager. And almost without exception, the chief administrator in every congregation is the pastor.

A business the size of a church cannot function without a leader. And the leader must always be the manager. Whether the pastor likes it or not, wants it or not, does it well or not, every pastor is a church administrator. Some are obviously much more competent than others, but every one of them is an administrator—a manager of the congregation for which they are also spiritual leaders.

Lowell Ditzen was absolutely correct when more than two decades ago he wrote in his *Minister's Desk Book* about the variety of interests, activities, and financial matters of the local congregation: "In meeting these needs, the minister cannot evade the role of the chief administrator of his church related to every aspect of the congregational life."

The minister *is* the chief administrator of the church. He or she is the manager, the one who must be capable of organizing and executing the programs of the church, discovering the needs, and preparing the best ways to meet those needs. The pastor must then also implement and direct the effort required to meet the opportunity and challenge to minister.

The minister who manages well will be certain that relationships between people remain harmonious and that proper regulatory procedures are approved and used to guide the common life of the congregation.

Pastors in tune with their communities know far better than anyone else in the congregation the many questions, problems and opportunities that confront the people. The pastor knows best the complex and changing conditions of the neighborhood and surrounding community. Indeed, the pastor is in a unique position to influence the life of the congregation toward meaningful ministry in a way unmatched by any other member of the church or of the staff. The need for capable, intelligent, sensitive administration of the local congregation's total life demands the best possible leadership. The pastor is in that place, like it or not.

Pastors make many decisions as they manage. Sometimes they get approval, sometimes they just act, often they are criticized. But they do manage either way, right or wrong.

Of course others manage, too. In smaller congregations volunteers take on assigned responsibilities. In larger congregations, paid staffers with expertise in needed areas are hired to carry out the ministry in specialized ways. Like a fine orchestra, the pastor is the conductor, carefully guiding all these people with all their varied skills and responsibilities into a symphony of harmony that fulfills the mission of the church.

And some pastors manage better than others. Administrative skills must be learned. They require practice, attention to the tasks at hand and considerable study. Clergy who are unwilling to learn how, reluctant to manage, delegate, and plan, will not be able to administer. Ministry requires skills in Greek translation, bible interpretation, social awareness, interrelationship spontaneity, and excellent preaching skills. But that is not enough where programs must be developed, budgets built and raised, buildings maintained, and a staff kept informed and occupied. The pastor must also be a trained and competent administrator. The life of the church will depend on that skill.

Skill Development

Thus, clergy concerned about their own management skills may want to look around at what others are doing, how their peers manage, how successful churches are being led. Except for learning from peers, one of the most effective ways to develop administrative skills is to observe lay members of the church—by seeking them out and asking for help, trusting them for their competence and professional expertise. After all, business leaders, corporate executives, and public officials have achieved the respect of the community and their colleagues through their ability to deal with people, develop new ideas, and handle a multitude of complex situations. They are successful administrators. Clergy will do well to listen to them.

Educational courses can also be helpful in developing or improving administrative skills. Community colleges offer courses in basic managerial skills. A few seminaries, although far too few, offer elective courses in management techniques and administrative skill development. Without adequate training, clergy quickly discover limits to their ability to manage a new congregation, even though their preaching skills are fine-tuned and well-honed.

A few key lay leaders can prove to be an especially valuable learning group. Sensitive clergy can test out their new ideas on these trusted leaders. Are these leaders impressed? Is their reaction favorable? Will the idea fly? Touching base with these trusted friends can avert errors in judgment and provide potential support for controversial programs. Where loving respect and mutual trust are cultivated, the practical wisdom of effective administration can be learned from these nonministerial colleagues.

Administrative skills are cultivated by careful development of those techniques that best search out the facts, explore the possibilities, and reserve judgment until an informed decision can be announced. Exploring the opportunities, evaluating the situation before and now, contemplating the impact on events yet unknown, and just avoiding snap decisions or independent actions is a learning process toward development of better management skills. "Seat of the pants" administration works sometimes best for the disorganized pastor because it is better than nothing, but planned administration offers the minister an opportunity for more acceptable and effective ministry. When people understand, when they are involved, when they experience careful planning, their response to management will be supportive and popular.

Good administrators work well under pressure, neither crumbling nor flying off the handle. Calm reassurance, careful response, and a sympathetic ear can provide opportunity for an aggressive program or decision not otherwise popular or liked. Anger, obvious resentment, shouting, tears, undeserved criticism can all set back dramatically what may have otherwise been possible under a more subdued and loving response.

In times of excitement, the minister's competent administrative attitude will come through loud and clear. Knowing the facts always strengthens a position and lessens tensions. The careful administrator does his or her homework and remains prepared, ready for the onslaught of those who would tear down and destroy programs, people, and ideas so strenuously supported by the leadership.

And isn't that precisely where prayer and meditation become a minister's chief allies? Seeking strength from the Almighty, remaining close to Jesus, and putting confidence in that trust will assuredly give strength to the pastor to quiet troubled parish waters. This strength can also help the pastor promote potentially controversial programs, assuage the fears of frightened, orphaned children, calm the anguished cries of those who suffer without cause or purpose, or listen quietly to the needs of those who hunger, who are threatened, beaten, depressed, or forgotten. Church administration is not all business—it is also caring and loving, praying and hearing.

The pastor-administrator undoubtedly will be thoroughly familiar with constitution, bylaws, regulations and past actions of the church, but will also be understanding, sympathetic, and loving, too. The ideas are not antithetical. They are compatible in the life of the pastor who is chief administrator—manager of a congregation. The pastor who manages will not ignore one to the exclusion of the other, but in all humility will strive to exemplify the presence of Jesus Christ in making administrative choice—decision and pronouncement.

Lowell Ditzen, pastor emeritus of the National Presbyterian Church in Washington, D.C., and author of two extensive books on church management, summarizes the administrative role of the minister as both "servant" and "leader":*

> The officers and lay leaders of the church will look to the minister for ideas and will consider with care the recommendations he will make for the development of the congregation. The minister will seek to be wise as the serpent and as harmless as the dove. The minister will "listen" as much as speak. Having a conviction about democratic processes and the importance of each individual's outlook and experience, the minister will consider with respect the thoughts and evaluations of others.
>
> The minister will be free from pique and hurt feelings when proposals made may not be accepted.

---

*From the book, *Minister's Desk Book* by Lowell R. Ditzen, © 1968 by Parker Publishing Company, Inc., West Nyack, N.Y., page 10. Used by permission.

The minister will enlist others when a matter of major importance is to be presented to the Official Board, so that prior evaluation can be given to the matter and support has been gained when the matter is presented for group consideration.

The good administrator will see that all those who are related to a project or a program are adequately informed.

The good administrator involves as many people as possible in the cause and the programs which he supervises. The minister will be aware that all individuals are sensitive, and that every person wants to feel important. Therefore, the understanding minister will give continuous encouragement and prompt and warm expression of appreciation for able work done in the service of the church.

Perhaps the key to the great administrator is found in the frequency with which he seeks to unlock the doors to the presence of God and the guiding spirit of Jesus Christ. As the minister does this, his heart and mind are strengthened with the humility and wisdom that exposure to such perspective and grace alone can give. Cultivating those graces, the minister will be one to radiate breadth and harmony and joy. The minister's spirit will cause others to be free from "littleness" and narrow self-interest. Objectivity and the excitement that come in working for a cause that is greater than one's self begin to permeate the Official Board and the entire parish. There then come high direction and blessing to all.

Principles of Management for Ministry

Management, someone has observed, is nothing more than getting things done through people. Clergy, of all the professionals, constantly deal with all sorts of people and, therefore, should be best at management. In truth, they may be worst. For clergy deal with a lot of people, but not for getting things done, rather for doing things for people. Nevertheless, the effective ministerial manager will gather together those people—as staff or volunteers—through whom things will get done for the building of the kingdom.

Techniques and principles of management for ministers are not really any different than they are for any manager and are just as important as they are for any administrator. Consider the following:

Setting objectives

Every task must be defined and understood, at least implicitly if not specifically. If you aim at nothing, that is precisely what you will hit. Without objectives—written, clarified, debated, and understood—church leaders will surely wander and meander, heading off only into uncharted waters of distrust, uncertainty, criticism, and problem creating. To avoid all this, there must be direction, a goal, a sense of purpose, and statement of mission.

Certainly the Scriptures are central in the life of any congregation. Adherence to the Word, acceptance of it, and worship of God Almighty become the sensitive guides to developing objectives for outreach, worship, and education in the life of the congregation. Our objective is also to reach, teach, and touch people, to provide worship, to admonish and love the erring, to challenge each other to a greater witness in stewardship and proclamation. To proclaim and to reach out become important objectives of the church manager.

Adherence to the approved constitution of the denomination, as well as the local church, sets the tone for satisfying the underlying requirements of this first principle.

Response—responsibility

So what does God want the church, you, or the pastor to do? To be in church at worship time and carefully perform once more the ritual that has no variation or change or enthusiasm? Hardly. More. Our response is a continuing responsibility for all the people committed to reaching and touching people with the gospel through worship, teaching, outreach, and visits. The ministry is the proclamation of the gospel. Our responsibility is to proclaim.

14

Someone gets the job done. The official board, tutored by the pastor, determines the objectives of the church. Each level of leadership, each committee, adopts its own objectives, determines the activities needed to carry out that goal, and assigns responsibility to persons to get the job done. And the job is then done, not by a pastor impatient for a committee to act, but by assigned people, people with good communication and effective relationships, people with authority to act. Everyone—volunteers, board members, staff—and not just the pastor, is responsible for determining congregational objectives and then seeing to it that they are carried out. The manager of all that—the pastor—coordinates, administers, manages.

Unity

Unity is not union. In management, unity is the act of cooperating in getting the task done. It is not holding hands to show a oneness in the spirit. To achieve stated goals, the members of the organization must work together. Some actions are far more important than others. To major in the minors devastates church growth and mission.

Who cares, for example, what color the drapes are in the parsonage master bedroom? (The pastor's spouse, who else?) But what about the hungry vagrant squatting outside the church door? Who cares if the hymnals are all tidy and square in the racks? But what about the Oriental family two blocks down the street that has no heat on a cold January day? If certain action is required to get a job done, managers will recruit all necessary groups to work in accomplishing the goals, solving the problem, or finding some space heaters (and letting the pastor's spouse worry about bedroom curtains!). A church gets things done when it purposes to work—not at odds or singly—but together to do the thing *needed* doing. The pastor will delegate, manage, and administer until the matter is done.

Simplicity

The acronym KISS—keep it simple, stupid—is an apt if crass reminder that tasks kept simple are more likely to be done, that assignments simply stated are more likly to be completed, and that delegation of responsibilities simply described are more likely to be fully understood.

Complex organizations are confusing and often ineffective. To be understood and effective, the church must retain simplicity of organization. All leaders and no followers never gets the job done.

The people

Every congregation consists of people. Without the people there is no church. "Where two or three are gathered together in my name," said Jesus. People do the work in the church. And the pastor is one of those people, too. So is the official board, the staff, and every other member on the rolls. Even the people who are not yet on the rolls are the people of the church, too.

But in order to manage the church and the people who must do the work to get the job done, responsibilities must be assigned by the manager. The assignees must do the work. Some people can do one job, others something else. Effective church staffing includes well-trained key personnel. A church's strength often rests with its staff and pastor. These people, properly trained, administer the program, do the tasks, and produce the results. They share the load, are committed, are trained administrators and managers—the pastor is the leader.

Delegation

Pastors who cannot delegate authority cannot manage effectively. A committee charged with responsibility must have the authority to command—to act and to make decisions. Nothing happens if the committee cannot decide without pastoral approval and action. A pastor who must do it all has not learned to delegate authority nor acknowledged his or her physical inability to do everything. Clergy tend to be workaholics when they cannot delegate or let others do the job. So what if the chairs are not properly aligned some Sunday morning? Better to be with family than lining up chairs. So what if the air conditioning is not turned on soon enough to be comfortable on Sunday morning? Next time it will be a concerned property committee chair person, under pressure to do it right, who will get it done, not the pastor.

But unless authority is delegated along with the responsibility assigned, nothing will happen. Most pastors fail to delegate authority for fear they will lose control. But one person or only a few cannot and should not do everything in the church.

Supervision

Managers supervise. They must supervise to be certain assigned tasks are being completed properly, on time, accurately, and as expected. Assigning a responsibility and then forgetting the people involved is foolish administration and bad stewardship. A manager knows what staff, volunteers, or committees have done or plan to do. All staffs need guidance to accomplish their group's objectives. Getting the job done in the chuch requires supervision from people who then become more effective servants. And that is also a good stewardship of people. For the clergy, that is good management by minister-managers.

Control

Too many clergy try to supervise too many people, too much staff, and too many committees. It can't be done effectively. The span of control that a pastor can manage is limited by the skill and capacity of the pastor, by the latitude of supervision by the pastor (a close watch or no watch), by the nature of the church, and by the type of supervision expected by the official board. Too many people cannot be managed. A proper span of control for pastor or other manager enhances ministry.

A Job or a Role?

Is the Minister-manager's Function a Job or a Role? Is It to Be or to Do?

Lyle Schaller responds to that question in "Job or Role? To Do or to Be?" from *The Clergy Journal:**

"Our first task is to draw up a job description for this new position of associate minister," declared Herb Adams, as he chaired the first meeting of the newly constituted pastoral search committee at Trinity Church. "After we agree on the job description we can begin to build a list of candidates for the job." This marked the beginning of the process as Trinity Church sought to move from several decades with only one pastor into a new era in which that congregation would be served by two ministers.

"When Harold Anderson came as our new minister back in 1973, it seemed to all of us that it was an easy transition, even though he followed a fifteen-year pastorate," reflected one of the leading lay persons at St. Paul's Church. "When he left in 1980, while we all hated to see him go, we assumed that it would be easier for someone to follow a seven-year pastorate than to follow a minister who had been here for 15 years, so we anticipated another easy transition. We sure were wrong! Even though he was an excellent pastor, Harold's successor experienced so much dissatisfaction that he resigned after less than three years, and now we're back to looking for a new minister again. I can't understand what happened."

"Perhaps I can offer a partial explanation," suggested a staff member from the denominational office. "Harold's predecessor concentrated most of his time and energy on four roles here at

*Reprinted from *The Clergy Journal,* September 1983. Copyright 1983 by Church Management, Inc. Used with permission.

St. Paul's—preaching, administrator, teacher and builder. During those 15 years you experienced two very successful building programs as well as several hundred excellent sermons.

"When Harold Anderson came as your new minister, he greatly expanded the number of roles he filled. He served this congregation as preaching teacher, administrator, pastor, cheerleader, confidant-to-persons-with-problems, shepherd, chief evangelist, reconciler, innovator, celebrant, tribal leader, father figure, counselor, fund raiser, mediator and lover. He filled all the roles his predecessor had filled, except builder, and by the time he came, you needed a fund raiser, not a builder. In addition, he filled a dozen other roles, and these were mostly relational or people-centered roles, such as counselor, pastor, lover, shepherd and reconciler, that had been vacant for 15 years. No wonder it was such an easy transition!

"When Harold left, you called a new minister who filled four roles, teacher, pastor, preacher, and theologian-in-residence. The role of administrator was vacant for the first time in at least 22 years. All of those relational roles such as friend, counselor, shepherd, lover, reconciler, pastor, mediator and confidant that Pastor Anderson filled so well for seven years were left vacant. Almost as serious, those leadership roles of cheerleader, tribal leader and innovator also were left vacant when Harold's successor was called. Some of us were a little surprised he lasted 33 months."

These two incidents illustrate a point that often is overlooked in parish life. There is a vast difference between a job, which is represented by the verb *to do* and a role, which is represented by the words *to be*. The calling of a minister is to a vocation in which the primary emphasis is on the role of being and a secondary emphasis is placed on the job of doing.

The importance of this distinction for both the clergy and the laity can be lifted up by four examples.

Recent years have brought an increasing demand for a systematic and regular evaluation of the minister's performance. All too often the basic approach for these efforts has been to attempt to prepare a job description outlining what the pastor is expected to do, prepare criteria for measuring the level of performance and develop a procedure for matching performance against the expectations contained in the job description.

The central flaw in this business-like procedure is that a minister is called first to be and secondly to do. Instead of thinking in terms of a job, it is more appropriate to think in terms of a role, or more precisely, a number of roles.

If and when a parish decides to create a process for the evaluation of the pastor, the focus should be on that word *role*, rather than on a job description. One beginning point might be to list all the roles that need to be filled. Which ones can and should be filled by lay volunteers? Which ones match the gifts and talents of the current (not the previous) pastor? Which ones can and should be filled by someone else on the staff, such as the church secretary? Which are the most important roles for our current pastor to fill? What are the tradeoffs?

A second fallacy in many of the current efforts at pastoral evaluation is the assumption that a single system will fit all congregations. For example, in thousands of smaller parishes the people place a high premium on such relational roles as friend, shepherd, lover, model-of-a-committed-Christian and confidant. By contrast, in many very large congregations there often is a widely-shared expectation that the senior pastor will excel in such functional roles as preacher, administrator, teacher, celebrant, organizer, and community leader. The ranking of the importance of various roles often must be adjusted to fit the personality and needs of a specific parish.

A third limitation of current evaluation efforts is an indirect result of the past. We now have a reasonable level of competence in evaluating the performance of a person in a job such as typist, plumber, accountant or barber. We have yet to develop an equivalent level of competence in evaluating the performance of a person in a role such as friend, father, wife, lover, husband, mother, counselor, reconciler or shepherd. Thus we are tempted to attempt to use criteria and procedures developed for evaluating job performance to evaluate role fulfillment. Frequently that will not work.

A second example of the value of this distinction is in the calling of a new pastor. Which roles did the predecessor excel in as pastor? Which roles were largely unfilled by the predecessor? What are the priorities on roles that we see for the next pastor? What will be the response of the members if the next pastor does not fill some of the roles that were filled exceptionally well by the predecessor, but that the pastoral search committee now identifies as low priorities for the next pastor? Will someone else fill those roles? Who? If not, what will be the probable consequences?

Likewise, the committee responsible for filling the newly created position of associate minister at Trinity Church would be well-advised to think in terms of roles rather than to attempt to prepare a job description for that new position. What are the roles not being filled by the current pastor that need to be filled? Which ones could be filled by lay volunteers? Which ones should be filled by the new associate minister? What roles should be at the top of the priority list for the new associate minister?

A Church Constitution and Bylaws

A sample congregational constitution and bylaws that can be adapted for use by any church group is available from the Board of Publication of the Lutheran Church in America, 2900 Queen Lane, Philadelphia, Pa. 19129. Ask for the "Approved Constitution for Congregations."

Included in the complete sample congregational constitution are the following topics:

Preamble
Article I—Name and Incorporation
Article II—Confession of Faith
Article III—Congregational Function
Article IV—Relation to the National Church Body
Article V—Membership
Article VI—The Pastor
Article VII—Congregational Meetings
Article VIII—Elections
Article IX—Church Council
Article X—Officers
Article XI—Organizations within the Congregation
Article XII—Discipline of Members
Article XIII—Bylaws and Amendments

CHAPTER 2

MANAGING THE CHURCH: ITS ORGANIZATION AND STRUCTURE

THE CHURCH'S PROGRAM simply cannot proceed without competent administration. And the chief administrator in every congregation is the minister. Yet, organization charts have little meaning unless the chief administrator is properly trained and able to direct all of the programs, budgets, and properties of the congregation. Church organization is not only a chart. It is a chart that comes alive by the way in which the administrator administers.

Too often clergy are not properly trained in seminary to administer. Church administration is often learned on the job. And by the very nature of the job of being pastor, what seems an inordinate amount of time for administration is a necessity. Pastors must administer, like it or not, trained or not. If somehow all clergy could have a meaningful, intensive course in practical church administration, struggling young clergy would be better able to relate the primary business of the church with the need for mundane church administration tasks.

No one questions that the church's business is spiritual; it is not business, at least not primarily. But in the process of being spiritual the church must conduct its business efficiently. Otherwise, even the spiritual purpose may be forgotten. Sound theology not only affirms the spiritualness of the church, but also affirms that the will of God should be done efficiently and in good order when fulfilled in the congregation.

Church administration is an inescapable necessity. After all, churches do have land, buildings, money, organs, furnishings, vehicles, kitchens, and equipment. The program of the church includes Christian education, weekday schools, neighborhood outreach programs, worship services. Responsible stewardship of the rich resources of a congregation—abilities and talents, money and property—requires careful, efficient, and aggressive church administration skills.

Caring clergy relate to the needs of people. Sensitivity to those needs, however, requires competent administration if those needs are to be satisfied. There is no escape from the obvious—a competent administrator must be responsible for overseeing the variety of needs, programs, and resources of the typical congregation.

The minister is the prophet, the priest, the executive, and the resource leader of the church, assisted by a variety of competent and dedicated volunteers. The spiritual and the material combine in that leadership to fulfill the stated mission of the church.

Every Member an Involved Member

"Who's in charge here anyway?" John Thompson was a new member of the parish, but he kept getting mixed signals about who was really in charge. It seemed the pastor made all the decisions, hired all the staff, and retained veto power over every committee decision. Yet, an official board was regularly elected and installed, committees met, and matters seemed to move smoothly.

But a recent meeting of disturbed members suggested all was not well. "The pastor's too autocratic," complained Susan Smith. "He rejects suggestions that do not match his ideas."

"He hires and fires and asks no one if he can or should. Sure the staff is great, but why was the part-time pastor dismissed last week? Something wrong?" asked Sam Brown. He obviously didn't know.

"My committee has come up with some dandy ideas for church programs, but the pastor insists on doing what he wants done. Our committee plans are often torpedoed by his veto." That was Leon Jones' assessment of the current problems.

One principle of successful administration is to include every member in the life of the church's activities. Churches that operate on democratic principles allow the members to share in the decisions and the implementation of programs. Leaders keep the members informed of policies and programs, seeking their reaction and their support. Domination by the pastor or a lay leader will be avoided in those congregations that seek to include every church member.

"Who runs the church?" should be answered simply and plainly—the people run the church. But the pastor and key lay leaders share in the administration. The pastor is administrator, but the members are involved in those congregations where good administrative techniques are followed.

Participation in the life of a congregation begins with baptism. At that moment the person (child or adult) becomes part of that fellowship, a "participating" member of the church. Not only is the Sacrament an acknowledgment of acceptance into the kingdom, but it is also the beginning of a long relationship that brings member and church together in a variety of programs, activities, and experiences. Reception of the child into active, adult membership is a moment of significance as that member now becomes acquainted with and involved in leadership opportunities. Every new member, every confirmed member, every person formally received into the membership should come in with an understanding of what the church is all about. Contact with peer groups of similar age and interests should be offered. Challenge to participate in fellowship, in education, Christian service should be regularly announced. Lay participation in the life of the church begins when members are *challenged* to share with others their lives, their resources, and their enthusiasm for the gospel.

Domineering leaders do not cultivate relationships to church life that are meaningful and useful. *Sharing* leaders challenge each member to share, to lead, and to participate.

But participation in the life of the church is not limited to doing things. It is also a matter of helping members to stay close to one another, to know each other—to feel wanted, needed, and important. Acknowledgment of birthdays and anniversaries, recognition of work done, achievements accomplished, or milestones reached keeps members in touch with others and helps them know they are a wanted part of the group.

The Pastor Is the Leader

Someone must lead. That is a fundamental principle of good administration. The answer to "Who's in charge here?" is probably the pastor. Indeed, a strong church organization depends on the strengths and weaknesses of the pastor as leader. There is no choice.

Thus, the apex of the church administration pyramid, says Lowell Ditzen, is the minister who must be the "servant in the role of administrator. With humility, docility, and a kindly interest in each parishioner and his service in the church, the minister needs to be familiar with all aspects of the church life. No detail of the care and fabric of the church, no aspect of financial life, and no phase or activity of the church program will be outside his concern."*

---

*Reprinted with permission of Macmillan Publishing Company from *Handbook of Church Administration*, page 5, by Lowell R. Ditzen, © Lowell R. Ditzen, 1962.

But the pastor is not dictatorial nor pawn. The pastor leads. The pastor listens. The pastor shares. The pastor administers. The pastor seeks the advice of associates and of members before making recommendations for action. The pastor accepts criticism—the pastor listens and learns; he or she is a leader, standing firm on conviction, leading out of strength, dedicated to the gospel, attentive to the lay leaders, receptive, free of pride or resentment—a spirit of love and humility and service to others.

Have you ever noticed that those congregations that seem alive and vibrant, active and aggressive are congregations with a goal? And how is that goal achieved? By leaders committed to planning. The good administrator has a vision, and that vision is shared, infused, promoted, explained, and kept front and center.

The minister must be the leader closest to the action, operations, and tone of the church. It is he or she who paints that vision, says Lowell Ditzen, and inspires the congregation to find the best, positive way to make the picture. But visionaries do not by themselves make effective church administrators. Clergy with vision must also be able to implement those dreams.

Procrastination in relationships will do a pastor in more quickly than a bad sermon. "Do it now" gets things done now, not later. Again, a word of appreciation, and acknowledgment of the anniversary of a death, a special birthday, a contribution to the church—all of these build bridges between pastor and people. Loving attention, courtesy in conversation, a listening ear, careful response to needs and actions stimulates member support. The vision is achieved by careful, immediate attention to the needs of the people.

There is no one set pattern of time management that will be effective for all clergy. No one can tell the pastor exactly how much time is needed or when sermon preparation should be done, marital conferences held, administrative duties done, hospital visits made, or other calling done. Each of us has a responsibility to evaluate primary responsibilities, abilities, and emphasis. Careful adherence to routine is vital for successful time management.

Many clergy insist that they cannot plan their time because of the innumerable and incessant daily interruptions. Nevertheless, a careful outline of the day's proposed activities will help get the job done even in the midst of constant interruption.

One pastor I know develops a daily plan of "things to do." The list is organized from most-important to least-important or sometimes from least-liked to best-liked. As the day progresses, items completed are checked off. Interruptions may slow down getting the job done, but not the order. Eventually, then, all is accomplished. Incompleted tasks become the first tasks for the following day.

Settling first on jobs that are not particularly liked gets them out of the way. Clergy who dislike writing letters and prefer study for preaching, should get all correspondence done first thing, then reserve time later to do the pleasant tasks of sermonizing.

Some clergy are "early persons," functioning best in the early hours of the day. Other clergy are "night people," getting into full swing only as the sky darkens. Knowing when work is done best, clergy should schedule their intensive work accordingly.

One senior pastor insisted that all staff people keep a time log of all their activities for one month. Each day those staff persons could evaluate precisely how their time was spent and note the time wasted and the tasks undone. Professional persons, such as attorneys and accountants, regularly keep a daily tab on how each fifteen-minute block of time is spent. That is essential for billing clients for time spent. Perhaps clergy should maintain the same discipline, not for billing out their time, but for recognizing their stewardship responsibility of time and effort on behalf of the congregation.

It goes without saying that the pastor's time must be carefully organized around family and personal needs as well. Workaholic clergy will have personal problems with children and spouse sooner or later. In fact, careful time management begins with the family, not the church. It begins with clergy and spouse sharing in the planning of life. Too often clergy offer counseling advice to young couples about family budgets, sexual relations, spiritual life, but neglect their own wives or husbands, fail to pay bills, and never pray. Those who teach must also do.

21

Careful planning of time includes time for family. Careful planning of resource management involves family, too. Spouse, clergy, and children are all dependent on intelligent, careful, and shared planning of limited clergy incomes. Since spending always rises to the level of one's income, it frequently makes little difference how much income the pastor receives (if it is fair and reasonable) somehow it never seems to be enough.

In the management of family resources, therefore, frugal living or a change in one's standard of living may be required of clergy. Generous pay increases can be a temptation to spend more rather than an opportunity to save more. Yet, additions to salary can often be carefully set aside, saved in part, and later used for some special project or pleasure. Limited incomes require careful management. Constant complaining about not enough to make ends meet may suggest poor management and unreasonable spending goals, not inadequate salary.

Developing a careful family budget will help in making do with limited resources. Clergy simply cannot expect to maintain the same standard of living as many of their members, and they certainly shouldn't try. Families who are forever trying to "keep up with the Joneses" never succeed, but often go bankrupt in the process. The "Joneses" are always a step ahead. Frustrations over unpaid bills and overdrawn bank accounts are eliminated with careful administration of resources.

Perhaps less can be spent on movies, less on eating out, less on pop and snacks. Frittering away loose pocket change is expensive. Walking rather than riding, limited magazine subscriptions (the library has them anyway), a smaller automobile, omission of cigarettes, liquor, even expensive foods cuts costs dramatically. Clergy families who cannot make ends meet should review one of the various resources listed elsewhere in this book. My book *Making It on a Pastor's Pay* offers many specific suggestions for clergy on spending less and maximizing their own available resources.

The bane of many clergy's successful administration of the church's programs is still the constant interruption that interferes with planning times for personal devotions, visitation, counseling, marriages, conferences, sermon preparation. Yet, the skilled administrator who has planned will be able to counter those interruptions more effectively. Instead of controlling the pastor, the pastor controls the time more efficiently in spite of those interruptions.

Managing time is, however, only one aspect of efficient management. Organizing the way in which tasks are done is equally essential.

Indeed, the good church administrator has a workshop where the work of planning and doing ministry is well-organized. Every pastor has a library. But many libraries are in such disarray that much time is wasted looking for appropriate materials. A little time spent to organize books by subject matter or call number will save countless hours of searching. A system is important. The workplace must be arranged in an organized manner if it is to be used efficiently.

Some clergy maintain sermon illustrations from their readings on 3 × 5 cards. One of my seminary professors had thousands of such cards filed by topic that contained illustrations gleaned over fifty years of reading. Complete information about source, author, volume, date, and page was always entered on each card along with the illustration. Many clergy today can clip and file specific illustrations published by various authors, such as Clyde Chesnutt's *Windows of Truth* newsletter of illustrations. Using a computer rather than 3 × 5 cards offers a modern technique for efficient maintenance of an illustration file.

The well-organized pastor also puts desk, typewriter, file cabinets, and telephone in efficient positions to avoid motion time-wasters. Up-to-date files offer a handy resource of current material. Desks piled high with files and papers do not suggest an organized office. Yet someone has observed that a clean desk suggests not enough work, a full and cluttered desk too much work. Some people do equate a cluttered office with hard work and the spic and span place with low initiative and not enough work. Nevertheless, I am convinced that many well-organized pastors do keep their desk tops clean just so they can get more work done!

Well-organized sermon files facilitate research and avoidance of repetition. Chronological files perhaps offer the best cross-reference. And, of course, a computer listing of sermon titles, topics, and text will pull up at a moment's notice whatever sermon is needed.

Appointments are still another matter. Timeliness in keeping appointments is imperative. It is absolutely inexcusable to be late without the courtesy of a call to apologize for a delay. A competent secretary can keep appointments on schedule. Desk top calendars are useful, but I have always found a pocket appointment book the most helpful. That way, no matter where I am—at home, in my office, traveling—I know what's coming up and when it is coming up. I can make commitments on the spot. I can plan other events best when I have in my pocket every commitment for the near future.

Some clergy find a daily card helpful on which the pastor or secretary has listed the day's appointments. Steven Fleming's "Daily Organizer," as described in *The Clergy Journal*, is the best I've seen. (See pages 24 and 25.)

The Official Board

The minister is the chief administrator, but participatory administration in a church involves all the members. Efficient administration, however, generally limits the actual leadership to a few elected persons. This is the Official Board, Vestry, Church Council, Session of the church. This is the group that leads, motivates, implements, and ends up doing most of the work. It is also where the "buck stops." Any organization using democratic principles will select some of their group to run the show at the pleasure of the total membership.

An official board is the Board of Directors. They are the trustees authorized to make policy decisions and govern the affairs of the church between congregational meetings. The number of people varies by tradition. But every group has a president or presiding officer (often the pastor), vice-president, secretary, and treasurer. The officers may also be the executive committee.

The activities of many congregations are controlled by a book of discipline adopted by the denomination. Other congregations are controlled by constitutions approved by denominations.

Officially, therefore, either by discipline or constitution, an official board is established and continued according to set procedures. Complete explanations of the functions of the official board are given in these documents.

The official board is responsible to the membership, having received its authority from the congregation. It is accountable to the congregation for all its actions. To fulfill that responsibility the official board must organize itself and then report its actions to the congregation just as the pastor should report his/her actions to the official board on a regular basis.

Thus, the official board may organize itself in the traditional committee format representing the basic program ministries of the church. Of course, additional committees may be appointed from time to time to meet certain specific additional tasks.

For example, committees may be needed to organize the youth work, or develop internal communications networks, fellowship opportunities, memorial gift opportunities, a five-year long-range plan.

All committees are important for the life of the congregation. How well they function will be reflected in the members' attitudes toward their church. Committees are committed to finding ways for a church to advance its goals. A pastor that dominates the committee decision-making process will disrupt the usefulness of the committee and frustrate the members. Committee members serve when they believe their suggestions are taken seriously by the pastor and the official board.

An official board does not act unto itself in an ivory tower of defiance. Members of the board must be willing to listen to those who elected them. Sometimes official board meetings are open to the congregation, which gives everyone a chance to be heard. Committee members must then be sensitive

NOTES: _____

_____

_____

_____

_____

_____

_____

_____

_____

_____

_____

_____

MILEAGE: *begin*_____ *end*_____

*Reasons for trip:*_____

_____

_____

_____

Total Business Miles today: _____

DAILY ORGANIZER   DATE _____

THINGS TO DO TODAY!

1 _____

2 _____

3 _____

4 _____

5 _____

6 _____

7 _____

8 _____

9 _____

10 _____

Page 4

Page 1

TODAY'S SCHEDULE & APPOINTMENTS

Bkfst _____

8am _____

9am _____

10am _____

11am _____

Noon _____

_____

1pm _____

2pm _____

3pm _____

4pm _____

5pm _____

Dinner _____

_____

7pm _____

8pm _____

9pm _____

10pm _____

EXPENSES TODAY: _____

_____

_____

_____

PHONE CALLS TO MAKE TODAY

Name   Phone number

_____

_____

_____

_____

_____

_____

_____

_____

_____

_____

_____

_____

_____

_____

VISITS AND STOPS TO MAKE: _____

_____

_____

_____

_____

_____

_____

_____

_____

Page 2   Page 3

25

to the stated concerns of duly elected representatives. The members want to know that the official board is keeping in touch with its constituents and has listened to their ideas.

Responsive leadership encourages communication between members and the official board. The board should explain to members making suggestions why their ideas were not adopted, offer opportunity for dialogue between committees and congregation, and most important, express appreciation to those persons who have been involved in church projects and ministries.

Your official board may be administered by any one of several styles from autocratic leadership to free-rein leadership. In one extreme the pastor runs the show and gets things done; in the other no one does anything—things just happen. Somewhere in between should be a happy medium.

The Division for Parish Services of the Lutheran Church in America, for instance, identifies six different ways in which an official board may function:
1. The official board plans and decides; the official board members implement.
2. The official board decides; committees propose and implement.
3. Committees plan and do; the pastor represents the official board.
4. The official board looks to the pastor for almost all decisions and actions.
5. The official board sets policies; the pastor informs and guides.
6. The official board oversees and funds; the pastor implements.*

But no official board acts in only one way. Truth is, on some issues, the official board does decide, on others the committees decide. Sometimes decisive action by the leadership will resolve the problem; other times a casual approach will be the better direction. Leadership styles vary and official board membership changes. Thus, official boards change, yet by whatever means they lead, communication with and involvement of the membership is crucial to a successful leadership style.

Which style is best for your congregation? That depends. Some will want to share; others will want to be told; still others will be decisive. But regardless of the style of leadership, the official board has responsibility for leadership—in other words, it must lead.

Who Are the Leaders?

It should be and is an honor to be elected to the official board of a congregation. But with that honor comes responsibility. The most effective official board leaders will be those with creative leadership abilities and a deep interest in the life of the church. Most official boards will function best with generalists. The special interest people can serve on committees of their interest.

But there are many types of leaders in a congregation. Yet, every official board must act as a body—sharing and cooperating. Each member is in partnership with the other. None can act independently of the group without violating proper and appropriate conduct. This is the management committee of the congregation. It must function as a committee, not as twelve separate decision-makers. Of course, each member makes a unique contribution, but it is still one body, one committee, one group acting for the whole.

The official board members agreed to be nominated and, if elected, to serve. With the honor goes the responsibility to serve, to act, to do—not passively, but actively, aggressively, intensely. The role of the official board member includes:
1. Commitment to the confession of faith of the church and a willingness to learn more about that church.
2. Commitment to attend all scheduled meetings, to make excuses for not attending, and to be active in the conversation of meetings.

---

*Reprinted from *Member of the Council*—A Church Council Guidebook, © 1982, Parish Life Press, Philadelphia, Pa., page 13. Used by permission.

3. Commitment to become well-informed on the issues, and to help, not hinder, the decision-making process.
4. Familiarity with parliamentary procedures.
5. Willingness to question and offer constructive criticism on actions that appear wrong.
6. Upholding strict confidentiality until issues are made public.

The official board plays only one role, but that role is critical toward getting the job done by helping the people to work together and resolving all the problems that are part of the life of any congregation. The official board is a team and must work like a team if it is to be successful.

Team building is accomplished by attention to detail, especially the setting of the meeting. Sit on comfortable chairs around a table facing each other. Be certain the lighting is good, temperature comfortable, ventilation good. Prohibit smoking. Use visual aids (chalkboard, etc.) to explain issues. Brainstorm together, divide into smaller groups, have individuals express their concerns, and evaluate the way the group makes its decisions.

With a slate of officers to lead—president, vice-president, secretary, treasurer, and committee chairpersons—the official board can act. Organizing committees assist in better administration. Careful consideration by the official board for all committee appointments is better than a free choice system by each chairperson. Committee appointments made simply on the basis of expressed interest may not create the strongest group to carry out the various goals and ministries of the congregation.

A job description for all staff persons is expected. Just so, each official board member should have a job description, too. People need to know what they are expected to do if elected to the job. Care must be exercised, however, because a job specification too complex will discourage prospective leadership. A job description too skimpy will not be helpful.

A job description tells what the job is all about, what is expected, what has to be done. A job specification lists the qualifications—education, experience, judgment, aptitude—of the person elected to the job. An official board should prepare careful listings for all officers and committee chairpersons. Good church administration requires a statement of expectations for those elected to lead.

Qualifications for Board Members

1. Active church member (confirmed or adult).
2. Leads exemplary Christian life-style.
3. Possesses leadership skills.
4. Accepts the teachings of this church.
5. Accepts the Scriptures as the Word of God and the norm for Christian living.

Responsibilities of Board Members

1. To attend all regular and special meetings of the board.
2. To assist the pastor in the care of the poor, the sick, the distressed.
3. To practice a generous stewardship of time, ability, and money.
4. To promote peace, unity, and purity within the church.
5. To promote brotherhood, fellowship, and loyalty among members of the congregation.
6. To explore new areas for Christian service and support.
7. To share regularly in the worship experience of this congregation.

Responsibilities of Officers (in addition to those of a board member)

1. President: to preside at all meetings of the board and congregation.
2. Vice-president: to preside at meetings of the board or the congregation when the president is unable to do so.

3. Secretary: to keep accurate minutes of all meetings of the board and the congregation, to serve as archivist for the congregation.
4. Financial Secretary: to keep records of all individual contributions, to report regularly to the board.
5. Treasurer: to keep financial records of the congregation, to receive and disburse all funds, to make proper payment of benevolence offerings to designated organizations, to report regularly to the board, to arrange for an audit of financial records.

Job description for committee chairpersons*

Responsibilities—
  prepare agendas
  arrange schedules
  help organize the committee
  lead meetings
  participate in group discussion
  work out differences
  bring discussion to conclusion
  present challenges
  persuade peers
  explain new plans and possibilities
  ask and answer questions
  relay messages
  review literature
  prepare reports
  follow up on committee actions
  counsel committee members
  consult with others, especially the professional staff
  attend the committee meetings
  represent the committee at council
Desired skills and interests—
  communicate effectively
  able to challenge and involve others
  listen with empathy
  sensitive to others
  get along with others
  make logical decisions
  able to read, write, analyze, interpret, and explain
  able to plan and present proposals
  have a special interest in the concerns of the committee
  be committed to the committee's cause
  willing to spend the time needed to chair the committee

How Do the Leaders Interact?

Committees do most of the work for any congregation. The official board appoints, assigns responsibilities, and expects an accounting. But committees function only as the official board gives careful instruction. Generally, the official board cannot do everything by itself. It must delegate work with the committees by:
1. giving careful directions.
2. appointing persons interested in that ministry.

*Reprinted from *Member of the Council*—A Church Council Guidebook, © 1982, Parish Life Press, Philadelphia, Pa., page 22. Used by permission.

3. giving complete responsibility to the committee for work to be done.
4. expecting results; the committee is appointed for a purpose, not just for the sake of meeting.
5. letting the committee decide and act within the guidelines given to the committee.
6. thanking participants.
7. seeking an evaluation from committee members on progress and results.
8. making the committee a true partner in ministry.

The pastor's relationship to the official board is important. In some congregations the pastor serves as the executive administrative officer while lay leaders serve as officers and chair the board meetings. In other groups, the pastor may be president of the congregation and chair all board meetings. Congregations faced with the choice of leadership style should make that decision prior to seeking a new pastor. Since pastors do have their own preferences, it is best for the congregation to review the advantages and disadvantages of the pastor's various possible roles without getting tied up with personalities.

Advantages when the pastor is president and chief executive officer:
1. more efficient administration by full-time staff person.
2. pastor can control the decision-making process more easily.
3. strong pastoral leadership can move the congregation ahead more effectively.

Disadvantages when pastor is president and chief executive officer:
1. pastor may dominate and control too much.
2. lay leaders are denied key leadership role.
3. ideas inconsistent with the pastor's plans may be ignored.
4. constructive criticism of pastoral leadership may be more difficult.
5. lay leaders may not know how or be willing to lead between pastorates.

But the relationship between pastor and official board must be one of partnership—not competition—of working together, not opposing each other. Consider:
1. Pastor Sam complains that no one does anything, that he is expected to do it all. "I don't understand," he grouches, "no one does anything. I'm supposed to mop the floors, set up the tables for women's meetings, type the bulletin, run the mimeo, mow the lawn, even put the flowers on the altar. I sweep the floors, clean out the hymnbook racks, open the church doors for every event, and turn off the lights. And then the official board expects me to be out calling at least four nights a week plus Saturdays. If I don't stick around from beginning to end for some member's wisdom tooth extraction, I'm criticized for not caring. All this 'busyness' is getting me down. I'm ready to quit. No one else does anything. They tell me what to do."
2. Pastor John also says the official board is a bunch of do-nothings. "I work hard at keeping this church going. Just look at the increase in offerings, the new members, church attendance, a new building. I did all that because no one else would." "And that's just the problem," chimes in board member Smith. "That pastor does everything. I can't do anything anymore. I'm not needed. Everything I once did is now done by the pastor." "I'm overworked," complains the pastor, "maybe I just ought to quit."
3. "This pastor makes all the decisions," complains board member Roscoe. "Of course, things get done, and no one seems to care. He's such a good guy that the milquetoast we have for board members just let him run all over them. He treats them like a bunch of kids instead of executives like they are. He rewrites all the annual reports, he tells the committees what to do (and vetoes any changes to his own plans), and he makes grand plans for programs and puts them into action without even asking the board. No one complains because the church looks successful. He runs the ship, twenty-four hours a day, seven days a week. Criticism is simply not tolerated."
4. "Everyone likes him," exclaims board member Allen. "That's because he's always buttering us up. He's so godlike and self-righteous, a father figure to anyone that wants him. And he's always

hugging everyone, like it or not. Birthdays are remembered, the old folks are made over like you wouldn't believe, and whoever he really likes gets their names in the newsletter most often. He plays the game to the hilt and then cannot understand why some people still don't love him when outwardly he seems to be sincere and dedicated. It's sick."

Membership in the church is a mutual mission of understanding and ministry. It is not the pastor's church; it is not the member's church. It is the church of all the people—working together in harmony, respecting each other, striving to build, witness, and share. Autocratic pastors (even when hiding behind their insecurity or contrived piety) do damage the same as domineering lay leaders who create havoc and drive out a good pastor-leader.

The professional leader should be professional. And the board members should complement that professionalism, not oppose it. Competence, theological training, knowledge of the church, and special training mark the pastor as the leader. But the lay people are there, too. Partnership in ministry is responsible leadership and administration.

The Agenda

A good official board meeting doesn't just happen. It is planned, starts on time, gets to the point promptly, offers opportunity for debate, and then ends at a reasonable time.

"They don't start on time anyway," complained Deacon Jones, "so I always arrive fifteen minutes late." Don't wait for latecomers. Begin at the appointed time. Soon everyone will show up on time because they know the meeting will start.

"Can you imagine? One hour to debate whether the sidewalk behind the parsonage needs repair?" Let committees handle routine maintenance. Concentrate board time on policy (keep the property in repair) not on the details (one square or two squares). Board time is too valuable to waste on trivia. So is the pastor's time!

"No one ever seems to know what needs to be done. Not once have I seen an agenda." Plan the meeting carefully. Propose an agenda, adopt it, and then stick to it. Random ramblings will quickly dampen leadership spirit.

"When Herman Schmidt starts on that treasurer's report, it'll be thirty minutes before he stops reading all the bills he's paid, what's still due, how much cash balance there is in every fund, and how the bank made a mistake and he found it." Write out reports, distribute before the meeting, ask for comments, and move on to the next item. Never, never read the bills paid or due to be paid because that's why the congregation approved the budget!

"Art Wagner is forever coming up with some off-the-subject comment and then the whole discussion strays." Limit discussion. Stick to the subject. Move decisively.

A good agenda provides for reports, resolutions, motions, assignments, appointments, reviews, and opportunity to approve or disapprove. Try this:

Agenda for Official Board Meeting

Call to order
Opening devotions, prayer
A learning opportunity
Roll call, minutes, financial reports
Communications
Committee reports, action
Unfinished business
Other new business
Announcements, assignments, comments
Date, place, and time of next meeting

Generally, who ever chairs the meeting is responsible for proposing the agenda. The pastor and lay leaders should consult on the agenda before the meeting. The board should approve. Set the order, specify beginning and ending times for the meeting, set debate time limits, set priorities of items, distribute agenda copies in advance, and monitor progress during the meeting.

Control and action can best be achieved by using parliamentary procedures within reason. Strict compliance to *Robert's Rules of Order* inhibits discussion. Action by motion offers yes and no choices. Decision by consensus can avoid complicated parliamentary snarls. Indecision can be resolved by referral.

Proposals for board action are probably best made by committee leaders, not by the pastor or staff. Careful minutes—a record of actions—should be completed without exception. Distribution within a few days to the board permits prompt review of actions taken and a reminder of assignments. Minutes distributed just prior to the next meeting are generally ineffective for follow-through action.

Boards that fail to communicate their actions are regarded with suspicion. A brief report should be put in the next newsletter after the meeting. Talking to persons especially affected is good. Letters can communicate actions taken. The minutes might be shared with any interested persons. Boards should not depend upon or trust the grapevine. Messages become garbled the third or fourth time around. Concerned boards might study resources on effective ways to communicate just to avoid possible misunderstandings.

The Organization

Many congregations prepare an organizational chart that shows the lines of relationship within the membership. Such a chart helps to show who is responsible to whom. And that is important. Without a chart some may believe they are responsible to the pastor, when in fact they are responsible to some other staff person.

When new board members are elected, the following service of commissioning would be appropriate:

A SERVICE OF RECOGNITION AND INSTALLATION OF MEMBERS OF THE OFFICIAL BOARD*

Instructions

1. If officers and board members sit at the front of the sanctuary, they can more easily step out as a group when called.
2. In the roll call of official board members and officers, the names of newly elected persons are called first, then the names of the continuing board members and officers.
3. When names are called, the persons should turn, facing the congregation so that the members will be able to identify each.
4. An appropriate theme might be the importance of volunteerism in the ministry of the church in the life of the community.
5. The statement of faith of the church, Apostles' Creed, or some other affirmation could be used appropriately as a part of this service.

---

*Adapted from a service prepared by Dr. John Thompson, emeritus pastor of the Congregational Church of Christ, Sarasota, Fla., and published in *The Clergy Journal*, May/June 1978. Used with permission. Copyright 1978 by Church Management, Inc., P.O. Box 1625, Austin, Tex. 78767.

Introduction

In the churches of our faith and order, much of the responsibility for the ministry of the church is entrusted to the laity. In like manner, this congregation, seeking the guidance of the Holy Spirit, has chosen persons to serve in their appointed places—to be associated with their fellow members already so serving, and with the pastor and other members of the staff. In preparation for their installation let us hear the instruction of the Apostle Paul to all of us:

Scripture: Romans 12:4-8

Minister:

We celebrate our varied gifts of the one Spirit. In their commitment now, may they complement one another to build up the Body of Christ to the full maturity that was in him.

All:

Praise be to God for the creativity of his love in the many gifts manifest among us.

Minister:

Let us give attention to the roll call of the officers and board members elect: (names of newly elected officers and board members are read).

Officers and board members-elect:

Having been nominated by the Personnel Committee and duly elected by the congregation at its annual meeting, we do now present ourselves for installation.

Charge to the officers and board members-elect:

God's call has been sounded through his church. You have been responsive to this call. In these moments you come offering your gifts of personality, talent, energy, and time in ministry through this congregation. May your position of leadership be not just a job to be done, but an opportunity to grow in all Christ-like graces; in new relationships, may you celebrate the church; in service, may you discover life's meaning.

Response of officer and board members-elect:

If there is something I can do, I want to do it. I want to do it wholeheartedly as unto the Lord. I will need the trust, prayers, and encouragement of my fellow officers and fellow members. I now commit myself and the gifts of God's love and grace to me, that with the quickening of his Spirit, I may become that instrument of his to which the church is calling me.

Charge to the continuing officers and board members:

Will you officers and board members previously chosen as leaders pledge your cooperation and support to these newly elected officers and board members that together you may give effective leadership to this congregation? May you stand in response.

Response of continuing officers and board members:

We receive these our fellow officers and give ourselves in a renewed sense of loyalty to the ministry in which we share.

The commitment of the staff:

As members of the staff, it is our privilege to serve as co-ministers with you who are leaders in the life of this congregation. Our first responsibility is to equip you for ministry. We are here to instruct, to counsel, to support, but not to usurp your ministry.

The charge to the congregation:

What response would you, who are members of this congregation, make to your fellow members whom you have duly elected to positions of leadership? If you wish to respond, rise, indicating your desire to stand in commitment with these fellow members.

The commitment of the congregation to the board members:

We, as members of this congregation, sense our responsibility in supporting your leadership. "We *are* members one of another." We are called to minister to each other, as well as a church to the world. Together, we need to discover what God is calling this church to be and do. We need to dream together, study together, worship together, serve together. Together, may we exalt Christ, the head of the church, and for the ministry we share, may we experience the light and strength of God's own Spirit.

All:

Once we were no people, but now we are God's people; once we had not received mercy, but now we have received mercy, that we may declare the wonderful deeds of him who called us out of darkness into his marvelous light (adapted from I Peter 2:9-10).

The pastoral prayer of installation for church officers and board members:

Our heavenly Father, the giver of every good and perfect gift, we rejoice in the gifts which you have given to us: the different talents, the diverse opportunities of education, the varying experiences that life affords. We praise you for the enrichment that comes to the life of the church as these gifts are enthusiastically committed and faithfully exercised. We thank you for these men and women who have answered the call to Christian service through election to leadership responsibilities in this congregation, and who come in these moments dedicating their different gifts to your ministry.

O Lord, bless those who lead this congregation as officers with insight into the truth, love for people, a zeal that never flags, and a strength that comes from a consciousness of your presence. As a congregation, may we receive all these officers as servants of yours and give ourselves in loyal support to the program which they project to the different areas in which they have responsibility. Confronted with demanding responsibilities, we do not ask for lesser tasks but for a faith equal to our tasks. Increase in each of us the ability to receive the fullness of your grace and truth expressed in Jesus Christ. In all things, may we build upon Christ, the chief cornerstone, that we may be as living stones built into a spiritual house.

O you who cares for all people and for all conditions of people, we lift to you the common life that we share as a congregation: heal our infirmities, awaken us to our great opportunity, strengthen aspirations to serve. Where there is illness in our families, we pray for health. Where there are problems that perplex us, we pray for knowledge of your will and the courage to follow it. Where there is sorrow, either in the present or in remembrance, we pray for the strength of your comfort. Be with those who serve your church in other lands that theirs may be a faithful witness to your love for all persons. Strengthen the leaders of this nation and all world leaders in concern for truth, justice, and righteousness. Be with those who risk their lives in bringing the gospel of reconciliation to the troubled areas of our world. For your sake and for the sake of all of those for whom we have responsibility, we pray. Amen.

Church Records

Effective administration of the church organization requires records—for legal matters, historical interest, good order, information. And every church administrator maintains some kind of records. But careful administration requires that records be maintained accurately and carefully. The following suggests the kinds of records a congregation may wish to maintain:

Minutes

Minutes of meetings of the congregation must be kept. Considering their extreme importance to the local congregation and potential significance for the larger judicatory group and even in matters of legal authority, they should be kept accurately.

The secretary takes the minutes and types up a copy after the meeting. The first draft should be reviewed by the pastor and lay leader of the board for any change and approvals. Copies should be made promptly and distributed to all board members with a permanent copy placed in the official minutes book. Corrections may be made at the next board meeting. Distribution of copies beyond the board membership should be by board action only.

Annual reports

Good church administration requires regular review and reports on previous actions. Responsible church leaders will insist on annual reports as a record of past action. In a sense the annual reports become the historical records of the life of the congregation. Thus they should be as complete as possible, even lengthy. Done in an attractive way, they can be a useful annual tool of reporting the exciting happenings of ministry.

All standing committees, special committees, auxiliary groups, officers, and staff should report on their progress and activity during the past year.

Statistical reports

Statistical reports are always useful to test the progress and vitality of a congregation. Comparisons with past activities indicate progress since then. Reports of the number of baptisms, funerals, weddings, confirmations, communions, board elections, and church attendance are also needed. Most congregations maintain official records. Statistical records offer an opportunity to compare.

Membership records

Too many pastors maintain membership records in their own heads. Aside from the church directory, seldom do congregations maintain exhaustive records on their membership. The computer, however, now makes that recordkeeping less complicated and easier to maintain.

A membership record will include just about every conceivable fact about each member that is possible to obtain. Without a computer, that information is put on cards and maintained manually. Here are items that might be included in a computer membership/ministry data file:

Household unit record number	Family surname
Area/group code	Street address
Street address supplemental field	Town or city
State or province	Zip code
Title	Phone number

Household unit type
Date of last visitation
County of residence code
Household optional fields
Person record number
Member surname
First name
Membership status
Member participation
Membership date
Family relationship
Sex
Birthdate
Birthplace
Ethnic origin
Citizenship status
Military status
Envelope number
Register number
Baptism status
Baptism date
Congregation baptized into
Date of first communion
Confirmation status
Confirmation date
Congregation of previous membership

Location of congregation
Church activities
Time/talent/abilities
Time available
Member optional field
Marital status
Wedding date
Date of spouse's death
Name of spouse
Occupation
Occupation title
Employer
Employer's address
Employer's phone
Educational level
Church education attainment
    history
Grade level
School code
Sunday school status
Visitor's name
Member assigned
Visitor's comments
Current church relationship
Last communion date
Last attendance date

An appropriate form must be developed so that the information can be gathered properly for new members. Computer-based systems will require a specific format. Congregations keeping manual records can develop their own (preferably) or secure denominational bookstore forms. An appropriate change sheet may also be required.

Parochial reports

The permanent records of the church must be kept in appropriately bound volumes. Usually the parish secretary maintains that record.

The permanent records will include the names of all pastors of the church, with dates for installation and duration in office. Photographs and biographical information should be provided.

The elected members of the board and all officers should be listed with dates of service noted.

A chronological membership record will list the names of all persons when they become church members. Full name, method of reception, date, and baptismal information should be recorded promptly. At dismissal or transfer, notation should be added.

All baptisms, confirmations, marriages, and deaths need to be properly recorded.

The archives

Historical documents should be preserved in a place of permanent storage. Appointment of an archivist, some one interested in the church's history, will insure that this record is maintained. The charter, the articles of incorporation, deeds to properties, and other legal documents should be kept.

Past records of memberships, ministers, board members, baptisms, marriages, and deaths are all part of that permanent record. Old books, documents, news items of future historic significance, photographs, newsletters, bulletins, special correspondence, minutes, and blueprints of all buildings are some of the items to be included.

Proper care and storage is important. Check with a museum curator for proper procedures in preserving old documents. Keep a safe-deposit box for valuable historical documents.

Financial records

All of the financial analyses made by the church treasurer should be kept. While the annual report does include that information, a separate record is helpful when analyzing prior years. All cash receipts, cash disbursements records, cancelled checks, and deposit slips can probably be discarded after ten years, maybe less. Individual member contribution records must be retained for at least three years so that any questions raised by the Internal Revenue Service about a member's giving can be checked out and verified.

Family history files

Older congregations with older members can develop quite an historical record of the families that have been members. In addition, these files can include all current data on members, including their personal expressions of interest in the life of the church.

Other files

A prospective membership file can be maintained by a volunteer with information given to the pastor on a regular basis. The computer can do this conveniently.

Sunday church school membership files are needed for active Christian education administration. Other groups or organizations should have information files on participants.

And adequate records are required to keep tab on memorials, endowment funds, photographs of church activities, and the confidential files of the minister—plus any other records deemed important for retaining.

The Church Office

Efficient operation of the church office is imperative for effective church administration. A poorly organized office will impede careful administration. Proper equipment that is properly placed will enhance the church's operation.

Communication system

The availability of a variety of telephone systems from differing vendors has been confusing. But a good system is required for efficient and dependable communication.

A receptionist can be an effective central operator in directing calls to the proper person. However, direct lines to some offices is advisable, as in the pastor's case. A direct line to the pastor's office will reach the secretary first without also going by the central operator.

Put telephones wherever they will best serve the staff and volunteers. Control toll calls with proper equipment. Develop rules for use of the telephones and clear instructions on how they are to be used. It is important that staff members not in the office on a given day receive their messages.

A telephone company could analyze your church's needs.

Interoffice memos

Staff must share information in order to keep informed. The telephone is useful; personal conversation is best; but memos may be required in some cases. A central mailbox will aid in the distribution of blind carbons, individual memos, copies of minutes, and other documents.

Interoffice memo pads are available at an office supply store.

Equipment

Office equipment should be placed where it will be easiest to use, close to wherever other equipment is used. Efficient office management requires careful placement of equipment: the copier should be near the line of traffic; the mimeograph and printing supplies near the duplicating equipment; typing paper close to typewriters; the mail room centrally located with necessary postage scales, sealers, tape, etc.

Filing equipment should be close to the offices. Careful selection of file cabinets to fit in with the office decorations can enhance the appearance of otherwise drab file drawer cabinets.

Church computer terminals should be located on the desks of staff members.

Supplies should generally be kept in a supply closet with careful inventory control. A vault or safe-deposit box can be used to protect valuable papers. However, the use of a bank box is preferable over a vault in the church office.

Addressing equipment in the modern large church office is generally computer operated. No equipment should be maintained in the pastor's office, no matter how nice it looks or how often the pastor is responsible for its operation. A separate room if available for the address files and equipment is important. A specific staff person should have responsibility for maintaining and updating the church's mailing list. (In smaller congregations with limited space, some equipment may of necessity be required in the pastor's personal office.)

Not many congregations use mimeograph equipment anymore because often the church secretary simply types a master and takes that to a photo copy place for duplication. It can be less expensive and is certainly more efficient.

However, some congregations maintain their own printing equipment. Whatever equipment is used should be of the finest quality. Nothing detracts more from a positive appreciation of the church than sloppy, poorly done printing. In today's market, the price for quality reproduction is so small that there is no excuse for less than perfect bulletins, newsletters, and other documents.

Many clergy use dictating equipment, although a fast typist can use a word processor almost as efficiently. Typewriters are a necessity, of course. Good electric memory typewriters quickly pay for themselves in time saved and quality production.

An automatic letter opener can be helpful for churches with a great deal of mail. Adding machines or printing calculators are necessary for financial officers, as well. Folding machines and coin counting machines are often standard equipment in larger church offices.

Many church office machines are dispensable. That is, when they cease to function they are replaced, not repaired. But typewriters and computers need repairs. Service contracts are especially important for sophisticated typewriters and larger computers.

Church administration is not only the process of managing the church through staff and programs, but also the care of equipment, maintenance of records, and attention to the properties and monies of the church. In a subsequent chapter, property management and financial recordkeeping will be discussed.

CHAPTER 3

STAFF RELATIONSHIPS AND SUPPORT

THERE MAY COME a time in the life of a congregation when the minister simply can no longer do everything. Most congregations, therefore, do have support staff—paid professionals who assist the pastor.

A modest start is in order. Perhaps the congregation needs to hire a part-time custodian, a part-time secretary, an organist, and eventually, a part-time director of Christian education. Eventually, as the congregation grows, those part-time positions become full-time and soon a second pastor is added. If a school is added to the program, teachers, cooks, and bus drivers must be hired. Nursery helpers may be required, along with receptionists, bookkeepers, and many others who may be hired to keep the church program functioning—to assist the membership in fulfilling its mission.

So how much staff should a congregation have? That depends of course on needs, finances, and the desire for more staff. It may also depend on just how willing volunteers are to work without being paid.

No one can authoritatively tell you how much staff you ought to have. Perhaps a church with five hundred members ought to have a multiple staff while a church with only three hundred members ought to have at least a part-time sexton and a part-time music leader. But with sixteen hundred members it may well be that there ought to be two clergy, a director of Christian education, two secretaries, two sextons, a full-time organist and choir director, and a part-time financial secretary. Take your pick. You must simply decide what you need, what you can afford, and how you wish to administer your programs.

Besides the size of the congregation, the geographic distribution of the church's membership, its financial resources, and the attitude of the clergy leadership all make a difference. Certainly the plans for the future mission of your congregation must be considered. Thus, some congregations with one thousand members still have only one full-time minister, a part-time secretary, part-time lay assistant, part-time custodian, and part-time social worker. Other congregations of equal size may have three clergy, full-time secretaries, full-time sextons and other staff. Much depends on the pastor and the thrust of the congregational programs.

A parish changes. Needs change. Congregations grow and decline. Neighborhoods change, pastors change, financial stability changes. Thus church programs and staffing must be responsive to that change—to the needs and the problems of the congregation. A pastor must be conscious of what is happening to the people. Changing programs and a changing direction in mission go with a changing age group and changing mix of people. Staffing needs change also. Thus the staff must be flexible.

Flexibility means cooperation with others—a helping attitude, a positive spirit about the work of the church, and a willingness to pitch in and to do what is best for the congregation. The thinking pastor will demonstrate that there is no part of the church life that he/she is not willing to participate in. The pastor must be familiar with everything, ready to take over if necessary, even to putting up chairs and tables when the custodian has forgotten. That spirit, that attitude, that action is vital to the creative growth of the caring congregation.

Techniques for Selecting Staff

Good administrators will develop careful techniques for determining staff needs and for selecting staff personnel. A sudden crisis, emotional appeal, or inspiration is not sufficient cause for a pastor to go off and hire new staff. Nor is someone's personal need for a job sufficient to justify hiring a staff person when no congregational need has been demonstrated for the task. And no church administrator would add staff until the congregation, through the official board, had properly studied, evaluated, and approved the need for the position. Even an authoritative pastor seeing the obvious need for additional staff will be prudent about selection in order to avoid criticism. Selecting additional staff must be done in an orderly and careful way.

A personnel committee (staff relations committee, pastor-parish relations committee, mutual ministry committee) provides an excellent opportunity for developing good procedures for selecting needed staff.

The personnel committee

Purpose: To administer all programs relating to staff employee relationships and needs, employment and dismissal, benefits administration.
Membership: Six members, staggered terms, three years each, appointed by the official board.
To whom responsible: The official board
Qualifications of committee members:
—administrative experience
—knowledge of needs of the congregation
—a spirit of tolerance and support of employees
—experience in office procedures, especially personnel administration
—tactful, yet aggressive in dealing with problem people
Responsibilities:
1. To draw up job qualifications and job descriptions for all staff positions.
2. To oversee the process of selection of candidates to fill specific staff positions.
3. To maintain personnel files on all employees.
4. To employ and dismiss employees with approval of the official board.
5. To supervise an annual evaluation of all employees.
6. To recommend annually to the official board compensation arrangements for all employees.
7. To serve as the grievance committee for all employee complaints.
8. To create a personnel policies manual and a staff relations statement.
9. To maintain all confidential personnel files.
Whenever the official board determines the need for a new staff person, the personnel committee must act. Applicants must be found, interviews conducted, job qualifications and descriptions set forth, specific responsibilities described, compensation and employment details agreed upon, final approval of the congregation or board secured, and a contract signed.

A job qualification and description statement should be prepared for all existing staff positions as well as for any anticipated positions. A frequent updating of these statements will be important.

The qualifications for any job are important. Thus a description of abilities and aptitude needed, as well as spirit and attitude expected, are listed first on a job description. Then responsibilities associated with the position are listed. The application form should include all necessary information for a careful evaluation of the person's qualifications: age, education, experience, family, religious orientation (if that's important to the job), aptitude, ability, skills, interests, etc.

When advertising for a position, the personnel committee should describe briefly the job and its qualifications. The staff opening should be circulated first among present staff, then to the membership, perhaps also to the judicatory office, and then to the general public.

A brief notice such as the following might be distributed. More specific details would be available in the church office from the committee:

STAFF POSITION AVAILABLE

OFFICE SECRETARY, part-time, Christ Church. College degree preferred. Experience in business and office management required. Superior typing skills needed; shorthand helpful. Experience in use of computer word processors essential. Desire person with strong Christian commitment, cooperative spirit, pleasing disposition, with ability to relate to a variety of situations and individuals. Contact the pastor, 513-453-6875.

OR

STAFF POSITION AVAILABLE

CUSTODIAN, full-time, large church building, Christ Church. Handyman skills desired. High school education required. Strong Christian commitment necessary. Willing spirit, cooperative attitude, with ability to get along with others. Must respond to requests for a variety of maintenance and custodial tasks. Includes Sunday morning. Contact the pastor, 516-453-6875.

Careful attention to references listed on the job application cannot be overemphasized. While references listed will always be those people the applicant knows best and expects will provide the best recommendations, nevertheless, each should be contacted. Conversation may reveal some flaw or undesirable characteristic not suitable for a church employee. If the church is going to ask for references, it is only courteous to follow through and seek a recommendation or comment. Needless to say, such information will be kept in the strictest confidence.

In the case of an organist applicant, for example, or a clergy person, the personnel committee may request permission to visit the church where that person is presently employed in order to assess skills. Such a visit must be done, however, with the greatest sensitivity so as not to embarrass or interrupt the applicant.

Interviewing

Interviewing is a skill that requires careful attention to detail and an awareness of personal feelings and emotions. Skilled interviewers will be prepared to ask specific questions and to let the applicant do most of the talking.

Two or three persons, rather than the entire committee, should conduct the initial interview. A large group can be unsettling to a candidate. The applicant who appears qualified then can meet later with these same persons as well as the larger group. Basic background information is obtained from the application form. The interview is intended to discover attitudes, explore personality traits, question motivation, reveal spiritual maturity.

Having a prepared set of questions available at the interview will make the interview easier. An informal setting and approach insures a relaxed atmosphere and more cordial response to questioning.

APPLICATION
FOR
EMPLOYMENT

(PLEASE PRINT PLAINLY)

To Applicant: We deeply appreciate your interest in our organization and assure you that we are sincerely interested in your qualifications. A clear understanding of your background and work history will aid us in placing you in the position that best meets your qualifications *and* may assist us in possible future upgrading.

PERSONAL   Date _____

Name _____ Social Security No. _____
          Last   First   Middle

Present address_____ Telephone No. _____
              No.   Street   City   State   Zip

Are you legally eligible for employment in the U.S.A.? _____   State age if under 18 or over 70. _____

What method of transportation will you use to get to work? _____

Position(s) applied for _____ Rate of pay expected $_____ per week

Were you previously employed by us? _____ If yes. when? _____

If your application is considered favorably on what date will you be available for work? _____ 19_____

Are there any other experiences, skills, or qualifications which you feel would especially fit you for work with our organization?_____

_____

_____

_____

RECORD OF EDUCATION

School	Name and Address of School	Course of Study	Check Last Year Completed				Did You Graduate?	List Diploma or Degree
Elementary			5	6	7	8	☐ Yes ☐ No	
High			1	2	3	4	☐ Yes ☐ No	
College			1	2	3	4	☐ Yes ☐ No	
Other (Specify)			1	2	3	4	☐ Yes ☐ No	

(Turn to Next Page)

List below all present and past employment, beginning with your most recent

I

Name and Address of Company and Type of Business	From		To		Weekly Starting Salary	Weekly Last Salary	Reason for Leaving	Name of Supervisor
	Mo.	Yr.	Mo.	Yr.				
	Describe the work you did:							
Telephone								

II

Name and Address of Company and Type of Business	From		To		Weekly Starting Salary	Weekly Last Salary	Reason for Leaving	Name of Supervisor
	Mo.	Yr.	Mo.	Yr.				
	Describe the work you did:							
Telephone								

III

Name and Address of Company and Type of Business	From		To		Weekly Starting Salary	Weekly Last Salary	Reason for Leaving	Name of Supervisor
	Mo.	Yr.	Mo.	Yr.				
	Describe the work you did:							
Telephone								

IV

Name and Address of Company and Type of Business	From		To		Weekly Starting Salary	Weekly Last Salary	Reason for Leaving	Name of Supervisor
	Mo.	Yr.	Mo.	Yr.				
	Describe the work you did:							
Telephone								

I hereby give permission to contact the employers listed above concerning any information you deem relevant.

Signed _____

If there is a particular employer(s), you do not wish us to contact, please indicate which one(s). _____

_____

PERSONAL REFERENCES (Not Former Employers or Relatives)

Name and Occupation	Address	Phone Number

MILITARY SERVICE RECORD

Were you in U.S. Armed Forces? Yes _____ No _____ If yes, what Branch? _____

Dates of duty: From _____ To _____ Rank at discharge _____
               Month   Day   Year   Month   Day   Year

List duties in the service including special training _____

_____

Have you taken any training under the G.I. Bill of Rights? _____ If yes, what training did you take? _____

PLEASE READ AND SIGN BELOW

The facts set forth in my application for employment are true and complete. I understand that if employed, any false statement on this application may result in my dismissal. I further understand that this application is not and is not intended to be a contract of employment, nor does this application obligate the employer in any way if the employer decides to employ me. You are hereby authorized to make any investigation of my personal history and financial and credit record through any investigative or credit agencies or bureaus of your choice.

In making this application for employment I authorize you to make an investigative consumer report whereby information is obtained through personal interviews with my neighbors, friends, or others with whom I am acquainted. This inquiry, if made, may include information as to my character, general reputation, personal characteristics and mode of living. I understand that I have the right to make a written request within a reasonable period of time to receive additional, detailed information about the nature and scope of any such investigative report that is made.

_____
Signature of Applicant

To Applicant: READ THIS INTRODUCTION CAREFULLY BEFORE ANSWERING ANY QUESTIONS IN THIS BLOCKED-OFF AREA. The Civil Rights Act of 1964 prohibits discrimination in employment because of race, color, religion, sex or national origin. Federal law also prohibits discrimination on the basis of age with respect to certain individuals. The laws of most States also prohibit some or all of the above types of discrimination as well as some additional types such as discrimination based upon ancestry, marital status or physical or mental handicap or disability.

DO NOT ANSWER ANY QUESTION CONTAINED IN THIS BLOCKED-OFF AREA UNLESS THE EMPLOYER HAS CHECKED THE BOX NEXT TO THE QUESTION, thereby indicating that for the position for which you are applying the requested information is needed for a legally permissible reason, including, without limitation, national security requirements, a bona fide occupational qualification or business necessity.

☐ How long have you lived at present address? _____

☐ Previous address _____ How long did you live there?_____
No.   Street   City   State   Zip

☐ Are you over the age of eighteen? _____ If no. hire is subject to verification that you are of minimum legal age

☐ How do you wish to be addressed? Mr.____Mrs.____Miss____Ms.____

☐ Sex: M _____ F _____   ☐ Height: _____ft. _____in.   ☐ Weight: _____lbs.

☐ Marital Status: Single _____ Engaged _____ Married _____ Separated _____ Divorced _____ Widowed _____

☐ Date of Marriage _____ ☐ Number of dependents including yourself _____ ☐ Are you a citizen of the U.S.A.?_____

☐ What is your present Selective Service classification?_____

☐ Indicate dates you attended school:

Elementary_____ High School _____ College _____
            From   To   From   To   From   To
Other (Specify type of school) _____
                                                                                                 From   To

☐ Have you ever been bonded?_____ If yes. on what jobs? _____

☐ Have you ever been convicted of a crime, excluding misdemeanors and summary offenses, in the past ten years which has not been annulled or expunged or sealed by a court?_____If yes, describe in full _____

☐ Do you have any physical condition which may limit your ability to perform the particular job for which you are applying?_____

If yes, describe such condition and explain how you can perform the job for which you are applying in spite of it._____

_____
_____

☐ Do you have any physical defects which preclude you from performing certain kinds of work?_____ If yes. describe such

defects and specific work limitations._____

☐ Have you had a major illness in the past 5 years?_____ If yes. describe_____

_____

☐ Have you received compensation for injuries?_____ If yes. describe _____

_____

☐ List any friends or relatives working for us, other than spouse_____
                                                                                                 Name(s)

Employer may list other bona fide occupational questions on lines below:

☐ _____
☐ _____

APPLICANT — Do not write on this page
FOR INTERVIEWER'S USE

INTERVIEWER	DATE	COMMENTS

FOR TEST ADMINISTRATOR'S USE

TESTS ADMINISTERED	DATE	RAW SCORE	RATING	COMMENTS AND INTERPRETATION

REFERENCE CHECK

*Position Number	RESULTS OF REFERENCE CHECK	*Position Number	RESULTS OF REFERENCE CHECK
I		IV	
II			
III			

*See page 42

This *"Application for Employment"* is prepared for general use throughout the United States. Our legal counsel has advised us that the material outside the colored blocked-off area complied with all Federal and State fair employment practice laws and with the Fair Credit Reporting Act. However, the various fair employment practice laws and related statutes and the interpretations of them change frequently, and neither V.W. Eimicke Associates, Inc. nor its counsel assume any responsibility for the inclusion in this *"Application for Employment"* of any questions that may violate local and/or State and/or Federal laws. Users should consult their counsel about any legal question they may have with respect to the use of this form.

Interview questions

1. What is your interest in the position?
2. Do you believe you have a capacity to respond to a variety of needs, to grow in the position, and generally to take the initiative to do what needs to be done in the best interests of the church?
3. Is there anything else we should know about you that is not listed on the application form?
4. Do you have questions of us?
5. Do you understand our expectations of you if you are selected for this job? Do you know the job responsibilities?
6. When will you be available to begin working with us if you are selected?
7. How can we assist you in moving, transportation, and housing if you are selected?
8. How do you react under pressure? Is your personality generally pleasing? Are you tactful, understanding—not abusive, curt, or negative?
9. What is your Christian commitment?

All applicants should receive a copy of the job qualifications and specifications. But it must be emphasized that job specifications may not remain as precise as at first set forth. While it is certainly the intention of the personnel committee and the other staff to follow through with any assignments delegated to the new employee, it must be understood that church needs may vary, programs will change, and the unexpected is more likely to happen than the planned. Job specifications are set forth to outline expectations, but needs of the people set the dynamic for staff response in a specific situation.

Employment of any staff must be done carefully and cautiously. Whether it is a new pastor, the custodian, or a secretary, the church is about to make a commitment that will be difficult to undo if things fail to work out satisfactorily. Likewise, the applicant makes a commitment to the church. It may seem to be only another job at first glance, but it is truly a commitment to a different kind of task than one would secure in a business.

Making a Job Offer

When an offer is finally made to an applicant, the personnel committee should carefully explain in writing the various benefits, conditions, and terms of employment. A copy of the employee manual should be given to the candidate.

Employment offer checklist

Checklist for items to review upon offering employment:
1. Exact beginning salary to be paid.
2. Exact date of review and first salary adjustment.
3. The pay period—weekly, semi-monthly, monthly.
4. Days of employment, hours of employment.
5. Moving arrangements and reimbursements of costs.
6. Reimbursement policy for professional expenses including the use of a personal automobile.
7. Pension plan participation.
8. Health and accident plan insurance premium payments.
9. Holidays, vacations, sick leave days, leaves without pay.
10. Who the employee is responsible to.
11. Housing provisions.
12. Social security tax or allowance.

If all is agreed by the personnel committee, a recommendation is made to the official board. The board may also wish to interview the candidate before authorizing the employment.

If the congregation and/or the official board authorizes the personnel committee to proceed with the employment under the terms of the job description and financial conditions imposed, the committee hires the applicant.

Often the congregation approves the new position by including an amount in the budget to cover the costs for the new employee. Then when the official board authorizes the personnel committee to make a choice, the committee may decide and only then report its actions to the official board and the congregation.

It is a good idea to send the applicant a written invitation to become a part of the staff of the church. Such a "call" or "contract offer" formally sets forth the terms of employment and is signed by the proper church official and the employee. Oral employment agreements tend to be forgotten, misunderstood, or rearranged. A written contract spells out the exact agreement and can be used later during job evaluation.

Normally, it is appropriate for the pastor, chief executive officer, or the president of the congregation to issue a sincere letter of invitation to the applicant along with the call or contract outlining the commitment of the congregation to the employee and the responsibilities of the employee to the congregation. A letter or response from the new employee, as well as a returned signed copy of the call or contract should accompany that response. The congregation and all staff should be informed promptly of the acceptance of the position by the applicant.

CALL OR CONTRACT OFFERING EMPLOYMENT

To (Name of applicant) _____,
Grace to you and peace from God our Father and from the Lord Jesus Christ.

At a meeting of the members of (name of congregation or official board) _____
_____ you were duly chosen to become (position, i.e., secretary to the pastor, associate pastor, etc.) _____. By authority and on behalf of this church, we, the undersigned, do hereby now extend to you this formal call (or contract) and earnestly urge you to accept it.

You are to fulfill all of those responsibilities listed in the job description for the position to which you are called (list name of position) _____. In addition you are to respond to the needs of the congregation in those areas of your expertise and to otherwise respond to the requests of the senior pastor as required. You are to conduct yourself in a manner that is consistent with Christian principles of living and to perform your duties in accordance with the confessions and orders of (name denomination of church) _____
_____.

For our part, we pledge ourselves to work with you to fulfill your responsibilities, to increase our understanding of your abilities and interests, and generally to assist you in every way possible so that your ministry and work can be fulfilling for you and useful to us, and helpful in the building of the kingdom of God in our community.

In the name of this church (show name of church) _____
_____, we pledge to you our prayers, our love, and our esteem. For your temporal support and comfort, we agree to pay to you the following reimbursements, benefits, housing, and salary:

1. Reimbursements (list items, i.e., car expenses, professional expenses, etc.)
2. Employee benefits (list items, i.e., pension plan, health benefits plan, social security, vacation, etc.)
3. Housing (state housing arrangements to be provided, if any)
4. Salary (state initial amount of salary)

In testimony whereof, we have subscribed our names this _____ day of _____ A.D., 19____, by authority and on behalf of the congregation issuing this call (contract).

_____

Authorized officer

_____

Secretary

Seal of Congregation

LETTER OF INVITATION TO NEW EMPLOYEE

Dear (name of applicant) _____,
I am pleased to inform you that at a meeting of the official board of (name of congregation) _____ a unanimous decision was made to extend to you a call (or contract) to serve on the staff of our congregation as (name of position) _____. Congratulations on your selection! We look forward with eagerness to your participation with us in the work of the church.

The official board has asked that I send to you the enclosed copies of the formal offer, requesting that if you accept this offer, you sign both copies, keeping one for yourself and returning the other to me in the self-addressed stamped envelope enclosed.

I personally look forward to the contribution that I believe you will be able to make to the life of this congregation and sincerely hope that you will accept our offer and join our team.

May the blessings of Almighty God continue to be with you as you make your decision.

All best wishes.
Sincerely,

(Senior Pastor)

Orientation of New Employees

The first day on a new job is always the most difficult day for a new employee. Careful introduction of the new employee to surroundings and staff is important if a positive attitude about the job is to be maintained.

For a small staff, an informal hour or so in conversation at the beginning of that first day will help to break the ice and set the tone for positive relationships. In a larger staff the new employee should be introduced to all other staff members as soon as possible. When this is done by the minister, it can be an effective way to make the new employee feel like an important member of the staff. This introduction also emphasizes to the other staff that the minister believes this employee is important as a person and that the job to be done is important also. If there is a regular break time during the day, that too is a good time to get acquainted and for other staff to learn more about the new employee.

The official board may wish to get acquainted with the new employee in some special way. The personnel committee may arrange for a gathering or informal get-together for just that purpose. The employee should meet those persons or committee leaders with whom he/she will need to work most closely.

Informing the congregation of new staff appointments can be done in several ways—certainly the parish newsletter should include an announcement and a brief statement of background and job responsibility. An informal reception following a worship service or a coffee hour during Sunday school time could be considered. Or the minister may wish to make an announcement from the pulpit. In one way or another the congregation needs to be informed. It is the responsibility of the personnel committee to see that that is done promptly and appropriately.

Staff members will need to be aware of the needs of the membership in all they do. Careful attention to detail, recognition by name, follow-through on requests for information, courteous responses to inquiries, and reports to the senior pastor about pertinent information on any members must be encouraged. The staff is an extension of the senior pastor's ministry to all members. How staff reacts to the membership reflects on the membership's perception about the entire staff.

Recognition of staff birthdays, anniversaries, or special achievements can be conveyed to the membership also. Reports to the membership of professional recognitions of staff persons—publications, awards—will indicate the professional proficiency of staff and of activities beyond the local congregational program.

And finally, the personnel committee must continue to review the new employee's work, assisting as needed, but also reassuring that staff person and all staff of their importance to the total work of the church. Appreciation, when sincere, cannot be expressed too often.

Evaluation of Personnel

Periodic review of employees is important for the staff person, as well as an assurance to the congregation that staffers are responding to the needs of the people through their assigned responsibilities.

Of course, if employees are told when hired that such an evaluation will be done, they will not be as intimidated by the process a year or so later. The purpose of the visit must be stressed as simply an attempt to be certain all things are mutually satisfactory with respect to job assignment. A periodic review avoids the unpleasantness of always dealing with personnel problems only as they develop.

Here is a checklist of guidelines for such an evaluation:

1. Advise the employees of the date, time, and purpose of the forthcoming review. Evaluations are for the purpose of mutual review for employee and employer.
2. Make the evaluation objective and without personal prejudice or bias.
3. All conversations must be kept confidential.
4. A written report should be prepared promptly by the evaluator and copies distributed to the personnel committee and the senior pastor.
5. Any changes in job responsibilities should be discussed promptly and immediately implemented.
6. Follow-up evaluation of proposed changes should be arranged and done on schedule.
7. A record of the review, action taken, and any recommendations for change should be placed in the personnel file of each employee.

Staff Supervision

Staff teamwork does not just happen. It must be nurtured. And even though staff will always relate to each other somehow, that relationship can be enhanced by good administrative techniques. A positive, upbeat spirit is crucial to the effectiveness of staff relations with the church members. Communication is essential to good management. The pastor must keep the staff fully informed about his/her own plans, about the plans and actions of the official board, and about the activities of other staff.

Good church administrators (pastors) communicate to and with their staffs in many ways. The typical way for that to happen is with staff meetings. Many staffs meet at least once a week, some less frequently. A staff of two or three probably meets informally several times a week, yet an occasionally planned staff meeting could be useful in pulling together loose ends.

A larger staff may meet formally each Tuesday morning (or any day) for thirty minutes or so. Perhaps a luncheon meeting works best. While the first thing Monday morning may seem desirable, a Monday afternoon or Tuesday meeting gives all staff a chance to pull together the events of the previous weekend, prepare necessary reports, and give thought to the rest of the week before meeting with other staff.

The purpose of any staff meeting will be to:

1. Inform each other about what has been going on in the life of the church.
2. Review the progress of existing programs.
3. Review immediate future programs.
4. Stimulate creative suggestions from staff about the life and program of the church.
5. Correct errors, resolve staff problems, and encourage staff toward program improvements and self-assurance.
6. Assign new or different responsibilities to staff.
7. Encourage sharing, motivate commitment, support each other.

An informal agenda for most staff meetings will offer opportunities for all present to speak up. However, an agenda and a set of minutes from each meeting will facilitate an efficient meeting.

AGENDA FOR STAFF MEETINGS

1. Prayer for guidance and concerns for others.
2. Review of the church calendar, dates, and schedules.
3. Building equipment arrangements for special events.
4. Church office procedures; inventory of supplies; printing, addressing, and mailing schedules.
5. Visitation needs and assignments to staff.
6. Next Sunday's schedule, assignments, and special needs.
7. Review of church programs, committee activities, and plans.
8. Business from prior meetings.
9. New items, concerns, problems, other reports.
10. Date and time for next meeting.
11. Closing prayer.

Staff support can be undergirded by various activities. A daily worship opportunity can indeed inspire a sense of commitment and lift the spirits of the staff. It is a good way for anyone to begin the workday, but it is especially fitting that in the church this time of prayer and meditation together is planned. A variety of methods can be used. In one church a fifteen-minute worship experience is open to any one in the building at 9:00 A.M. each day. Staff are encouraged but not required to participate.

Some church staffs gather for social events—a picnic, a luncheon, or even an evening in the pastor's home. This is time for fun together, time to get better acquainted, time to share.

Staff Relations Manual

Some congregations find a staff relations manual helpful. That is not the same as a personnel policies manual. The latter is a description of policies and procedures relating to staff employment and compensation. A staff relations manual describes the way in which staff relate to each other and to the senior pastor.

Beginning on page 50 is a sample staff relations manual used by one congregation.

STAFF RELATIONS MANUAL*

Our role as leaders in the life of this congregation can be summed up in the words of St. Paul: "Each has his own special gift from God, one of one kind and one of another." Our concern is for people within and without the walls of what we call the organized church. In our committee service to all people whom God must love, we find ourselves and the mission of the church.

The church is a means of God's salvation to the world and we are his instruments each with our own talents. It is the cause and purpose for which we are organized that is "the first and last item."

1. As members of the staff of Christ Church we function together in a team ministry. We are one working fellowship serving in and for a cause greater than ourselves, either individually or corporately. Our chief loyalty is to Jesus Christ, the great head of the church, for whom we labor in this particular place. At the same time, we seek to fulfill our calling through a humble and loving ministry to those with whom we work and the congregation we service.

2. Our loyalty to one another is a reflection of our loyalty to Christ. Our emphasis in this mutual responsibility is on unity, harmony, and cooperation. We mutually stimulate each other, develop program together, worship, and work and play together, so we will have a part in causing the church to move forward, fulfilling its destiny in the world. Accomplishments are achieved by the total staff. However, each individual will have certain areas for personal achievement but most always will be well complemented by the total staff.

3. Every team must have a captain. This is the role of the senior minister. He is called by the congregation to administer the entire program of the church for which he is ultimately held responsible. Obviously, this is not something one person can do alone. Thus, we have a team of individuals, trained and qualified, to serve in particular areas of specialization, with responsibility for that area. At the same time, every aspect of the church is a concern of the entire staff. As we share together in this intense relationship of a group ministry we develop a sensitivity to each other and our work, which expresses itself in a unique rapport with one another and with the entire congregation.

4. We carry a heavy load, individually and together. Each person's time is extremely valuable in the economy of service. Respect for the work and study time of each person is important. Plan carefully and in advance. Seek to avoid changes in schedules once established and the ensuing last-minute pressures. Anticipate problems and conflicts and have practical suggestions in advance where possible. Attention to all details is of utmost importance. Doublecheck rather than take a chance.

5. Let us operate together as economically as possible. We are all servants of the church. We should never be miserly; neither should we be careless. Thoughtful ordering is important. Careful use of equipment and supplies is essential. Simple practices of economy can show marked saving in the budget at the end of the year. Plan generously, but with as little waste as possible.

6. If acute problems develop, it may be best to consult with the senior minister. Where problems come up in a given area of responsibility, use good judgment in working them out. Call on the minister for aid or counsel only when the problem is complex or may be a matter involving other areas of the church life.

7. Regular staff meetings will be held to discuss programs, projects, and details of administration. Questions, reviews, and announcements should be cleared through this mutually shared time. It is essential that we keep each other informed. Free communication, both formal and informal, gives us insight into the various activities and the spirit behind them.

8. Help to see that the church is neat and in good order at all times. An immaculate church indicates Christian concern for the appearance of God's house. Encourage others of the congregation to leave areas of activity neat, attractive, and uncluttered. Please see that your desk gives the appearance of order.

9. The personal touch is important in maintaining good public relations. The way we deal with people personally, by telephone or by letter, represents our entire church and its good name. In the service of the Master, we deal in service. Every contact we make, the way we make it and how we handle it, speaks for all of us.

10. Let us deal with our common faults, mistakes, and needs in Christian love and charity. Above all, let us seek to be creative and always helpful. At some points, dialogue in depth may help ease tension and renew spiritual bonds.

11. In order to have a uniform understanding of administrative procedure, these points of policy are noted:

a. Any special time-off periods should first be discussed with the minister. Regular days off have been established and as nearly as possible normal personal needs should be cared for on these days. Vacation plans will be worked out individually with all members of the staff by the senior minister.

---

*From the book, *Minister's Desk Book* by Lowell Ditzen, © 1968, by Parker Publishing Company, Inc., West Nyack, N.Y., pages 84-86. Used with permission.

b. Salaries are determined by the personnel committee, taking into consideration total church budget and all factors relating to a particular position. Salaries are personal and if for any reason there may be need for discussion, this should be done with the senior minister.

c. Staff hours will vary because of the particular demands of the various areas of service. Each person will want to establish and maintain his own discipline in regard to a pattern of working hours and then give his best. Each person who has a specific time commitment will want to do his part by being on time. Any departures from what has become our regular schedule should be noted with the office so that one may be contacted in case of an emergency or callers may be informed where one can be reached or the expected time of arrival. Keep the church office informed during regular working hours when you leave your point of contact for any length of time.

d. Messages taken for another member of the staff should be placed on that person's desk immediately. Report every telephone call to the person for whom it was intended, even if no message was left. Return all telephone calls promptly.

12. Programs.

a. Recommendations from the staff regarding any aspect of the church should be cleared through appropriate board committees. Where such reference is not feasible, the senior minister will present the recommendations.

b. All activities and programs for which staff members have responsibility should start promptly. Be present in advance of every appointment to see that all is in readiness. At times when a staff member cannot be present for a meeting where he has responsibility, another should be notified and briefed completely.

c. All committee meetings and activities or any use of the building should be noted in the parish date book.

d. Personal use of church equipment should be approved by the business administrator. The borrowing of equipment can be done only by keeping with the principles outlined by the maintenance and operations committee.

e. All supplies are ordered through the administrator, so that a proper inventory and budget check can be accurately maintained.

Staff Retreats

Many church staffs find an annual retreat helpful in pulling together the activities of the previous year and for doing some intensive planning for the coming year. Selecting a place away from the church office offers an opportunity for concentration without interruptions. A two- or three-day event, carefully planned, can be inspiring.

Often such a retreat includes the official board. In that way the church leaders are involved directly in hearing of progress and developing plans. An annual retreat offers a way to coordinate the church calendar for the entire church year and to establish or review matters of policy and program.

For any staff retreat program the minister is the key leader who inspires creative innovation in programming and a steady progression toward the objectives of the retreat.

A carefully developed agenda by staff can make the days together extremely useful. There should be no limitations on what can be discussed, but objectives for the retreat will keep the discussion from wandering.

STAFF/OFFICIAL BOARD RETREAT SCHEDULE

First Day
1:00 p.m.	Settle in
2:00 p.m.	Opening devotions/worship/prayer
2:15 p.m.	The minister sets the tone
2:30 p.m.	Group discussion on agenda & objectives
3:00 p.m.	Break for coffee, talk, etc.
3:30 p.m.	Review of the church program to date, information about everything that has been going on in the church

51

4:00 p.m.	Recreation and personal time
6:00 p.m.	Dinner
7:30 p.m.	Small group sessions to brainstorm about possibilities for the new year
8:45 p.m.	Break for coffee, etc.
9:00 p.m.	Identification of specific areas of concern
9:45 p.m.	Evening devotions, refreshments, conversation

Second Day

7:30 a.m.	Breakfast
9:00 a.m.	Devotions
9:15 a.m.	Consolidation of ideas, development of plans
10:00 a.m.	Break for coffee, etc.
10:30 a.m.	The calendar is put together, assignments are made, work schedules developed, priority listings made of proposed programs
11:30 a.m.	Worship with Lord's Supper
12:00 noon	Adjournment

Personnel Policies Manual

It will help the church staff to put in writing the personnel policies affecting the staff. The personnel committee has the responsibility of implementing the personnel policies authorized by the board. A manual of instructions will define the manner of salary payment, vacation time, days off, benefits, housing, expense reimbursements, etc.

The *Personnel Policies Manual* is different from the *Staff Relations Manual* in that the latter relates to relations between staff; the former deals with employment contract agreements and work responsibilities.

PERSONNEL POLICIES MANUAL

I. *Introduction:* This manual sets forth the personnel policies of Christ Church. While individual contracts and job descriptions are definitive (where in conflict with this document), the *Personnel Policies Manual* sets forth the expectations of the church and its employees with respect to employment and compensation agreements. This manual may be amended from time to time. All staff may request current copies of this manual following any change. Responsibility for maintaining this manual in a current status is that of the personnel committee. This manual is applicable for all staff persons.

II. *Reimbursements of Professional Expenses.* The principle of reimbursement followed by Christ Church regarding any expenses incurred by any staff person on behalf of the congregation shall be reimbursement in full. Only those expenses that have been previously approved by the senior pastor or included in the church budget shall be reimbursed. The congregation shall provide a church-owned automobile to all clergy staff and pay all costs. Nonclergy staff shall be reimbursed at twenty-six cents per mile for all church business miles, not including commuting costs from home to church and return.

III. The following *employee benefits* shall be available to all staff, as may be applicable:

1) *Pension plan:* The church will contribute to the pension plan of the denomination the required amount for all full-time employees. All contributions shall be vested immediately to the employee, and the congregation shall have no further claim on such contributions. Employees desiring to make additional tax deferred annuity contributions must sign the appropriate salary reduction agreement with the treasurer.

2) *Health benefits:* The full premium costs for health, accident and dental insurance for the employee and all dependents will be paid by the church. Payments will continue for up to one year following termination of employment. Only the denominational plan will be used.

3) *Social security taxes:* All required social security taxes, including the employee's portion, will be paid by the church. All clergy will receive a social security allowance equal to the maximum social security self-employment tax, payable monthly. Income taxes will be withheld as required except that clergy must request to have their income taxes withheld since the Internal Revenue Code states that such withholding is not required.

4) *Medical expense reimbursement plan:* All full-time employees participate in the church's approved medical expense reimbursement plan. The plan provides for reimbursement of up to $1000 of any noninsured medical costs per year per employee for expenses of the employee or dependents. If more than one member of a family is an employee, the $1000 limitation is available for each employee. Reimbursement will be made upon submission to the treasurer of appropriate receipts. Generally unused funds at year-end cannot be reimbursed to employees, according to recent IRS rulings. The unspent funds could be carried over to the following year, however, to be used as needed for such expenses.

5) *Malpractice insurance:* The church provides a malpractice insurance policy for all employees. The premium is paid by the church. The protection afforded by this policy offers defense counsel and judgment payment for any suit brought against any employee for malpractice claims as an employee of Christ Church. The policy does not cover claims for suits for actions done outside church employment.

6) *Life insurance:* The church provides a $50,000 group term life insurance policy on the life of all employees. Beneficiaries must be designated by the employee. Upon termination the employee may continue the policy at his/her own expense upon application to the insurance company.

7) *Vacations:* All employees are entitled to vacation time. Payment is not available for unused vacation since all employees are encouraged and expected to use all of their vacation time for rest and recreation. Clergy staff shall have thirty days of paid vacation annually. Other full-time employees shall have fourteen days of paid vacation annually. Full-time employees with at least five years of service will receive twenty-one days of paid vacation time and employees with at least ten years of full-time service shall receive twenty-eight days of vacation. Part-time employees do not accrue vacation time or seniority.

8) *Holidays:* The church offices will be closed on the following days. Employees shall receive full pay for such days: New Year's Day, Martin Luther King's Birthday, President's Day, Monday after Easter, Memorial Day, Independence Day, Labor Day, Columbus Day, Election Day, Veterans' Day, Thursday and Friday of Thanksgiving week, Christmas Day and the next work day thereafter, normally December 26, and New Year's Eve.

9) *Work week:* The normal work week is Monday through Friday, 8:30 A.M. to 5:00 P.M. each day, except as otherwise designated. Clergy are encouraged to take at least one day off each week for personal pleasure.

10) *Sick leave, disability:* All employees accrue one day each month for paid sick leave days up to a maximum accumulation of sixty days. Accumulated, unused sick leave will be paid upon termination or retirement. The church provides a short-term disability plan, after sixty continuous days of disability, equal to 60 percent of monthly pay. At the end of the first year of disability, the denomination's long-term disability plan benefits will be applicable. Part-time employees do not accrue sick leave benefits.

11) *Maternity/paternity leave:* Maternity and paternity leave for full-time women and men employees, without pay, shall be granted for no more than six consecutive weeks at the birth of a child.

12) *Continuing education:* All employees are encouraged to pursue continuing education experiences that may be helpful for maintaining and improving skills in their present positions. The church will pay the cost of such education upon evidence of satisfactory completion of the course, seminar, lecture, or workshop. All continuing education reimbursements must be approved by the senior minister prior to registration or attendance.

13) *Sabbatical leave:* Clergy staff shall be entitled to a three-months sabbatical leave with full pay and benefits upon completion of each six years of service with the church. All costs plus salary will be paid by the church for an approved course of studies useful to improving the minister's skills in ministry at Christ Church. Recipients of this benefit will be expected to continue their service to Christ Church for at least one year following the sabbatical.

14) *Tuition for dependents:* The church will pay full tuition costs for up to four years of college education for children of full-time employees with at least five years of service.

15) *Keyperson insurance:* A term life insurance policy is maintained on the lives of all clergy employees. Upon the death of the insured, one half of the policy amount will be payable to Christ Church, the other half to a beneficiary designated by the employee. Coverage is equal to four times the annual cash salary (including housing) of the employee.

16) *Housing equity fund:* All employees who live in church-owned housing shall be paid an annual housing equity allowance of 10 percent of cash salary. Payment will be into a trust fund established by the church, with the contributions to accumulate at interest, payable to the employee only upon termination of employment, disability, retirement, or the purchase of a home. At the employee's death, payment will be made to the designated beneficiary.

17) *Group automobile insurance:* All employees may participate at their own expense in the church's group automobile insurance plan.

18) *Travel insurance:* The church pays the entire premium for a twenty-four-hour $100,000 travel insurance policy on the lives of all full-time employees. Payment is made upon the death of the employee in an accident whether on church business or personal travel.

19) *Worker's compensation:* The church pays all required premiums for full worker's compensation coverages for all employees.

20) *Unemployment compensation:* As a nonprofit organization, the church does not participate in state or federal unemployment plans. However, the church will pay three months of full salary as severance pay to any clergy terminated for cause. All other employees shall receive six weeks severance pay when terminated for cause. Resigning employees shall not receive severance pay.

21) *Child care:* Employees with preschool children may use the child-care facilities of the church without cost. School-age children of full-time employees may attend the church's parochial school without cost.

22) *Annual physical examination:* All clergy employees and all other full-time employees over the age of fifty-five are required to arrange for an annual physical examination. Full-time employees ages thirty-five to fifty-five are required to arrange for a physical examination at least once every two years. All costs will be paid by the church.

23) *Moving expenses:* Any employee required to move from one home to another upon employment by Christ Church shall have all moving expenses reimbursed by the church.

24) *Leave without pay:* All full-time employees may take up to one month's leave annually without pay. Prior arrangements must be made with the senior minister.

25) *Office hours:* The normal workday will be 8:30 A.M. to 5:00 P.M. unless other schedules are assigned. The church office will be closed on all holidays. On Sundays, staff will be available in the church office from 7:30 A.M. to 12:30 P.M., as assigned.

26) *Legal and financial planning:* The church will pay up to five hundred dollars annually for each full-time employee for legal and financial planning services.

IV. *Housing.* All full-time clergy staff will be provided housing, either in church-owned housing or with a housing allowance, whichever the minister prefers. Nonclergy staff shall not receive housing. The amount of a housing allowance for clergy in their own homes or in the parsonage shall be requested by each minister and properly designated by the official board. Wherever possible, a housing allowance will be paid.

V. *Salary.* All employees shall receive a fair, equitable, and comparable salary for their work. The personnel committee shall annually review all salaries and make recommendations for adjustments to the official board. The annual budget shall show employee compensation for all employees in one lump sum without detail. The congregation will not be asked to consider individual salaries, but a listing of compensation paid to all employees shall be available upon request for review by any active member of the church.

VI. *Grievance Procedures.* All employees are entitled to a review of employment-related complaints. If an employee has a complaint, the matter should be reviewed with the supervisor first. If not resolved, the employee may take the matter to the personnel committee. If still not resolved, the matter may be appealed to the official board, with their agreement. The official board's decision shall be final.

Improving Staff Effectiveness

In addition to the numerous suggestions already made for assisting staff to be effective employees, there are other additional ways in which to improve staff activity.

All supervisors, especially the senior minister, should retain an open-door policy toward employees. While the weekly staff meeting may provide a forum for new ideas, the senior minister should encourage staff to make suggestions anytime for improving services and work efficiency. Of course not all ideas can be accepted, but all should be received and given a prompt response, yes or no. Any suggestions to the personnel committee, the official board, or to supervisors should be considered. Good ideas can be passed on directly to the appropriate committee for recommendation and implementation.

An effective staff will keep careful records of staff decisions and suggestions. Staff meeting minutes are important for action starters. Even notes of casual conversations can be used to improve effective communication. A card or pad for quick notes can be carried by all staff to note suggestions from members or staff.

Communication must be planned if a staff is to function effectively. Reports from departments ought to be shared with all staff, not just responsible staff, in order that all staff be informed about what is going on. After all, members may ask for information from the custodian, the secretary, or a pastor to a variety of questions: "Where is the paper collection? How do I enroll in the adult Bible class? Is there a cradle roll? Do you have a Mother's Day Out program? Can I get help for an aged father? Who arranges for weddings?" It is so very important that all staff be kept as fully informed as possible. Maximum effectiveness is achieved when all staff can respond to questions about future plans, class arrangements, routine scheduling, special programs.

"Write it down!" At best, staff effectiveness is enhanced when memos are passed to other staff requesting action. Oral communication is possible but not as effective since it can easily be forgotten. Instructions or comments from worshippers to the senior pastor following a worship service should be written down by a secretary unobtrusively standing near the pastor at the door. Or the use of a hidden tape recorder will help keep track of all requests and comments as people pass out of the church building. Also, telephone messages for staff out at the time of the call must be written down with clear instructions.

A daily schedule of staff hours is important to know who is where. An itinerary of clergy appointments during the week will be helpful to other staff in knowing the whereabouts of the ministers. A monthly schedule of travel plans informs all staff about who is in town, who is gone, and where they are. Open communication is very crucial to effective staff activity.

When the ministers aren't available, the staff must listen—report parishioners' responses, pass on comments, suggestions, complaints, and irritations, as well as compliments. Encouraging staff to observe congregational action and then respond to those reports can enhance the effectiveness of staff and create good relations between the senior minister and staff.

The senior minister is boss, but the boss needs to be open—to be a friend, a confidant, a willing listener, and above all a supporter and encourager. Staff responds to aggressive leadership that is open and helpful.

Bruce Lee says that today's professional employees are looking for something more than just a place to toil (*The Ledger,* National Association of Church Business Administrators, page 5, January 1984). They want a supportive environment where correction may indeed take place, but where the manager is truly interested in the individual employee. Lee goes on to say that if the employee cannot have confidence in the leader's ability to perform, then the employee's work may be less than expected. An employee, says Lee, has

1. "a right to be needed
2. a right to be involved
3. a right to a covenantal relationship
4. a right to be understood
5. a right to the ability to affect his/her own destiny
6. a right to be accountable
7. a right to know how well he/she is doing
8. a right to make a commitment
9. and a right to appeal."

Job Descriptions

JOB DESCRIPTION FOR THE SENIOR MINISTER

Summary statement of duties: The senior minister is elected by the congregation according to the rules and regulations of the denomination. He/she is the chief administrator of the church and responsible for the management of its programs, finances, property, and persons.

Qualifications:

1. Seminary graduate, ordained in this denomination.
2. Clergy member in good standing in this denomination.
3. Experienced manager (preferably of a larger congregation).
4. Skills in personnel management, fund-raising, organization.
5. Outstanding preacher (preferably with publishing credits).

To whom responsible: The official board.

Responsibilities:

1. Provide spiritual leadership to the members of the congregation through worship leadership, preaching, administration of Word and Sacraments.
2. Perform pastoral responsibilities for visiting the sick, consoling the bereaved, counselling the to-be-weds, and generally responding to the needs of people.
3. Coordinate all church activities.
4. Serve as president of the official board presiding at all meetings of the official board and the congregation.
5. Work with the various organizations of the church assisting them in program development and offer encouragement and inspiration.
6. Set an example of stewardship in personal living.
7. Train others in the oversight of the congregation's programs.
8. Arrange for proper accounting and reporting of the congregation's financial records.
9. Teach the confirmation classes.
10. Administer the Sacraments of Baptism and Holy Communion on a regular basis; provide private communion opportunities as requested.

11. Oversee the youth program and the Christian education program.
12. Direct church publicity, prepare the newsletter and the Sunday bulletin.
13. Represent the congregation in various judicatory meetings and ecumenical gatherings.
14. Supervise the church staff and encourage development in their areas of responsibility.
15. Submit quarterly written reports to the official board of activities, ministerial acts, and program plans.
16. Delegate responsibilities.

JOB DESCRIPTION FOR ASSOCIATE PASTOR

Summary statement of duties: The associate pastor shall support the senior minister in all pastoral responsibilities in harmony with the mission and objectives of the denomination and in conformity to the authority assigned by the official board.

Qualifications:

1. Seminary graduate, ordained in this denomination.
2. Clergy member of denomination in good standing.
3. Energetic, enthusiastic leader.
4. Administrative skills preferred.
5. Ability to work with youth.

To whom responsible: The senior minister.

Responsibilities:

1. Perform pastoral duties of Word and Sacrament as required.
2. Administer the youth program of the church providing skilled leadership and program planning.
3. Work with lay groups in developing evangelism visitation.
4. Assist the senior pastor in teaching confirmation classes.
5. Preach from time to time as requested.
6. Assist in the administration of the Christian education program serving as the staff person responsible for education development, coordination, and teacher training.
7. Represent the congregation in denominational and community activities as requested.
8. Share in the administration of the church program as requested by the senior minister.
9. Report quarterly, in writing, to the official board on activities and pertinent program responsibilities.
10. Do other tasks assigned by the senior minister.

JOB DESCRIPTION FOR SECRETARY TO THE PASTORS

Summary statement of duties: The church secretary shall assist the pastors in fulfilling their clerical responsibilities as requested, such as correspondence, directory maintenance, official record entries, appointments, and such other secretarial duties as may be assigned, including management of the church office.

Qualifications

1. Experienced secretarial skills, including typing at least fifty words per minute; shorthand preferred, word processing experience desirable.

2. Member of the congregation.
3. College degree.
4. Pleasant personality, conversational skills, ability to receive directions and carry out instructions.
5. Ability to supervise.

To whom responsible: The senior minister.

Responsibilities:

1. Maintain the church files and official records.
2. Produce the weekly newsletter and bulletins.
3. Handle all correspondence for the ministers.
4. Open, sort, and distribute daily mail.
5. Maintain an up-to-date church directory.
6. Prepare routine correspondence to visitors, for baptisms, memorial gifts, hospital letters, birthday cards from the pastors.
7. Prepare and distribute the minutes of the official board.
8. Prepare and distribute the annual congregational reports.
9. Receive telephone messages and relay them to proper persons.
10. Maintain the pastor's appointment calendar.
11. Complete other tasks assigned by the pastors.

JOB DESCRIPTION FOR BUSINESS ADMINISTRATOR

Summary statement of duties: The business administrator is responsible for the administration of the church's physical property and financial assets.

Qualifications:

1. Experienced businessman or woman.
2. Dedicated church person.
3. College degree in business or engineering.
4. Skilled manager of property, people, and money.

To whom responsible: The senior minister.

Responsibilities:

1. Oversee the maintenance and use of the physical plant and equipment.
2. Schedule the use of the building and equipment.
3. Coordinate the stewardship program and annual Every Member Response or Every Member Visit program.
4. Oversee the development of the church budget.
5. Schedule insurance coverages for the church's physical assets, determining and securing liability coverages as needed.
6. Delegate responsibility for an annual audit of the church's financial records.
7. Administer the congregation's employee benefits programs.
8. Maintain the church's financial records; administer those volunteers or paid staff responsible for the recordkeeping tasks.
9. Recommend needed maintenance and improvements.

10. Supervise the custodial staff.
11. Arrange for proper maintenance of the heating and air conditioning systems and all other special equipment.
12. Serve as purchasing agent for the congregation in securing necessary supplies, materials, etc.
13. Do other tasks assigned by the senior minister or the official board from time to time.

JOB DESCRIPTION FOR DIRECTOR OF CHRISTIAN EDUCATION

Summary statement of duties: The director of Christian education has overall responsibility for the entire education program of the congregation in accordance with the objectives set by the official board and the committee on Christian education.

Qualifications:

1. Master's degree in Religious Education.
2. Committed church person.
3. Member of the denomination.
4. Experienced teacher of children.
5. Creative, aggressive, innovative leader.

To whom responsible: The senior minister.

Responsibilities:

1. Provide complete oversight, supervision and planning for all of the schools of the church: Sunday church school, weekday church school, vacation church school, day school, nursery school.
2. Determine personnel needs for all of the church's schools; hire staff.
3. Strengthen relationships between church families and the education program through visits, calls, cards, letters.
4. Encourage educational personnel to develop contacts with parents and students beyond the classroom.
5. Arrange for teacher training opportunities, leadership schools, etc.
6. Review literature, equipment, and supplies needs and inventories.
7. Attend all staff meetings.
8. Submit written, quarterly reports to the official board.
9. Work with the Christian education committee in developing educational opportunities and programs.
10. Represent the congregation at various denominational and ecumenical educational events, seminars, programs.
11. Do other tasks assigned by the senior minister from time to time.

JOB DESCRIPTION FOR CUSTODIAN

Summary statement of duties: The custodian is responsible for the maintenance and personal appearance of the church building and facilities.

Qualifications:

1. Committed church person.
2. High school education.

3. Experienced maintenance skills.
4. Ability to receive instructions and carry them out.
5. Neat appearance, high moral standards.
6. Physical strength.

To whom responsible: The church business administrator.

Responsibilities:

1. Maintain a neat and clean church facility.
2. Maintain an adequate inventory of maintenance supplies.
3. Do routine maintenance.
4. Implement a preventive maintenance program for equipment, buildings, and grounds.
5. Unlock and secure the buildings each day, including Sunday.
6. Maintain the keys for all doors, equipment, etc.
7. Arrange for proper room setups as requested by organizations, committees and staff.
8. Do other assignments requested by the senior minister or the business administrator from time to time.

JOB DESCRIPTION FOR MINISTER OF MUSIC

Summary statement of duties: The minister of music is responsible for developing a music program for the church that will complement the liturgy, the preaching, and the spirit of the people. Specific responsibilities include providing music at all worship services and directing all church choirs.

Qualifications:

1. Master's Degree in piano, organ, or voice.
2. Experience in directing church choirs.
3. Ability to teach children as well as adults.
4. Pleasing personality, demonstrated ability to work sympathetically with a variety of individuals.
5. Master of the organ instrument.

To whom responsible: The senior minister.

Responsibilities:

1. Play the organ for all worship services, funerals, weddings, and other church events.
2. Direct all of the church choirs—adults as well as children.
3. Develop an overall music education program for the benefit of interested persons.
4. Maintain all musical instruments, including the organ.
5. Offer at least one concert annually for the benefit of the membership.
6. Work with the worship committee chairperson in developing meaningful music for worship.
7. Plan all music for all worship services, including hymn selection (in consultation with the preaching minister), preludes, postludes, anthems, special music, etc.
8. Do other tasks the senior minister may request.

JOB DESCRIPTION FOR FINANCIAL SECRETARY

Summary statement of duties: The financial secretary is responsible for maintaining the financial records of the congregation.

Qualifications:

1. Accounting or bookkeeping skills and experience.
2. High school diploma.
3. Committed Christian (not necessarily a member of Christ Church).
4. Familiarity and experience with the use of small personal computers.

To whom responsible: The business administrator.

Responsibilities:

1. Count, deposit, and record all offerings and receipts.
2. Maintain individual contributions records for all members' contributions.
3. Distribute offering envelopes and assign numbers.
4. Mail quarterly and annual statements of giving.
5. Keep records of all memorial gifts and other restricted funds.
6. Maintain safety of all securities.
7. Keep proper records of all receipts and disbursements.
8. Reconcile the bank statements.
9. Prepare payroll checks and necessary payroll tax reports and payments.
10. Maintain all benefit insurance records.
11. Prepare all checks for payment of all bills for signature by the treasurer or business manager.
12. Prepare written, monthly financial reports for the official board; prepare the annual financial statements.
13. Prepare necessary financial reports to committee chairpersons.
14. Promote sound stewardship practices among staff and church members.
15. Assist the business administrator, treasurer, finance committee, and senior minister in any other ways requested.

JOB DESCRIPTION FOR MEMBERSHIP SECRETARY

Summary statement of duties: The membership secretary is responsible for maintaining a current and up-to-date directory of the membership and for supervising the church office.

Qualifications:

1. Dedicated member of the church.
2. Experience in supervising other employees.
3. Penchant for detail; neat and precise.
4. Sensitive to the needs of people who want information.
5. Familiarity with the use of a personal computer for purposes of statistical recordkeeping of membership files.

To whom responsible: The secretary to the ministers.

Responsibilities:

1. Supervise church office details under the direction of the secretary to the ministers.
2. Arrange for baptisms, securing required information and making necessary record entries.
3. Arrange for weddings, providing for music, flowers, minister, reception area, and all necessary plans as required; sign and mail the marriage license to the courthouse; record necessary data for the church records.

61

4. Coordinate all details for funerals, making necessary record entries; arrange for food and transportation.
5. Supervise, collect, and maintain all files and records on new members.
6. Maintain all records for existing membership, including all family and church activity records; maintain mailing lists, make changes, prepare mailing labels, etc; be responsible for use of the church personal computer.
7. Prepare all mailings.
8. Prepare necessary membership statistical data for bulletins, newsletters, parochial reports, etc.
9. Organize needed information for the Every Member Response program including coordinating the assignment of visits, follow ups, and reports of visits.
10. Maintain the church directory.
11. Maintain personal family history records.
12. Maintain the official membership and ministerial acts records of the congregation.
13. Coordinate the work of the church office, assigning tasks and responding to membership inquiries.
14. Coordinate the church volunteer program with assistance from the director of volunteers.
15. Complete such other tasks as may be assigned from time to time by the senior minister or his/her secretary.

JOB DESCRIPTION FOR RECEPTIONIST

Summary statement of duties: The receptionist is primarily responsible for transferring all incoming telephone calls and for greeting visitors to the church building on weekdays.

Qualifications:

1. Charming, outgoing personality.
2. Pleasant voice when talking on the telephone.
3. Experience in meeting people and responding to their inquiries.
4. Dedicated church member.

To whom responsible: Secretary to the ministers.

Responsibilities:

1. Direct telephone calls to recipients.
2. Maintain the church calendar and staff travel itineraries.
3. Send publicity notices to newspapers.
4. Respond to visitors' inquiries.
5. Direct visitors to requested offices.
6. Prepare daily listings of room use.
7. Maintain the church bulletin boards—indoors and outdoors.
8. Compile church attendance records and prepare required reports.
9. Do such typing as may be requested by the secretary to the ministers.
10. Assist the business administrator in the preparation of stewardship materials, mailings, and reports.
11. Do other tasks requested by the senior minister or the secretary to the ministers.

CHAPTER 4

SELECTING, USING,
AND MANAGING
VOLUNTEERS

THIS CHAPTER IS about the recruitment, retention, development, and supervision of volunteer workers in the church.

Some friends were gathered for an afternoon barbecue. Conversation drifted to church work.

"It's no wonder Sally had a nervous breakdown," exclaimed her best friend Jane. "The way the church kept putting her on every committee for the last four years."

"Yeah," responded Sam, "you'd think they'd ask someone else occasionally."

"That's the trouble with this church," complained Howard. "It's always the same people who do all the work. I wish someone would ask me. I'm willing."

"Sure," chimed in Ed. "Since I retired last year, no one's asked me to help, and I've sure had the time to do something over there."

"It's one thing to usher or bake pies or mow the lawn," commented Sue, "but no one seems to know what needs to be done, or who does what, or who can do something."

"I think the pastor's got it all up here," spoke up Mildred pointing to her head. "But when he goes, who'll know anything then?"

"Somebody ought to get the volunteers organized," said Jane. "Then the pastor wouldn't always have to ask Sally to do everything. Surely somebody else can be a volunteer!"

Sound familiar? Probably so. There are able, willing, and generous volunteers in all congregations, but sometimes only a few do the work because no one has tried to coordinate a willingness to work and jobs to be done. No one has tried to inventory resources (people) or actions (jobs to be done). It's catch as catch can and the pastor is never sure anyone will really be around to do what needs doing.

Think about the members of your own congregation. Who are the volunteers and what do they do? It's easy to make a mental list of all the people who serve on the official board, teach Sunday church school, usher, sing in the choir, or work on committees.

It's easy to think about all the people you know who serve in the community as scout leaders, school board members, hospital aides, day-care helpers, and plenty more.

Many people serve and many people respond quite naturally. Remember Paul's "varieties of gifts" and "varieties of services" in his letter to the Corinthians (1 Cor. 12:4-5)?

Volunteers are those people who willingly and eagerly give of themselves to do whatever task needs to be done. Volunteers recognize a stewardship responsibility to give of their time, talents, and treasures in response to God's great gift of love in Christ for them.

Who Are the Volunteers?

So, who are the volunteers?

—They are the Sallys who are committed to getting a job done, asking for nothing except the satisfaction of achieving the goals they've set.

—They are the Janes, deeply involved in sharing responsibility for the mission of the church and committed to the task.

—They are the Sams sharing knowledge and skills with others in the church, offering service, bringing the people closer together in fellowship.

—They are the Howards willingly sharing and expressing their partnership in ministry, responding to the opportunity for identifying and putting to use the diversity of skills, abilities, and expertise of people around them.

—They are the Mildreds sharing time and talents and themselves simply to meet the needs of people, nothing more.

And why do they volunteer?

No matter how you define a volunteer, Christians generally always relate voluntarism to some service in response to the needs, goals, mission, and purpose of the church.

Surely the church is the essence of voluntarism. No one coerced us to join. No one promised us a good life, wealth, or health. No one threatened. We joined freely, accepting baptism and the covenant of grace. We have been called; we are part of that priesthood of all believers; we are the saints. But we came on our own through the call of the Holy Spirit. And here we are—a variety of persons with a variety of gifts and skills, which is exactly what Paul had in mind in Romans 12:6-8.

Thus, we are all God's people—clergy and lay alike. There is no distinction. We are all engaged together in the ministries of the church. Together, yet individually and in our own ways, we apply our Christian faith wherever we live and work and play. Some volunteers will minister in the community to meet a wide spectrum of human needs. Others may minister within the framework of the congregation, doing the jobs that need doing there.

Enough will probably never be done, but to whatever extent the volunteers in your church are intentionally fulfilling ministry, those members are responding to the Lord's command to make disciples of all nations, of all peoples.

Coordinating the Volunteers

The task, then, for the congregation is to harness all this existing, potential voluntarism into a manageable form so that the Sallys won't be burned out, the Eds will be found, and the Janes satisfied.

No matter the size of your congregation, somebody does try to get more members to serve; someone does know what some members are willing to do and how much time they have; someone does know why some members respond and others don't; and someone usually knows which Sally or Ed or Jane to ask to do a given job. Usually that's the pastor.

But no one probably knows how much time it takes to care for the church's volunteers—to get them to respond, to train them, or to support them. Yet people are the congregation's most valuable resource. It is not enough to know the church depends on its volunteers. The church must be intentional in taking care of the saints.

While coordination alone will never strengthen the ministry or motivate the Eds and the Mildreds to volunteer, it is the key to a responsible stewardship of an intentional volunteer ministry.

Surely you can see the efficiency involved in having someone responsible for coordinating the selection of committee members, teachers, ushers, and anyone else. Committee chairpersons may be responsible for selecting committee memberships, but without some coordination those committees won't be effective and the task of selection severely frustrated when just a few key workers are solicited by several chairpersons.

Coordination of volunteers involves the obvious:

—Knowing what jobs have to be done.

—Keeping tab on who is willing, who is doing what, and who has done what jobs and when.

—Helping members to find the places where they can serve.

—Knowing needs outside the church—in the community or larger judicatory—where the church's volunteers could be helpful.

—Alerting volunteers to resources and leadership opportunities in the community that could be supportive.

But who will coordinate? The pastor, historically, unless an intentional program is developed. Or perhaps the Sunday church school director can at least coordinate education ministry volunteers; the choir director looks out for choir members; the property committee knows who will mow. One way or another coordination is going on. But to improve the volunteer ministries in your congregation most effectively, you may want to consider selecting a volunteer coordinator.

Perhaps that will continue to be the pastor. It probably will be in the smaller churches. But it is better for someone else to be appointed to the task. The pastor, of course, always remains available for guidance, support, and information. And in larger congregations, a leadership committee can support, supervise, train, and work with the volunteer coordinator (VC) in coordinating the activities of all the members of the church—the volunteers. But a key to efficient management of the volunteer ministries is the selection of a competent person as coordinator. That option cannot be overlooked.

JOB DESCRIPTION—VOLUNTEER COORDINATOR*

1. *Purpose of the position:*
   a. To provide more members with the opportunity to serve as volunteers in the congregation and community.
   b. To coordinate the ways members are identified, recruited, trained, and supported in volunteer ministries.
   c. To contribute to the church's mission through volunteer services.

2. *Responsibilities and duties:*
   a. Encourage an awareness and commitment to lay ministry.
   b. Assist in describing volunteer jobs.
   c. Encourage the use of sensible recruitment procedures.
   d. Match people with skills and interests to the jobs that need to be done.
   e. Develop and maintain a volunteer filing system.
   f. Assist in developing the leadership program.
   g. Support volunteers with encouragement and recognition.

3. *Relationships:*
   a. Be responsible to the official board and the pastor.
   b. Build a working relationship with congregational leaders.
   c. Communicate with the congregation and key leaders.
   d. Establish relationships with voluntary action groups in the community.
   e. Establish relationships with the denomination's area volunteer coordinator services program.

---

*Adapted from *Recruiting and Developing Volunteer Leaders,* © 1979, Parish Life Press, Philadelphia, Pa., page 10. Used by permission.

4. *Time required:* Days _____ Length of service _____

5. *Qualifications:*
   a. A person who:
      1) Is committed to the mission of the church in the congregation.
      2) Has the ability to get along with people and win their cooperation.
      3) Has the ability to organize.
      4) Has experience as a volunteer.
      5) Has perseverance, enthusiasm, dedication, a sense of humor.

6. *Training suggested:*
   a. Study and use of denominational handbooks.
   b. Take advantage of counsel and leadership opportunities sponsored by the denomination's volunteer services divisions.
   c. Take advantage of community training opportunities.

Review the job description for a volunteer coordinator. Adapt this suggestion to the needs of your own congregation. A one-year commitment, renewable for another year, is reasonable.

Keep in mind that a volunteer coordinator does not take over recruiting volunteers and deciding what jobs need doing. The coordinator does not take over the work being done by others. A coordinator is part of the leadership team, supporting the ministry of committees, staff, and leaders. A good working relationship is imperative.

Once decided, tell the congregation about the new coordination program. Describe it fully. Tell about the leadership, the costs, the duration, the purpose, and the goals. Above all, explain why this position is so important in the life of the church.

Then go out and recruit the volunteer coordinator!
—write a job description
—specify qualifications
—develop a handbook of guidelines
—identify potential candidates
—interview candidates
—select the best suited person
—train the new volunteer coordinator

An Inventory of Volunteers

Who are your volunteers, and what are they doing? Before embarking on this ambitious program of coordination, you'd best know what it is you have to coordinate. Take an inventory of who is doing what.

Develop some worksheets (similar to the ones illustrated) to count how many people are doing something, what they are doing, and how many hours they do it. Get the big picture. Organize the inventory this way:

1. List all the committees, groups, and organizations in your church and count all the people involved.
2. List all the nonorganized ministries people do: lawn care, folding bulletins, visiting the nursing home, making coffee for meetings, etc.
3. What is the involvement of members in church activities outside the church? Count the jobs and the people.
4. Count the members involved in community programs: scouts, meals on wheels, child abuse prevention, alcohol rehabilitation, PTA, etc.
5. Put all of this information on your worksheet.

66

VOLUNTARISM INVENTORY WORKSHEET

Church Program	Youth	Men	Women	Total	Percentage of Membership
Leadership					
Official board					
Women's groups					
Men's groups					
Youth ministry					
Educational ministry					
Stewardship					
Finance committee					
Personnel committee					
Property committee					
Worship/music committee					
Social ministry committee					
Visitation ministry					
Etc.					
Individual Ministries					
Sick visitors					
Yard care					
Office help					
Coffee makers					
Shut-in care					
Etc.					
Outside Church Ministries					
Camp board					
Area council of churches					
Judicatory executive board					
College student ministries					
Etc.					
Nonchurch Community Ministries					
Local hospital board					
United Way campaign volunteer					
Girl & Boy Scouts					
School board					
Etc.					

But that listing only tells you how many people are doing what. It says nothing yet about how your members are most involved. Thus, so you'll know where your members are really doing the most work, compile an inventory of volunteer program hours per month.

Use the inventory of volunteer hours to list the total time spent on various church programs. Use the earlier inventory of people and assign volunteer hours to each program.

You may be pleasantly surprised at the number of hours your members are volunteering just for church programs. And that of course does not count all the hours beyond the church for other judicatory activities or community programs. At least now you'll know in which programs there is the preponderance of voluntary activity. It will also give you a key to the programs that may need some help from available volunteers.

INVENTORY OF VOLUNTEER HOURS

	Number of Volunteers	Hours per Month
Worship & Music Choirs		
Worship planning		
Stewardship Every Member Response		
Planning		
Education Sunday church school teachers		
Staff supervision		
Leadership training		
Home visits		
Witness Visits to prospectives		
Visits to members		
Property care Planning		
Yard work		
Building maintenance		
Personnel Committee Planning		
Interviews		
Evaluations		
Service Committees Planning		
Participation		
Other programs Planning		
Doing		
Evaluating		
Total hours of volunteer time per month		_____

What Are Volunteers Supposed to Do?

Without volunteers, the church would surely crumble because most of what is done in the church's ministries is done by volunteers.

George Scheitlin and Eleanor Gillstrom developed a volunteer model with eight aspects of volunteer activity:*

1. *The congregation's statement of mission:* This is a written statement that spells out what the congregation is all about, its purpose, its goals. It gives direction to parish planning and activities. And it provides a basis for evaluating the whole process of leadership development.

2. *The tasks necessary to carry out this mission:* Tasks that are clearly outlined make it possible for volunteers to know what needs to be done.

3. *The people with the skills and commitment to perform the tasks:* When people know what's needed to be done and their skills can be used, personal growth improves and there is a development of new interests.

4. *The file of potential and active volunteers:* An inventory file of who is, can or will do something becomes a clearing house for information and referrals.

5. *Recruitment procedures:* This brings together the person and the task—personal interviews seek to recruit the right volunteer for the right job.

6. *Training opportunities:* Sound leadership development is crucial for personal growth of volunteers as well as for preparing volunteers for their tasks.

7. *Ministries performed:* These are all the needs fulfilled by the volunteers—advocacy, program planning, policy making, consultation, teaching, counseling, visitation, etc. Recognition of services performed is essential to a continuing relationship and willingness to work.

8. *Mission evaluation of ministries and leadership procedures in light of the congregation's stated mission:* Continuous matching of people and tasks to accomplish mission.

WHERE ARE WE NOW? WORKSHEET**

In Mission—

1. Yes _____, No _____, we have a mission statement which gives direction to our ministries.
2. Yes _____, No _____, we use the constitution (or discipline) for direction of our ministries.
3. Yes _____, No _____, we regularly evaluate volunteer activity by our mission statement and constitution.

In Tasks—

1. List two tasks for each function:

	Regularly . . . Sometimes . . . Seldom		
a. Worship			
b. Learning			
c. Witness			
d. Service			
e. Support			
2. Which tasks still need job descriptions?			

In Skills—

	Regularly . . . Sometimes . . . Seldom		
1. Members are asked to complete a skills-and-service sheet or some other form listing tasks for which volunteers are needed.			
2. Members are informed about the ministry of the laity.			

*Adapted from *Recruiting and Developing Volunteer Leaders,* © 1979, Parish Life Press, Philadelphia, Pa., page 17. Used by permission.
**Ibid., pages 18-19.

	Regularly .	. Sometimes .	. Seldom
3. Attempts are made to discover the person's interest, motivations, expectations, and availability.			
In Recruitment—			
1. Recruitment is done through personal interviews.			
2. Job descriptions are used.			
3. The emphasis in recruiting is on helping persons find jobs that match their interests, abilities, and time.			
In Leadership Development—			
1. Every newly recruited person receives orientation.			
2. Every newly recruited person receives training for tasks which require it.			
3. Training opportunities are planned to both adequately deal with the subject and take into account the volunteer's time limitations.			
4. Volunteers are involved in the planning and evaluation of their tasks.			
5. Provision is made for babysitting to allow for participation in training sessions.			
6. The congregation takes advantage of leadership and training opportunities sponsored by the denomination.			
7. The congregation uses outside resources (people, media, events) to supplement its own resources.			
In Ministries—			
1. Someone cares about the volunteers, meets with them, and can be contacted when help is needed.			
2. The work of volunteers is appreciated and receives appropriate recognition.			
3. Volunteers have the opportunity to evaluate how they are doing.			
4. Volunteers are given opportunity for enrichment.			
5. Volunteers can "retire," or move on to a more challenging or different task.			
6. Volunteers have their expenses taken care of.			
7. Volunteers who serve in the community or at the judicatory level are known, recognized, and supported.			

Developing the Program

Start where you are. Examine each direction on the "Strengths and Weaknesses Worksheets" and select the place most logical for you to start your planning. Typically you'll do well to start with mission, because without knowing directions, it will be hard to assign tasks. But look first at where your congregation is in relationship to the directions. Use the worksheet "Where Are We Now?" Then test the strengths and weaknesses of each of those directions.

SELECTING, USING, AND MANAGING VOLUNTEERS

DIRECTIONS—STRENGTHS AND WEAKNESSES WORKSHEET*

Directions	Strengths	Weaknesses
Mission	Communicate through sermons	No congregational mission statement
Tasks	Committees are set up to carry out the mission	No clear job descriptions
Skills	We communicate need for volunteers	Not reaching enough people
File	Pastor has file of volunteers and uses it	Not enough names referred
Recruitment	Personal contact is made	Fail to match interests and abilities of person with task
Leadership Development	Encourage people to attend workshops	Seldom given adequate orientation—judicatory workshops rarely attended
Ministries	Recognize the service of some volunteers	Not enough recognition for some—no evaluation of service or need
Mission Evaluation	Regular evaluation of some key ministries	Evaluation of other current ministries seldom made

Then, having learned where you are and knowing which aspects are strong or weak, develop a strategy to deal with each aspect, write out a specific plan of action.

VOLUNTARISM STRATEGY WORKSHEET**

Determine where you would like to begin strengthening your volunteer program. Select that direction that seems to need the most work. Then list what needs to be done to develop that direction to a top priority item. Use this strategy worksheet to formulate your plans.

1. Direction to work on: _____
2. What needs to be done to develop this direction of voluntary activity? _____
_____
3. Details of what needs to be done to develop this direction:

Need to work on	This will be done how:	By (date)	By whom?	Job is done when
1.				
2.				
3.				

---

*Adapted from *Recruiting and Developing Volunteer Leaders*, © 1979, Parish Life Press, Philadelphia, Pa., page 20. Used by permission.
**Ibid., page 21.

Finally, establish good relationships with other leaders. Let the other church leaders know what the volunteer coordinator does. Tell the congregation, support the leaders, seek the assistance from staff to accomplish strategies for the voluntarism program. Just help everyone concerned understand what the volunteer coordinator's job is all about.

—Describe the purpose of the work and tell others what the coordinator wants to do.

—Clarify the role of the coordinator to avoid stepping on someone's toes.

—Spell out clearly the procedures by which the coordinator expects to be most helpful.

—Identify the persons or groups to whom the coordinator is accountable. Make sure everyone knows this.

—Identify the volunteer coordinator as a resource person rather than a volunteer ready to do the work of the committees.

—Arrange for adequate office space, telephone, filing cabinets, etc.

If no one has really coordinated all the volunteer activity in your congregation before, the most important first activity will be for the newly appointed volunteer coordinator to establish a good working relationship with everyone else. Nothing will devastate a program more quickly than perceived assumptions of authority over activities claimed by others. Sharing is crucial.

Keeping Track of Volunteers

So, how does the coordinator now pull together in one comprehensible file folder all the tasks that need doing and all the people willing to do the tasks? Some may argue that a file is not needed since needs and people seem to get matched up eventually. Of course they do, but because matching doesn't always take place (either in a mutually agreeable way or maybe even at all), a list of jobs and volunteers needs to be compiled. There are always more jobs, and there are always more volunteers. A file contains the information needed to match the two easily, quickly, and for the best match. A computer can be a handy tool for that process.

Use a volunteer job inventory notebook similar to the following:

JOB INVENTORY WORKSHEET

Program _____ Job _____		
Volunteer's Name	Telephone	Date Job Completed
1.		
2.		
3.		

List the names of persons who have done the job and who are now doing the job. With every change of personnel, add the new name. An historic record is then created with complete information about total voluntarism of the membership. Not only is this a record of who all worked at certain jobs (teaching, ushering, greeting, meal service, etc.), but it will always be clear which volunteers may be interested in doing this kind of job again.

Arrange this notebook alphabetically by program, or develop a master chart of accounts and sort by number. That way, new programs or new account numbers can easily be assigned and all pages quickly located.

For greater efficiency in knowing who has done what or is willing to do something, a time and talent form for every member may well be a crucial part of the volunteer coordinator's file. As part of the annual Every Member Response stewardship program, this form could be completed along with the financial pledge. Its purpose is to determine available skills and interests of the membership.

Filed alphabetically, the time and talent record provides ready access to every member's interests. Be sure to develop the form around the job needs of committees, working with chairpersons to determine the different tasks required.

TIME AND TALENT RECORD—
SKILLS AND SERVICE INTEREST RECORD*

(Print each page on one half of an 8½ × 11 sheet of paper. Statistical information from page one should be printed left to right at bottom of one 8½ × 11 page, the other pages printed the other direction. The page, when folded, will provide a booklet with three pages printed in small booklet format, cross-wise to the others so the folded sheet can easily be filed and information easily read.)

Page 1 information:

Ms./Mrs./Mr. _____

Address _____

Occupation _____

Work experiences _____

_____

Prefer to work with:

preschool___ school age___ teenagers___ young adults___ adults___ seniors___ handi- capped___ homebound___ no preference___ Transportation is ___ is not ___ available.

Date _____

Home phone _____ Business _____

Age range Under 18 (exact)_____ 18-20_____ 21-30_____ 31-45_____ 46-65_____ 65 +_____

Educational experience _____

Leisure activities _____

Time for volunteering: (hours)

Mon._____ Tues._____ Wed._____ Thurs._____

Fri._____ Sat._____ Sun._____

Page 2 information:

About Your Skills and Services

Witnessing to our faith in Jesus Christ takes many forms in daily life and in the community of believers.

Each year the official board and the committees of the congregation identify ways in which that ministry can take place. This form indicates the opportunities for members of our congregation to become involved in specific ways with the mission of our congregation.

Additional information about each of the opportunities for service are available from the volunteer coordinator at the church office. Job descriptions and qualifications have been prepared for each opportunity.

Our Volunteer Needs This Year

(Please check one or more volunteer services you would be willing to provide this year.)

Worship: Ushers__ Lector__ Assisting minister__ Altar guild__ Senior choir__ Junior choir__ Worship committee__ Acolytes__

_____

*Adapted from *Recruiting and Developing Volunteer Leaders*, © 1979, Parish Life Press, Philadelphia, Pa., pages 25-26. Used by permission.

Learning: Church school teachers for age 3__ Grade 1__ Grade 2__ Grade 3__ Grade 4__ Grade 5__ Grade 6__ Grade 7__ Grade 8__ Grade 9__ High school__ Youth ministry advisors__ Bible study leader__ Adult class discussion leader__ Education committee__ Vacation school teachers/helpers: Nursery/Kindergarten__ Grades 1 & 2__ Grades 3 & 4__ Grades 5 & 6__ Music__

Page 3 information:

Service: Social ministry committee__ Hospital visitation__ Homebound visitation__ Committee on congregational community responsibility__ Community council for human rights__ I am available for the following emergency needs:

_____

Witness: Evangelism committee__ Visitor to inactives__ unchurched__ special cares__ Committee on lay ministry__ World mission__ Interpreter (language)_____

Support: Stewardship committee__ Every Member Response visitor__ Leadership development committee__ Communications committee__ Congregational fellowship nights__ Program__ Refreshments__ Publicity__ Telephone__

Property: Painting__ Yard cleanup__ Carpentry__ Repairs__ Housekeeping__ Gardening__

Page 4 information:

Skills which I have and would like to share are:

_____
_____
_____

Skills I would like to develop are:

_____
_____
_____

My hobbies are:_____
_____

I would be interested in knowing more about the possibilities for service in the community__ in the area__ in the judicatory__ in churchwide agency programs__
My volunteer experience includes:
Church_____
_____

Community_____
_____

Matching jobs and skills in larger congregations could be a tricky business. Here's where a personal computer would be of enormous help to the volunteer coordinator. At the touch of a button, a complete listing of all those persons with a specific skill could be produced.

But whether the file is in a three-ring notebook, in a small 5½ × 8½ booklet, or in a computer, the information now on hand *must* be used. Refer names of interested persons to committee chairpersons. Respond promptly to requests for names. Contact volunteers when a job is to be done. Recruit other volunteers. Publicize the list. Above all, use the information. Don't forget that you have asked the members to tell you about their interests, talents, and willingness to do something. They will expect to be asked and used.

Add to the volunteer notebook job descriptions for many of the tasks that need doing. Use as much detail as possible. That will be extremely helpful to volunteers needing to know what's involved before agreeing to work. A standard job description form, such as the following, could be developed.

VOLUNTEER JOB DESCRIPTION FORM

Program:
Position description:
Purpose of job:
Responsibility of volunteer:
To whom responsible:
Time expectation:
Qualifications:
Training sessions:

A volunteer resource file would be a handy information packet to distribute to volunteers. Such a packet would include a copy of the church constitution, an organization chart of committees and staff, descriptions of the volunteer program, telephone numbers of key persons, job descriptions for the volunteer coordinator and for the job requested of the volunteer, articles on voluntarism, a report of volunteer activity in the congregation for the previous year, and articles on lay ministry. A general file of information on voluntarism should be maintained in the coordinator's office for the benefit of any interested persons.

Finding Volunteers

Volunteers able and willing to do the jobs required around the church don't just happen. A volunteer coordinator will need to recruit, train, and develop a plan for volunteers. The question is not the lack of volunteers but of controlling the flood of possible volunteers. By coordinating the task of seeking volunteers, recruitment of Sunday church school teachers, stewardship program visitors, gardeners, and bulletin stuffers will be a more satisfying experience for the leaders and for the coordinator—and especially for the pastor!

By using the volunteer file the coordinator can help identify the appropriate people for jobs. The file has information on everyone's prior experience, skills, and interests. Sorting by computer will bring up the names of qualified persons. The volunteer coordinator will be able to coordinate and ease the process of filling out committee lists and supplying workers for emergencies as well as planning programs. When the plumbing breaks, the coordinator knows the plumber by looking up the information in the file. When the air conditioning fails on a hot Sunday morning, the coordinator knows the engineers. When a member dies, the coordinator knows who can prepare food for the grieving family. When the pastor becomes ill on a Sunday morning, the coordinator knows the teachers and would-be preacher. He/she can call them! When the social ministry committee needs five people to help with the Mothers Day Out program tomorrow, the coordinator can match the need.

Once the volunteer coordinator has responded to standard program needs and crises calls successfully, congregational recruiters will begin to depend on the coordinator's files of information for personnel. More important, they will begin to search out ways to use the vast array of available skills already volunteered.

To motivate potential volunteers with a willingness to share, the coordinator must create an awareness among the congregation of the continuing need for volunteers. Too often, without a coordinator, congregations lapse into the problem that got Sally bombed out on church work. When people know the needs for volunteers and realize that a few dedicated members can't do it all, there will be more volunteers.

A personal interview with prospective volunteers for a specific job will get the best recruits and generate the most likely acceptance. For special tasks, the person-to-person contact is especially necessary. Over a cup of coffee, in the home of the member, or at lunch, the task can be carefully spelled out by the pastor or coordinator, clearly stating the time required, the training provided, and what is expected. The volunteer must have an opportunity to respond, of course. A prompt decision is likely, and thanks can be expressed in advance for willingness to do that job. A letter won't be the same, and a telephone call misses the expression of the eyes and mouth. But both can be an additional way to say thanks. Not every task needs a special interview to find the right person, but when the task is big—the EMR chairperson, Sunday church school director, choir director—eye-to-eye contact can make the difference in a yes or no.

Making Volunteers Leaders

Not all volunteers are the kinds of leaders you may want or need. Keep in mind that each potential volunteer leader is unique and already has a personal style that won't change much. The purpose of any training is not to teach new skills, necessarily, rather to help the volunteer to grow and mature in his/her ability to lead.

Development of special training programs in the various program areas must be coordinated with leaders responsible for those areas. The volunteer coordinator does not develop the program but does coordinate the selection of participants. Volunteers can be trained before or during their service, depending on what they are doing. Some won't need any training at all. The depth of training depends on needs, prior experience, interest, and difficulty of the tasks to be done. Every possible resource tool, person, and material should be made available to potential volunteer leaders.

A hearty thank-you

Those volunteers don't expect anything in return for their work, just the satisfaction of doing a good job that will be helpful to someone in need. But the wise volunteer coordinator will be certain that adequate amounts of praise are heaped on every volunteer. It is appropriate to greet volunteers with a smile when they show up for a job, listen to their ideas, display photos of them at work, and provide publicity materials to newspapers on outstanding voluntary activities. Give a small gift of appreciation. Have the congregation provide funds for volunteers to attend training sessions. Recognize volunteers all year long in special ways. And plan a recognition event—a luncheon for Sunday church school teachers, a steak dinner for choir members, a reception for EMR visitors, a party for property committee workers, or a coffee hour after the service for ushers. Send a birthday, anniversary, or special occasion card; write personal thank you notes; praise volunteers to their friends; plan a volunteer of the month celebration; have a volunteer and family picnic.

SERVICE AND PRAYER OF RECOGNITION OF VOLUNTEERS*

Leader: Let us give thanks to God for the love which he has revealed to us in Jesus Christ, and for all persons who embody his love in the church, in our community, and in the world.

---

*Adapted from *Recruiting and Developing Volunteer Leaders,* © 1979, Parish Life Press, Philadelphia, Pa., page 47. Used by permission.

76

Leader: Let us pray. O God, we thank you for your Son, who came into this world to serve, not to be served; who gave his life as a ransom for us, in love for us. Open our eyes to the needs surrounding us in this world, a world into which he came to save and to serve and to love.

Congregation: Enable us to serve that world in love.

Leader: O God, we thank you for all those persons who share their time and skills and resources with the rest of us in the ministries of this congregation and your church. Enable each of us, following their example, to witness more fully to your love to those with special needs.

Congregation: Help us to grow in our service to you and to your church.

Leader: O God, we give thanks to you for all those who work for justice and harmony and peace in our community. Help us to respond to the needs of all people everywhere that all may be fed and live in dignity and peace.

Congregation: Empower us with your grace that we may serve all our neighbors in love.

Leader: O God, we give you thanks for your whole church, for all those who serve in our denomination, and for our pastor and staff. Do not let us take any of them for granted.

Congregation: Strengthen those who serve us and you and the church wherever they may be in your vast kingdom here on earth.

Leader: O God, open our eyes to the many needs of your church and the world. Help us to see the opportunities for service that abound in this place. Enable each of us in our own way to respond in new and creative ways of ministry and service.

Minister: Almighty God, bless now these volunteers who come from our congregation to use their skills and their time and their resources and their energies in unselfish service to you. Help all of us to respond to the diverse needs of the world in which we live, help all of us to see the variety of needs in your church, and may we always remember that you sent your Son into the world to redeem each one of us.

Congregation: We commit our support to these volunteers and pray that you would enable us to be good stewards of all that we are and have, to the glory of your holy name. Amen.

Resources for Volunteer Coordinators

William J. Bannon and Suzanne Donovan. *A Manual for Developing Parish Volunteers.* Ramsey, N.J.: Paulist Press, 1983.

George E. Scheitlin and Eleanor L. Gillstrom. *Recruiting and Developing Volunteer Leaders.* Philadelphia, Pa.: Parish Life Press, 1979.

Marlene Wilson. *The Effective Management of Volunteer Programs.* Boulder, Co.: Volunteer Management Associates, 1976.

Eva Schindler-Rainman and Ronald Lippitt. *The Volunteer Community: Creative Use of Human Resources.* Fairfax, Va.: NTL Learning Resources Corp., 1971.

Anne K. Stenzel and Helen M. Feeney. *Volunteer Training and Development: A Manual.* Revised Edition. New York: Seabury Press, 1976.

National Center for Voluntary Action, 1214 16th St., N.W., Washington, D.C. 20036.

National Information Center on Volunteerism, P.O. Box 1807, Boulder, Co. 80306.

CHAPTER 5

PROGRAMMING

THERE IS VIRTUALLY no limit to the variety of programs, activities, and interests that the local congregation can generate. Indeed, a congregation can be so motivated that activity for the sake of activity seems to be an end in itself.

The women are busy baking pies and fixing turkeys for the monthly bazaar, the weekly Lions Club meeting, the men's weekly breakfast, the ethnic club's Friday dinner, the meals-on-wheels program, the snack for day-care center, the soup and sandwich Wednesday Bible study, and . . . and . . . and . . . and—it just never stops. All some congregations do is eat!

Look into the multipurpose room and there's always something doing there, too—aerobics, cub scout meeting, volleyball, bridge, dominoes, a garage sale, a talent show, gymnastics, basketball, children's play day, cancer bandage sewing, banner making, vacation church school, Rotary dinner, community theater, school board open meeting—you name it, church-related or not, something's always going on. A full time custodian is kept busy just changing the props and sweeping the floor.

The well-administered church will be full of activity of course, but it will be activity that builds the church, invites the people, and strengthens the mission of the church. It must be a place filled with activity that motivates men and women to come to Christ, to be conscious of the church's goals, and in some way to further—not trample—the great tradition of the Christian ideal.

The manager of all that—the pastor—and the board of directors of the official board—are the ones responsible for overseeing what goes on in the church building and what is done in the name of the church. The goal must be to keep the life and activity of the church firmly within the purpose of that building. Too many AA's, dancercize, Kiwanis, overeaters anonymous, ballet classes, parks department basketball, Scandanavian clubs, and highway department forums turn the church into a community center country club, not a church.

All of which is not to say that any of these activities are bad or that none should ever be permitted in the building. By no means. The building is there. Good stewardship of resources suggests it should be used and used often. But when the objectives of the church are no longer fulfilled by the activities there, the managers must review what is going on.

One way to fulfill the congregational objectives in all this activity is to hold a meeting (once or twice a year) of all the contact people from all the groups in the church and outside. This offers the pastor (and the official board) an opportunity to: (1) help each leader understand the overall objectives of the church's mission and that every activity in some way should extend the kingdom, (2) set forth the aims of the church as a means for furthering that basic mission aim, and (3) review the building use policy statement so that all respect and use the facilities appropriately.

PROGRAMMING

A Survey of Resources

Following are ideas for parish activities and programs you may want to try. At the outset you may want to find out something about your congregation's interests and desires. What do they want to do? How do they want the building to be used? What activities do the people believe are appropriate and useful in extending that purpose of mission? Try a survey form.

A SURVEY: What I would like to do; what I would like to see done.

Items	That's for me!	Do it!	Forget it, not appropriate to mission
Services:			
Babysitting			
Ushering			
Providing flowers			
Telephoning			
Work on church newspaper			
Audio-visuals			
Movie projection			
Sound system operator			
Welcoming			
Educational:			
Teaching—age groups:			
High school			
Junior high			
Junior (4, 5, 6 grades)			
Primary (1, 2, 3, grades)			
Kindergarten			
Nursery (1, 2, 3 yr. olds)			
Infants nursery			
Assistant teacher			
Librarian			
Pianist			
Worship leader			
Nursery school visitor			
Vacation church school			
Sunday church school			
Weekday church school			
Teaching training			
Office work:			
Private secretary			
General clerical			
Typing			
Envelope stuffing			
Mimeographing			
Photocopying			
Mailing lists			
Visiting:			
Stewardship			
Evangelism			

	That's for me!	Do it!	Forget it, not appropriate to mission
Visiting (continued)			
Visitors			
Shut-ins			
Music & worship:			
Sing in choir			
Direct children's choir			
Piano accompanist			
Play instrument			
Youth:			
Group leader			
Boy scouts			
Girl scouts			
Recreation leader			
Women's activities:			
Women's group			
Program leader			
Refreshments			
Wedding receptions			
Baking for funeral dinners			
Service projects			
Men's groups:			
Leader			
Serving in kitchen			
Making calls			
Dishwashing			
Traffic supervision			
Security			
Maintenance			
Groups participation:			
Youth group			
Men's group			
Women's group			
Adult singles			
Square dancing			
Camping			
Study interests:			
Prayer group			
Bible study			
Theology			
Parenting			
World missions			
Special skills:			
Art work			
Storytelling			
Handicrafts			
Photography			
Writing			
Carpentry			
Electrical			

Then use the church computer to evaluate results. List the volunteers, and get a consensus on the *Do its* and the *Forget its*.

Possible Parish Programs and Activities

Drama

Check the talent lists. You're bound to find people interested in religious, dramatic activities. It's a natural way to further the spiritual thrust of the life of people as well as a way to foster fellowship and fun.

Assign responsibility to an interested individual, and then gather the people who want to share. Maybe only a few will respond at first. No matter. Enthusiastic theatrics can be catching. And the program easily spills over into other areas of congregational life.

The obvious Easter and Christmas children's programs are part of that thrust. A major musical presentation by the youth will offer congregation and community an evening of fun and witness. Vignettes in Sunday school classes and women's meetings offer further opportunity for enrichment.

Not everyone wants to perform. Some will direct or write or choreograph or build sets. Others can do publicity, design programs, and telephone. What a variety of opportunities for service! Pageants, anniversaries, celebrations—even the worship service—all offer opportunity for expression and witness.

As with any activity, leadership is the key. The pastor, as chief administrator, must be involved at least indirectly, but must be supportive and interested.

Talent shows

Some prefer not to act, but perhaps sing, dance, or speak. A talent show full of church members of much or little talent offers an opportunity for witness and expression of conviction.

Often the youth sponsor variety shows to raise money, but seniors can be talented, too, and a talent show by the over-65 crowd could be a fun-building event as well.

Liturgical dance

Ballet-oriented men and women, young and old, can do interpretive dance. For groups that may be offended by dance at worship, call it interpretive movement instead. Then be as creative as possible in developing the skills of those who are interested.

As with any activity, leadership is crucial to a successful effort. But once organized, a group of young women or children, for example, can add tremendously to the beauty and meaning of worship, a women's meeting, a wedding, or baptism.

For more information on starting a liturgical dance group, write to Carol Donnan, Liturgical Dance Leader, c/o Church Management, Inc., P.O. Box 1625, Austin, TX 78767.

Lecture series

Many congregations find that a series of lectures by a well-known author can be a stimulating experience for the membership. Or not-as-well-known lecturers can stimulate some creative thinking among the membership on topics as varied as Central America, Bach, digging in Jerusalem, Ethiopian Coptic church design, or the annual seal slaughter.

A lecture must have a purpose that somehow or other strengthens the spiritual awareness of the congregation. A convenient time must be carefully selected. Select the location based on the expected crowd. The lecture will be doomed to failure in a room too small because people will be hot and crowded; in the too large room people will be lost and probably not hear too well.

Lots of publicity is needed for a successful series. Try radio and television stations, newspapers, other church buildings, flyers, and bulletin boards in the community.

Are questions permitted? What about tape recorders? Okay to take photos? Check with the speaker. Can everyone hear? Is it cool enough, not too hot? Any glare? Set a time to start and a time to end, then stick with it, don't waver. A late start irritates those who came on time; in overtime the crowd quickly fades away. The lecturer can stay afterwards for questions, but end the lecture at the announced time without fail, or even a few minutes early.

Plan transportation, meals, and lodging for speakers carefully. When the lecturer is rested and satisfied, the whole program will move better. Pay any honorarium promptly, the same day. Provide for a reception afterwards if that seems appropriate. Keep the official board informed and the people advised.

A music fair

In addition to dramatic events, musical events are popular activities in many congregations. Where several people are especially skilled, significant programming can be developed using local talent. But many congregations go beyond the membership to sponsor individual artists, choirs, or symphonies for the benefit of the congregation and the community.

Bringing in a big-name entertainer requires considerable organization and skillful promotion to insure a good response. If an extremely large crowd is expected, the church managers (the pastor) will need to enlist the help of many people to be certain that all goes smoothly. Someone needs to be in charge. If tickets or offerings are involved, a treasurer may be appointed. There will be need for volunteers to plan and manage ticket sales, ushering, hospitality, arrangements, transportation, seating, lighting, staging, and sound system engineers.

Even a church college choir concert will require efficient planning for housing, meals, publicity, church building heat or cooling, lights, etc. These events don't just happen. Planning is essential.

Try a church fair

Many congregations find that an annual bazaar, barbecue, or church fair offers a fun time that brings the membership together in festive activity of "togetherness." Successful church fairs, however, don't just happen, either. They are carefully organized and administered. While these activities often involve considerable time and effort, they are nevertheless hailed as being one of the best of all church activities planned. And their value, it is claimed, comes from the teamwork generated to get the effort done.

It is important, but often difficult, to keep the thrust of this kind of an effort spiritual. But the objective for the activity must be to strengthen the purpose for which the church exists. It will also strengthen friendships. Furthermore, the financial success may indeed go to support a worthier cause. Any nonchurch purpose shouldn't be tolerated for a church function. An annual church-related church fair seems often enough. Some congregations do hold church fairs even less frequently, believing that infrequency will help to strengthen church purposes more effectively than when scheduled every year.

Careful planning will involve a chairperson, several assistants, and then chairpersons of each booth, display, or activity. Enlist as many members as possible to assist with parking arrangements, cooking, selling tickets, setting up tables and chairs, publicity, cleanup, etc. Open and close the fair with prayer. The minister's presence and support will be helpful to the workers.

A county fair booth

Small town and rural area congregations often find that a booth at the county fair is an effective way to put the name of the church in front of the public. But recognition does not come easy because the work is usually long, hard, and hot. Frequently the membership loses interest after a few years, and only a few people end up doing the work.

But with careful administration and enthusiastic leadership, a food or refreshment booth can be a moneymaker, friendship builder, and good piece of publicity.

Administration includes appointing of chairpersons, assistants, treasurer, cooks, dishwashers, order takers, cleanup crew, facility maintenance group, and so on.

Nursery school, day-care center, mothers day out

Caring for the children of working mothers can be an important task for a congregation. Providing learning experiences for preschool children can mean a significant Christian witness to children and parents. And the Mothers Day Out (MDO) programs offer a real relief and service to mothers who want a few hours of personal time a few days a week.

Nursery school, day-care centers, and MDOs are good ministries, yet each has a slightly different objective, audience, and participation. For each, a board of directors can oversee the program and report directly to the official board. A director for each will be needed with different requirements and qualifications. Establishing a constitution or at least a statement of procedure for each program will be helpful.

Illustrated is an outline of directives that govern the nursery, day care, child development, and primary grade school in one large congregation.

ST. MARTIN'S LUTHERAN DAY SCHOOL BOARD HANDBOOK

(Outline of Contents)

The purpose of this handbook is to:

1. serve as a resource helping day school board members take action resulting in good school management, good relationships, accountability, and a successful school program that ministers to the needs of children and parents both in the congregation and in the community.

2. serve as the basis for training and orienting new board members.

3. serve as an official policy manual of St. Martin's Day School.

Introduction
  Concept of the Christian school
  Status of the Christian school board
    In the state
    In the congregation

Organization
  Relationship to the congregation per constitution
  The school board per bylaws
  The American Lutheran Education Association
Functions and administration of the day school board
  Administration
  School board
    Relationship
    Calling a principal

Policymaking functions
    Budget
    Pupil personnel committee
    Staff/support personnel
    Academic standards
  Ethics
    Principle
    Code
  Accreditation
Finance
  Budget
  Definition
    Sample budget form and treasurer's report
  Income
    Tuition
    Space reservation
    Fees
    Special drives
    Endowments, requests, special gifts and grants
  Fiscal policies
    The fiscal year
    Purchases and payments
    Records and reports
      Types of records
      Monthly statements
      Report to congregation
      Filing
    Inventories
    Auditing
    Past due accounts
  Maintenance and use of facilities
    Duties and responsibilities
  Insurance
    Comprehensive liability
    Worker's compensation
    Health insurance
    Student accident insurance
  Day school staff
    Qualifications
    Contract procedures
    Personnel policies and practices
    Retirement
    Substitute teachers
  Admission and attendance
    School age
    Enrollment priorities
    Enrollment documents
    Fees and reimbursements
    Attendance

Discipline
    Reporting to parents
    Cumulative records
    Promotion and retention
    Welfare
    Activities, social events
Education program
Schedules
Evaluation
Instructional arrangements
Guidance
Safety
Student activity program
Staff handbook
Promotion
Relations to parent organization
Relations with parents congregational
Relations among staff
Professional organizations
Relations with government & public service agencies

Special services for dedications and anniversaries

Using special occasions effectively can help members participate in the life of the church, let the community know about the congregation, and extend the ministry of the church. The effective manager will use every such event to further the work of the church.

People respond to special events that carry importance in their lives: dedication of a new church building, commemoration of those who have died the past year, anniversary of ordination, organization, or dedication, celebrations for the lives and achievements of special people.

But no special event takes place without careful planning. Significant occasions must be meticulously planned. Making sure that the audience only sees a flawless program is the goal of the efficient church administrator.

The following dedication service for a new sanctuary reveals careful planning with the organist, choir director, ushers, building project leaders, and all who have a part in the service.*

DEDICATION OF A NEW CHURCH BUILDING

MINISTER: The Lord be with you.

PEOPLE: And also with you.

MINISTER: Let us pray. To the glory of God, in thanks to the Lord of all, for the love, concern, and untiring efforts of our general contractor, fellow worker, and friend, blest and dedicated be this church building: in the name of the Father, and of the Son, and of the Holy Spirit.

PEOPLE: Amen.

---

*From *Dedication Services for Every Occasion* by Manfred Holck, Jr., Judson Press, © 1984, pages 11-14. Adapted by permission of Judson Press. For examples of thirty-five complete special occasion events and a listing of some thirty-three additional available services, write to Church Management, P.O. Box 1625, Austin, Tex. 78767.

(Having come to the doors of the church, the minister shall say:)

MINISTER: Let us pray. O Lord, God the Almighty, you are the same yesterday, today and forever. Open our hearts to your discerning Spirit, that all our prayers and work may begin and end in you; through Jesus Christ, your Son, our Lord, who lives and reigns with you and the Holy Spirit ever one God, world without end. Amen. Lift up your heads, O gates! And be lifted up, O ancient doors!

PEOPLE: That the King of Glory may come in.

MINISTER: Who is this King of Glory?

PEOPLE: The Lord, strong and mighty, the Lord, mighty in battle!

MINISTER: Lift up your heads, O gates! And be lifted up O ancient doors.

PEOPLE: That the King of Glory may come in!

MINISTER: Who is this King of Glory?

PEOPLE: The Lord of Hosts, he is the King of Glory!

MINISTER: Glory be to the Father, and to the Son, and to the Holy Spirit.

PEOPLE: As it was in the beginning, is now, and ever shall be, world without end. Amen.

SCRIPTURE: Genesis 28:16-19, 22

(Then shall the keys of the building be presented: The general contractor gives the keys to a representative of the Building Committee, who gives them to the vice-president of the congregation. The doors are opened.)

MINISTER: Since by the grace of God and under his good providence this house of worship has been provided to replace the one destroyed by storm, that it may be set apart for its proper use to be a house of God, a dwelling place for his honor and a house of prayer for this people, we open it in the name of God the Father, God the Son, and God the Holy Spirit. Amen.

PRESIDENT OF CONGREGATION: Peace be to this house and to all that enter therein. The Lord bless our coming in and our going out from this time forth and forever. Amen.

PEOPLE: I was glad when they said to me, let us go to the house of the Lord.

RINGING OF THE BELL

PROCESSIONAL HYMN: "Alleluia"

PRAYER OF CONSECRATION: Almighty God, whom the heavens cannot contain, but whose will it is to have a house on earth where your honor dwells, and where people may continually call upon you; be pleased to enter into this house, which we devoutly consecrate to the honor of your name. We set this house apart from all common and worldly uses as a temple and sanctuary of your presence, where we may gather for worship and fellowship; where we may celebrate new life in baptism and holy communion; where we may confess our sins and receive your forgiveness; where we may study your Holy Word; where we may administer the business of your church; where we may dedicate and rededicate our lives, our time, our talents and our treasures to you; where we may meet together as your family, to enjoy your gifts and blessings—food, drink, and mutual love; where we may come for quiet meditation and prayer; where we, too, may experience the presence of your Spirit, O God, and rise up to heaven in prayer, praise, and thanksgiving. Let the glory of God fill this house and the Spirit of God descend and dwell in our lives, through Jesus Christ our Savior and Lord. Amen.

RESPONSIVE DEDICATION LITANY

MINISTER: To the glory of God, the Father, to the honor of Jesus Christ, our Savior, and to the praise of the Holy Spirit, our Comforter.

PEOPLE: We dedicate this house.

MINISTER: For worship in prayer and praise, for the preaching of the Word and for the celebration of the Holy Sacrament.

PEOPLE: We dedicate this house.

MINISTER: For the comfort of those who mourn, for strength to those who are weak and for those who are tempted.

PEOPLE: We dedicate this house.

MINISTER: For the sanctity of the family, for the purity and guidance of childhood and youth, for the promotion of brotherhood and the building of Christian character.

PEOPLE: We dedicate this house.

MINISTER: As a tribute of gratitude, of faith and hope and love, an offering of thanksgiving and praise from those who have found salvation and experienced the riches of God's grace.

PEOPLE: We, the people of this congregation, consecrating ourselves anew, dedicate this house as a temple, for the worship of Almighty God, in the spirit and name of Jesus Christ, our Lord and Savior. Amen.

MINISTER: In testimony of our sincerity, let us unite in praying with the Lord's Prayer.

THE LORD'S PRAYER

MINISTER: Thus we dedicate and consecrate this building, and rededicate its furnishings in the name of the Father, and of the Son, and of the Holy Spirit.

HYMN: "The Church's One Foundation"

SCRIPTURE LESSONS: Romans 8:11-19, John 11:47-53

DEDICATION MESSAGE

THE PRAYER

THE BENEDICTION

(As used at Bethlehem Lutheran Church, Lund Community, Elgin, Texas, with the Reverend Alfred O. Hoerig, pastor.)

Such services, when planned and executed thoughtfully, will deepen fellowship and congeniality among the members. One congregation distributes ribbon bookmarks to all worshipers on an Easter Sunday noting the date and place of worship. Another congregation on the eve of its one-hundredth anniversary celebration distributed colored ribbons, marked by years, to members according to the year they joined the church.

An organ dedication offers an opportunity for special liturgical banners and activity about the place of music in the congregation. Another congregation published an attractive and descriptive booklet when the church purchased and dedicated a beautiful church site. Another congregation celebrated the installation of a new pastor with pagentry, procession, music, congeniality, and fellowship.

Educational ministries activities

The program of education in the congregation, for children and adults, requires careful attention. A special task force responsible for the entire educational program should oversee the activities. A Director of Christian Education often coordinates the activities.

ORGANIZATIONAL CHART FOR EDUCATIONAL MINISTRIES*

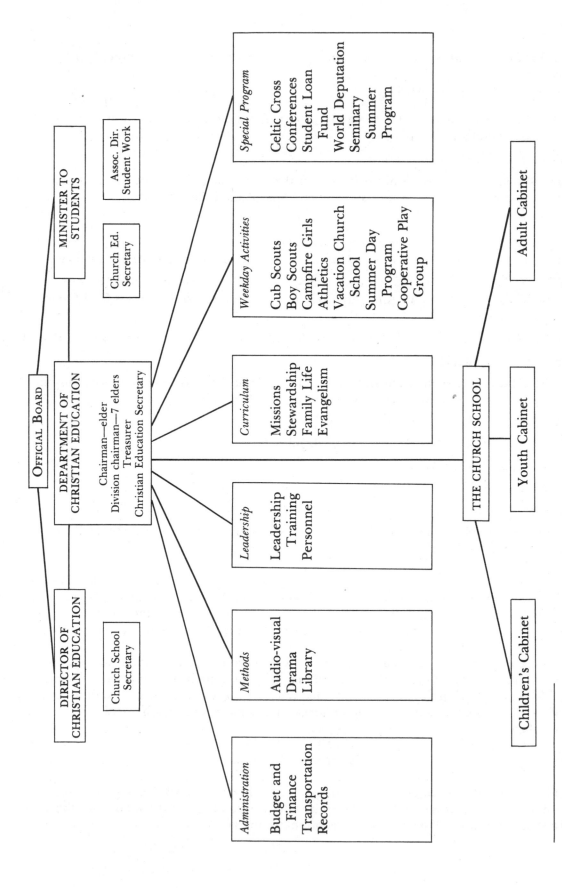

OFFICIAL BOARD

DIRECTOR OF CHRISTIAN EDUCATION

MINISTER TO STUDENTS

Church School Secretary

Church Ed. Secretary

Assoc. Dir. Student Work

DEPARTMENT OF CHRISTIAN EDUCATION

Chairman—elder
Division chairman—7 elders
Treasurer
Christian Education Secretary

Administration

Budget and Finance
Transportation
Records

Methods

Audio-visual
Drama
Library

Leadership

Leadership Training
Personnel

Curriculum

Missions
Stewardship
Family Life
Evangelism

Weekday Activities

Cub Scouts
Boy Scouts
Campfire Girls
Athletics
Vacation Church School
Summer Day Program
Cooperative Play Group

Special Program

Celtic Cross Conferences
Student Loan Fund
World Deputation
Seminary
Summer Program

THE CHURCH SCHOOL

Children's Cabinet

Youth Cabinet

Adult Cabinet

*Reprinted with permission of Macmillan Publishing Company from the *Handbook of Church Administration* by Lowell R. Ditzen, © Lowell R. Ditzen, 1962, page 121.

As with any committee or group charged with oversight and planning of programs, this task force should:

1. Include strong, dedicated, and creative leaders.

2. Be supported by the official board and know that the educational program is of primary concern to leaders.

3. Know the various parts of its program and responsibilities of leaders.

4. Have available for its work adequate professional leadership and staff.

5. Frequently evaluate the effectiveness of programs through reports, testing, one-on-one conversations with leaders and teachers.

6. Communicate regularly with the membership about the program, i.e., weekly notices about youth activities in the newsletter, recognition of teaching staff in a service of commissioning.

7. Develop a comprehensive schedule of events listing what is going on where and when during the year for the benefit of staff, students, and interested persons.

8. Consider the organization of a helping group of parents to assist in support of the overall program.

9. Develop, support, promote, and staff a variety of organizations and programs for the youth of the church on weeknights, weekdays, and weekends.

10. Sponsor family night activities where youth and parents share together in an evening of family fun, togetherness, and fellowship: family dinners, banquets, father-son and mother-daughter events, style shows, square dances, picnics—all for the purpose of strengthening relationships and extending ministry.

11. Organize specific age group programs for high school youth, middle age couples, senior members, singles, and children. Such groups can be organized with their own leaders and programs.

An invitation/evangelism task force

In a well-managed congregation, the pastor is not the only person responsible for contacting, inviting, and visiting prospective members. Often a special group of highly dedicated individuals are selected for this important activity. In one church, a group of men meets weekly for supper and then makes assigned calls, reporting back the same evening. In another congregation, the visitors meet for supper once a month, report on their calling experiences of the previous month, and receive assignments. In another congregation, selected leaders from specific areas are regularly assigned names of visitors to call and visit.

Organization of an invitation/evangelism group should include these steps:

1. Geographic division of the congregation.

2. Assignment of several callers to the areas in which they live.

3. Appointment of a leader and assignment of responsibilities.

4. Designation of a regular meeting time to motivate, make assignments, hear reports.

5. Insistence upon written instructions on how to make a visit, how to join the church.

6. Instruction of all members about the organization of the church, its purpose, its program, its schedule.

7. Availability of materials for distribution to families interested in the life of the congregation. (An attractive brochure will be especially helpful.)

8. Communication to the congregation, encouraging all members to invite their friends and neighbors to share in their church's ministry.

Shut-in task force

There are many persons simply unable to attend worship services or other activities at the church due to handicaps or illness. A special group of dedicated leaders can minister to these people.

89

Sensitive callers will be overwhelmed with the kindness and appreciation they receive from these closed-in people.

Regular visits on birthdays, anniversaries, and other special times mean much to shut-ins. An organized method for telephone calls can offer help or just a routine check on conditions. Transportation to church events, worship, community day programs, and children's Christmas programs can all be used to extend ministry.

The task force or committee should:

1. Include highly motivated and dedicated persons.
2. Involve creative leaders who can organize and plan appropriate programs, i.e., rummage sale, a movie, dinner out, visits to friends, an outing in the park.
3. Have available transportation vehicles.
4. Know the shut-ins.
5. Assign specific individuals to make regular calls.
6. Maintain complete records on the status, family, friends, health, and interests of shut-ins.
7. Develop a listing of contact persons and emergency helps in case of needs.
8. Provide tape recordings or video cassette decks of worship services to shut-ins.
9. Assist in the distribution of altar flowers following each worship service.

But the primary purpose of this program is to maintain close, friendly contact with those persons unable to share in the life of the congregation through their own active participation.

Hospitality

Many congregations sponsor coffee hours or a fellowship time on Sundays between worship services. This is often a welcome time for meeting friends, getting acquainted with newcomers, extending friendships to fellow members.

Often a committee or task force is assigned responsibility for organizing and administering this and similar events. Care must be taken to plan carefully, involving as many people as possible.

This group of volunteers is often also responsible for arranging special receptions or recognizing new members in special ways. It is a program intended to express the friendly nature of the congregation.

Ushers

The organization, maintenance, and management of the ushering program may vary dramatically from one congregation to another. In some places the first four men to show up on a Sunday morning are "volunteered." In other places a very detailed and carefully orchestrated procedure is developed to handle the necessary functions of sitting people, receiving the offering, and being certain that all is in readiness for worship. Ushers are responsible for preparing worshipers for a solemn and dignifying celebration.

An ushering task force may oversee the program and should be recruited from those who have expressed an interest. Training is necessary. Written instructions are essential.

The ushering group is often responsible for taking worship attendance. Sometimes it serves as a tellers' group to count the offerings. In any event, it should be trained to handle the routine and the unusual. Careful selection of men or women for this important task insures a successful operation.

A task force on spiritual life and devotion

The heartbeat of a congregation is the spiritual nurture of its people. Without that, a congregation flounders or is no more than a country club. While the development of spiritual maturity is part of

90

every program sponsored by the congregation, nevertheless, the official board may believe it important to appoint a specific committee with responsibility for developing ways in which such intentional nurturing can be done.

In cooperation with other committees, groups, or task forces, this supporting group is responsible for forming and supervising special Bible study groups, prayer cells or chains, spiritual life retreats, and programs on theology, religious tradition, or family devotional life.

Some congregations develop specially printed worship aids during Lent. One congregation developed a program for visiting in the home of each member during Lent for the purpose of promoting family devotions. Another group put together a daily devotional book written by the members. In other places the pastor's Lenten or Advent sermons are summarized in a small booklet of devotional aids.

This group can assist other leaders in preparing devotions and prayers for opening and closing of meetings. A book corner of selected devotional aids can be planned and supervised by this task force during special seasonal celebrations.

Baptisms, weddings, and funerals

The familiar Christian celebrations of life are an integral part of the life of every congregation.

1. *Baptisms*

Policies regarding baptisms may be established by the official board (although most pastors make their own plans).

The following ideas may help make baptism a significant occasion in the life of children, parents, and the larger family.

1. The minister should call as promptly as possible on a new mother at the birth of a child. Baptism can be encouraged by sharing on the process and meaning.
2. The pastor may wish to make a personal call in the home of the family when the decision to have the child baptized has been made. The pastor will then explain again, if necessary, the meaning and purpose of baptism as well as procedures for the service, leaving literature at the home.
3. The church secretary must obtain necessary information from parents for the official church records as well as the baptismal certificate. The certificate should be prepared and ready for signature as soon as the service is concluded.
4. Instructions to all participants—parents, sponsors, grandparents, friends—should be clear about photographs (preferably no flash pictures as these are distracting), where to stand around the font, where to sit during the service, what to say.
5. The church building should be in order, and warm water placed in the baptismal font when necessary.
6. The parents should gather as instructed.

One pastor has the parents, family, and friends walk in the opening procession of the worship service directly to the baptismal font for the baptismal service. Another pastor invites all the children to join the family and baby at the font. One pastor presents a small white New Testament to the newborn child with name on fly leaf and short note enclosed. Another pastor presents the child to the congregation by personally holding it up for all to see and admire.

A careful record of the baptism should be kept so that any inquiry can be verified.

2. *Weddings*

Most weddings require careful planning. A simple marriage needs little preparation, but large and elaborate weddings require more.

It is important that couples respect the requirements for use of the church facilities. Conversation with the pastor, organist, and custodian are important to avoid misunderstandings.

The following instructions are provided by one congregation in an attractive booklet given to every couple expecting to use the church.

WEDDING INSTRUCTIONS*

"Planning the Wedding Service"

St. Martin's Evangelical Lutheran Church
Austin, Texas

"Marriage is a holy estate, ordained of God, and to be held in honor by all. It becomes those who enter therein to weigh with reverent minds what the Word of God teaches concerning it."

Your desire to have a church wedding is indicative of the fact that you want to ask God's blessing upon your marriage. God will not withhold his blessing from you, if you will earnestly seek to accept the blessings he offers. To this end we suggest that you carefully study the order for marriage in the Lutheran Book of Worship, page 202.

The purpose of a *church* wedding is to share your joy with the congregation and to enable the congregation to join you in invoking God's blessing upon your marriage. The purpose is not to "put on a show" for your friends. Following this idea does not prevent you from having a beautiful wedding, but it does set certain limitations upon what may properly be done.

GENERAL ARRANGEMENTS

It is advisable to make wedding arrangements as far in advance as possible. As soon as the date of your marriage is determined, call one of the pastors to reserve the date on the church calendar. Non-members may not reserve a date more than two months in advance.

You may desire to use the Sanctuary for larger weddings or the Chapel if no more than 100 guests are expected.

The Fellowship Hall and Parlor are available for receptions and should be reserved at the same time the date is reserved.

It is expected that one of the pastors of the church will officiate at all weddings. Where it is the wish of the couple to have other clergy conduct or participate in the ceremony, they are to get the consent of the pastor of the church. It is understood that all clergy participating and ceremonies held in the church will have a Christian orientation.

The couple should arrange with the pastor for the counseling sessions. If either party has been divorced, this matter should be made known and discussed with the pastor.

The couple should also arrange an appointment with the organist to discuss the music.

OFFICIATING CLERGY

Guest clergy of your choice are welcomed to participate in your wedding along with one of our pastors and the invitation will be extended by our staff. The division of the ceremony will be made by our pastor in consultation with the guest clergy.

If clergy other than one of St. Martin's staff is to officiate, one of St. Martin's clergy staff will meet with the bridal couple and officiating clergy to help finalize the wedding arrangements.

DECORATIONS

The paraments (altar, pulpit, and lectern hangings) always remain in the liturgical colors for the season of the year in which the wedding is held.

---

*From the booklet, *Planning the Wedding Service*, as used at St. Martin's Evangelical Lutheran Church in Austin, Tex. Used with permission.

PROGRAMMING

The Chairperson of the Special Occasions Committee of the Altar Guild will contact you to assist you with decorations. Please inform the Chairperson about all decorations used in the church. The flowers are to be placed only in vases owned by the church. It is the responsibility of the bride and groom to pick up the liners and take them to the florist. A member of the Altar Guild will place the flowers in the vases and on the altar as this is *not* to be done by the florist. Artificial flowers should not be used on the altar.

After the ceremony an Altar Guild member will remove the flowers from the altar and do as you wish with them. If you wish to leave them for Sunday services, please let the church know so that it may be mentioned in the Sunday bulletin.

The Altar Guild member is also responsible for placing and removing the white satin kneeling pillow, owned by the church, and placing candles on the altar and in the candelabra owned by the church. If the florist supplies additional candelabra for the chancel, plastic protectors are to be placed under them. No candles are permitted in the aisles or on the pews. A pair of brass, nine candle, candelabra are available for rental from the church.

The use of nails, screws, and wire in decorating is not permitted except by special permission.

The above procedures apply both in the sanctuary and the chapel.

REHEARSAL

Where a rehearsal is necessary, approximately one hour should be allowed. All members of the wedding party, including parents and ushers should be present PROMPTLY.

MUSIC

The music should be in keeping with the dignity, beauty, and sacredness of a service of worship. There is much secular wedding music which, though it may be beautiful and acceptable for use at a wedding reception, is hardly in keeping with the purpose of a church wedding.

It is recommended that the church organist be considered first to play the service. The church organist is most familiar with the instrument and understands the type of music that is acceptable. If another organist is used, that person should consult with the church organist. In making remuneration to the organist and the soloist, bear in mind that you are purchasing professional service; that they do not merely spend the half-hour which the actual wedding takes, but the time required to select music, get to the rehearsal, the rehearsal time, plus the time before and after the wedding.

If the Lord's Prayer is sung by a soloist, it should occur at the designated point in the Order for Marriage as found in the hymnal. It is, however, liturgically proper that all present at the ceremony pray this prayer together.

PHOTOGRAPHS

The marriage service is a sacred service, which should have no intrusions such as come from the taking of pictures, particularly flash pictures. Therefore, we request that no pictures be taken after members of the bridal party have entered the nave of the church and are proceeding to the altar. Nor are pictures to be taken during the ceremony, unless it be a time exposure from the balcony. Pictures may be taken at the rear of the nave as the bride enters and as the bridal couple recesses. After the service is concluded, pictures may be taken in the chancel.

Professional photographers observe these rules. Friends and relatives of the couple are often unacquainted with them. They should be informed about these rules and requested to observe them.

In order to expedite the taking of pictures after the ceremony, it is well to give the photographer a list of the groups or persons you wish photographed. By planning to take the first pictures of the group involving the largest number of persons, some of the bridal party can be dismissed to attend to other things.

RECEPTIONS

Each wedding party is responsible for securing its own catering service, and making arrangements for food service and decorations.

Rice and confetti are not allowed within the building.

The use of alcoholic beverages is not allowed on church premises.

Receptions are to be terminated no later than 10:30 P.M. except on Saturdays when they are to be terminated no later than 9:00 P.M.

Details concerning the reception may be discussed with the Business Manager.

MISCELLANY

The marriage license is to be delivered to the church office in the week prior to the wedding ceremony. No weddings or receptions will be scheduled during Holy Week.

All arrangements for dressing room areas, setting up of reception area, and opening of the building are to be made with the Building Manager.

If programs for the ceremony are desired, the wedding party is responsible for securing these and having them printed. The pastor will assist in arranging the program material, if desired.

Holy Communion is not proper at a wedding ceremony unless it is offered to the entire congregation in attendance.

If an aisle runner is desired, it must be provided by the florist or caterer.

The florist and/or caterer should be instructed, when employed, to remove all equipment immediately after the wedding is concluded.

Taping of the ceremony is permitted by request. Equipment and operation is the responsibility of the wedding party.

FINANCIAL ARRANGEMENTS

Financial arrangements are established on the basis on the membership of the bride and groom at the time of the first appointment.

It is not the policy of the church to look upon weddings as a source of revenue; however, there are expenses connected with the operation of the various areas used for weddings and receptions.

All rental fees are to be paid at the church office prior to the rehearsal.

Please make all financial arrangements with the Business Manager.

Rental fees for the use of church facilities are as follows:
1. Weddings
   a. Members—No charge for use of the Sanctuary or Chapel
       Custodial service, $25
   b. Non-members—Sanctuary, $150
       Chapel, $75
2. Receptions
   a. Members—Fellowship Hall, $35
       Parlor, $25
   b. Non-members—Fellowship Hall, $150
       Parlor, $100
   (Note: these charges include custodial fees)
3. Personnel
   Fees for all personnel, except custodians, should be negotiated with each person involved.

INFORMATION FOR THE PHOTOGRAPHER

For the Wedding of: _____

Date: _____ Time: _____

at St. Martin's Evangelical Lutheran Church, 606 W. 15th St., Austin, Texas, 512-476-6757.

We welcome you to St. Martin's Evangelical Lutheran Church as a photographic recorder of this couple's wedding ceremony. Weddings that are held at St. Martin's are looked upon as a service of worship, whether conducted in the church facility or elsewhere.

You will want to familiarize yourself with these guidelines:

1. Before the wedding service please confer with the Pastor about the pictures which will be taken.

2. No flash pictures are permitted during the service. Pictures may be taken during the processional, recessional and poses before and after the service. Time exposures from the balcony or rear of the sanctuary are permitted during the service.

3. Please inform the pastors of any pictures in which they will be involved. It would be appreciated if these would be taken first.

4. The Parlor and courtyard are available for pictures of the wedding participants prior to and following the wedding ceremony.

5. Generally the bride dresses in the Choir Room (located in the basement under the main sanctuary) or in the Parlor (located in the northwest corner of the building).

6. The groom and best man generally wait in the Sacristy (located behind the altar) for a wedding that takes place in the Sanctuary or in the Church Library (located across from the Chapel) for a wedding that takes place in the Chapel.

Thank you for your cooperation. If you have any questions prior to the wedding date, please feel free to contact the church office.

INFORMATION FOR THE FLORIST

For the wedding of: _____

Date: _____ Time: _____

at St. Martin's Evangelical Lutheran Church, 606 W. 15th Street, Austin, Texas, 512-476-6757.

We welcome you to St. Martin's Evangelical Lutheran Church as florist of this couple's wedding ceremony. Weddings that are held at St. Martin's are looked upon as a service of worship, whether conducted in the church facility or elsewhere.

You will want to familiarize yourself with these guidelines:

1. Flowers and decorations must be in place no later than one hour preceding the wedding. Please check with the church office to schedule a time for decorating the church.

2. Altar flowers are to be arranged in the altar vase liners, which are available from the church. Since the altar flowers are not to be taller than the cross, you will want to make the arrangements no more than twenty-two inches above the top of the liner.

3. Altar flowers, corsages, and boutonnieres may be delivered to the Church Library located on the main hall between 15th and 16th streets.

4. The Altar Guild member will place flowers on the altar. Placement of flowers and decorations other than the altar flowers and the white kneeling pillow is the responsibility of the florist.

5. The use of nails, screws, and wire in decorating is not permitted except by special permission.

6. Plastic protectors for the carpeting are to be placed under all candelabra provided by the florist.

7. Artificial flowers are not acceptable for use on the altar.

8. Following the wedding, there is to be no activity (removal of decorations, flowers, etc.) until the church is empty.

9. Flower stands, etc. should be removed from the church building immediately after the wedding activities have been completed.

Thank you for your cooperation. If you have any questions prior to the wedding date, please feel free to contact the church office.

3. *Funerals*

The appropriate place for the funeral of a church member is in the church building. Because of local custom and the architecture of the building, it may be necessary to formulate a set of guidelines on funerals.

One church has published the following regarding funerals in the church:

ABOUT THE FUNERAL*

The funeral is a precious part of a minister's relationship with the people and a mediating influence involving the entire parish and often the community. This outline of procedures is prepared with the hope that all concerned with the funeral may make of it an occasion of comfort and satisfying strength to the bereaved.

The ministers of the Christ Church are available for funerals of such bereaved families as are connected with our church either as members or as relatives of members or simply those who look to Christ Church as their church home. The request for and presence of a minister brings the service within the influence of the church and makes the emphasis uniquely Christian.

Ordinarily, in the case of members and those closely related to the church, the ministers will have knowledge of the impending death and will sometimes be of assistance in the actual funeral

*Reprinted with permission of Macmillan Publishing Company from the *Handbook of Church Administration* by Lowell R. Ditzen, © Lowell R. Ditzen, 1962, pages 168-69.

arrangements (e.g., the order of service, Scripture, music to be used). They deem this a proper function of their total ministry.

The sanctuary and the chapel of Christ Church are available for funerals and memorial services for members of the church at no charge. There is but one regulation: If the casket is present in the service it be and remain unopened.

Nonmembers of the church may also use the sanctuary and chapel of Christ Church under the same conditions and under the further provision that one of the ministers of Christ Church be in charge of the service. A nominal charge for organist and custodian may be made at the discretion of the Board of the church.

There is no fee or honorarium charged or expected for the services of the ministers. This is part of the ministry of the church that they serve. It is hoped that this may be made quite clear to the bereaved by the mortician, and in no case should the services of the minister be made a part of the funeral bill. If the family wishes to express its appreciation in a monetary way, a gift to the church that makes possible the minister's service would be appropriate. A memorial fund, a tribute window, and many special items at the church have had the benefit of such gifts.

Because there is misunderstanding upon this point of funeral fees, especially among the nonchurch families, further elaboration may be necessary. A funeral involves much more than the preparation and conducting of a memorial service and the internment. Always there is at least one call and usually several calls upon the family between the time of death and the service, and always at least one call after the service. The service itself, sometimes requiring an internment at a distance, takes not only the minister's time but time away from other duties at the church that is entitled to that time.

Beyond this, however, is the further consideration of the funeral ministry itself. If the minister has adequately done what he is trained to do in the spirit of the God served, then the minister has deepened the dependence of the church family and has influenced the nonchurch family toward closer relationship with the church. The fee or honorarium becomes an intrusion upon this delicate relationship, while a financial response to the church itself may be a part of a proper response.

One further matter needs to be mentioned, one upon which both the morticians and the ministers must surely be in agreement: The wishes of the family are the major determining factor. Among Christians, funeral practices differ: for example, the disposition of the body by burial or cremation, the floral tribute or memorial gifts in lieu of floral tributes, the open or closed casket. In these matters the ministers will usually give support to the best judgment of the family and will be happy to confer with morticians if requested to do so. Surely each problem involving funeral procedures may be solved decently and in accordance with Christian principles.

Discussion of these or other matters connected with the Christian attitude toward funerals and Christ Church practices in connection with funerals will be welcomed by the ministers.

Approved provisionally by the Board, April 4, 19__.

At the word of the death of a member, the pastor will immediately make a call to console and comfort the family. Arrangements for the funeral service will begin. The church secretary will remove the name of the deceased from the roster and note the appropriate information in the official registry of the church. The fellowship committee will be notified and arrangements made for a meal for the family and friends following the services.

Appropriate notification of the death will be listed in the weekly newsletter and announced at the Sunday services. The pastor will call again soon after the service and other members will offer support and comfort in the weeks following the service. The pastor will call again on a surviving spouse or family on or near the anniversary of the death. And once a year, usually All Saints' Sunday (first Sunday in November), all deaths during the prior year are remembered.

CHAPTER 6

MAINTAINING PROPERTY AND PLANT

MINISTRY IS DONE in many ways in a congregation. Effective ministry is enhanced by church property that is well-kept. A congregation witnesses something of its life-style and its relationships by the appearance of its property. And people are impressed by the appearance of a congregation's property.

The property committee, therefore, is a responsibility of significance for the life of the congregation. Organization of its work dare not be slovenly or haphazard. This committee requires the most responsible attitude of stewardship possible in planning, care, maintenance, repair, inventory, oversight, administration, and planning of all that is required to manage the assets of the congregation. Without possessiveness but with responsibility, committee members should exercise careful leadership in using church property to further the mission of the church.

The property committee's success will be measured by the impression of people who are worshiping in the building, visiting, or who may be passing by.

Responsibilities

Each congregation will develop its own list of property committee responsibilities. Included in any listing, however, will be some or all of the following ideas:

1. In general. Oversight of the care, repair, protection, maintenance and improvement of all church property: real estate, buildings, and equipment.
2. Equipment. Care, protection, maintenance, and repair of all equipment, including oversight for purchasing, installation, dismantling or sale of all congregational-owned or leased equipment, including vehicles (cars, vans, buses, trailers, etc.)
3. Grounds. Oversight for maintenance, care, and protection of all outside areas, including landscaping.
4. Personnel. In consultation with the personnel committee, (1) develop and maintain job descriptions for work relating to property, (2) employ necessary workers to accomplish that task, and (3) recruit, enlist, and supervise volunteers to carry out functions of the committee.
5. Records. Maintain complete listings of all assets, copies of all plans and specifications, insurance coverages, warranties and guarantees, contracts, inventories, preventive maintenance, and repair schedules.

The various checklists, charts, and forms used in this chapter have been adapted from *Property Committee Manual,* © 1977, Parish Life Press, Philadelphia, Pa. Used by permission.

6. Memorials. Provide frequent listing of approved memorials or gifts for paintings, furniture, windows, altar ware, musical instruments, and other equipment.
7. Finance. Recommend to the official board all actions required to implement contracts, leases, and agreements; oversee fulfillment of terms of all contracts, leases, and agreements; submit budgetary needs to the official board for personnel, repairs, equipment, care and protection of properties; maintain appraisal lists and, as desired, depreciation schedules on all properties.
8. Reporting. Submit regular, written reports to the official board on (1) the status of all properties, (2) work done and planned, and (3) recommendations to be acted on by the official board.
9. Leadership. Assume responsibility for long-range planning for buildings and grounds improvements in consultation with other appointed committees.

The Committee

Proper care, maintenance, and protection of church property will be possible only when carefully selected volunteers are asked to commit themselves to the task. All members must be committed to the program of the church as well as understand its mission, program, and physical needs. Ideally, most groups in the congregation should be represented on the committee. Each member should possess necessary skills, interest, and experience to oversee or even to do the work required, such as:
1. Practical experience in (preferably professionally) and knowledge of building maintenance, construction, carpentry, electrical, plumbing, traffic and parking, sanitation, housekeeping, yard care and landscaping.
2. Supervisory skills, business experience, and legal knowledge as required.
Work on church property is not limited to members of the committee. Often members need to be brought into the work as their skills are needed. Willing volunteers should be sought for necessary tasks, but care in selection of those skilled for the job must be exercised. Not everyone willing to do a job can do it. Matching interests, skills, and tasks requires careful screening.
The key to a successful committee will be selection of a chairperson—someone dedicated to the task, committed to the church, skillful in leadership capacities, and experienced in property management. The committee leader is responsible for planning and coordinating the activities of the committee, watching the budget, recruiting volunteers and paid staff, and chairing the monthly committee meetings.
A property committee functions best when its structure consists of subcommittees responsible for specific functions—specific people assigned for specific tasks. Delegating responsibilities relieves the chair person or even a handful of volunteers of the tasks required. (And it always avoids involving the pastor in the task of property management.)

Committee responsibilities and relationships

Generally, most property committees will have five key areas of responsibility or subcommittees:
1. Building maintenance, care, and repair.
2. Grounds maintenance, care, landscaping, parking.
3. Equipment maintenance, care, purchase, and disposal, including all vehicles.
4. Use of property and documentation of safety and insurance.
5. Housing (pastor and other staff) care and maintenance.
Since the property committee cannot function by itself, it must develop relationships with all the other committees of the church. It must work closely with those who use the facilities, who need additional facilities, and who are responsible for programming, worship, fellowship, and education.
The official board establishes policy on asset management. The property committee implements those policies. The minister must convey to the property committee an understanding of ministry

and the work of the congregation. Ministers should not do the work of the property committee; they must communicate needs and schedule events. The property committee makes certain the facilities, equipment, and grounds are ready.

As the congregation seeks financial commitments from the membership, the property committee must provide information on opportunities to give for special needs. The finance committee must be appraised of financial needs not met with special gifts, of annual budget requirements, and estimated funds needed for maintenance of facilities.

Space and equipment needs for the educational programs of the church must be arranged by the property committee. Safety rules, care, and use of equipment by the education committee, for example, will be in response to the property committee's proposals. The proper maintenance of building and equipment also enhances the work of the worship committee through cleaning, sound equipment, safety guidelines, organ maintenance. Activities of other groups—social ministry, women, men, youth—must be conveyed to the property committee to facilitate the use of the facilities.

Buildings

Volunteers assigned the task of maintenance and protection of the congregation's buildings, including the parsonage, rectory, manse, or pastorum, must be able to respond to all mechanical needs, cleaning, inspections, safety of the buildings, and protection of property.

Tasks for this area of responsibility include:

1. Development of job descriptions for custodian, sexton, and others needed to care for the congregation's property.
2. Recruitment of volunteers needed to complete those duties assigned by the official board.
3. Development of a statement on the use of property by members and other committees.
4. Supervision of regular (every six months minimum) inspections of all buildings, structures, and equipment—including maintenance of necessary records to record needed repairs, maintenance, replacement, and completion of those tasks.
5. Frequent inspections (weekly) of all facilities and equipment care, cleanliness, fire hazards, proper equipment storage, lights, and heat off or on.
6. Keys management listings of users—who has what key to which door?
7. Development of guidelines to encourage user care of supplies and equipment, as well as periodic disposal of items no longer needed.
8. Review and periodic inspection of all fire and safety devices in accordance with local codes and regulations.
9. Supervision of all paid or volunteer personnel of buildings and grounds.
10. Development of property budget needs.

PMI (Preventive Maintenance Inspection)

Many congregations fail to care for their equipment properly. The lack of periodic preventive maintenance inspections aggravates minor problems into later serious problems. A carefully kept schedule of inspection and work done is responsible stewardship of the congregation's resources. Use the illustrated form as a checklist of what needs to be examined inside and outside the buildings.

PMI (PREVENTIVE MAINTENANCE INSPECTION) CHECKLISTS

Outside inspection checklist:

__Check for roof damage; inspect ridges, valleys, and condition of roofing materials.
__Look for damaged or clogged gutters and downspouts.

__Inspect spark or lightning arrester condition.
__Check condition of paint or other exterior protection.
__Look for any open mortar joints.
__Check any loose masonry.
__Note any open joints that need caulking or sealing.
__Look for badly weathered trim and wood.
__Check condition of doors and hardware, including storm and screen doors.
__Check condition of windows, trim, frames, storm sash, screens, including hardware and putty.
__Renew caulking around doors and windows.
__Replace cracked glass, broken glass.
__Check door and window weather stripping.
__Inspect all electrical lines as well as external outlets, switches, and receptacles.
__Look for broken steps, sidewalks, railings, or other hazards to walkers.
__Check condition and operation of fire escapes; keep these uncluttered.
__Remove inflammable rubbish, weeds, or grass next to building.
__Check exterior faucets for leaking.
__Make sure that drainage around buildings is satisfactory.
__Remove graffiti from walls.
__Check condition of foundation; look for cracks and areas of crumbling; is the foundation closed to prevent a fire from burning grass or leaves starting in the building?
__Look for building damage from shrubs, vines, or bushes; prune or replant as needed.
__Check for water, wind, or frost damage to plantings.
__Inspect storage of materials next to buildings; are materials well protected from weather and theft?
__Check condition of air conditioning units, cooling towers, and coolers.
__Check flashing, vents, and air vents.
__Make certain all entrances are clean and uncluttered.

Inside Inspection Checklist

__Check condition of paint or protection on walls and ceilings.
__Note cracks, crumbling plaster, missing tile, or damage to wallboard of walls or ceilings in all rooms.
__Check for easy operation of all doors and windows.
__Note any missing hardware from doors and windows.
__Are doors provided with panic hardware in compliance with local building codes?
__What is the condition of floors, floor coverings, or carpeting in all areas?
__Check for wear, damage, and cleanliness.
__Check walls and ceilings for cleanliness.
__Check all electrical outlets, lights, and switches.
__Check the condition of air conditioning units.
__Check all exit signs for illumination, visibility, and good order. Are they in compliance with local code and sufficient in number?
__Check condition of all chalkboards, bulletin boards, etc., for proper attachment to walls.
__Are instructions clearly posted about what to do in case of fire at various places and locations in the building?
__Check the proper placement and condition of fire extinguishers.
__Check on first-aid kit and its availability with necessary contents and emergency numbers posted.
__Check all storage areas and rooms for cleanliness, neatness, and lack of combustible materials.

__Check out heating plant and furnace room for cleanliness, neatness, and compliance with local codes and requirements.

__Are oil mops and rags stored properly to prevent spontaneous combustion?

__Are remote storage areas such as under staircases clear of combustible materials?

__If smoking is permitted, are ash trays available in meeting rooms and lounge areas? Are they used instead of wastebaskets?

__Check for water damage and leaks.

__Check for dry rot, termites, and rodents.

__Check the condition of pews, tract racks, storage cabinets, appliances, and other fixtures in need of repair and care.

__Check all interior woodwork and trim for conditioning and protection needed.

__Check all cabinets, files, etc. for content, neatness, and orderliness.

__Check all inside plumbing for leaks and proper operation.

Look around now. Does the church seem clean? Is it safe and attractive? Will its appearance welcome visitors? Is it bright, cheerful, and comfortable? Keep those questions in mind as you go through your routine checklists.

Now that the general items have been checked off, take a look at specific rooms and areas:

1. *Entrance Way*—Of all the areas in the building, the narthex, vestibule, entrance way demands special attention. First impressions as people enter the building will affect their impressions of the rest. Check the list carefully. Ask the ushers to recheck prior to each service.

__Are the walks, steps, and thresholds in good repair and clean?

__Is there an easy access to the building for the elderly? The handicapped? Are there adequate ramps or railings? Is there another entrance that is or can be equipped with special ramps or lifts, well-marked and identifiable?

__Are adequate and orderly facilities available for hats, coats, umbrellas, rubbers, overshoes? Are these areas adjacent to, but not causing congestion in, normal traffic patterns?

__Do the doors open out and easily? Are they locked securely? Is there adequate weather stripping to keep out drafts?

__Is the narthex well-lighted, clean, neat, and orderly?

__Are the literature racks, display tables, bulletin boards, and member boxes neat, orderly, clean, kept updated with new and current materials?

__Is the guest book prominently located and easily accessible?

__Are book storage areas, cabinets, and display tables kept clear of unused articles and outdated materials?

__Are these areas being used for the purposes intended?

2. *The Sanctuary*—Worship is enhanced in an area pleasing to sight, smell, and body comfort.

__Are the heating, cooling, and ventilation equipments noisy?

__Is there good air flow distribution and circulation?

__Does the system adequately provide the necessary cooling, heating, and ventilation?

__Do the lighting fixtures enhance or detract from the worship service?

__Do the organist and choir have good lighting?

__Is there enough light; is it well-distributed without glare?

__Are the pulpit and lectern lights adequate for the pastor? Do these lights bother worshipers?

__If there is a rheostat on the lights in the chancel and nave, does it function properly?

__Do the chancel lights enhance or detract from the chancel?

__Who is responsible during worship for the operation of the system?

__Are microphones free from feedback?

__Are speakers properly placed for total distribution of sound throughout the nave?

__Are there hearing aids for those who are partially deaf? Are these aids and their location properly marked?

__Are banners changed so that the ones displayed are always appropriate for the occasion or church year season?

__Are pews free from sticky varnish or paint?

__Are the pews securely fastened to the floor?

__Are the pews in good repair and clean? Slivers and cracks can result in damage to the clothes of the worshipers. The undersides should be free from chewing gum.

__If there are pew kneelers, do these operate quietly? Are the pew racks attached firmly and free from squeaks?

__Is the aisle and floor covering soundproof? Is it in good repair?

__Are windows clean and in good repair? Can extreme glare or sunlight be controlled?

__If the windows are vented, do the vents operate easily?

__Do classrooms and meeting areas give a good indication of their function?

__Are the floors clean and in good repair? Are ample wastebaskets available?

__Are storage cabinets, shelves, chalkboards, tack boards, and other equipment being used well, in good repair, and kept orderly?

__Is the lighting adequate? Are there sufficient electrical outlets for audio-visual equipment?

__Is the classroom space being used wisely?

__Do classrooms provide adequate space and such environment as to foster learning in accordance with the latest educational standards?

3. *The Parish Hall*—Frequent use of large areas for meetings, fellowship, meals, and other events requires extra care for safety, cleanliness, and attractiveness.

__Is the area clean, orderly, and inviting? Is it serviceable and adaptable?

__Is it properly equipped for various needs?

__Is there adequate storage for various equipment needed in its utilization?

__Are the floors and walls in good repair?

__Is the area adequately heated, cooled, and ventilated?

__Does the area comply with local codes regarding sanitation and safety?

__Is there one or more well-marked and functioning emergency exits?

__Is the area easily accessible to the kitchen and a good flow pattern for food service established?

__Are fire extinguishers and first-aid kits readily available?

4. *Kitchen*—Special care is required of a church kitchen, even one used infrequently. Inspect for cleanliness and neatness.

__Are instructions on use, care, cleaning, storage, and local fire regulations prominently posted?

__Is there scrupulous compliance with fire and building codes and regulations?

__Is the kitchen area kept clean and orderly?

__Is proper ventilation provided?

__Are the heating, plumbing, and electrical supplies in good order?

__Are all kitchen items, including appliances, properly cleaned and stored?

__Are there provisions for adequate waste and trash disposal?

__Is the kitchen limited to use as a storage space only for items that are related to kitchen use?

5. *Special Areas*—A parlor, lounge, or specially appointed room often serves a multiple of needs: receptions, meetings, study groups, casual conversation. Comfortable furniture, bright and cheerful decorations, cleanliness and order are essential.

__Do the lounge facilities meet the needs of the congregation?

SAMPLE INTERIOR CHURCH INSPECTION FORM

Page_____

Name of congregation _____ Room_____

Inspection by _____ Date_____

ITEM	CONDITION, CHECK APPROPRIATE COLUMNS					SPECIFIC INFORMATION & REMARKS
	OK	Needs Paint	Needs Cleaning	Needs Repair	Needs Replacement	
CEILING						
Light fixtures, bulbs, etc.						
Vents						
Tile						
Acoustics						
Plaster						
NORTH WALL						
Electrical outlets, switches, lights						
Vents: air and heating						
Curtain rods						
Drapes						
Tapestries						
Built-in storage cabinets, shelves						
Built-in glass cases, planters						
Doors						
Windows						
Chalkboards						
Bulletin boards						
EAST WALL						
Electrical outlets, switches, lights						
Vents: air and heating						
Curtain rods						
Drapes						
Tapestries						
Built-in storage cabinets, shelves						
Built-in glass cases, planters						
Doors						
Windows						
Chalkboards						
Bulletin boards						

| ITEM | CONDITION, CHECK APPROPRIATE COLUMNS | | | | | SPECIFIC INFORMATION & REMARKS |
	OK	Needs Paint	Needs Cleaning	Needs Repair	Needs Replacement	
WEST WALL						
Electrical outlets, switches, lights						
Vents: air and heating						
Curtain rods						
Drapes						
Tapestries						
Built-in storage cabinets, shelves						
Built-in glass cases, planters						
Doors						
Windows						
Chalkboards						
Bulletin boards						
SOUTH WALL						
Electrical outlets, switches, lights						
Vents: air and heating						
Curtain rods						
Drapes						
Tapestries						
Built-in storage cabinets, shelves						
Built-in glass cases, planters						
Doors						
Windows						
Chalkboards						
Bulletin boards						
FLOOR						
Tile and carpets						
Finish						
Electrical outlets						
Air & heating vents						
Other fixed items attached to floors						
GENERAL ITEMS						
Thermostat controls						
First-aid kit						
Safety/Fire regulations, exit signs						
Dry rot, termites, rodent damage						

SAMPLE INTERIOR CHURCH INSPECTION FORM

Page_____

Name of congregation _____

Inspection by _____ Date_____

ITEM	CONDITION, CHECK APPROPRIATE COLUMNS					SPECIFIC REMARKS
	OK	Needs Paint	Needs Cleaning	Needs Repair	Needs Replacement	
ROOF						
Flashing						
Vents/Hatches						
Ridge/Valleys						
Eaves/Gutters						
Sealants						
Spark and lightning arrestors						
NORTH ELEVATION						
Mortar joints						
Caulking						
Loose siding or masonry						
Doors						
Windows/Louvers						
Vents/Hatches						
Trim:wood or other						
Steps/Railings						
Storms/Screens						
Downspouts						
EAST ELEVATION						
Mortar joints						
Caulking						
Loose siding or masonry						
Doors						
Windows/Louvers						
Vents/Hatches						
Trim: wood or other						
Steps/Railings						
Storms/Screens						
Flashing						
Downspouts						

ITEM	CONDITION, CHECK APPROPRIATE COLUMNS					SPECIFIC REMARKS
	OK	Needs Paint	Needs Cleaning	Needs Repair	Needs Replacement	
SOUTH ELEVATION						
Mortar joints						
Caulking						
Loose siding or masonry						
Doors						
Windows/Louvers						
Vents/Hatches						
Trim: wood or other						
Steps/Railings						
Storms/Screens						
Flashing						
Downspouts						
WEST ELEVATION						
Mortar joints						
Caulking						
Loose siding or masonry						
Doors						
Windows/Louvers						
Vents/Hatches						
Trim: wood or other						
Steps/Railings						
Storms/Screens						
Flashing						
Downspouts						
GENERAL						
Foundations						
Fire escapes						
Drainage						
Plumbing leaks						
Inflammable materials next to buildings						
Electrical outlets, lights, wiring						
Shrubs, vines, bush damage						
Termite/Rodent damage						
Improper storage of materials						
Entrances, clean, uncluttered						

FIRE PREVENTION AND EXTINGUISHER CHART*

DEPARTMENT	HAZARD	PREVENTION	PROTECTION	
			Extinguisher	Location
Heating plant	Ignition of exposed woodwork	Insulate exposed woodwork	A	1
	Disposal of ashes	Metal cans	A	1
	Fuel oil spills	Good housekeeping	B	2
Chimneys and flues	Defective pipes, flues	Replacement	A	1
	Soot accumulation	Annual cleaning	A	1
	Ignition of exposed woodwork	Insulate exposed woodwork	A	1
Electric wiring—organ motor, etc.	Improper extension or alteration of wiring	Approved installation by competent electricians	C	1
	Overfusing, arcing, sparking, etc.	Approved equipment plus proper maintenance	C	1
Candles, open flames	Presence of combustible material	Caution: use only in closed areas free from people	A	2
Decorations	Accidental ignition	Flameproofing: use of nonflammable material	A	1
Kitchen	Heating equipment: ranges, ovens, etc.	Approved insulation of floors and woodwork	A	1
	Grease in hoods and flues	Frequent cleaning, approved construction	B	1
	Grease in ovens or on stoves	Reasonable care	B	1
	Blower system	Approved installation	C	1
Storage	Presence of combustible material	Good housekeeping, adequate ventilation	A	1
Cleaning and polishing materials	Flammable liquids	Storage in fire-resistant locker or cabinet	B	1
Oily or paint-soaked rags or waste	Spontaneous ignition	Immediate disposal: self-closing metal cans	B	1
Waste paper and refuse	Combustible material	Good housekeeping	A	1

KEY TO ABOVE CHART

A—Fires in ordinary combustible materials such as wood, paper, textiles, etc. Soda-acid, foam, loaded stream and anti-freeze solution extinguishers recommended. The vaporizing liquid extinguisher also can be used effectively when there are no air currents to dispel the extinguishing vapors.

B—Fires in flammable liquids, greases, etc. Foam, vaporizing liquid, carbon dioxide and loaded stream extinguishers recommended.

C—Fires in live electrical equipment. Vaporizing liquid, carbon dioxide extinguishers recommended.

1—One extinguishing unit for each 2,500 square feet of floor space and within 50 feet of travel distance from any point.

2—One extinguishing unit directly at the point of hazard.

*Prepared by Church Management Safety Research Institute, Cleveland, Ohio.

___Is there suitable lighting?
___Are the areas properly heated, cooled, and ventilated?
___Are the areas on special thermostat control so they can be used independently, apart from the rest of the building?
___Are the areas inviting and free from clutter?

6. *The Offices*—Since the most frequent amount of continuous church activity probably takes place in the church office, care of the facility is an ongoing, daily concern. Adequate space, equipment, and personnel in an attractive setting will enhance the effectiveness and the efficiency of the volunteer and paid staffs.
___Is there sufficient and orderly storage for supplies and parish records?
___Are the furnishings adequate to perform various adminstrative tasks? Arranged for most effective usage?
___Is the office equipment on a regular maintenance and replacement schedule?
___Is the office equipment properly stored?
___Are the offices clean, neat, and attractive?
___Are emergency instructions posted prominently?
___Remove unnecessary storage of articles or materials not related to administration.

7. *Other Areas*—Storage areas are needed, but their usefulness depends on periodic reorganization. Encourage members who use storage areas to clean out what they no longer need and to rearrange remaining items neatly. Periodic fire and safety inspection of all storage areas is essential. Special youth rooms, boiler rooms, and equipment storage sheds should be inspected and cared for, also.

The custodian—qualifications and responsibilities

The property committee group, responsible for maintenance and care of the buildings, must arrange for proper custodial care of those facilities. In smaller congregations, the minister is often required to move tables and chairs, pick up trash, clean chalkboards, and shovel snow. In larger congregations, people are hired to do those jobs. Nevertheless, in every congregation someone has the job of custodian, sexton, or janitor. And it is that person's activities that create the positive atmosphere for worship, meetings, or fellowship. Careful selection and use of a custodian—member or otherwise—could be significant toward fulfilling the ministry of the church.

1. Qualifications and experience:
   ___Ability to relate well with other people.
   ___Ability to receive instructions and carry them out.
   ___Possess good health, character, and be a dependable, responsible person.
   ___Possess working knowledge of building maintenance and construction methods.
   ___Ability to work with tools and make small repairs.
   ___Possess knowledge of heating and air conditioning equipment or show proven desire to become familiar.
   ___Possess experience of two or more years in one of the building trades.

2. Duties and responsibilities:
   ___Become familiar with buildings, their structure, and functioning of all equipment.
   ___Develop and follow a cleaning schedule—all rooms once a week, all offices once a day, including emptying of wastebaskets and dusting of furniture.
   ___Keep all floors cleaned; vacuum, dust, sweep, mop, buff, and wax as needed.

___Keep all glass cleaned; wash windows, pictures, glass cases, doors, etc., as needed. (Stained glass windows should be cleaned professionally.)

___Wash painted walls and woodwork at least once each year; handmarks and other marks should be removed as often as necessary.

___Clean and straighten rooms after all meetings.

___Keep stairways and hallways clear of stored articles, clean and well-lighted at all times.

___Keep toilet rooms clean, sanitary, and attractive at all times; keep necessary toilet supplies available; do not use these areas for storage.

___Keep the kitchen walls and windows clean and orderly; remove paper, garbage, and other refuse each time kitchen is used; washing and storing dishes, however, is not the sexton's responsibility, since that duty (as well as the responsibility for cleaning of appliances after use) belongs to the groups using the kitchen.

___Clean the sanctuary, the narthex, and the chancel after each service, including picking up pencils, paper, and litter, removing used bulletins, collecting communion glasses, and putting hymnals back in the racks; vacuum, sweep, or remove any excessive dirt or mud from the floors.

___Gather up lost articles such as gloves, purses, jewelry, and turn them into the church office.

___Keep baptismal font clean and ready for use.

___Pick up any papers or trash in the buildings and on the grounds.

___Clean and sweep walks, patio areas, and benches as needed; never allow snow and ice to accumulate on walks and steps.

___Be familiar with church calendar in order to make necessary preparation for all meetings.

___Arrange rooms prior to meetings, provide for adequate ventilation, heating, or cooling during meetings; avoid interrupting meetings to close or open windows.

___Unlock the buildings and rooms at specific times (at least thirty minutes prior to events unless specific instructions provide for different opening times).

___Turn on the lights for evening meetings.

___Have special equipment available and ready when requested.

___Close and lock buildings after all meetings.

___Check that all water is off, all lights are off, all stoves are off, all windows closed and locked. (If it is a late adjourning meeting, make arrangements for someone to assume this responsibility.)

___Be familiar with and understand the furnace and air conditioning equipment. Consult with competent technicians to determine best method of operation, purpose of each control—regulator, safety device, and valve. Keep buildings at proper temperature for optimum efficiency for heating or cooling. Keep furnace rooms clean and orderly.

___Know fire and safety regulations, and practice the procedures in the regulations as well as other standard safety procedures.

___Make weekly fire inspections of buildings and grounds. Remove all noted hazards, and report the action taken to the church office.

___Make repairs day-by-day as needed.

___Keep tools clean, in good condition, and appropriately stored.

___Keep all equipment in proper storage areas.

___Report to the buildings and structures subcommittee anything that may be a serious problem or will become one.

___Replace all light bulbs as needed, and report anything that indicates a serious short or overtaxed electrical wiring.

___Care for the lawns, shrubs, and hedges. Keep them fertilized, watered, and trimmed. Rake leaves, pick up limbs, twigs, and trash.

__Take good care of all yard tools and equipment.

__Keep mowers sharp and adjusted; put everything away when not in use.

Grounds

An attractive outside will encourage people to come in to see an attractive inside. While a beautifully landscaped yard won't feed the hungry, it may entice some otherwise reluctant giver to respond to the need for food, impressed by the congregation's stewardship and care of its own facilities. All persons are motivated to enter our church buildings for a variety of reasons. But until they come in there's really not much we can do to share with them the mission and ministry of our program. An attractive outside helps to get them inside our comfortable buildings where they can then finally hear and respond to the message we proclaim.

This group is responsible for the care and maintenance of the lawn, shrubbery, landscaping, church sign, parking area, sprinkler system, outside lighting, and trees. Its tasks include the following:

__Maintenance of parking areas, patios, fountains, and fences.

__Care of lawns shrubs, trees, flower beds, including necessary watering, fertilizing, trimming, and replacement.

__Control of insects and rodents.

__Repair and maintenance of outside lights.

__Repair and maintenance of sprinkler system.

__Repair, maintenance, and replacement as needed of all church signs, including signs along nearby streets or roads.

__Traffic control in parking areas, including requesting police assistance as needed.

__Control the weeds.

__Supervision of full- or part-time salaried employees and volunteer workers who work on grounds, landscaping, and parking areas.

__Develop a regular schedule of maintenance and repair for the grounds and parking areas.

__Provide for snow removal.

__Provide for adequate drainage and grading as necessary.

__Maintain the play and recreational areas.

__Prepare an annual budget of needs to accomplish the tasks of this group of the property committee.

1. *Landscaping and Grounds*—What is planted has to be cared for, too. Good stewardship principles insist that enough money be spent on landscaping for an attractive outside but not so much that it becomes elaborate. Easily maintained lawns and shrubbery should be the goal. However, always keep plans flexible so more can be added, if needed, or something can be removed.

Grounds care includes:

__Maintenance of accurate markings for property lines, and if necessary, resurvey of the property.

__Maintenance of overall general appearance of grounds.

__Maintenance and repair as necessary of all fences, walls, signs, ornaments, patios, outdoor fireplaces, and outdoor meeting areas.

__Control weeds, insects, and rodents.

__Provide adequate fire control and safety of grounds.

__Remove dead trees, limbs, branches, garbage, rubbish, and other materials that detract from the appearance of the grounds.

__Provide upkeep, maintenance, and repair of all outside electrical, plumbing, and sprinkler systems.

2. *The Church Sign*—How can the congregation expect to attract visitors if there is no church sign? Some church buildings are identified only by their cornerstones. Not much better are church buildings with antiquated, inadequately lighted, hard-to-read, poorly placed signs. Money spent on an attractive, easily read sign can reap rewards untold. The church sign is a "sign" that the members care, that the members *want* people to know about their place, that they are proud of their building.

Consider, then act:

__Are the signs in a good location, attractive, and readable? Keep encroaching tree branches and overgrowing shrubs trimmed.

__Are the outside bulletin boards and signs on the church building well-lighted? Equipping them with a time switch saves time and effort.

__Is information correct and current on the church sign? Do the church signs have the church's name, pastor's name, and congregation's phone number, and time of services?

__Are bulletin boards and signs in good repair?

3. *Parking and Lighting*—Adequate nighttime lighting and sufficient parking are this group's responsibility, also. Check the light timers frequently to be certain they come on and go off when they are expected to. Stop back frequently and look over the lighting—does it enhance and accentuate without glare or unevenness? A lighted church can be a silent witness to your caring concern. It can be for safety, too.

Parking lots need lights, too. Do they work? Do they cover the area? Are they adequate?

Check the parking lots. Many congregations have off-street parking, others don't. Good parking can impress visitors. No parking may discourage visitors. Paved parking is probably most economical over the long term.

Consider these tasks for parking lot maintenance:

__Make certain that parking is adequate and in accordance with local codes.

__Properly paint and stripe parking spaces or stalls. This should be done in accordance with latest codes. To accommodate more cars, mark a special area for small cars.

__Make certain that parking spaces are reserved close to the entrances for the handicapped; be certain marking is clear.

__Provide for easy access and exit to parking areas.

__Post legible and concise signs for good traffic flow and for maximum safety.

__Control speed by posting prominent speed limit signs; construct speed control "bumps."

__Provide traffic control for congested situations. Contact the local police department for assistance if parking areas exit into main thoroughfares.

__Repair all ruts and "chuck holes."

__Resurface when necessary with gravel, crushed materials, sealcoat, sand, or asphalt.

__Keep all cracks in concrete areas sealed with tar.

__Remove grass and weeds from paved areas.

__Keep parking areas clear of rubbish such as papers, cans, bottles, and other unsightly items.

__Keep parking areas clear of obstacles that may cause persons to trip, such as concrete parking curbs. Use curbs only at the edges of parking areas where no curbs are present.

__Make certain that parking areas are well lighted for all activities.

__Arrange for adequate snow removal from parking areas.

__Regularly grade nonpaved parking areas.

__Make regular inspections of parking areas, and take the necessary action to correct all discrepancies and repairs noted.

__Stay within the lines of the adopted budget, but develop priorities for short- and long-range parking plans.

Equipment

Many congregations have equipment they don't know they have. The task of the equipment group includes listing inventory, assessing needs, purchasing equipment, and disposing of unneeded, discarded, and obsolete equipment.

These tasks are necessary:

__Annual inspection and development of schedule for care, repair and replacement; annual inventory and marking; annual current valuation of all equipment, personal property, and vehicles.

__Purchase and replacement of equipment, personal property, and supplies, including memorials.

__Suggested list for items on a memorials gift list.

__Supervision of all full- or part-time salaried employees and volunteers in carrying out group tasks.

__Preparation of an annual budget of needs to accomplish the tasks for this group.

1. *An Inventory and Appraisal of Equipment*—If the congregation doesn't know what it has, it can't know what it needs. Adequate insurance coverage can only be determined from a listing and an appraisal of what the congregation has. Thus, an annual inventory and appraisal is crucial to the stewardship of the congregation's assets and resources. General equipment: those items in constant use, and special equipment: those items infrequently used and usually requiring an operator—are to be listed. A careful record of maintenance, disposal, and replacement must be maintained for good control.

   Secure an inventory and appraisal form from your denominational publishing house (or local business office supplies store) to maintain this important record.

2. *Automobiles, Vans, Buses*—These vehicles represent large investments. Their proper maintenance must be looked after by this group of the property committee. Develop a standard procedure for use of vehicles. Keep a regular schedule of maintenance. Secure a maintenance record form from an auto supply store.

3. *Organs and Pianos*—Special care is required for musical instruments. Musicians familiar with pianos and organs should be consulted. These guidelines will be helpful:

__Have a service contract for periodic service and tuning.

__Keep the organ room clean and locked.

__Keep the organ console closed and locked when not in use.

__Protect the organ and piano from extremes of temperature and humidity. Never let the temperature go below 50 degrees F. In cold weather or damp climates keep a small electric heater in the organ room.

__Do not permit organs or pianos to stand in sunlight, near heaters, radiators, or steam pipes.

__Protect instruments from excessive humidity by using a chemical or mechanical dehumidifier. An electric light bulb left burning will help.

__Protect the instruments from rodents, moths, and other destructive insects.

__Do not let anyone play the organ or piano unless trained.

__Do not let students use the instruments to practice except under the guidance of a teacher.

Purchasing

The property committee can be responsible for purchasing, not only those items needed for buildings and grounds maintenance, but also those items needed for the general programs of the church. In larger congregations a purchasing agent is probably used. A business administrator may take over that function. In smaller congregations the pastor is often involved in coordinating the buying. But where a functioning property committee takes responsibility for its duties seriously, it may act as the purchasing group for the congregation. Generally, it is a good idea to have one person do all the buying for the congregation. That avoids duplication in purchases and usually gives the congregation the best prices, quality, and service.

Those responsible for purchasing should consider the following items when purchasing goods or services for the church:

__Determine the need for an item or service. This is usually done by a requesting committee based on their prior request to the official board for budget amounts.

__Determine the quality of the item or service needed.

__Ascertain how much (quantity) is needed.

__Secure a written request from the committee or person needing the item for authority to make the purchase.

__Consolidate, where possible, the requests from various departments in order to make a quantity purchase.

__Seek out possible vendors, review their services, and negotiate with them for the purchase of goods on a routine basis.

__Determine how the goods purchased will be shipped and delivered.

__Analyze proposals received from vendors, select the vendor desired, place the order.

__Follow up on the order to be certain the item will be received in adequate time for effective use.

__When the item is received, check the invoice, and inspect the goods to be certain all is in order.

__Approve the payment invoice.

__Store the merchandise in an appropriate location.

__Include the goods in the inventory of items on hand.

__Review the way in which the items purchased have been used to determine the effectiveness of the purchasing activity.

Effective organization of the congregation's purchasing procedures will help to make proper use of available resources. The property committee has responsibility for making certain that the congregation does in fact get "the right item, of the right quality, in the right quantity, at the right time, at the right place, and from the right vendor." Good stewardship principles require that the congregation pay no more than necessary for the goods and services it needs.

Building Use and Insurance

The volunteers on this group of the property committee must set forth the guidelines adopted by the official board for the use of the church facilities by members and others. It will also review necessary protection coverages for continuing use of the facilities and will provide for protection of documents.

Generally, this group's tasks can be defined as follows:

__To recommend to the official board policies and changes in existing policies concerning the use of the property and equipment.

__To coordinate the use of all property with the other congregational committees, groups, and organizations, as well as with other groups from outside the congregation.

__To make certain that all those using the congregation's facilities are operating within the law and in accordance with the current local, county, state, and federal safety codes and regulations.

__To prepare all necessary leases, special use agreements and other appropriate contracts.

__To make an annual appraisal of property.

113

__To make quarterly inspections of fire extinguishers, safety devices, and exits; to provide updating as needed of safety and fire regulations for property users.

__To provide for adequate and proper insurance coverages in consultation with the finance committee.

__To be familiar with current tax law requirements related to building and property use.

__To file for any necessary tax exempt status where appropriate.

__To maintain careful records of all documents related to church property, including plans and specifications of structures with provision for safekeeping of all original or certified true copies.

__To prepare annual budget needs to accomplish these tasks.

Guidelines for building use

Congregations should develop and distribute to potential building users some kind of public statement about building use. All members and potential users should have copies of this document. Official boards should take action to develop such guidelines upon recommendation of the property committee. The matter should not be left to the whim of the pastor or the chairperson of the property committee. The matter should be set forth by the property committee, approved by the official board.

Church use policy statements help to stress the congregation's attitudes toward its property and equipment as tools that help to fulfill its mission. A consistent pattern of use and a periodic review of those guidelines will assist the property committee in maintaining the building for the primary benefit of the members.

SAMPLE STATEMENT OF BUILDING USE POLICIES*

Christ Church
Adopted by the Official Board on January 1, 19__

The purpose of Christ Church's building, grounds, and equipment is to serve its membership, its neighborhood, and the community; to provide for maximum use for the greatest service. These policies are authorized and published in order that all might know the conditions governing the use of our facilities and equipment.

SCOPE

The use of the building, grounds, and equipment shall be confined to religious, educational, social services, and other character-building functions.

ADMISSION CHARGES AND COMMERCIALISM

No group or organization shall be permitted to charge admission or conduct fund-raising activities of a commercial nature. Free-will offerings may be received.

FUNERALS

The church buildings, grounds, and necessary equipment shall be available without charge (except cemetery lots and care) to members of the congregation as well as to nonmembers.

Adapted from *Property Committee Manual,* © 1977, Parish Life Press, Philadelphia, Pa., pp. 35-36. Used by permission.

WEDDINGS

Church facilities shall be made available for weddings to members of the congregation, as well as to nonmembers. It should be understood that the setting of the sanctuary and chapel shall not be changed in any manner.

1. *Equipment.* Equipment shall not be moved from its regular places without authorization. Arrangements must be made to return all equipment to its regular place. All kitchen equipment including dishes and silverware is to be washed, cleaned, and returned to storage areas immediately after use.

2. *Decorations.* No tacks, nails, tape, or other material that will deface church property shall be used. Flowers, candles, cords, etc., must have bases or stands to support them. Decorations such as streamers shall not be attached to walls, pews, chancel rails, or ceilings in a manner that will leave permanent marks.

3. *Flowers.* As soon as a florist has been selected, notify the church office so that an understanding may be reached regarding the time and policy on decorating. If no florist is involved, then those responsible for flowers and decoration should notify the church office for the same reason. This applies to all members and nonmembers.

4. *Removal of flowers and decorations* should be done immediately after the wedding so that facilities are ready for the next scheduled activities.

5. *Alcohol and Tobacco.* No alcoholic beverages are to be served on the premises. Smoking is restricted as posted.

6. *Costs.* The facilities of the church shall be made available for members without cost. For nonmembers a flat fee of $_____ will be charged for the use of the facilities and equipment. This fee covers normal use of electricity, temperature control, as well as the general wear and tear on the facilities and is not designed for profit or moneymaking. Honorariums for pastor, organist, and custodian, as well as fees for special services such as catering, decorations, and cleaning should be paid directly to the individuals involved.

7. The official board reserves the right to restrict the privileges of anyone who violates these regulations.

ORGAN-PIANO

These instruments shall be available for practice to persons studying under a teacher. No charge shall be made to members of the congregation. Nonmembers are expected to pay $_____ per hour for practice use of these instruments. Practice hours must be arranged in advance and followed to avoid conflict with congregational programs.

OUTSIDE GROUPS AND ORGANIZATIONS

Outside groups and organizations may use the church facilities if their purposes are considered worthy and if their programs do not conflict with scheduled congregational activities. Decisions concerning worthiness are determined by the property committee in consultation with the pastor and the official board. The facilities may be made available to organizations without cost, on a flat fee basis, on a lease agreement, or on a contract basis—depending on whether the outside group or organization is nonprofit or profit-oriented.

LOANING EQUIPMENT

Loaning equipment such as chairs, tables, dishes, projectors, screens, tools is not encouraged to groups or organizations for use on other sites. However, these items may be borrowed for church-related functions, if cleared through the property committee and properly checked out with persons designated. No items shall be loaned for private use.

GIFTS

Before memorials and gifts are purchased and offered to the congregation, the official board and the property committee should be consulted to determine that these memorials and gifts harmonize with design and purpose to the church facilities. Used items such as furniture, carpets, mowers, and automobiles shall not be accepted as gifts unless arrangements are made in advance for their use or disposal. All memorials and gifts received, which are to be part of the church buildings or its facilities, shall become without qualification the property of the congregation.

In developing a policies guideline statement, the following considerations are important:

__Limitations on use of the building and equipment for specific purposes.

__Priorities for use.

__Instructions for care and cleanup of equipment.

__Instructions regarding storage.

__Instructions regarding use of equipment.

__Names and telephone numbers of the persons to contact in emergencies.

__Special operating instructions or charges for providing personnel to operate special equipment.

__Charges for damages of facilities and equipment.

__Checkout procedures for equipment and building use.

__Regulations for safety, fire, and traffic.

__Policy statement on the use of alcoholic beverages and smoking.

__A statement, acknowledging receipt of guidelines, to be signed by persons requesting specific uses.

__Procedures to follow for nonmembers in requesting special use of facilities.

__Charges for use of facilities for nonmember groups, for use of equipment, and for providing qualified operators of certain equipment, as well as for janitorial and/or cleaning services.

__Statement regarding required deposit and insurance.

__Specific statements about any agreements or contracts that need to be signed.

Many congregations do indeed permit their facilities to be used by other groups. Such sharing may be a good use of buildings not otherwise used by the congregation. Again, careful guideline statements must be developed to be certain that all users and all members are informed and so that there are no misunderstandings.

CHAPTER 7

COMMUNICATIONS

EFFECTIVE CHURCH MANAGEMENT is carried out best when communication techniques are carefully developed and used. The most obvious ways to communicate are through the church newsletter and the Sunday bulletin. Many congregations may also use other procedures.

The press release or newspaper article can effectively communicate to the general public. Trouble is, though, that the people who read the religious news section of the newspaper are church goers already. They may only be looking for news about their own church.

All congregations communicate with the use of bulletin boards, inside and outside. The best impression is made by a bulletin board that is always current and attractively arranged.

Radio and TV are popular tools for communicating. Churches are generally limited in the use of this media because of costs. But the success of TV religious programming is clear evidence of just how well religion has done on TV. Two or three congregations in a local area may be able to broadcast their services on TV, and a few more may be able to do so on radio. They are the ones that are reaching the masses.

Advertising pays, sometimes, for churches. Direct mail to the neighborhood can produce surprising results. Posters, broadsides, and brochures also offer an effective means of telling the story. Yet word-of-mouth remains the best way to communicate. Pastors know that a visit in the house always does more good—for clergy and parishioner—than a formal telephone call.

The Committee

But communicating by the church doesn't just happen. It must be planned. News releases don't get written, direct mail planned, or the newsletter put together without careful organization of the church office and a commitment to meeting deadlines by the staff.

Thus, a public relations committee may be useful in supervising the promotion of the church. Since such a committee is normally a constitutionally specified standing committee, its lifetime is controlled by the official board. A public relations promotion program can be most effective when the membership of the public relations committee includes members with public relations experience.

A job description for a member of the public relations committee might be something like the following:

THE PUBLIC RELATIONS COMMITTEE JOB DESCRIPTION

Purpose: The public relations committee is responsible for developing and using ways to tell the congregation and others about the church.

117

Membership: Six members appointed by the official board, staggered terms; two from the board, four from the congregation.

Qualifications of members:

1. Dedicated and active church member.
2. Experience in public relations and communications techniques.
3. Energetic, positive attitude about the church.
4. Knowledgeable about the church and its program.
5. Inquisitive, aggressive, professional.

Responsibilities:

1. Plan for, organize, and supervise the entire PR program at Christ Church.
2. Develop objectives, format, and style for the weekly church newsletter; delegate responsibilities for editing and publication.
3. Delegate responsibilities for creating the weekly Sunday bulletin.
4. Plan and make appropriate contacts for news releases about the church's program.
5. Delegate responsibility for the outdoor bulletin board; supervise frequent change of indoor bulletin boards.
6. Develop and obtain TV and radio exposure of church events.
7. Approve advertising plans.
8. Arrange and delegate responsibility for any direct mail campaigns for area residents.
9. Oversee preparation of posters, broadsides, and brochures that tell about the church and its programs.
10. Know the local newspaper religion editor; arrange appropriate contacts with the pastor and others responsible for writing newspaper copy.
11. Arrange for such other communication possibilities as may seem appropriate.

The involvement of the public relations committee in specific programs depends on the size of the congregation and committee and on the willingness of committee members to be involved. In larger congregations the committee of six members is good; in smaller congregations a three-member committee may function well. Delegation of committee responsibility will defuse the burden for doing everything from one person.

The Church Newsletter

Ross W. Marrs, pastor of First United Methodist Church, Bloomington, Illinois, describes the church newsletter preparation procedure:

HOW TO WRITE A CHURCH NEWSLETTER*

by Ross W. Marrs

Everybody is looking for simple gimmicks that will ensure successful communication in the church. There are none.

Getting the attention of a random selection of persons who congregate in any church is a formidable task. Only a clear, persistent, well-designed, carefully constructed program of sharing information that includes as many options as possible, including word-of-mouth, posters, letters *and* newsletters, will even begin to accomplish the task.

Church newsletters can be a useful and effective tool of communication and the following guidelines are offered for coming up with an effective newsletter:

1. Make it a *new* sletter. Yesterday's information is not news. There is nothing to be accomplished by telling everybody about last week's social, or how many made it to the picnic. A newsletter ought to be forward looking. Events on the verge of happening should be brought into view. Attention should be focused on what is about to happen. Keep the minds of the congregation in a spirit of anticipation.

2. In addition to a *calendar* of coming events, run special articles highlighting important programs about to occur. Be sure to give such events several weeks of coverage. The larger the congregation the more lead time will be required. Start the publicity toward the back of the newsletter and gradually move it to the front. Then on the last week make it "front page" material.

3. *Let programming groups write their own material.* No one can write a better article than someone who helped plan it and has a stake in it. Don't let the newsletter become a tool of employed staff. Use it by and for the congregation. Set your rules. Let them know that you expect the material from them and exactly when it is due, and to keep it brief and to the point.

4. *Use attention-getters.* Large clear headlines, line drawings, pictures, if you have the capacity. The front page can be used to highlight what is inside. Remember, few persons read all of such a newsletter. They want to read only what is meaningful to them. Help them find it. Examples: The youth can always have the same space. Specific groups and programs in expected location. And vary the format. Print some pages right to left, others top to bottom. This will slow down getting through the newsletter and more will be seen.

5. *Send it regularly.* Weekly is always best. But however often it is sent create expectancy. Hit and miss and random mailings will lead the congregation to thinking that the newsletter isn't very important. And plan for it to be mailed so that it always arrives on the same day. Friday and Saturday are preferable days.

6. *Keep it upbeat.* Negative reporting, cajoling or pressuring pleadings, begging articles and threatening implications serve only to demoralize a congregation. Let the congregation know that they are part of a going church, a winning team, and invite them to join in. Anyway, people know you're not going to cancel Bible Study or Choir, so why threaten it?

7. *Keep it cheap.* Cheap paper, cheap printing processes, volunteer help, bulk mailing. Use these and everything you can to keep it inexpensive. Stay away from the fancy stuff: color mixes, half tones and the like. If you need this kind of publicity let the local newspaper do it for you. Remember, your readers are going to pitch it as soon as they have given it the once-over anyway.

8. *Use other people's material.* Why reinvent the wheel? If your district or conference headquarters prints materials which you can acquire free or at little cost, get them and let them ride along.

9. *Don't crowd your luck.* When holidays have everybody's attention riveted elsewhere and it's fairly clear what you are doing, shut it down. Go to the Sunday bulletin. After all, most of them are in church then anyway. If your newsletter is going to get buried in Christmas cards, lost in the shuffle of holidays or ignored at vacation time, then send out an issue that is clearly marked on the front: "This is a two-week issue" or "Keep this issue handy. No newsletter next week."

10. *And one last thing.* There are times when reporting can be helpful, when the congregation has done a good job on a special offering, when a special program has succeeded—let them know. Too often we are apt to offer a kick in the rear to our congregations in an effort to stir them to do better. There is nothing like a good strong pat on the back to keep morale up.

So, keep them informed every way you can, as often as you can, as clearly as you can and as happily as you can.

For a more thorough explanation on developing a church newsletter, read George W. Knight's book, *How to Publish a Church Newsletter,* (Nashville: Broadman Press, 1983).

The Sunday Bulletin

The Sunday bulletin in most congregations conveys several types of information:
1. The order of worship.
2. Events for the day and week.
3. Items of inspiration and spiritual enrichment.
Those responsible for developing the Sunday bulletin, usually the church secretary, will set forth

their own procedures for getting the job done on time and done well. Some ideas for church bulletin management include:

1. The Sunday bulletin editor, usually the church secretary, should establish deadlines for receipt of all materials, including worship information from the music director and minister. Strict adherence to deadlines is important for church bulletin preparation.

2. The bulletin is still printed on the church's mimeograph in some congregations. But in many places it is done by an outside quick print service, on the church's own electronic stencil mimeograph, or even a desktop offset duplicator, or a photocopy machine. The use of equipment will depend on the money the church wants to invest in quality and time savers.

3. Church bulletin covers may be produced by the congregation and thus, probably, will be the same each week. Or if you want to provide photographs and a message of inspiration on the cover, all denominational publishing houses offer a Sunday bulletin service. These are, of course, professionally done and offer an extremely attractive format for your worship outline.

4. Be certain you include the date, the name, address, and telephone number of the church someplace on every bulletin (in fact that information should be included on anything that goes out of the church office). A prominent front-page location helps to identify the bulletin quickly. Of course, those who attend church know all this, but bulletins sent to shut-ins or used in visiting are not much help without good identifying information.

5. Most Sunday bulletins distributed as worshipers enter the sanctuary are for the purpose of outlining the order of worship and for listing significant activities for the day and week. It can be helpful to worshipers if the bulletin also includes some message of inspiration, admonition, or a religious thought. A printed cover may provide that, but the minister can add another note. A paragraph about the sermon can introduce the topic to worshipers.

6. Strangers and visitors depend on the Sunday bulletin to get them through the service. They should be welcomed with a special message and information. Include the names of the pastors, organist, choir director, and others participating in the service. Instructions on communion practices, signing the attendance sheets, etc., make being a visitor more comfortable.

7. Some pastors include comparative attendance and offering statistics in the bulletin. Others list the names of official board members. The educational staff is often recognized with a listing of teachers. The other church staff names may also be included.

8. Some congregations combine the Sunday bulletin with the weekly parish newsletter. That is certainly a time saver and does provide the membership with the Sunday schedule prior to Sunday. Combining the two does eliminate a separate piece of material and is most likely less expensive. For greater exposure and emphasis on special events, however, two pieces are more effective.

Managing the PR Program

The media is one of the most effective ways to tell a story or to promote an event. John William Zehring, vice-president for development at Bangor Theological Seminary, Bangor, Maine, describes how a church can get the most mileage out of the local newspaper.

HOW TO MANAGE PR FOR YOUR CHURCH*
by John William Zehring

Whether you are planning a church retreat, Bible study, social concerns work project, or a jog-a-thon, the activities of your church can be enhanced by good PR. The right publicity can help you to raise money, recruit members, increase attendance or participation, and inform people about the activity.

*Reprinted from *The Clergy Journal,* September 1982. © Copyright 1982 by Church Management, Inc. Used with permission.

There is also a higher purpose to public relations: if your church's primary goal is to nurture the Christian faith or extend the Kingdom of God, then letting your light shine via PR supports that important objective.

You, as pastor, are involved heavily in public relations either by design or default. To say nothing is to say something.

The executive of any organization is always considered the chief public relations officer. Of course, others may be involved in carrying out specific PR tasks. But it can't be assumed that they know how. Hence, your job is to equip them and provide vision to guide the public relations of the church.

There are two types of PR campaigns. The first is a one-shot approach to promote a program or event. The second is the on-going public relations of a church which has two basic objectives: a) furthering the name recognition of the church, and b) paving the way for recruiting members and raising funds.

Most non-profit organizations recognize PR as crucial to the success of recruitment and fund-raising, for people are more inclined to support or join an organization they have been hearing about. When an organization does not have good name recognition, people tend to lump it together with all other similar organizations and not recognize its distinctions. Public Relations becomes an important tool, therefore, for accomplishing the financial, membership, educational, programmatic, and spiritual objectives of your church.

But effective PR doesn't just happen by itself—it must be managed. The best campaigns usually result from people who have answered some key questions, planned carefully, and have chosen the right "vehicle" or media for their message. In fact, not to have a PR component to your major activities may lead to responses like "Gee, I didn't even know about . . ." or perhaps even failure of a potentially good idea.

Some publicity campaigns—and the bowling parties, concerts, or religious education programs they serve—fail because the wrong publicity was used. The message simply didn't get to its intended audience. Others do not get results because they neglect an important reality: your news or announcement competes with others for the attention of editors or readers. It must earn the space it's given, for free. Hence, the message must get across quickly and grab the reader's attention.

If you find yourself in charge of promoting your church's mission or if you supervise someone charged with planning an event worthy of broader attention, consider some of the following strategies for managing an effective public relations campaign:

PR STRATEGIES

1. Answer the Key Questions

WHO do you want to reach? All religious folk in town? Singles? Families? Potential donors? Church members? Who is your audience? Generally, the more specifically you can aim, the more effective your results. It may seem ironic, but those PR approaches pointed like a shotgun at everybody often reach nobody. It's the ones beamed like a laser beam to a particular audience that hit the target most often.

WHAT do you want to say? Re-write and edit until it is concise, clear, and as short as possible. You ought to be able to summarize your message in a sentence. If it isn't clear to you, it won't be clear to readers. Say too much and you'll lose the reader; too little and the reader will not be fully informed.

WHEN must it be done and submitted to meet deadlines? You can't expect to send a news release to the newspaper and see it in print the next day. Determine how much "lead time" you need to get your publicity through its channels.

WHERE should your message go? Radio? Church bulletin? Weekly paper? It's easy to overlook an important source. It's also easy to overshoot your goals and spend more time saturating the media when a simple approach would do.

WHY do you need publicity? The purpose of PR is to affect others into taking some kind of action. What are you trying to motivate the reader or listener to do? Give money or join your church or participate in a project? When someone says . . . "We ought to get some publicity," ask "why?" If you can answer that, you will have a more convincing case to make to the media.

HOW can you get the work done and who should do it? By a committee or a person? What needs to be done in what order? And what if you are in charge of the PR and you've never tackled something like this before?

It shouldn't be difficult to remember those key questions, for they are the ones asked by reporters: Who, What, When, Where, Why, and How. And when you present your message, these are the very questions you should answer for the reader.

2. Develop a Media Plan and Timetable

If you have answered the questions above, you're on your way to a successful media plan and timetable.

A media plan is just what it sounds like: your plan of attack. Writing it out helps you think through what you want to do and see the overall picture of your campaign. It also helps you to prioritize your goals: what should be done first, second, and so on.

3. Personalize Your Campaign

The more personally you handle your efforts, the higher the payoff. It's tempting to sit behind a typewriter and churn out impersonal announcements. Some of that is necessary, of course. But if you can add a personal touch, you will learn more about effective public relations and have a better chance of your releases being used. For example. . . .

—Ask around at church for ideas and contacts. Check with your official board, business executives, or professionals of the congregation to see if they know any media contacts you can call upon. Or, perhaps they can place a friendly phone call to alert the media contact that your release will be coming.

—Visit the religion editor of your local paper. Call first to arrange a meeting time, then go in, introduce yourself and hand deliver your news release. Perhaps you can provide some additional background which could serve as the basis of a feature story. Editors are alert to local possibilities for news and features and may even spot an angle you've missed. They are usually pleased to have you visit for fifteen to twenty minutes and your personal approach gives an importance to the release. It's also quite interesting to talk with someone at the paper, see their "shop," and make an acquaintance that might be useful for future programs run by your church.

—Arrange for a reporter to do an article about your event. This is *always* preferable to a simple news release, for it means the paper is taking a personal interest and will usually provide more space and attention to help you meet your goals. If you think there is more to your event than naming the date, time, and place, call up the religion editor (or city desk) and ask if they would be interested in doing a story on it.

—Provide taped (or live) interview to local radio stations. These are called "actualities" in the business and they are to radio what photographs are to newspapers. Suppose, for example, that you get a ten to twenty second tape of the activity's leader describing the special significance of your event. Call the radio station's news director (they prefer calls over letters), describe the event and the facts (who, what, when, where, why, and how), and tell them you have a twenty-second actuality of the activity's leader saying that it's a touching and spiritually significant play that makes the audience laugh, cry, and feel religious. If it's done well (and don't worry about technicalities of taping—a simple machine does fine), you've got a chance of getting "on the air."

—Call in story ideas to editors and news directors. Ideas are the lifeblood for print and electronic journalists who are always on the lookout for a good story. None will think you a pest, even if only one out of ten succeeds—that's not a bad batting average. Provide tips regularly for feature stories, for when one comes through, it will be worth its weight in gold and will do more for the church's public relations than a year's worth of paid advertising.

4. Prepare a News Release

This is a simple one or two page announcement of the facts. See the box for a sample format for how it might look. Make your release look as professional as possible: short, all the facts, typed perfectly and proofread.

There is a way of writing used by reporters called the "inverted pyramid," which is useful for news releases. Basically, that means putting the most important material first, the least important last. Like an up-side-down pyramid, the base (now at the top) is a description of key facts. When editors cut—as they inevitably must—they cut from the bottom up, leaving intact those key facts. The inverted pyramid makes their job easier, which makes your job more likely to succeed.

5. Prefer a News or Feature Story to Paid Advertising

For two reasons. First, cost. Why pay for something you can get for free? Second, credibility. Ads are self-serving, which is why you pay for them. Readers skim over them or neglect them much more frequently than a good news or feature item. Ads have their place, of course, especially when they are intended to be paid announcements. But in most cases, the effort to arrange a news or feature story will be repaid many times.

6. Follow-up Your Campaign by Measuring Results

It is helpful to get some measure of your success so you will know what works for future PR campaigns. This might range from a simple observation of attendance from nonregular attenders to a questionnaire handed out as people leave, polling them about where they saw the event announced and if that was the reason they came. In some events, there may even be opportunity to ask people which media announcements motivated them to action. Knowing where you succeeded will help next time in aiming carefully for the most effective media and eliminating those that aren't necessary.

—Remember to include photographs for newspaper releases and actualities (10-20-second tapes) for radio releases. While not crucial, they will get you more space in the paper or time on the radio. And more space or time means more attention. For photos, on-the-spot candids are better than mug shots.

—The most potent tool for publicity is creative writing. Editors hate to rewrite and edit PR, so make it as good and complete as possible.

When writing a news release—

. . . Use shorter sentences.

. . . Prefer the simpler word over a more complex word.

. . . Keep polysyllabic words of three or more syllables to a minimum.

. . . Action verbs are better than the verb "to be" or "to have." For example, use "performed, facilitated, educated, created, etc.," instead of "she did, he was" and so on. As you re-write your "copy," spice up your writing with action words. Write tight!

. . . Have someone else check your writing for clarity and simplicity. Another reader can add insights to pep up writing or to spot something that might be left out.

. . . With radio releases, aim for the ear, not the eye.

. . . Give news value to your publicity. Describing a church car wash is PR. But explaining how the church is raising money for a sick child's expensive operation via the car wash may have potential for a companion story. It never hurts to call the religion editor to ask if they would be interested in covering a story on the sick child, adding a human interest angle, and running it side by side with your news release. Whenever you can do some research get behind a story and find an extra slant, you multiply the impact of your publicity.

. . . Grab the attention of the reader in the lead (the introduction) and interest him or her in reading further. Work hard on the first few lines, drawing the reader into the article. Some writers begin with a catchy anecdote or a provocative question. It's worth your time to create a powerful lead. Otherwise, the reader may skip your announcement entirely.

. . . Create a desire for action. How do you want your reader to respond? If attendance or raising money is the answer, write your release so the reader is motivated to fulfill your hopes. That's the very reason for your efforts!

Sample News Release

NEWS RELEASE
FOR: Name of organization   CONTACT: Your address, telephone

FOR IMMEDIATE RELEASE

Richmond, IN May 1, 19__

TEXT: Indent 8 spaces instead of five. Use 8½ × 11 paper, one side only. Work name or organization or event into lead in such a manner that lead wouldn't work without it. Give news value. Show benefit to reader. Double space. Limit paragraphs to 4 or 5 sentences.

Keep to 2 or 3 paragraphs. Cover who, what, when, where, why or how. Use 1½" to 2" margins. Keep to about 200 words. If 2 pages, never jump in mid-paragraph. Keep short and tight, but not at expense of creativity. Proofread.

If two pages, type "–more–" at bottom of p. 1 and "ADD 1" in upper left corner of p. 2. Don't type "page 2." Conclude with "–30–" or "###."

Checklist of possible sources for PR

Church: Sunday bulletin, church newsletter, bulletin board, pulpit announcements, posters, announce in groups, announce in classes, direct mail to specific audience.

Newspaper: community announcements in daily, weekly, or "shopper" papers; religion page story/announcements; news/feature pages (via news editor).

Radio: Community bulletin board announcements, news (with actuality).

Other churches: Ask other churches to announce in their bulletin, newsletter, from pulpit or with posters; send delegation to other churches to announce in person during worship services.

Other sources for PR: Posters or signs in local shop windows; TV, but must have significance for viewing audience, by arranging coverage or sending slides/video cassette with release; posters at local schools (ask permission from principal); announcement in denominational publication, by region if possible; local cable TV, especially in towns that have small, local cable TV stations which feature publicity announcements; word of mouth advertising, which is the most effective way of all when you ask group members to spread the word, call friends, and tell everyone they meet.

A media plan

ACTIVITY: Christmas Play
DATE, TIME, PLACE: December 22, 8 P.M., First Church Fellowship Hall
BACKGROUND INFORMATION: Information on play and reason for its selection.
  Local tie-in (written by townsperson).
  Human interest angle, if any.
  Details on directions to church, parking, costs, childcare (make it sound easy to get there and attend).
AUDIENCE: All members of First Church.
  Members of neighboring churches/denominations.
  The religious community at large (others in your town like to be attracted to such a play).
PURPOSE OF PR: To invite attendance.
MEDIA: Announced in church newsletter, weekly bulletin, from pulpit two Sundays before play. Posters
    around church.
  Mail announcements and posters to other Protestant churches in the community, inviting them to
    attend. Ask to have announced in the youth groups, weekly bulletins, and pulpit announcements. A
    personal, handwritten line or two on a form letter helps to get results. Send three weeks before play.
  Daily newspaper. Send news release to religion editor three weeks in advance. Ask to have reporter or
    reviewer "cover" play, along with photographer.
  Weekly newspaper. Send release to "Community Announcements."
  Local radio stations. Send news release one or two weeks in advance to "Community Bulletin Board."
  Ask all members of youth group to spread the word.
ASSIGNMENTS: List which persons will be responsible for each of the above tasks.

Bulletin Boards

."If you don't tell them, they won't know." I never cease to be amazed at the number of congregations that have no outdoor signs—no identification at all to tell the passerby what or who they are. How can you ever expect a visitor to show up if there's nothing to tell them who and what you are?

Next worse, however, is the faded outdoor church bulletin board that is hopelessly out-of-date, hard to read, grown over with weeds, and obviously unattended. That says something about how much people at that church care—not much!

An attractive, well-kept church building and grounds is crucial in giving visitors an initial positive attitude about your church. It's no reason to join or not join, but people are favorably impressed when facilities are neat and clean. Even an old building can be spruced up at little cost with some paint and a few shrubs.

But along with that beautiful building goes the church sign. Say what you want about the mission of the church, you will still get more people to come inside when they can easily see and read an attractive church sign.

The sign identifying the church building needs to say nothing more than the name. Time of services, perhaps the pastor's name, will be helpful. *But it is the name of the church that is important.* No one really cares about the sermon title for next Sunday, and usually any message is too long and too small to be read driving by in an automobile anyway.

Design and build a custom-made church sign, prominently located, that tells anyone driving by what you are. You may discover that replacing that old bulletin board with an attractive new sign could help boost church attendance!

Churches have other outdoor bulletin boards and signs. Placing church direction signs at prominent street corners (with permission of city and property owners) can be helpful. However, these signs must be maintained and checked periodically. Beat up, rusty signs may give direction, but they don't make a very good impression.

Some churches join in with other churches to place a sign of welcome at the city limits. That defeats the purpose for identifying your place since people are not likely to stop their cars and try to pick out the church sign for their denomination. In a cooperative spirit it can be useful, but not as a directional aid to the location of your building.

Indoor bulletin boards are another matter. Their purpose is not to identify and give direction, but to inform, inspire, and educate. Assigning a volunteer with creative abilities and artistic interests to maintain hallway and narthex bulletin boards is important. Here are a few do's and don'ts:

1. Keep all boards attractive with current information.
2. Remove or rearrange anything that has been the same for more than two weeks.
3. Use bright colors, neat art work, poster-quality printing.
4. Avoid clutter. Keep it simple, direct, easy to read.
5. Use pertinent and interesting data. Make the boards personal for organizations or even for a member whose outstanding achievements or service should be recognized by the community.
6. A special board with recent thank yous, notes from visitors or members on vacation will interest many members.
7. A board especially for educational ministries can highlight church activities in the Sunday church school, vacation church school, weekday church school, nursery school, day school, and elsewhere.
8. Using a thermometer for financial or attendance goals can work for a few weeks. Eventually, however, no one sees it anymore and its effectiveness is lost.
9. Posting photos of new members (large enough to see a few feet away) can help people identify newcomers.
10. Mount a bright light above the bulletin board. Don't depend on overhead room or hallway lights. The same switch used for the room can be used for the board light so it won't be left on inadvertently.
11. Locate the most important bulletin board materials just a little below average eye level. That way the bifocal crowd can read it comfortably without tilting their heads backwards!

Direct Mail

For many congregations it's a new thought—junk mail promotion. But for growing churches it has been an effective tool for communicating and inviting. Direct mail is used aggressively by anyone anxious to tell a lot of people at the same time about a new product. Churches are doing the same with direct mail, telling a lot of neighbors about an old product that is just as new today as it ever was. The gospel message can be conveyed third-class, nonprofit, bulk rate. It is not limited to the pulpit, anymore.

The purpose of any direct mail campaign is to tell the neighborhood about your church. It is to inform. It won't convert; it may not even get anyone to the church building. But it does inform, it does advertise, it does make known, and it does say who you are and where you are.

Thus, the all-important focus of planning a direct mail effort is in developing an attractive brochure. The second focus is to determine the target audience. But unless the piece mailed is effective, it won't make much difference who gets it.

Obviously a direct mail program will not be a monthly event, at least not to the same people. Once a year to every home in the neighborhood may be sufficient. Sent too often, it will create a negative response, especially from church goers elsewhere. But a program of targeting specific areas each month avoids the one-time all-out effort. A regular program is easier to manage.

A direct mail brochure should have the following characteristics (this is different from the brochure that you send to new residents, as described in a later chapter):

Elements of a direct mail brochure

1. Keep it simple, direct, to the point, uncluttered.

2. As much as possible, include all pertinent information on the outside, i.e., if a #10 envelope is used, just left of the address put pertinent information or if a self-folding mailer, next to the address and on the back side. Some people won't open up the piece. You've got to catch their eye before the piece is tossed into file 13.

3. A photo of the church building will help to identify your place. Name, address, telephone number all go in the most prominent location, "up front, center." After all, that's what you want to tell most.

4. Then, in a brief description on the inside fold extend an invitation (briefly!). The pastor's photograph may be useful. State worship times. Perhaps a brief listing of activities that will interest people in general can be helpful, such as youth groups if your community has lots of teenagers, or a senior citizens program in a community of retirees, or child-care facilities in a community with young working mothers. Tell the people what your church can do to help them. Know the needs of the people in your area and then target that interest.

5. An attractive one color, three fold, 8½×11 self-folding piece should be just about right for the budget and the audience. An envelope may not be opened, so don't use one. Of course, a staple gets in the way, too. Avoid that. Try to avoid closing the piece, but check first with your post office.

6. Try a postcard, 8½×3¼. It can't help but be noticed—the whole thing—with minimum effort.

7. Use the local library to find books that help in designing direct mail.

Selecting the names that you will use for your direct mail is the second most important task. Names and addresses can be rented and that's what you will do, at least at first. Check with a mailing shop in your town about the availability of a list. Find something that includes the names of the people. "Occupant" is too impersonal. A name, even a computer-printed label with a name, is better than something addressed to "Resident."

The list you rent will be arranged by ZIP code order. So you can select the ZIP codes where most of your members live or your church is located and use that. With the new ZIP+4 codes, you'll even be able to rent lists for specific streets and blocks. Select names of residents near the church, since that is your obvious target area and the place where you are most likely to get a response. The farther you get from the church building, the less likely there will be any response. Expect to pay fifty dollars to one hundred dollars per thousand names for a one-time rental use.

If you can garner a cadre of volunteers, pressure-sensitive labels may be best. Those are the kind you peel off and stick on. No fuss, no muss. Or for less money you can rent a list on plain paper, one address above the next or four across a larger sheet. These must be cut and affixed with paste by a special machine available at your printer's place.

Your mailing piece will need the correct postage paid imprint and return address. As a nonprofit organization you'll pay less postage than a commercial business pays.

Advertising

Yes, it pays to advertise, insists Al Stauderman, who writes:*

You need to use the finest facilities available to you to keep your community aware of the place of your church in its life. Advertising is important. The best advertising, of course, is by word of mouth as your parishioners "talk up" the church and live out their faith in their daily lives. The pastor is also able to help the congregation by participating in public life, serving the community freely, and representing the church well. Your church building itself can be a good advertisement or a bad one.

But beyond all this, you need to use the public press and all other media to establish a high recognition factor for your church. Aside from news . . . you will find that it pays to pay to advertise. Taking a paid advertisement in a small newspaper is a symbol of your support for that paper and is likely to influence their willingness to give you space for news. A paid advertisement in a large newspaper, which really doesn't need your ad, is both a prestige item for your church and a way of reaching a wide audience of readers.

To be effective, a newspaper advertisement must be clear and straightforward. It should not be cluttered with too many words or deal with too many different topics. Let the ad tell about your Sunday services; if you have a weekday program, take a special ad on a different day to announce it. Trying to put too much information into one church ad may lead readers to skip over it, since the competition for attention is keen.

On a typical Saturday "church page" a dozen or more churches may be represented by paid advertisements. Your ad should have some distinctive factor to make it stand out among the crowd. This might be the use of special type, but you need expert guidance if you go this route. It could also be the use of some striking slogan or an excerpt from your sermon, but here you risk trying to pour in too much and therefore losing the attention of the reader. Best is to have some special logo, photograph, or drawing that makes your ad distinctive and that can be repeated over and over, thereby increasing the recognition factor. People who are actually looking for information about your church will soon recognize your particular format. Since many newspapers use photo-offset production, a simple drawing can easily be reproduced. If your paper still uses letterpress, they will make a "cut" of your drawing or photograph for a small cost. The metal cut can be used over again many times.

Don't think that you can advertise once a year and have people remember your church. One secret of successful commercial advertising is constant repetition. We see some commercials on TV so often that we become tired of them, but whether we like them or dislike them, we remember them. Advertising for recognition takes hold when it's pounded home time after time. And even the fiftieth time an ad appears may be the first time some newcomer spots it!

Special Brochures

Many congregations develop special leaflets and brochures for promoting a wide variety of causes and concerns. Several of these are described elsewhere in this book, but here is a further sampling that may help to stimulate your thinking and planning for promotion.

1. *The education program.* Use an attractively designed leaflet to tell people about the educational programs of your church. Many members may have no idea what you do or what you have or who is involved. Succinctly describe the program's overall objective; list each school, i.e., Sunday church school, vacation church school, etc., with the name, address, and telephone number of the director and show who's responsible—the education committee (list their names). You'll want to include a brief description of each program, times they meet, and the leaders.

2. *Stained glass windows.* An attractive brochure describing the symbolism of each window and telling something of the windows' history and technical data will be of interest. If you're eager to get more windows, the leaflet could be a low-key fund-raiser, too.

---

*From *40 Proven Ways to a Successful Church* by Al Stauderman. Copyright © by Abingdon Press, 1980, pages 41-43. Used by permission.

Sample Newspaper Ads

Sunday Services 8:45 & 11
Nursery Provided

RINITY CHURCH

United Methodist
9625 N. Military Tr.•Palm Beach Gardens

COMMUNITY CHURCH

Park Ave. at 5th St.   Lake Park

INVITES YOU TO WORSHIP WITH US EACH SUNDAY

Jr. Hi., Sr. Hi., Adult Sunday School	9 a.m.
Divine Worship	10 a.m.
Youth Sunday School	10 a.m.

Walter W. Wynkoop, D.D., Pastor
Mrs. Jane Mudgett, Music Director

St. John's Church

Sunday School 9 a.m.
Worship Service 10 a.m.
241 Cypress Dr., Lake Park
(2 Blks. west of Hwy. One)
848-3142

"Your Church"

NORTH PALM BEACH, FLORIDA

WORSHIP SERVICES 8:00 & 10:45 A.M.
BIBLE STUDY (ALL AGES) 9:15 A.M.
(NURSERY at all Services)
PASTOR'S FORUM 9:30 A.M.
COFFEE FELLOWSHIP 9:00-9:30 A.M.

Sermon: "Things That Cannot Be Shaken"
Guest Preacher
Dr. Albert P. Stauderman
848-4737

555 U.S. HIGHWAY ONE

Just north of Twin City Mall

WEEKDAY NURSERY
KINDERGARTEN PROGRAM

---

*From *40 Proven Ways to a Successful Church* by Al Stauderman. Copyright © by Abingdon Press, 1980, page 43. Used by permission.

3. *History and architecture of the building.* Some people like to know when the building was built, if there were additions, fires, relocations. For historical purposes, such a leaflet might include photos of earlier buildings, cornerstone and dedication service participants, interesting or unusual aspects of the building.

4. *Special services.* Leaflets telling about special Lenten or Advent services are often produced each year by growing churches. These can be used not only as worship aids or promotional pieces for the services, but they may make useful tools for handouts to prospective members. A three-fold 5½ × 8½ folder can tell the story quickly.

5. *Occasional papers.* Some congregations provide descriptive papers on topics of interest to special groups. A staff-written paper on the importance of teacher training, for example, may be distributed to the educational staff. Reprints of an article on effective ways to improve breathing when singing can be secured from the publisher and distributed to music department staff and participants. A paper explaining the need for an additional minister might be circulated to the membership including information about past selection methods and a word about the office of the ministry. A paper detailing the status of the pipe organ, its history, use, and current need for improvement could be useful and interesting.

6. *Special programs.* A series of lectures, a fine arts program, opportunities to hear good music, see fine paintings, or experience meaningful drama may all be written up in carefully designed, attractive leaflets.

7. *Newcomers.* A brochure of pertinent information for the benefit of new residents in the community can be an effective public relations piece. Another brochure specifically for visitors and prospective members is also useful. Both types of leaflets are fully described in a later chapter.

8. *The Every Member Response.* Special brochures may be developed specifically for the annual EMR program. Special programs, projects, and needs can be carefully set forth.

9. *Church furniture.* If there is a special symbolism attached to the altar, reredos, pews, pulpit, or other church furniture, descriptive leaflets can inform the people.

10. *Specialized programs.* Newsletters to members in the armed services, to a singles ministry group, and to the Sunday church school are all examples of specialized promotional pieces that help to tell people about the church.

More Advertising

The local telephone directory may be the most effective advertising your church can do. Visitors will find your church name some place, but they will never remember the telephone number. And almost all potential visitors will call the church at least once to find out the time of services, even though the times of services are shown on the church sign.

In the Yellow Pages you have an excellent opportunity to single out your congregation through special graphics and advertising space. It may cost more, but the exposure more than pays the added cost. As a minimum, your listing should be in bold type, as large as possible. Box the information. Include address, times of service, nursery facilities, and day school programs. List the pastor's name, also.

Hotel and motel church directories have limited impact, but if the cost is right (probably nothing), the church should be listed. Just don't expect a big rush of transients on Sunday morning!

Seasonal listings in your denominational magazine could be useful if you are located in a popular tourist area. Scattering your business card in mobile parks, recreation areas, and even local public facilities, if permitted, are all ways to keep the church's name out front. Response will be hard to count, but contacts can be made.

Recognition

Public relations is not limited to advertising, publications, and attractive brochures. For the church it must include a program of recognition that is sensitive toward what others continue to do. Perhaps public relations is, therefore, a way of promoting the church by telling people about what's happening as well as thanking them for doing something worthwhile for the benefit of other people. Everyone wants to feel that he/she is making a worthwhile contribution to the life of the church and wants to know that that is appreciated. Acknowledging that service is just good PR!

And there are many ways in which good PR is done by caring church administrators and ministers.

Some significant ways of expressing appreciation:

1. Personal expression of appreciation, one-on-one, is always the most effective method, but not always possible.

2. A personal telephone call is good but often fails to convey body language. Yet, a call to the Sunday church school director to express appreciation for an excellent Christmas program the day after can do a lot of good. A call to the head cook after an especially well-managed and delicious church banquet builds confidence and strengthens relationships.

3. The letter is the normal means used by clergy to express appreciation. Correspondence that shows genuine thanks for jobs well-done is always appreciated. Care must be exercised, however, to keep the letters personal even though they may be routinely churned out of the word processor.

Letters of appreciation or recognition are always appropriate for those persons:

—creating an outstanding music program
—organizing a field trip for a group of sixth graders
—contributing a special gift
—transporting elderly members
—supervising the VCS program
—ushering faithfully for a month, year, or more
—running the mimeograph
—contributing legal counsel
—keeping church finances
—maintaining the church library
—directing the children's choir
—attending worship services (as visitors)
—and the list goes on. . . .

Whenever and wherever people do special things or regular things for a long time, a note of appreciation is always in order.

4. Acknowledgment of all contributions of record is standard practice in most congregations. In addition to the standard reporting of financial contributions, one pastor (with one thousand members) always sends a form letter of thanks to all contributors and then pens a brief personal thank-you to each—that's effective PR! Special gifts deserve special thanks from the pastor or officers.

5. Recognition at worship services and in church publications also acknowledges appreciation. Listing names of volunteers and leaders in the newsletter or bulletin on a periodic basis is helpful. Done regularly, say a different group each week, the appreciation is more often expressed and acknowledged. Special luncheons for special groups acknowledging their contributions of service builds positive relationships. Costs are repaid many times over in continued, dedicated service.

Sermon Publication

It may be more of an ego "trip" than anything, but in some congregations, the pastor's sermons are often published and distributed to interested persons. On the other hand, this practice may produce considerable pressure on the pastor.

Yet, the traditions of some congregations are so imbedded with linking successful preaching with publication of sermons that official boards often make such publication a condition of the hiring or call of the minister. It is often believed that distributing published sermons will help promote the congregation and draw members and money. Good preaching does indeed bring people through the front door. But sermons preached are never the same as sermons published.

If there is a demand or requirement for sermon publication, the minister must not be expected to do the job. A secretary should prepare the manuscripts from tape recordings of the sermon. The manuscript must be approved by the pastor, with changes made as required.

Distribution depends on official board policy and the pastor's personal preferences—should copies be given to all members, to those not attending, or just to whoever picks one up? How about the local hospital, the seminary, or the church college as distribution points? What about the students in college or those in the armed services? And who pays for this? A special sermon publication fund may be needed if the program is greatly expanded. Its worth, however, must always be evaluated with respect to good being done to promote the church or help the people.

A printed brochure may be the most effective means, but an 8½ × 11 mimeographed sheet does the job, too.

Directories

Publication of an annual listing of names, addresses, and telephone numbers of the entire membership is important. The up-to-date directory is an effective tool for encouraging communication between members. And with the use of computers, a directory can be as current as needed.

Using the mimeograph does limit the frequency of a directory printing. However, a computer printout made after a periodic updating of data, can be done in letter quality and reproduced quickly by photocopying at a quick print shop. Secretarial time should be limited to updating current files, not typing the whole list all over again.

An annual directory may be enough for most members, but frequent users of the directory (such as staff) need interim updated listings. But annual directories often contain more than just a listing of names and addresses. The directory may be a compendium of useful information for many members. Information can include:
1. Photos. A pictorial directory includes photos of every member willing to be photographed. (That helps tremendously in putting names and faces together.)
2. Names of spouses, children, and the occupation of adult members.
3. Listing of all staff with appropriate positions and phone numbers, with photos.
4. Brief historical data about heritage and tradition.
5. A listing of special events, a calendar of activities, and special worship services for finger-tip access to what is going on.
6. Names of all officers, committee chairpersons, and their telephone numbers.
7. A brief statement of purpose for each organization, dates and times of regular meetings, names and numbers of contact persons.
8. Rules regarding the use of church property.
9. Names of ushers for the year.
10. Worship details for all Sundays such as themes, special music, sermon topics, preachers, communion, special observances.
11. A form of bequest to the church.
12. The annual budget, a statement about benevolences.
13. How to donate flowers for the altar.
14. Policy regarding the child-care facilities.

Attendance Records

There are many ways of securing information about people for purposes of caring, communicating, and responding to needs.

Almost all congregations maintain cards in pew racks, convenient for worshipers to use as needed. The most frequent card is a visitor card that urges nonmembers to give their address and telephone number and express their interest in the congregation. That information helps the clergy make follow-up calls.

Pew cards also include communion cards, prayer cards, special envelopes, announcements, etc. Care should be exercised that the card rack not appear as a trash can. Two or three cards should be sufficient. And children should be urged to use some other scratch pad!

A guest book properly attended by a host or hostess can be an effective way of helping visitors feel welcome. Then it is, of course, a source of names and addresses of prospects. Follow-up cards, letters, and calls are appropriate. Visits by out-of-town relatives of members may be acknowledged. Personal letters should be distributed to obvious prospects.

Attendance pads help to record who was in church, but also, when passed down the pew, help people to get acquainted with newcomers or others not previously known.

A coffee hour is good PR, too. The fellowship and casual conversation offers an opportunity to get acquainted and to share mutual concerns with others. A hostess/host or fellowship committee should be responsible. The coffee hour's location should be close to the sanctuary.

Letterheads

Every letter that goes out from the church office is a PR piece. The letterhead of an organization says a lot about the group, so considerable care should be exercised in designing the church stationery. Basic information is required—name, address (both location and mailing), telephone number with area code and name of pastor. Names of other staff may also be included.

Art work on letterheads should be tasteful. Simple, easily read letterheads are best. A logo may be appropriate. Two-color on other than white high-quality paper can be impressive.

Special note paper ("From the Pastor's Desk"), post cards, and routine stationery for mimeographing can all be tastefully created. Printers can help suggest quality at affordable prices.

CHAPTER 8

STAFF COMPENSATION

WHAT ARE YOU paid? How do your people add it all up on the church budget? And how does it compare to the pay of your lay leaders, to the pay of other clergy, to the pay of professionals in your community? The way in which the pastor's compensation is defined will make a difference on how much pay you really receive. Chances are, you receive less than you realize.

In some congregations, whoever is responsible for setting pay may take a lump sum, say $30,000, and tell the pastor, "How do you want the money divided up?" That's awful. It's unfair; it's not very creative; and it won't end up being much real pay for you either.

In other congregations, those responsible for pay plan recommendations may determine salary at, say, $20,000, car allowance at $2,000, and pension costs at $3,000, recommending that the church pay $25,000. That's unfair, too, because salary is perceived to be $25,000, not what it really is, $20,000.

Still other congregations may decide to boost salary 5 percent, leaving all else as is. That's also not very fair because it assumes the previous year base salary was adequate in the first place. Sure, it's more money for you, but is total pay now fair, equitable, and really based on a present evaluation irregardless of what's been paid in the past?

Forward-thinking congregations will quickly recognize that a total cost package of limited dollar amounts is not an appropriate way to make intelligent salary recommendations. The total cost for having a pastor is not the same as total compensation. Real compensation is always less than the congregation's cost for having a pastor. Salary is always less than total compensation.

When a congregation has aggressive leadership, those lay leaders will make a diligent effort to pay what is fair and equitable on the basis of what the pastor is really worth. Of course, total costs simply can't always be known in advance. And once determined, final costs may be too large a strain on the church budget, but then the matter of too low pay is revealed for what it really is, an inability to pay, not a lack of confidence in the pastor's ability to handle a variety of problems and respond creatively to the needs of people in the church. Some congregations simply cannot afford the pastor they now employ. It just may be costing too much. But to cut pay deliberately because budgets are inadequate puts the financial burden on clergy, not on the church. Seeking affordable leadership is a more honest approach than intentionally downgrading the present more capable leadership.

Good compensation planning requires a diligent search for finding adequate resources to pay the pastor. But compensation planning also requires a careful analysis of the whole package—an awareness of what is involved in clergy pay, a knowledge of tax laws that affect clergy, and some perception of expectations of both clergy and church.

When Pay Is Too Low

1. It's hard enough to make ministry work when there's enough cash in your bank account to go around. But too little pay could really interfere with the way you minister to your community of believers. You're not after a big bundle, just enough to take your worries off your pocketbook and keep them on the job. Take home too little, though, and your work may suffer while you worry about how to make ends meet. Your ministry could take a downturn just because you are so worried about your own personal finances. That's when your congregation will begin to feel the pinch of low pay, too.

You want to do a good job, but you need to be able to support your family to do an effective job. You worry about many things and many people. And that's no more than normal in most jobs where we try to do our best and satisfy the requirements of our employers. But burdening the normal tensions of job-related work with balancing the family budget makes a good job less likely. Employee and employer alike suffer the consequences together. Personal money worries exacerbate even the normal pressures of a job and do interfere with efficiency and productivity.

2. The public's view of clergy pay is, sad to say, stereotyped. Most people know that you are probably underpaid or at least assume that is the case. And for many, although by no means all pastors, that is all too true. Why else are ministers offered discounts at the local department store or on trains and airlines, given free tickets to sports events, and offered cash gifts by prominent parishioners, businesses, or the local undertaker?

How well I remember the vegetables and meat and butter and eggs from parishioners in the rural parish I once served. Summertime garden produce overwhelmed my wife. And the local meat clubs saw to it that the pastor wasn't forgotten at the weekly calf butchering either. In those days it took only a few calls around the parish to fill our cupboard when groceries got scarce at home. I knew where to visit when the annual pounding was still months away.* I suspect, though, that those people gave us all that food because they had more food to give away than money. It was their way of making a gift to the church, and they were proud that they could. But I got the food rather than more money because my pay was too low. And the community knew my pay was low, too.

Maybe that wasn't so bad out there in the country. But less understanding nonchurchgoing city folk often take a dim view toward the church when they know or at least believe they know the pastor is underpaid. Believe me, you can improve the image of your church in your community by letting it be known you are paid fair and square as pastor. It will enhance the effectiveness of your ministry.

3. Low-paid clergy can't help but develop rather negative attitudes toward their congregations. Perhaps it's not a conscious attitude you'd have. You're not likely to move off to another parish right away because you failed to get a boost in pay; but the nature of low pay, of feeling you're not getting what you ought to get, is bound to create some negative feelings. It's inevitable. It's the kind of thing that eats into your enthusiasm and dedication for getting on with the church's work.

On the other hand, pastors with salaries above the average, or at least reasonably adequate for the work expected in return, are satisfied. Of course, pastors usually want more pay, don't most workers? But knowing that ministry is at least appreciated with a fair and equitable pay, even though it'll never make the pastor rich, probably satisfies. Not many pastors really do complain about their pay.

Still, if your congregation pays you a minimum salary or pays just enough to get them by, you probably won't be happy no matter how satisfying the job is, how friendly the congregation may be, or how willing the membership pitches in to get things done. Somehow or the other, money influences all of us, preachers, too. And too little money influences us more than too much whenever we balance

---

*A pounding is when gifts of food are given to a new pastor or given annually at a special event, usually a surprise party. This is a typically rural practice.

out the family checkbook. Ministry is enhanced by positive attitudes. Your pay is crucial to your optimism toward the job.

4. Inflation has a way of eating up those happy surplus funds we once budgeted for a Caribbean cruise. It simply costs more money to live today (and travel) then it did a year ago or even six months ago. Budgeting for doctors, groceries, and vacations becomes more and more difficult.

Compound the effects of inflation on top of your low pay, and you get a picture of the almost impossible task of keeping your head above water financially. It's well-nigh impossible. So, no matter how well you may be able to manage your family's finances, budget, or cut costs, sometimes you simply will not be able to meet your financial commitments if your pay is too low.

Nor with low pay can you afford to participate in community affairs; send your children to a private church-related college (although financial aid based on need makes this much less difficult); pay for piano lessons, orthodontists, and opticians; or even buy pop and peanuts at the high school football game (even if the tickets were free.)

Everything just costs too much. And since food is the primary concern, dollars obviously go there first. Housing probably is taken care of by your congregation, so shelter of some sort (usually quite adequate) is not your financial problem. But the frustration of not having enough money to pay for what's considered basic plus a little more, the pressure from kids to keep up with the neighbor's kids, and the incessant spiraling of costs persist in getting in the way of your ministry.

Some of your lay leaders will see the wisdom of a careful review of salaries paid to staff members. Continuing to pay you too little simply aggravates your financial problems. Inflation can hurt you if your congregation refuses to recognize its impact on your own finances.

5. Perhaps you have to moonlight to make ends meet. That takes time from ministry and the congregation's programs are likely to suffer. Of course you're not hired on a twenty-four hour basis, in spite of the fact that some of your members may think so. Since you do have some leftover hours, perhaps you may use them to try to earn a few extra bucks. And of course you may do that. But that is not the main task for which you are paid.

Most of us who serve in the parish ministry, however, realize that it's not an eight to five job, not by any means. We simply cannot limit our workweek to forty hours. Most of us probably wouldn't even want to. The emergencies, interruptions, and multitudinous array of meetings simply prevent any pastor from ordering a work schedule into neat blocks of eight hours each day, for only five days a week.

Moonlighting, therefore, poses a precarious threat to effective ministry. It blocks out time when a pastor simply cannot respond to parish needs because another need (that of bolstering a tottering bank balance) is more pressing than the matter of a property committee meeting at the church. It threatens ministry to the congregation

6. By now your spouse is probably employed, just to help make ends meet. It may be a case of necessity. And that's not so surprising, really, especially now that most women are holding down paying jobs. Many spouses are employed outside the home to fulfill their own ambitions, to "do something worthwhile," or to make ends meeet. Yet the minister's wife has traditionally been of exceptional help in ministry. Many pastors and spouses are involved together in making ministry effective where they serve, yet only one gets a pay check.

That kind of cooperation from a spouse was once expected, but not so anymore. In fact, many spouses resent any expectation from the congregation that they be part of the team. The minister is called to ministry, not the spouse. So that when a spouse works outside the home, the congregation simply loses out on what could have been an important assist to ministry.

7. The old cliche that "those who have, get more" is especially true in retirement for low-paid vs. higher-paid clergy. In those denominations where contributions to a pension plan are a percentage of salary and benefits paid are based on accumulations in the plan, the low-paid pastor is still, in retirement, at the end of the line. Low pay equals low contributions equals low pension. There's just no way around it; what was inequitable in the parish continues into retirement.

Now, not all denominational pension plans work that way. Some plans require a percentage contribution, but the base is calculated as the average salary for all the pastors in the conference or district. Thus, congregations paying low salaries put into the plan on behalf of their pastors the same dollars as the congregations with higher wage scales. The end result is intended to offer an equal dollar pension to all pastors whether their salaries were high or low. It is a way to equalize pensions and not burden low-paid clergy with the double curse of a low pension, too.

8. One of the temptations facing clergy, if pay is low, is that of going into some other work—leaving the ministry, finding a job someplace else that pays more. It's not that clergy dislike ministry; it's just that they can't afford it anymore. A new job in a different place will probably pay more. When pay is low, the church is no longer competitive and cannot attract some of the best candidates.

If that's your predicament, before you make a switch check out one of the clergy professional career planning centers to help you reevaluate your professional goals. If you have other skills, this will be helpful. If you don't have other skills, this kind of evaluation is imperative before you decide ministry pays too little and you want no more of it. A chance at retooling could be helpful, but a switch just to switch because of low pay could be no better than what you now have.

9. Competition for positions within the parish ministry is probably as severe now as it has ever been. A sudden decline in the organization of new congregations, the leveling of growth rates for existing congregations, the merging of other congregations, and the general financial struggles that all congregations face, has created a surplus of pastors. The preponderance of vacancies is no longer there.

The demands for pastoral leadership has its ups and downs. There will always be a need for clergy; it's just that sometimes there are more candidates than there are places. The sizeable number of women seminarians today produces a much tighter market than ever, also.

But at the center of most dissatisfactions with ministry is money, and specifically low pay. You can be sure that bright young men and women are going to think twice before making a commitment to ministry if their vision of the pastor is the traditional "low-paid but dedicated servant of the Lord." They may be just as dedicated, but they don't want the low pay.

Conversation between Clergy and Lay Leaders

Good compensation planning requires good conversation between clergy and lay leaders. A cursory review of salary while the pastor is outside the room is degrading to the minister and unprofessional for lay leaders. Lay leaders should talk openly about pay. That's the only way church and clergy will understand why pay is set at the amounts proposed. Smart congregational leaders will want to be certain that they know clergy expectations and that clergy know their own.

Setting pay can be a cumbersome event. Lay leaders probably scrutinize each benefit, each item, then add it all up for a grand total called "compensation." Of course that grand total is not salary. And if lay leaders would compare that total with the pay *they* get, it's like comparing apples and oranges. They are just not the same.

It is natural for lay leaders to compare their own pay with their pastor's pay. It can be a good comparison. But, since they don't generally add in to their pay the value of various fringe benefits and expense reimbursements, they should not add that into clergy pay for comparison. What is the salary? That's the comparative figure, not including car allowance, pensions, health, and whatever. Compare salary with salary. That's fair!

Planning your pay, therefore, involves more than just dividing out a total lump sum of available dollars. It must also include an evaluation of performance and some decisions on specific payment principles. On the basis of a careful evaluation and those agreed upon principles of pay, a fair and equitable compensation plan can be put together. Instead of just a flat dollar amount to be divided out, it will include careful consideration of reimbursements, benefits, housing, and salary.

A small committee is usually the best forum in which to develop a plan. Call it a pastor parish relations committee or a mutual ministry committee, or whatever, but that group should have primary responsibility for putting a pay plan together. Then the committee recommends the plan to the official board and supports it before the congregation. This small committee, however, becomes the advocate for the pastor.

This conversation should be in progress during the summer months if typical salary changes are made in January each year. By October the official board should have the recommendation. And the congregation would act whenever the budget is approved, usually in December prior to the beginning of the new year.

Obviously, it is important for pastor, committee, board, and congregation to know the financial commitments on compensation before the fiscal year begins. Annual church meetings in January that adopt budget retroactive to January 1 create a lame-duck time when technically the church has no budget and nothing should be spent. Good planning techniques require the budget be in place (and new board members elected) before year's end.

The small committee will then review the four basic components of the pay plan: reimbursements of professional expenses, supplemented benefits, housing, and salary.

Reimbursements

Fairness has already been mentioned in this chapter a number of times, fairness as to how a congregation pays for your ministry to them. Perhaps nowhere else in compensation planning than in the area of reimbursements are clergy treated so unfairly. Indeed, the typical professional expense reimbursement arrangement is to pick some arbitrary figure, assign that to this category of costs and go on to the next item. For all the good that does, the congregation may as well have added that amount to salary and not even fretted over how much car allowance, book allowance, or continuing education allowance was best. It really doesn't make much difference unless a careful review is made of needs and a principle of full reimbursement is adopted.

And that's the key—full reimbursement of all professional expenses incurred as pastor of a congregation. There is no reason why clergy should have to pay out of salary any costs for professional expenses. Those costs are the congregation's responsibility for having a pastor. They are budgeted costs.

Therefore, the very first compensation principle to be adopted is one of full reimbursement of all professional expenses. And I can think of no reason why it should not be the congregation's policy with respect to all employees, including the pastor, to provide reimbursement for those expenses—not an allowance, but reimbursement.

For income tax purposes, an allowance or reimbursement is fully taxable income unless the employee has substantiated the use of the allowance or reimbursement and repaid to the employer any unused portion. If fully taxable because expenses have not been substantiated or the unused portion has been retained by the employee, then the full allowance or reimbursement is reported as part of income on page 1 of Form 1040, and all expenses are deducted only on Schedule A and are subject to the 2% exclusion.

If expenses exceed an allowance or reimbursement that has been fully substantiated, the excess expenses also are deductible only on Schedule A and are subject to the 2% exclusion. Thus ministers required to report professional expenses on Schedule A may not be able to deduct any or may deduct only a portion of those expenses. It is only when the pastor is reimbursed for specific expenditures that the congregation can be certain all expenses will be deducted and no excess allowances will be taxable.

Specific reimbursement of expenses is not taxable income, and the expenses are not deductible. One offsets the other.

Since the Internal Revenue Service generally insists that most ministers are employees for income tax purposes, clergy use Form 2106 "Employee Business Expense" to report their professional expenses, including car expenses. The form provides instruction on how these expenses are to be offset by any allowance or reimbursement.

Self-employed ministers would use Schedule C "Profit or Loss from Business or Profession" to report allowances/reimbursements and expenses. The tax consequence is different from that for an employee now because on Schedule C all excess unreimbursed professional expenses are deductible.

Ministers who live in a church-owned parsonage pay no mortgage interest or real estate taxes on that house, of course. Since home-owning ministers are able to deduct mortgage interest and real estate taxes on Schedule A, most of them will be able to use Schedule A to list unreimbursed professional expenses (subject to the 2% of adjusted gross income floor). But employee ministers who no longer have a home mortgage—even homeowners and including those in parsonages—may not have enough deductions to use Schedule A and will therefore not be able to list unreimbursed professional expenses anywhere on their tax return.

The largest single professional expense that ministers incur in their profession is that of operating a personal automobile on church business. And in the typical pay plan, the car allowance is entirely inadequate to cover those costs.

The most satisfactory way to get full reimbursement of costs for getting around the parish is for the congregation to own the automobile and pay all the expenses. That way, the pastor has no tax problem. All costs are paid. Salary stays intact and isn't used to repair the car, buy gasoline, or pay for insurance. The congregation does that, as it should, if it expects the pastor to drive around visiting people. Even if the car is used for personal miles, some congregations may not expect any reimbursement. But the IRS does say that there is taxable income to the minister for personal miles if no reimbursement is made to the church.

Unfortunately, not many ministers enjoy that kind of reimbursement plan, as reasonable and sensible as it is. Most clergy receive a flat monthly car allowance, an entirely inadequate way of reimbursing a minister for car expenses on the job. That allowance, be it $300 or $400 a month, every month, every year, usually is not enough, and the pastor must then pay out of salary part of the costs for using a car on church business. That simply should not happen.

A mileage reimbursement, if adequate, might be better, since such a reimbursement might more nearly cover the actual costs of driving a car, including replacement. But the preferred method for implementing the principle of full reimbursement is for the congregation to provide the automobile—all expenses paid. Any personal miles can be reimbursed to the church, if requested.

Ministers should be very familiar with the way car expenses can be shown on an income tax return. Too often they may do things the easy way and simply deduct the government's automatic standard mileage allowance amount. That can be done, of course, and it is easy, but it may cost more tax than if the minister took the time to keep records and deduct actual expenses instead.

The actual-expense deduction method is certainly much more complicated than the simple automatic mileage-allowance deduction method. When deducting actual expenses the minister must not only keep track of business miles driven, but also of all expenditures. Then the proper depreciation amount must be calculated.

All automobiles, new or used, put into service after 1980 and before 1987 were eligible for the Accelerated Cost Recovery System method of deducting depreciation. Automobiles purchased after 1986 are subject to the Modified Accelerated Cost Recovery System. If either method is elected, that precludes the car owner from using the automatic mileage allowance deduction.

Cars purchased after 1986 are not eligible for an investment tax credit and must use the modified ACRS, 20% first year, 32% second year, and decreasing rates after that for six years. The method is called a 200% declining balance method, including straight line depreciation in the last years. While the rate is set for five years, the required use of the half-year convention (deducting only ½ depreciation the first year) requires six years to get the entire deduction. Cars purchased prior to 1987 using the ACRS method can deduct depreciation in only three years—25% the first year, 38%

the second year, 37% the third year. The 1986 Tax Reform Act set the current limitations.

When the minister uses a personal automobile to drive around the parish, using the automatic-mileage deduction method is certainly the least complicated way of doing things. The only record needed is miles driven. Deducting actual expenses is more complicated but often results in a lower tax bill. Having the congregation own or lease the car is still the best—it eliminates the record keeping (except for proving business miles driven), the complicated tax calculation, the use of Form 2106, and provides for a full reimbursement of professional expenses. The full reimbursement is the goal for compensation planning and, as a second benefit, offers a tax break, too.

When pastors could use Schedule C to deduct all their professional expenses, there was really no tax problem with respect to deducting those expenses. They were all shown on Schedule C and dutifully deducted in full. Now, however, since ministers are really considered employees for income tax purposes according to the IRS (but self-employed for Social Security tax purposes), there is the possibility that some of those unreimbursed professional expenses cannot be deducted due to Schedule A limitations. Ministers who use Schedule C are more likely to be audited by the IRS just because they may be paying less tax than would be required if they were using the Schedule A approach.

Employee or Self-employed?

There continues to be considerable confusion about whether clergy are employees or self-employed. Most clergy have always thought that they were self-employed just because they paid the self-employment social security tax. And thus the use of Schedule C has become the norm for clergy in listing income and professional expenses.

But the IRS, as early as 1978, has stated that for income tax purposes clergy are employees, even though they are required to pay the self-employment social security tax. This means that Schedule C is not appropriate and Form 2106 and Schedule A must be used to deduct expenses. This is simple enough, except that when expenses cannot be itemized, the minister ends up paying more tax being an employee than being self-employed for income tax purposes. Hence, there is considerable reluctance on the part of most clergy to change. Yet IRS has been very specific in their requirements.

On March 13, 1978, the IRS issued a statement from its Washington, D.C., office through a publication called *Tax News:*

Earnings which a duly ordained, commissioned, or licensed minister received from ministerial services are deemed to be income from a trade or business and are treated as earnings from self-employment for purposes of social security coverage. However, in most instances a minister who is employed by a congregation on a salaried basis, is a common-law employee, not a self-employed individual. In addition to their salary, ministers receive directly from individuals fees for performing marriages, baptisms, and other personal services, which would be income from a trade or business even if the recipient were not a minister, and would be earnings from self-employment in any case. The correct way for these ministers to report their income is as follows:

(A) A minister should receive from the church a W-2 showing the salary received. Travel allowances would be included in this amount unless the minster is required to "account" to the employer church for the expenses. A rental allowance is not required to be reported on the W-2, provided the entire amount of the allowance is excludable under Section 107 of the Code. However, we prefer that the rental allowance be reported on Form W-2; and if it is reported on the W-2, it should be separately stated and properly described. The salary should be reported as any other wages on Form 1040 with travel expenses included on Form 2106, and any other unreimbursed expenses on Schedule A.

(B) The minister should attach a Schedule C to the Form 1040 showing income and expenses related to self-employment.

(C) Schedule SE should be attached to the return and should show in Part I, line 2 income from Schedule C on line 2 and income from the W-2, plus rental and utilities allowance also on line 2.

For your further information, even though their income is exempt from the withholding provisions of the law, duly ordained, licensed or commissioned ministers who are considered to have an employer-employee relationship with a church may request that income tax be withheld from the salary under the voluntary withholding provisions of section 3402(p)(1) of the Code. The minister could also request additional withholdings under section 3402(i) to cover amounts due under the Self-Employment Contributions Act of 1954.

Currently, in IRS Publication 517 "Social Security for Members of the Clergy and Religious Workers," a sample income tax return is shown, describing how an employee minister would complete Form 1040. In addition, Rev. Rul. 80-110 provides instructions for clergy who are employees to receive a W-2 form and to deduct professional expenses for the self-employment social security tax computation, even if such expenses are not deducted on Schedule A.

Clergy must decide therefore which they are, employee or self-employed. IRS says clergy are employees for income tax purposes, even though they pay the self-employment social security tax. And IRS makes that decision on the basis of its definition of a common-law employee.

Regulations to the Internal Revenue Code provide that:

Generally the relationship of employer-employee exists when the person for whom services are performed has the right to control and direct the individual who performs the services, not only as to the result to be accomplished by the work but also as to the details and means by which that result is accomplished. That is, an employee is subject to the will and control of the employer not only as to what shall be done but how it shall be done. In this connection, it is not necessary that the employer actually direct or control the manner in which the services are performed; it is sufficient if he has the right to do so. The right to discharge is also an important factor indicating that the person possessing that right is an employer. Other factors characteristic of an employer, but not necessarily present in every case, are the furnishings of tools and the furnishing of a place to work to the individual who performs the services. In general, if an individual is subject to the control or direction of another merely as to the result to be accomplished by the work and not as to the means and methods of accomplishing the result, he is not an employee (Reg. Sec. 31.3401(c)-1(b)).

That means, generally, that if the "means and methods" by which you do your work are subject to the right of control of your congregation-employer from whom you receive your compensation, then you are an employee.

Certainly, if you are employed by an institution of the church, such as a college, you are an employee. Even if you are a parish pastor, you are probably an employee because your employer provides you with a place to work and generally controls what you do. In some denominations the congregation has little authority over hiring and firing the minister, but they, like all other congregations, do pay salary, provide for a pension and health plan, reimburse expenses, and otherwise handle compensation as though the pastor was an employee. It will be hard for most parish pastors to convince the IRS that they are not employees.

On the other hand, if you are a free agent and can do as you please with respect to those for whom you work (provide your own work space, set your own work habits, are not under the control of or regularly paid by an organization, and receive no employee benefits) then you may be self-employed for income tax purposes. In any event, all clergy pay the self-employment social security tax.

Either way, you must decide what you are.

Note: On May 26, 1987, the Small Tax Case division of the U.S. Tax Court, in the case of *Cosby vs. Commissioner of Internal Revenue,* has ruled that, under the facts of that case only, United Methodist ministers appointed to local churches are self-employed, rather than employees. The decisions of the U.S. Tax Court under the "Small Tax Case" procedures are not considered a binding precedent and thus need not be followed in other cases.

If you are self-employed

Many ministers probably consider themselves to be self-employed for income tax purposes because they pay the social security self-employment tax. They generally determine their own work schedule, goals, and tasks. They have no income taxes withheld. And because professional tax accountants often suggest the use of Schedule C as the best way to list a minister's professional expenses (contrary to what the IRS has said), ministers go right on saying they are self-employed. Perhaps that's the way you do things now.

If that's what you claim to be, self-employed, then all of your unreimbursed professional expenses would be listed on Schedule C, including travel, entertainment, and continuing education costs.

Income will be reported to you and to the IRS by your congregation on a Form 1099, including salary and car allowance but not housing allowance. Unspent housing allowance is reported on Form 1040, line 21. Self-employed ministers will not have income taxes withheld.

And if you are self-employed but have insufficient expenses to itemize on Schedule A, you can still receive the full standard deduction on a joint return as well as deduct all of your professional expenses on Schedule C. Self-employed ministers do not lose out on any deductions.

If you are an employee

Clergy who follow the IRS's ruling and complete their income tax returns as employees (even though paying the self-employment social security tax) may end up paying more income tax.

An employee does not use Schedule C for listing unreimbursed professional expenses. Only self-employed persons can do that. Thus, in order to deduct any unreimbursed professional expenses, the employee minister's itemized deductions must exceed the standard deduction. All professional expenses, including car expenses, that are not reimbursed, if sufficient to exceed the standard deduction (along with other itemized deductions), are deductible only on Schedule A. But even then, they are deductible only to the extent that they exceed 2% of adjusted gross income.

At year end, an employee receives a W-2 wage form from the employer. The W-2 will show cash salary, car allowance, and any Social Security allowance. It will not show housing allowance or other reimbursements. However, the congregation must report, in box 16, the amount of contribution made to a tax-sheltered annuity 403(b) type pension program. Withheld income taxes will be reported, but since the pastor cannot have Social Security taxes withheld, there is no FICA wage or tax withheld to be reported.

If you do have specific self-employment income—honorariums from weddings, funerals, baptisms, and the like—these are reported on Schedule C. Any expenses incurred to earn that income can also be shown on Schedule C, but salary from your church goes on Form 1040, line 7.

For clergy employees who cannot deduct all of their unreimbursed professional expenses, this procedure does present a problem. The solution, so that you can get all your expense deductions while still taking the standard deduction, is to have your congregation set up a professional expense reimbursement fund. Even if it means reducing your salary, you will probably save on taxes by having the fund. Then, when you spend money on books, postage, or supplies, you will be reimbursed out of the professional expense reimbursement fund. That way the reimbursement and the cost is not reported anywhere on your tax return. On the other hand, an allowance for professional expenses paid to you monthly would be taxable income, but you could deduct expenses that exceed the allowance only if you itemize.

That principle of full reimbursement of professional expenses will certainly provide you with the best tax benefit. But if your congregation is reluctant to pay for those costs, for whatever reason, you will still be better off in having your salary reduced some to set up such a reimbursement fund out of which the treasurer can pay the costs. Anything left over at year's end can be paid to you as a fully taxable bonus.

You can choose for yourself, but the trend is certainly toward clergy being considered employees for income tax purposes while they continue to pay the social security tax at the self-employment tax rate.

Supplemental Benefits

The first thing that you and your congregation need to do is make a decision about the way in which your professional expenses will be reimbursed.

The next thing you need to talk about is all of your supplemental benefits. Here you will want the small committee to establish certain principles for the benefits to be provided. Rather than setting dollar limits at the outset, specific benefits should be selected first as those most appropriate and fair, with costs determined once all principles are established. You may be able to convince your congregation to provide more or other benefits than those listed here. The dollar value of benefits in the typical employee's pay package in industry may be anywhere from 20 percent to 40 percent of salary.

Pension plans

There may be at least six different ways in which you go about planning for retirement income. For most of these ways your congregation can help you by providing the funding through salary reduction plans. In others, it's up to you to make the necessary arrangements.

Planning for retirement income is important. And the sooner you begin that process the better. Retirement funds, once begun, multiply and grow significantly. And surely when you do reach retirement you will need some income. It is not too soon to begin your planning, even if forty years down the pike seems an impossible distance.

1. *Church pension plans.* Most congregations already provide a pension plan for their ministers—either voluntarily or because it is required of all congregations. Certainly you should be involved in a church pension plan from the very beginning of your ministry.

Most church pension plans require a contribution by the congregation. Many require a contribution by the pastor, also. And in some the member can make additional contributions, thus helping to build up a larger accumulation at retirement.

Furthermore, many church pension plans also include a long-term disability provision and survivor benefits. Some add a group term life insurance program. And many pension plans include as part of the overall premium the costs for health insurance as well. You should be informed about the pension, disability, survivor, and life insurance plans available through your denomination's plan. Write to your pension board for information.

Most church pension plans are organized under section 403(b) of the Internal Revenue Code. These plans offer significant opportunities to defer income taxes on the contributions and on the earnings of the fund until received in retirement. Such plans are often comparable to the TDA or TSA (Tax Deferred Annuities or Tax Sheltered Annuities) offered by commercial companies that solicit memberships from employees of nonprofit organizations.

2. *Tax sheltered or tax deferred annuities.* In addition to the contributions that you might make to your church pension plan, you can also make contributions to a commercial TSA or TDA account with some other insurance company, such as Ministers Life or Presbyterian Ministers Fund. You may even be able to make additional TSA contributions to your own pension plan. But there is a maximum amount that you are permitted to make—generally 20 percent of your cash salary. However, various exceptions often permit larger contributions, especially for older clergy. Write to your pension board for further information and clarification.

142

Contributions to a TSA can only be made by your employer. Such contributions cannot be made personally. The payments may come as an additional fringe benefit on top of your other benefits and salary, or you may enter into a salary reduction agreement with your congregation (only once a year) reducing your salary and having the congregation make the payments for you as though they were the congregation's own payments.

TSA contributions can be made only from income earned from a nonprofit organization. Lay as well as clergy employees may participate. But only employees of nonprofit organizations may make contributions through their employers. Thus clergy who consider themselves as self-employed and not employees of their congregations would not, presumably, be eligible to participate in the typical TSA denominational church pension plan.

3. *Individual Retirement Accounts (IRA).* All clergy, the same as all employees, may personally contribute to an IRA account or annuity. Your congregation cannot contribute for you. It is your contribution and when made you will be eligible for a deduction on Form 1040. Currently the maximum contribution and deduction is limited to $2000 or earnings, whichever is less, for each spouse with earnings. If your spouse has no earnings, you may make a $2250 total IRA contribution to the accounts for yourself and your spouse.

However, if adjusted gross income is too large, deductions for IRA contributions may not be allowed. For persons filing a joint return there is no deduction when adjusted gross income exceeds $50,000; on a single return, $35,000. Incomes below $40,000 and $25,000 respectively do not disallow a deduction. For adjusted gross income between $40,000 and $50,000 on a joint return, and between $25,000 and $35,000 on a single return, the deduction is phased out.

4. *Keogh (HR 10) retirement plans.* If you have substantial self-employment income—royalties, business income, fees, etc., but not including salary from your employing congregation—you may put up to 20 percent of that income, not to exceed a $30,000 contribution, into a Keogh type of self-retirement plan. The contribution is deducted on Form 1040.

5. *Social security.* You pay the self-employment social security tax (SECA—Self Employment Contribution Act). All clergy do, unless they have received an exemption for religious reasons. You do not pay the FICA social security tax (Federal Insurance Contributions Act). Thus, your congregation cannot pay any part of this government insurance tax for you. The pastor must pay the tax personally using Schedule SE of Form 1040.

Clergy income that is subject to the self-employment social security tax includes salary, car allowance, professional expense allowance, housing allowance or rental value of the parsonage, any social security allowance and all other taxable income reduced by car expenses and professional expenses (whether or not those expenses were deducted on Schedule A).

It is important for you to be aware that housing is subject to the social security tax even though some tax advisors have incorrectly suggested that it may not be because of a Supreme Court case (Rowan vs. U.S.). That case, now confirmed by the Social Security Act Amendments of 1983, refers only to section 119 of the Code—housing provided to employees, not necessarily ordained, for the convenience of the employer—and not to section 107, which affects clergy specifically. The case also refers to FICA taxes, not SECA taxes.

Perhaps your congregation is already helping you meet the increased costs of social security. Many congregations do provide financial assistance to their pastor for meeting the payments of this large tax. A social security allowance is often paid. Since there is no way that the congregation can pay this tax on behalf of the minister, the best that can be done is to supplement the pastor's pay by providing an allowance of this type. Direct congregational payment to IRS is not possible.

The massive 1983 social security tax amendments bill has already cost clergy dearly, and more costs are coming in future years. The tax rate for those self-employed will climb steadily in the next few years to 15.3 percent in 1990 when it will be exactly twice the rate of employees.

An attempt was made in Congress in 1983 to give clergy the option of being employees or

143

self-employed, but the measure failed. Such a change currently would have cost the pastor and congregation more in social security taxes than did the self-employment tax alone. But by 1990 the difference will be only slight and undoubtedly there will be a significant push to designate clergy as employees for social security tax purposes then. That becomes especially significant now that congregations have to pay social security taxes on wages paid to all other employees anyway.

As is obvious from the following table, the social security tax rate for self-employed, including clergy, goes to 15.3 percent by 1990. That will be offset some by a business expense deduction of one-half the tax, but even so it is significantly higher than the employee tax, thus an apparent inequity to those clergy who really consider themselves employees anyway.

SOCIAL SECURITY TAX RATE TABLE

Year	Employee		Self-employed			
	Old Rate	New Rate	Old Rate	New Rate	Tax Credit	Effective Rate
1984	6.7%	6.7%	9.35%	14.00%	2.7%	11.3%
1985	7.05	7.05	9.90%	14.10%	2.3%	11.8%
1986	7.15	7.15	10.00%	14.30%	2.0%	12.3%
1987	7.15	7.15	10.00%	14.30%	2.0%	12.3%
1988	7.15	7.51	10.00%	15.02%	2.0%	13.02%
1989	7.15	7.51	10.00%	15.02%	2.0%	13.02%
1990	7.65	7.65	10.75%	15.30%	-0-	**

**The 1990 effective rate cannot be determined now because the rate is applicable to a lower amount (usually) and because of the business-expense credit then applicable.

Perhaps now more than ever, a social security allowance would be appropriate. If you don't already have this, you may want to make arrangements for it. Since the self-employment social security tax is rather unfair to clergy who are employees, the allowance becomes all the more important.

In 1990, ministers will pay a net Social Security tax rate of 15.3%, compared to the 7.65% paid by employees. To equalize that difference, congregations should pay an allowance equal to at least the difference between those two tax rates. That way, the minister's out-of-pocket costs for Social Security will be no more than for an employee, ignoring the taxes on the allowance. Paying an allowance to the minister equal to what the congregation would have paid anyway, if the pastor were an employee, seems fair. Furthermore, even with that larger tax payment, ministers do not receive any greater benefit. Benefits are related to the wages upon which the tax is paid, not the tax paid.

There are some who say, however, that this is not really unfair. After all, clergy and others who are self-employed have gotten off cheaply in the past because their total contributions to the Social Security Trust Fund have been less than for the employee-employer, and for the same benefits. Congregations also have gotten off too cheaply in the past!

A fair allowance toward your social security tax would be for your congregation to pay you an amount equal to the additional social security tax paid over that of an employee *plus* whatever more is needed to cover the social security and income tax due on the allowance. (The allowance is fully taxable income.)

For higher paid clergy, that cost to the congregation could turn out to be significant, even if only the employer's share of taxes were paid. Nevertheless, without a very generous addition to the salary, clergy simply may have less take-home pay now due to this added tax rate change in social security.

Of course it will always be argued that a pastor in the 18 percent federal income tax bracket, for example, saves $1,296 of income tax because of a housing allowance that is, for example, $7,200 and

144

tax free. But that savings is not new; the higher social security tax rate is new. Thus, net take-home pay compared to previous years will still be less unless the congregation makes a substantial salary increase available.

If your congregation wishes to provide you with an allowance that will cover not only the difference between what employees and self-employed pay as well as cover your additional social security and income taxes on the allowance, the following formula may be used:

The allowance (A) equals the tax rate difference (RD) times the sum of salary (S) and the allowance (A), plus the sum of the self-employment rate (SER) and the income tax rate (ITR) times the allowance (A).

$$A = RD(S + A) + (SER + ITR)A$$
$$A = [RD(S)] \text{ divided by } [1 = RD = ITR = SER]$$

Here is a summary statement of income subject to the social security tax along with a listing of those incomes subject to income tax and that are shown on the W-2.

	W-2	Income Tax	Social Security Tax
Salary	yes	yes	yes
Housing allowance or parsonage	no	no	yes
Utilities paid by church	no	no	yes
TSA contributions by church	no	no	no
Social security allowance	yes	yes	yes
Pension payments	no	no	no
Health insurance	no	no	no
Car allowance	yes	yes	yes
Deduction for car expenses	no	yes	yes
Professional expense allowance	yes	yes	yes
Deduction for professional expenses	no	no, unless expenses are itemized	yes
Honoraria	no	yes	yes

6. *Private investments.* If you are financially able, you will have been making regular deposits into a savings account or making investments of some kind so that when you retire, you will be able to supplement your income from church pensions, social security, TSA and IRA accounts, and Keogh plans with investment income. Obviously, your congregation is not involved in this planning. But its importance cannot be underestimated or ignored. You will enjoy your retirement far more if you have taken the time and effort to put aside now—even if you think you cannot afford to do so—monies that will earn interest or grow in value and be available for your use after you retire.

Insurance plans

Your future financial security is not assured with only a retirement plan. Insurance coverages are essential to protect you against financial disaster due to unexpected losses. Your pension plan is extremely important, but an adequate insurance program is likewise crucial. You can save tax dollars by having your congregation pay some of those premiums for you.

1. *Life insurance.* Your congregation can pay the premium for you on up to $50,000 of a group term life insurance without those premiums being subject to an income tax. Premiums on coverages in excess of the $50,000 are currently taxable at an amount calculated from specific IRS formulas based on your age.

If you have other life insurance premiums paid for you by your church, those premiums are probably taxable income, even though they are an important fringe benefit. The premium is taxable if you have ownership of the policy and can control the designation of beneficiaries. Of course, the

145

congregation may take out a key person life insurance policy on your life just to protect its own interests, not your family's. Since ownership of that type of policy is with the congregation—they may designate your spouse as beneficiary for part of the policy amount, the church for the rest—the premiums are not taxable income to you.

2. *Health insurance.* Critical to the financial security of your family, or any family, is an adequate health, accident, and disability income plan.

Most pension plans for clergy include a disability benefit plan. If not, then you should be certain that your congregation obtains for you a disability income insurance protection plan policy. You will want a policy that pays to you a benefit equal to a specific percentage of your salary. Also, the policy should begin paying by at least the fourth month of disability since your congregation should assume continued salary and housing during those initial three months. Social security disability benefits are available after six months of total disability. Extra disability insurance premium payments by a congregation are usually not subject to income tax since they are often considered part of most pension or health benefit plans.

A health and accident policy is a must for you. The Internal Revenue Code under current law provides that the payment of such premiums by an employer are not taxable income. Thus your congregation should be paying for you and your family all of your health insurance premiums.

It is difficult for most clergy to amass enough health costs to take an itemized deduction on Schedule A. You'll only be allowed to deduct the amount of unreimbursed health expenses that exceeds 7.5 percent of your adjusted gross income. It may pay you to get your congregation to reduce your salary and pay all of your family health insurance protection coverage for you.

3. *A medical expense reimbursement plan.* Since the medical expense deduction has been substantially reduced, you may want to talk to your congregation about a medical expense reimbursement plan. Under a properly designated plan, your congregation can pay all or part of the unreimbursed medical expenses incurred by all of your congregation's full-time employees and their families without such payments being taxable income to them. The following resolution is suggested but you should check with your own legal counsel before asking the congregation to set up such a plan.

SAMPLE RESOLUTION FOR ESTABLISHMENT OF MEDICAL EXPENSE REIMBURSEMENT PLAN*

WHEREAS, _____ church desires to arrange for the payment, directly or indirectly, of medical expenses, to the extent not compensated for by insurance or otherwise, in the event of personal injuries or sickness, to _____,
his/her spouse, and dependents as defined for Federal income tax purposes, up to a maximum of $_____ each during the employee's employment by the church;

AND WHEREAS, notice of knowledge of this Plan shall be reasonably available to all employees;

AND WHEREAS, this Plan is established in order that the payments by _____ _____ church and the receipts by the above-named employee(s) shall be within the purview of Section 105 of the Internal Revenue Code of 1954 and the United States Treasury Department Regulations thereunder;

THEREFORE, BE IT RESOLVED THAT THE ABOVE DESCRIBED PLAN SHALL; 1. Be, and hereby is, adopted on behalf of the above named church by its official board; 2. Become effective as of _____; 3. Continue in effect until terminated by like resolution.

AND THEREFORE, BE IT FURTHER RESOLVED, THAT the officers of this church shall be authorized to execute this Resolution by all necessary and proper means.

Warning: Drafting of resolutions should be done by the church's attorney.

---

*From the article "A Medical Reimbursement Plan" by Manfred Holck, Jr. in *The Clergy Journal*, 1983 November/December issue. Used with permission. Reprints of the complete article are available from Church Management, Inc., P.O. Box 162527, Austin, Tex. 78716.

Continuing education costs

Many clergy engage in some kind of continuing education program. That assists pastors in being more effective leaders. Most congregations encourage their pastors to take the time for such studies and pay for those expenses. A reimbursement plan offers considerable incentive for clergy to be involved in continuing education programs.

Your continuing education costs, when they help you to maintain and improve your skills as a pastor, are fully deductible, but only if you itemize deductions on Schedule A. Travel expenses in connection with your continuing education would be deductible in any event on Form 2106. Thus, if you have to pay some of those nontravel costs yourself, you just may not be able to deduct all of them.

However, if your congregation reimburses you for those costs, then you can be certain of the tax benefit. Getting reimbursed for specific expenses or having the congregation pay those expenses directly for you means the costs are not shown anywhere on your tax return nor is the reimbursement income. If you are unable to itemize deductions, just because you don't have enough deductions to exceed the standard deduction currently permitted on a tax return, having the congregation pay the costs directly gives you the deduction anyway and you can still claim the entire standard deduction. Full reimbursement of professional expenses will generally save you tax dollars.

Be sure the congregation provides not only the money but also the time for continuing education. Two weeks annually, in addition to vacation, is appropriate. Then, after six years in that congregation, you might request a sabbatical leave of three months, in addition to vacation, with full pay and all benefits. That will provide you with a good large block of time to do concentrated study.

Vacation, time off, holidays, sick leave

You should get appropriate time off from your work, the same as other employees get. There's no tax benefit involved in such time off, but that time will help you to rest and rejuvenate. No one is expected to work seven days a week (although some clergy still do), so be sure you know what your congregation expects. You're paid for a forty-hour week. Stick to it. If your congregation expects more time from you, expect more pay. Other employees receive time and a half for overtime. Require a day off each week. Expect to take holidays. And be sure your congregation has developed a sick pay plan, written down in the personnel procedures handbook.

An equity allowance

If you live in the church-owned house, you are paying "rent." You know that. Some of your members may not. But it is obvious that when you leave or retire from that congregation, you take no housing equity with you. It all stays with the congregation for their benefit. Yet, someday, you will still have to provide your own housing when parsonages are no longer available to you. Any equity that the congregation has accumulated on the house stays with the congregation even though you have really "paid" for that house all the years you were there.

Concerned congregations provide their pastors with an equity allowance as one way to help them accumulate some money toward the down payment on a home. Such an allowance really has nothing to do with the housing allowance, since it is applicable only to clergy in church-owned housing. It is nevertheless a significant additional income benefit and should be considered by the congregation that requires the minister to live in the parsonage.

An equity allowance is additional income. Keep that in mind. Depending on how it is paid, it may or may not be currently taxable income. If it is paid directly to you to be invested in an IRA or other investment, the amount is fully taxable and is included on a W-2 and in gross income. It may then be deducted as an IRA if proper contributions were made to such a plan by the pastor personally. When the allowance is not paid directly to you and is actually set aside in a separate fund, it is not current taxable income just because it is not available to you as yet. Only when the fund, including the interest it has earned, is paid to you—at retirement, death, disability, moving, or buying a home—is the full amount taxable income.

In the meantime, the congregation can set aside the funds in a separate CD or savings account or mutual fund in the name of the congregation. You may want to have a signed contract regarding the accumulation and distribution of that fund, as a protection of your own assets.

The amount of that fund can be whatever you and your church agree upon. Usually the tax deferred contribution is related in amount to (1) an increase in the value of the parsonage, (2) principal payments that would have been made to reduce a home mortgage, (3) a percentage of salary, or (4) some combination of these.

Other benefits

You may have already thought of some other benefits than those listed.

Your congregation may want to provide you with a scholarship fund to be used to send your children to college. That can be a very generous and noble offer. But the payments by the church on behalf of your children are probably taxable income.

It would be important to receive those contributions on a regular basis, all in the same amount. The investment income earned by the fund is taxable only to the donee when withdrawn. Even a scholarship fund for the benefit of just the pastor's children would throw up an immediate red flag to the IRS. A careful review of this matter with a tax consultant is necessary.

A discretionary fund can be a very useful tool in your ministry. Care must be exercised that you account separately for payments into the fund and out of the fund, so that these payments are not counted as part of your income. Such a fund could be used to pay for your professional expenses, as well as expenses in ministering to other people.

Malpractice insurance has become increasingly popular for clergy who do a lot of counseling. Free legal assistance and financial planning are also two other benefits that some clergy have requested.

Housing

Probably the most significant tax benefit available to a minister are the housing provisions under Section 107 of the Internal Revenue Code. That section specifies: "In the case of a minister of the gospel, gross income does not include: (1) the rental value of a home furnished to him as part of his compensation; or (2) the rental allowance paid to him as part of his compensation, to the extent used by him to rent or provide a home." Compared with the tax you would have to pay without that tax provision, Section 107 becomes a very significant item for reducing tax liability.

Your congregation, however, must take appropriate action or the benefit will not be available to you at all or only of limited value to you. Using Section 107 carefully can actually mean an increase in your net take-home pay, without costing the congregation anything more for salary costs.

A parsonage or a housing allowance?

The parsonage for the minister's family has been part of congregational life for a long time. Historically congregations have simply expected their pastor to live in the church-owned house.

In recent years, however, more and more congregations have been paying a housing allowance to the pastor in lieu of providing the rent-free use of a church-owned house. The reasons are varied. Some congregations have converted the parsonage adjacent to the church building into educational space. For others the parsonage has become old and in need of extensive repairs, so it has been sold or torn down. In yet other situations, pastors have requested a housing allowance and the congregation, agreeing, has sold the parsonage and paid a housing allowance instead.

Recent economic conditions, which have made selling a home more difficult, have tended to halt the continuing increase in home ownership among clergy. Second thoughts are now being had by those who routinely have suggested the home ownership route. Higher mortgage rates have also discouraged some clergy from borrowing money to purchase a home, if they could even afford the monthly payments. And then the IRS has put a clamp on the deductions of mortgage interest and real estate taxes that makes home ownership from a tax standpoint even less attractive.

But for whatever reason, many congregations now are faced with the decision of whether to continue the parsonage principle of a rent-free house for the pastor's family or to pay a housing allowance instead.

Facing that choice, congregations and pastors must decide. The merits of each individual case, of course, will determine the final decision, but there are important advantages and disadvantages either way.

The parsonage

A parsonage can often be a good bet for the pastor's family. Here's why:

1. In a parsonage you won't have to bother with maintenance and costs and leaky plumbing. That's the congregation's responsibility, at least theoretically. If the congregation owns the home, then as landlord, it should assume responsibility. An advantage to living in a parsonage is avoiding repairs and maintenance.

2. Adequate homes for purchase may simply not be available in a small community. If that's the case, then the parsonage may be the better choice anyway, assuming its condition meets your family's expectations. A good house, not a drafty barn, should be provided.

3. To own a home outside a neighborhood of similar homes, such as in the country, may not be wise financially. Selling, when matters come to that, could be a problem. The market may just be too thin. A parsonage avoids that risk.

4. If If you are the kind of pastor that likes to get out of a situation in a hurry, that's possible in a parsonage. No messing around trying to sell a home. You just pack up and leave! It's the "quick and easy" way to leave a problem congregation. (It may be a quick and easy way for a congregation to remove you, too!) A parsonage also offers you the opportunity to consider the call to another congregation without being influenced by the fact of home ownership. If a new call is accepted, moving out of the parsonage is easy; selling a house may not be so easy.

5. If you are going to worry about a potential loss on the sale of your own home, you may want to think twice about moving out of the parsonage. If that's going to bother you, the parsonage may be better than a housing allowance.

6. A parsonage may be quite elegant, a better home than you could ever afford. If you like fancy living and an elegant home, then such a parsonage may be the better choice. Most pastors simply cannot afford to buy the same house that the congregation can buy for them. But then again, your parsonage may not be so great after all!

7. If you have a problem coming up with a down payment for a home, then you will need to stick to the parsonage plan. Of course, a congregation could help, but if financing for a home seems impossible or unrealistic, you must stick to the parsonage, anyway.

8. In a parsonage, the congregation may, in some states, be able to avoid the payment of real estate taxes. The same house owned by the minister means real estate taxes must be paid, hence more cost.

9. There may be some pastors, including yourself, who simply don't want to bother with all the problems and potential headaches of owning a home. In fact, your family may be so comfortable and at ease in the parsonage—enjoying the benefits that go with such tender, loving care from the congregation—that you may have no desire to own your own home.

10. And now that IRS has clamped down on the deduction for mortgage interest and real estate taxes (Revenue Ruling 83-3: denying a deduction on Schedule A), the relative tax advantage of home ownership over being in the parsonage is narrowed considerably.

A housing allowance

In spite of all these good reasons for staying with the parsonage, there are some weighty arguments for going the other way, too. Some pastors do want a housing allowance. Here's why:

1. Perhaps most important, an allowance gives your family the opportunity to live wherever you want to live. No one decides the kind of home you will live in. The choice is yours if you want to buy a ranch rambler, a two-story modern, an old house, or a real barn of a place. You may do what you like, limited only by your pocketbook.

2. Of course, buying a home means building up equity. As mortgage payments are made, regularly each month, savings are accumulating, principal is being reduced, and some day the mortgage is paid off. Making those same payments for rent leaves nothing at the end. Equity build-up is the strength of home buying.

3. In your own home, you and your spouse can paint the kitchen polka dot yellow, the front door bright red, and the bedroom ceiling baby blue; scatter bean chairs, pillows, and hammocks in the living room, if you want to. You can keep things as neat as a pin or live in a constant clutter, if that's what you want. In your "castle" you have no obligation to the congregation. Which is not to say you shouldn't use some common sense about appearance when members do come to call. But it is *your* home, and you can do with it as you like.

4. If you don't like to move all the time, you can make certain those moves are less frequent by buying a home. One just does not pick up their marbles and stomp away if there is a home to sell. Homeowning pastors probably tend to stay put longer than the family in the parsonage.

5. Owning your own home may offer your family greater opportunity for participation in community affairs. After all, homeowners pay real estate taxes! Your complaints about the use of taxes may be more readily heard now that you are paying taxes. Your outspoken complaint on the use of tax money may now be heard because you are making a personal financial commitment to the programs. You pay taxes, too!

6. During the past several decades, home ownership has been one of the most effective hedges against inflation. Not so, however, during an economic recession. But generally, as the inflation rate moves ahead, the market value of most homes has steadily increased as well. Of course, the value of the parsonage keeps on going up, too, but that isn't much help to the pastor. Owning a home makes it easier to finance each successive house as a pastor moves from place to place.

7. Your family will quickly gain practical experience in home ownership the moment you move into your own home! No longer can you call the parsonage committee in the middle of the night to fix a leaky faucet. The termites are your problem. Frozen pipes, clanky heaters, and ice on the roof must be taken care of by you. Drapes, curtains, rugs, carpets have to be cleaned, not by the committee, but by you. Home ownership gets you involved, of necessity!

8. A significant advantage of home ownership is a mortgage! As a mortgage holder and homeowner, along with many of your other members, you may be able to relate much better to the

problems and frustrations of the membership. When members complain about the high cost of a mortgage and reduce their giving accordingly you can sympathize with, although not justify, the excuse. When the member insists the lawn must be mowed on Sunday morning, you realize it must be mowed, but through personal experience can offer alternate suggestions.

9. Home ownership offers your family real financial security. Should you, as principal earner, die first, your surviving spouse has a home. Your spouse won't have to move. If proper insurance protection was arranged, the house will be fully paid for. But most important, the congregation cannot insist your spouse move in order to make room for the next pastor's family, as would be the case in the parsonage.

10. The same benefit comes with retirement. If you own your own home, you don't have to move out of the congregation's home. You can stay or go as you like. Besides, by then your home may be all paid for—no rent to pay in retirement, no down payment to arrange—monthly payments are over and you have a place to live.

11. There are certain income tax advantages, as will be explained later, to all clergy homeowners, in addition to those enjoyed by lay homeowners. Clergy may exclude from taxable income all of any properly designated housing allowance used to provide a home. That means that if your compensation includes $10,000 for a housing allowance, for example, and that money is used for that purpose, the entire $10,000 may be excluded from taxable income! Lay members have no such privilege (except for employees who are provided housing for the convenience of their employers under section 119 of the Code). When you have a housing allowance, it can mean a substantial tax savings for you. Of course, the rental value of the parsonage is also excluded from taxable income.

Finally, whatever choice you make, keep in mind that home ownership, if that is your choice, is a big decision. It involves the considerations noted above, but it also involves a lot more. You must consider location, taxes, schools, age of the house, maintenance problems, proximity to town, neighborhood, and a whole host of other items. Staying in the parsonage may be the easiest route, but having a home of your own may fulfill your fondest ambitions and offer you and your family the greater joy.

If you have the choice, consider the alternatives carefully, and then, satisfied that you made the right choice, enjoy that way. A parsonage or a housing allowance offers significant benefits to live the way you want to live.

Who can use section 107?

Not all those who call themselves ministers or even who are ordained may take advantage of section 107.

The regulations provide that in order to qualify for the exclusion, the home or rental allowance must be provided as remuneration for services that are ordinarily the duties of a minister of the gospel. Examples of specific services cited in the regulations, the performance of which will be considered duties of a minister of the gospel for purposes of section 107, include "the performance of sacerdotal functions, the conduct of religious worship, the administration and maintenance of religious organizations and their integral agencies and the performance of teaching and administrative duties at theological seminaries."

The regulations further state that section 107 is applicable only to duly ordained, commissioned, or licensed ministers of churches.

Furthermore, whether the service performed by a minister is really in the conduct of religious worship or the ministration of sacerdotal functions depends on the tenets and practices of the particular church or denomination. Any service performed by a minister in the exercise of ministry must be under the authority of a religious body constituting a church or denomination.

In cases where a church or denomination ordains some ministers of the gospel and licenses or commissions other ministers, commissioning must establish a status that is the equivalent of

151

ordination and is so recognized by the church. That is, the individual, upon being commissioned, must be invested with the status and authority of an ordained minister, fully qualified to perform all of the ecclesiastical duties of such a minister in that denomination.

Thus, services, rendered by an individual minister in the conduct of religious worship or the ministration of sacerdotal functions, are considered services in the exercise of ministry, whether or not they are performed for a religious organization or an integral agency. Such religious activities, however, must accord with the tenets and practices of a particular religious body constituting a church or denomination.

Services rendered by an ordained minister of the gospel who is employed as a teacher or administrator are considered duties of a minister of the gospel only when such services are done for an organization, which is an integral agency under the authority of a church or denomination.

Ministers performing services according to an assignment or designation by their church are considered ministers of the gospel, even though the services are not being performed for an integral agency under the authority of the church.

Ordained ministers who perform teaching and administrative duties at theological seminaries are considered ministers of the gospel for purposes of section 107 but only if the seminary is an integral agency of the church or the minister was assigned by the church to perform that duty.

How much housing allowance?

That all depends. The amount of housing allowance varies by pastor. The amount of housing allowance that can be excluded from taxable income also varies by pastor. And the two amounts are not necessarily the same, even for the same pastor.

The general rule is this: the amount of housing allowance that a pastor receives in any one year cannot exceed the fair rental value of the home in which the pastor lives (furnished, plus utilities). Furthermore, the amount of housing allowance that can be excluded from taxable income cannot exceed the allowance itself or the amount actually used *to provide a home,* or the fair rental value, whichever is lower.

So, I don't know how much housing allowance you will need or can justify. It all depends on how much you expect to spend "to provide a home," your housing allowance, and the fair rental value of your home. The amount of income that you will be able to exclude is the lesser of those three items.

Any amounts spent in excess of the allowance are not excludable; any allowance not used is taxable income.

Many congregations review their pastor's compensation each year, as they should, including the provision for housing. But you should not let your congregation tell you how much of your compensation will be for a housing allowance. It may not be enough to cover your expenses, thus depriving you of a potential income exclusion, if you could have, in fact, justified more.

You should insist that your congregation set a total amount for salary and housing combined, and then let you suggest how much should be designated for housing depending on your personal circumstances.

Some lay leaders will insist that $5,000 a year, for example, is sufficient to provide the kind of house that their pastor should live in. And maybe a $5,000 allowance plus $18,000 salary is designated. That's a total salary item of $23,000.

But with a housing allowance, a pastor can pick and choose the house that fits the fancy of the family. It's not the congregation's house. It's the pastor's home—bought or rented to suit their needs. It can be a big red barn of a place or a tiny bungalow, an architectural monstrosity or a typical ranch house, in the city or in the country. One purpose of an allowance is to give the pastor the freedom to make a personal choice about where to live.

152

And that choice may require more or less money than what the congregation thinks the pastor should spend for housing. But now it's the pastor's business, not the congregation's, as to what ought to be spent on housing. The congregation has given up that responsibility.

According to the IRS, the amount of that housing allowance now has to do with the rental value of the home selected and the amount spent to provide a home. It has nothing to do with what the members think should be done.

Thus, if you are purchasing a home, you should be able to tell your lay leaders just how much of that $23,000 income, for example, is to be designated as housing allowance. If you can justify $7,000 under the rules, then your official board should not tell you that that cannot be done, that $5,000 is all that can be allowed. That's not true. To limit the allowance to the lower figure could cost the pastor $400 more income tax (20 percent tax bracket times $2,000).

In that example, then, as long as the rental value of the pastor's home, furnished, and the cost of utilities do not exceed $7,000, the amount is quite proper and can be designated. Housing allowance is officially designated as $7,000 and cash salary as $16,000.

Then, the pastor must keep careful records to justify the exclusion of the allowance from taxable income. Only what is spent is excludable. So, if $5,500 is spent to provide housing—mortgage payments, taxes, furnishings, repairs, utilities, and all the other costs—the pastor may exclude $5,500 of that $23,000 salary from taxable income. The rest, $17,500, is taxable income.

On the other hand, if $7,500 happens to be spent to provide housing, then only $7,000 can be excluded and $16,000 of income is subject to tax.

In any event, if the original $5,000 allowance had been required, the pastor would have overspent either way and thus been penalized by the congregation by having to pay more income tax than was necessary.

To emphasize: it is important that a congregation determine the total amount it expects to pay for base salary and housing combined, but then permit the pastor to request how much of that total should really be designated as allowance, limited only to the fair rental value of the pastor's home.

How much housing allowance is needed depends entirely on what the pastor expects to spend and the fair rental value of the home. Each of us has a different situation. Only you, as pastor, can really decide how much housing allowance will be needed.

Of course, a housing allowance can be used only to provide a home for qualifying ministers. Thus, no part of an allowance can be used for housing not used by the minister as a principal residence.

In the case of a duplex, for example, the minister may use the allowance for the half not rented out. So costs need to be identified. Only those that apply to the pastor's residence half are a justifiable use of the housing allowance. Costs that cannot be specifically identified, such as insurance, taxes, or mortgage payments, should be divided in half (if both sides are substantially the same size, otherwise in proportion to square footage).

In other words, the allowance you receive can be used for all costs associated with living in your side of a duplex. Costs and income associated with the rental side are treated the same as for any kind of rental property. Costs paid in connection with the purchase of a condominium are certainly also an appropriate use of the housing allowance. However, your housing allowance cannot be used to pay for a future retirement home while you are living in the parsonage.

It is well to plan for retirement housing, but the housing allowance can be used only to provide a home that is the principal residence of the pastor. If a parsonage is provided and lived in by the pastor's family, even if only part of the time, this is, indeed, the principal place of residence. Any allowance paid to the pastor would be appropriately used only for expenses in the parsonage.

How does one determine rental value?

Clergy living in a church-owned house, as well as those receiving a housing allowance, must estimate the rental value of their homes.

153

The fair rental value of the parsonage, manse, or rectory is includable in income subject to the social security self-employment tax (as is any housing allowance received).

The maximum amount of housing allowance that clergy may receive is the fair rental value of the home they live in, furnished, plus utilities.

The most acceptable way to determine rental value is by securing an appraisal from a qualified real estate person. The Internal Revenue Service may insist, upon audit, on such an appraisal if your own estimate appears inaccurate or unreasonable.

You can simply ask a real estate friend for an opinion on the rental value. Or you can look around your neighborhood to see what the rent for other comparable houses might be.

A popular rule of thumb suggests that a reasonably accurate guess can be made by using a figure equal to 1 percent per month of the fair market value of the home. Thus, a $60,000 home might rent unfurnished for $600 a month.

The rule may not always be applicable, however, and you will have to assess the reasonableness of your estimate. A $150,000 home, for example, probably would not rent for $1500 a month but for a much lower figure.

For those who live in a parsonage and who furnish the home on their own, the 1 percent rule is generally acceptable for rental value of the parsonage or furnishings. For those clergy who receive a housing allowance, the housing allowance need not be limited just to the rental value of the unfurnished home. According to the IRS, the maximum housing allowance may include a rental value of furnishings also.

Thus, a pastor in a $60,000 personal residence with $12,000 worth of furnishings and $2,500 a year utility costs may be able to secure a $10,000 annual housing allowance (no matter the size of salary). That is 1 percent times $60,000 plus 1 percent times $12,000 plus the cost of utilities. The allowance is excludable from taxable income to the extent used.

How to set up a housing allowance correctly

The proper designation of an allowance in advance of its use or payment is required in order to qualify for the exclusion.

Three documents are useful. First the minister should make a request to the official board requesting an allowance and stating the amount desired. A statement regarding the estimated fair rental value will be helpful. A listing of expected expenditures is not necessary.

Second the official board must pass a resolution authorizing the designation of the housing allowance. The following form is acceptable:

The board on the _____ date of _____ 19_____, after considering the statement of the Reverend _____ setting forth the amount of fair rental value of the home the Reverend _____ _____ occupies, furnished, plus the cost of utilities, on motion duly made and seconded, adopted the following resolution:

Resolved that the Reverend _____ receive compensation of $_____ for the year 19_____ of which $_____ shall be designated as a housing or rental or parsonage allowance. (If the minister is to receive the rent-free use of the parsonage, then also state: the Reverend _____ shall also have the rent-free use of the home located at _____ for the year 19_____ and for every year thereafter as long as the Reverend _____ _____ is pastor of this church.) The parsonage or rental or housing allowance shall be so designated in the official church records.

Third, the secretary by letter informs the minister of the action taken.

How can you use the housing allowance?

A housing allowance may be used for all expenditures required to provide a home, with the exception of the cost of food and maid service.

Thus, the allowance may be used for the down payment on a new home, taxes, mortgage payments, interest, insurance, repairs, utilities, furniture, furnishings, yard care, etc. Any unused allowance is taxable income. Amounts spent in excess of the designated allowance are not deductible.

Perhaps the single largest item for which an allowance may be used is home mortgage payments. But if the mortgage is paid off, the housing allowance is no longer being spent for that purpose. Nothing then can be excluded for house payments and rental value. Homeowning clergy will simply be paying more income taxes than when mortgage payments were required.

That means that a lot of pastors who are paying on a mortgage pay less income tax, all else being equal, than those who have the foresight, fortitude, discipline, and ability to pay off their mortgage. The housing allowance rules tend to encourage indebtedness by pastors.

Refinancing one's home and then using the allowance for those new payments has been done by some clergy whose mortgages just recently got paid off. Money received from that refinancing has gone for down payments on a second home, into savings, perhaps into securities. But the loan was not secured in order "to provide a home," thus upon audit IRS may find that mortgage payments on such a loan do not qualify as proper expenses.

If you live in a parsonage*

The proper designation of a housing allowance for clergy who also receive the rent-free parsonage is appropriate. And to the extent used for furnishings and other expenses required to provide a home, that allowance is excludable from taxable income.

Needless to say, the tax savings can be significant. Assume a $15,000 salary with unfurnished parsonage provided and all utilities paid by the congregation. Assume further that the minister expects to spend $1,000 during the year for additional furniture, some drapes, minor repairs to the front steps, grass seed, and a new TV—none of which will be reimbursed by the congregation.

If no allowance is designated, the minister has $15,000 of income subject to tax. On the other hand, if salary can be reduced to $13,800 and a $1,200 rental allowance designated, then, to the extent used, $1,200 may be excluded from taxable income.

For a minister in the 20 percent tax bracket that simple designation will save that pastor's family $240 in income tax. The congregation can actually boost the pastor's take-home pay by $240 this way. (The rental allowance cannot, of course, exceed the difference between the rental value of the home furnished and unfurnished.)

This action can be justified by referring to Section 107 of the code. In that section of the code the value of the parsonage is not restricted either to an unfurnished home or a home with furniture provided. It is the fair rental value of the minister's home that is excludable from taxable income, with the rental value of a furnished home being excludable the same as an unfurnished home. And presumably, if the basic house is the same in each instance for two pastors, the rental value of the furnished home will be greater than the rental value of the unfurnished home. Yet, in either instance, the total value is excludable.

It would appear, therefore, to be somewhat unfair and clearly not the intent of Congress in voting Section 107 if the minister with the unfurnished home (who must now secure his or her own furniture

---

*Adapted from *Housing for Clergy* by Manfred Holck, Jr., © 1982 by Ministers Life Resources, Minneapolis, Minn. Used with permission.

in order "to provide a home") cannot receive a rental allowance to equalize the difference in those two rental values. The minister should also be able to exclude from taxable income, to the amount used to furnish that home, the same total value as the pastor in a parsonage with furniture provided.

As noted previously, there was a time, prior to 1954, when a housing allowance was fully taxable, but the rental value of the rent-free home provided by the congregation was not. Code Section 107 removed that inequity. And by that action Congress intended to provide equity between pastors in parsonages and those with allowances. Fairness is satisfied, therefore, for the minister who receives a rental allowance and those ministers who are provided the rent-free use of a parsonage, including the church-owned furniture.

Pastors living rent-free in an unfurnished parsonage can maintain that same fairness between those receiving a rental allowance and those receiving a rent-free furnished home, when they are permitted to exclude from taxable income the rental value of their parsonage, plus the rental allowance received to purchase furnishings. If Congress really intended in section 107 to put all clergy (those receiving a rental allowance and those given a rent-free parsonage) on an equal basis, a rental allowance for furnishings is equitable and defensible.

Furthermore, Rev. Rul. 71-280, which sets the maximum amount of permissible housing allowance, states specifically that a rental allowance may not exceed "the fair rental value of the home, furnished, plus the cost of utilities." Clearly, a rental allowance may include a value for the furnishings in that home paid for and provided by the pastor. Once again, that maximum puts the minister receiving a rental allowance on an equal basis with the minister in a rent-free completely furnished parsonage.

It is also clear that a rental allowance may be used for a variety of personal expenses, including the purchase of furnishings, but excluding food and maid service, in order "to provide a home."

Thus, the maximum value of a minister's home that may be excluded from taxable income is the rental value of the home including furnishings. Then, if that value is received through a church-owned parsonage, plus a rental allowance for furnishings where the allowance is used for expenditures for furniture and other nonreimbursable expenses "to provide a home," all clergy are treated equitably, as intended by section 107.

Finally, IRS Publication 17, "Your Federal Income Tax," describes how clergy may exclude parsonage rental value or rental allowance used.

> If you are furnished a home as part of your compensation, the rental value of the home and the utility expense paid for you are not income to you. However, the rental value of a home, and related allowances must be included as earnings from self-employment for purposes of the Social Security self-employment tax.
>
> A rental allowance paid to you as part of your compensation is not income to the extent it is used by you, in the year received, to provide a home or to pay utilities for a home you are furnished. . . . Expenditures to provide a home include the amounts spent for rent, to buy a home, to provide furnishings for the dwelling, for appurtenances to the dwelling such as a garage, and for utilities.

Even the IRS in its own booklet does not limit the exclusion to either a rental value or a rental allowance. In fact, the opposite is true. The IRS suggests the possibility of a home being furnished, plus related allowances being paid. The value of utilities is generally included in the rental value for social security self-employment tax purposes, as are other allowances designated for other expenses required "to provide a home," such as for furnishings.

Therefore, since a rental allowance may be used to purchase furniture, furnishings, yard care, repairs and other costs, pastors in unfurnished parsonages may receive a supplemental rental allowance to be used for those same housing costs not otherwise provided by the congregation.

As stated, a rental allowance for the pastor in a parsonage could offer a significant tax savings since that allowance is excludable from taxable income to the extent used "to provide a home."

A rental allowance for furnishings may not exceed the difference between the fair rental value of the parsonage furnished and unfurnished. An additional payment may be provided by the congregation for the allowance, or salary can be reduced by the allowance amount. The allowance is excludable from taxable income to the extent it is spent. Unspent allowance is taxable anyway; any overexpenditure is not deductible, the same as for any housing allowance.

To report your allowance to IRS.

The housing allowance (or fair rental value of a parsonage) is not to be reported to IRS either on a W-2 form, if such is issued to the pastor, or on a Form 1099, because it is not compensation subject to tax. On the minister's tax return, only any unused allowance is reported. Otherwise, the housing allowance or rental value of the parsonage is not reported for income tax purposes (except that a record of expenditure must be kept to verify, upon audit, the use of the allowance.)

For social security self-employment tax computation purposes, however, the allowance or the fair rental value of the parsonage is included in taxable income.

Salary

Whatever your cash salary, it ought to be sufficient and a fair indication of your worth as pastor to your congregation. Perhaps your people considered your age and experience as well as the size of your congregation when they set your salary for the new year. My guess is, though, that you would have preferred that they considered your ability to relate to other people and to solve all the problems that come up to you every day. Or perhaps the wages paid to other professionals offered the bench mark by which your salary was set. Indeed, the median wage paid to all wage earners in your community is one criteria that is frequently used. The median salary paid to the ministers in your denomination is another basis.

You are probably more impressed by a merit increase in pay than by a routine cost-of-living increase. Actually, you should get both—one to maintain your purchasing power, the other to express the congregation's approval of what you are doing.

Your congregation will have to decide, of course. If they pay enough, you stay; if they don't pay enough, you may leave.

Pay plans run the gamut, but the basics are still the same. Have your people consider reimbursements first (full reimbursement of all professional expenses), supplemental benefits next (all appropriate benefits, full payment by the church), and finally housing and salary. Understand with your lay leaders the reason for each; establish the principles that should be applicable; consider the costs; and arrange the budget. Some conversation with your congregation will help for mutual understanding in the development of a successful plan for the year.

What your congregation pays you is their business, of course. But when they have finally considered the possibilities, examined the issues, understood all the tax consequences, and know how to distinguish between what is pay and what is simply another cost for having a pastor, they will be able to put a financial plan into shape that is useful to you.

Some pay plans illustrated

There's nothing magic or really unique about any pay plan. But an illustration often helps to stimulate thinking. Here are some pay patterns that, when modified, may suit your ideas very well.

157

A suggested pay plan

First of all, here's a typical arrangement developed on the basis of the pastor's age, years of service to the church, and size of congregation. It's easy to figure.

—Minimum salary for senior pastor (80 percent to associate)

Years of service	Adult Members Up to 300	300-600	600-900	Over 900
Up to 5 yrs	$15,850	$16,785	$17,720	$18,650
6 to 10 yrs	18,650	19,580	20,515	21,450
11 to 15 yrs	21,450	22,380	23,310	24,250
Over 15 yrs	24,150	25,180	26,110	27,040

—Free use of a church-owned home or housing allowance equal to at least 40 percent of base salary.
—Car allowance equal to at least the government's mileage allowance or free use of church-owned auto.
—A minimum of 15 percent of the sum of salary, housing allowance, and any social security allowance to be paid by the congregation to a pension plan.
—an allowance for social security taxes equal to the maximum self-employment social security tax applicable each year.
—A health and death benefit insurance plan, all premiums to be paid by the congregation for the pastor's family.
—At least four weeks vacation.
—Two additional weeks for continuing education with tuition payments made by the congregation.
—A three-month sabbatical for each six years of service with the same congregation.
—And, full reimbursement for all professional expenses.

Another pay plan

Beginning with the first year in ministry, basic salary is $260 a week, increased by $10 a week for each year in the ministry. Reimbursement for automobile expenses is set at twenty-five cents a mile, including the cost of replacement. A provision for social security tax allowance is set at 10 percent of salary and housing. The pastor is provided with a parsonage and all utilities or a $5,000 housing allowance. Pension plan contributions are 12 percent of salary and housing. Health coverage is $700 a year. A book and study materials allowance is also recommended, for which $500 a year is anticipated.

For a congregation using that pattern, cost would be something like this (no consideration assumed for inflation):

	First Yr.	Tenth Yr.	Twentieth Yr.
Base salary	$13,520	$18,720	$23,920
Car allowance	3,750	3,750	3,750
Social Sec. allowance	1,850	2,370	2,890
Pension plan	2,650	3,390	4,130
Health insurance	700	700	700
Book allowance	500	500	500
Housing allowance	5,000	5,000	5,000
Costs to church	$27,970	$34,430	$40,890

Obviously that would not all be income to the pastor. The pastor's net take-home pay is much less than the congregation's total cost for having a pastor. Here is what the real income, supplemental benefits, and expense reimbursements in this situation would be like:

	First Yr.	Tenth Yr.	Twentieth Yr.
Real income:			
Base salary	$13,520	$18,750	$23,920
Soc. Sec. allow.	1,850	2,370	2,890
Housing allowance	5,000	5,000	5,000
Net take-home pay before taxes	$20,370	$26,090	$31,810
Fringe benefits:			
Pension plan	$ 2,650	$ 3,390	$ 4,130
Health insurance	700	700	700
Book allowance	500	500	500
Benefits	$ 3,850	$ 4,590	$ 5,330
Reimbursements:			
Car allowance	$ 3,750	$ 3,750	$ 3,750
Cost to church	$27,970	$34,430	$40,890

Yet another pay plan*

In yet another plan, you can be paid at a rate comparable to the median family income of the area in which the congregation is located. The plan includes three steps: an agreement on a pay range, adjustment to that range according to the complexity of assigned responsibilities, and development of a fair rate of remuneration based on job proficiency.

Step One: The minimum of the pay range should be the median family income of those persons living within the geographical area served by the church, adjusted downwards for favorable tax benefits uniquely available to pastors. Median salaries in the area must be adjusted for inflation, depending upon the years for which they were applicable.

Because you receive the free use of a parsonage or a housing allowance and are able to exclude the value of either from taxable income, thus reducing tax liability, a downward adjustment of the median should be considered according to this plan. Allowing for further real estate tax savings for a minister in a parsonage, the median is reduced further. The maximum rate of the range should be 150 percent of the minimum calculated.

Step Two: Assigning a factor of one to ten for less to greater complexity, your job assignment should be evaluated. These elements might be rated in this way: Newly formed congregation, size of congregation, level of education in the congregation, racial-ethnic problems in the congregation, counseling problems in the congregation, degree of expected pastor participation in the church program, difficulty of the mission field, proficiency of lay leadership, level of secretarial and staff help, aid received from other pastors in the area. Out of a possible one hundred, the percentage points above fifty would increase the minimum-maximum range upwards. Less than fifty would lower the range.

---

*This three-step pay plan is adapted from Harold Sedrel's "Salary Guide for Pastors," produced by the Presbytery of Great Rivers, Ill., United Presbyterian Church, USA. Used with permission.

Step Three: A fair rate of remuneration would finally depend upon your proficiency on the job. Consider: education—liberal arts degree, seminary training, graduate work; experience as a pastor, length of service with this congregation; abilities as shepherd, teacher, counselor, administrator, and representative of Christ in the community.

Then, using these criteria, a fair rate of remuneration is set somewhere between those established ranges. For example, assume that the median salary for your geographical area as determined by the Bureau of Labor Statistics is $24,280.

If the fair rental value of the parsonage is $4,000 (or a housing allowance of that amount is used), tax liability in the 22 percent range is reduced by approximately $880 for federal taxes, perhaps $400 for state taxes in the 10 percent range. Property taxes (estimated at $1,200) are also avoided in a parsonage (or as part of excludable housing allowance).

The weighted estimated median family income for the year, therefore, might be reduced from $24,280 to $21,800 ($24,280 less the sum of $880, $400, and $1,200), which becomes the minimum pay range. The maximum would be 1.5 times as much or $32,700.

If the complexity of the job is rated to be 55, then the pay range should be adjusted upward by 5 percent, assuming a 50 percent complexity as normal. The pay range is now $22,890 ($21,800 times 1.05) to $34,335 ($32,700 times 1.05).

If a fair rate of remuneration is then based upon proficiency at the job, and that is assumed to be at a midpoint between the minimum and maximum adjusted range, a remuneration (cash salary and housing) would be tagged at $28,612 ($22,890 plus $34,335 divided by 2).

Budgeting pay plans

You know how people compute clergy income. They take all the items listed on the church budget that are paid to the pastor, draw a line, add it up and assume that is total pay. It is not, of course, but the members believe it to be so and wonder why the pastor complains about a low salary!

Since salary is not the total of compensation items, benefits, and reimbursements, it should be made clear to your official board just what is compensation and what is not.

After all, the congregation's costs for having a pastor is just not the same as the pastor's income. It's not all take-home pay. Sure the cost is the same to the congregation either way. But for the pastor, it is important that the congregation be aware of salary, separate from its total cost for paying for a pastor. Unless your congregation is aware of the *true* income that you receive as their pastor, they will assume that your income is far greater than it really is.

An effective way to clarify this kind of distinction is to list the congregation's expenses for having a pastor in more than one budget classification. After all, your congregation doesn't list postage under salaries, and benvolences are not a part of office expenses. Neither should car allowance paid to you, for example, or mortgage payments on the parsonage be part of your salary on the church budget. These are unrelated to compensation and should not be shown in the same category of expenses as your salary.

Thus, only base salary and housing allowance should be included in the professional salaries category of the church budget. The congregation's payment of pension contributions, health insurance premiums, and other supplemental benefits should be listed as part of employee benefits along with the costs for providing similar benefits to other employees.

Reimbursements for your professional expenses should be included among the congregation's budget line expense items, not as part of salary. Thus, car allowance is in fact part of the congregation's administrative costs. Postage or supplies are part of the church's costs for doing business. Payments on the parsonage mortgage are debt-retirement costs.

Here's a way that all of this can best be shown on the church budget:

ANNUAL BUDGET (highlighting costs for having a pastor)

Benevolences		$13,500
Ministry		
Salary for pastor		15,000
Employee benefits		
Pension plan contributions	$3,120	
Social security allowance	1,433	
Health insurance premiums	850	
Annual physical examination	150	
Equity allowance	200	5,753
Service		
Pastor's discretionary fund	$ 500	
Other costs	400	900
Administration		
Car allowance	$1,200	
Book allowance	100	
Continuing education allowance	500	
Key person life insurance	200	
Employee scholarship fund	500	
Other costs	2,000	4,500
Program costs		5,100
Property maintenance		
Parsonage utilities, repairs	$1,800	
Other costs	4,000	5,800
Debt retirement		
Church mortgage	$2,000	
Parsonage mortgage	3,600	5,600
Total budget		$56,153

Reducing Staff Income Taxes

So, how do you convince your lay leaders of ways to help you avoid paying taxes you do not owe? You do it by having them put together a pay plan that offers the best tax advantage without really costing your congregation a whole lot more, if anything at all.

Here are some of the things you can encourage your lay people to do for you as they put together your compensation arrangement for next year:*

---

*Adapted from *Tax Planning for Clergy* by Manfred Holck, Jr., © 1984 by Prentice-Hall, Inc., Englewood Cliffs, N.J. Used with permission.

Example 1: Amounts spent by a minister to provide a home in excess of a rental allowance are not deductible. *Solution:* Have the congregation agree on a total amount of compensation for salary and rental allowance combined, permitting the minister to specify, within the Internal Revenue Service allowed limits, that part of the total to be designated as allowance. Too much allowance is better than not enough. *Result:* No additional cost to the congregation, with possible significant additional income exclusions and tax savings to the minister.

Example 2: If the congregation owns the parsonage, but the minister must buy furniture and pay for utilities, only the rental value of the home is excluded from income. The minister will pay tax on the income used to buy that furniture and pay those utilities. *Solution:* Designate a part of the minister's base salary for rental allowance, not to exceed the rental value of furnishings and cost of utilities. *Result:* The minister can also exclude from income any allowance used to buy furniture or pay for utilities. This action cuts income taxes, yet costs the congregation nothing!

Example 3: The tax on personal contributions made to certain denominational pension plans can be deferred only through a salary reduction plan. *Solution:* Reduce salary by the minister's contribution and have the congregation pay the entire amount. *Result:* A cut in the minister's income tax at no cost to the congregation.

Example 4: Health insurance premiums paid by a minister are generally deductible only if he or she itemized deductions and medical expenses exceed 7.5 percent of adjusted gross income. *Solution:* Have the congregation pay the entire premium by designating that amount as a special allowance. *Result:* A full deduction, in effect, for that premium payment whether or not the minister itemized deductions—and at no extra cost to the congregation if salary is reduced. (It would be much better, however, for the congregation to pay that full premium without reducing salary. It's still not taxable income to the minister and only a nominal increase in total congregational costs.)

Example 5: Group term life insurance premiums personally paid by the minister cannot be deducted. *Solution:* Have the congregation pay that bill, too, along with the health insurance premiums, and in the same way. *Result:* More tax-free income to the minister for premiums on the first $50,000 of coverage only.

Example 6: Social security self-employment taxes keep going up and ministers (as well as others self-employed) are digging deeper than ever into their pockets to pay those taxes. *Solution:* Have the congregation designate an allowance for social security tax each year equal to the maximum self-employment social security tax. *Result:* The minister's take-home pay remains unchanged as the tax goes up. Any increases in costs can be absorbed more readily by the congregation. It's a small built-in salary advance each year for the minister. (The allowance must be paid to the minister, not IRS, and it's taxable income.)

Example 7: A minister normally spends more to operate a car than is received in reimbursement. Of course, the excess costs can be deducted, but all the same, that means cutting into salary to pay those extra costs. *Solution:* Provide a car, with all expenses paid, to be used for the minister's *exclusive* use on church business. *Result:* Pay isn't reduced by excess costs coming out of the minister's pocketbook. Further, the congregation is doing what's fair—it's reimbursing the minister in full for church-related professional expenses. Besides, the whole matter can then be ignored for tax purposes.

Example 8: The minister has professional expenses (in addition to car costs)—such things as books, magazines, tape recording equipment, pulpit robes, professional dues, and home entertainment of church guests. True, these expenses are usually deductible, but they're still expenses. *Solution:* Have the congregation provide full reimbursement for all professional expense costs. *Result:* The congregation pays the proper costs for having a minister, and the minister can ignore the matter for tax purposes. (Of course, good records need to be kept so that full reimbursement can be requested.)

Example 9: Many ministers participate in continuing education opportunities to improve their skills. But that costs money, too. The cost is deductible, but it's still another expense. *Solution:* Have the congregation pay all or part of those costs. After all, it's for their benefit. *Result:* This will cost the congregation something more, but it relieves the minister of paying out-of-pocket costs and eliminates any possible tax question concerning the legality of the claimed deduction.

Example 10: Many congregations offer their ministers a fixed monthly automobile allowance. For tax purposes, ministers generally can deduct their actual costs or use the government's automatic-mileage allowance deduction. Yet the allowance is artificially fixed and often has no bearing on costs for operating a car in that community. *Solution:* Have the congregation pay a mileage allowance equal at least to the government's automatic-mileage allowance deduction. *Result:* The allowance is geared to miles driven and thus more nearly to the costs incurred. The mileage deduction is still applicable, or actual costs can be deducted. And it probably won't cost the congregation much more that way than under the "allowance" way. At any rate, it'll be a much fairer reimbursement plan.

Example 11: Ministers often incur medical expenses that are not covered by insurance and are not deductible. *Solution:* Have the congregation set up a medical expense reimbursement plan for all full-time employees, not to exceed a stated maximum, say $1,000 a year per family. *Result:* Such reimbursements generally are not taxable income to the minister or the other employees.

Evaluation

Congregations large and small struggle with the task of evaluating the work that their pastor is doing for them. Often that struggle is no more than a rehash of all the things the people like about the minister or dislike. Seldom is the evaluation any kind of systematic approach to what the pastor really does all day long.

And that's probably not all bad. Actually any attempt to evaluate the pastor may be doomed from the start since evaluation is such a difficult task. However, evaluation forms have been developed by other groups, and you may wish to examine some to see if you would like for your leadership to evaluate your work. Write to the Alban Institute, Mt. St. Albans, Washington, D.C. 20016, for more information.

(For a complete explanation of the maximum Tax Sheltered Annuity contribution which an employee of a nonprofit organization may make through the employer in any given year, a detailed worksheet and description of the law should be available from your church pension board.)

CHAPTER 9

CHURCH FINANCE AND RECORDKEEPING

JUST HOW YOUR congregation goes about securing its funds, keeping a record of those funds, and then spending those funds can indicate how concerned the leaders of your church are about its financial program. In a very real way, your congregation can actually express its own church accounting philosophy and its stewardship attitudes by the way financial records are kept and money is spent.

What your congregation spends, for example, may well indicate its interest in particular areas of the church's program. Adequate salaries and allowances may indicate a healthy concern for staff members' welfare. Sufficient funds allocated to the church schools may show a strong concern for your educational program. Advertising accounts may indicate an active public relations program. Increased amounts for janitorial services may show a concern for the upkeep of the physical plant of the church and the proper maintenance of its property.

Attitudes toward a stewardship of church accounting may also be seen in the actual financial records your church keeps. Inaccurate, messy records show little concern for a proper accounting or reporting to the congregation. If your congregation is really interested in the work of the kingdom of God, then its financial system must necessarily be good. Even mailing statements to members about their contributions reflects some misconceptions about what stewardship and church fund raising is all about. A statement suggests we owe money to the church. We don't. We give because we want to give. A report not a statement best reflects how well we have met our commitment to give.

Then, how your congregation's financial records are actually kept, how your congregation's money is spent, and how your congregation is kept informed about its giving all demonstrate, in a large part, your congregation's concern over its financial resources. That concern is reflected in the impact your congregation makes on the life of its members and the community it serves.

Whenever money is received or paid out or when services or merchandise are received or purchased, a business transaction takes place in the accounting sense. When funds are received by the church and expended for benevolences, services, supplies, debt payments, or for any other purpose, business transactions are involved. The administration and maintenance of a congregation is a business operation. Obviously, then, your congregation has a responsibility to use the best known business procedures available.

Good business procedures are important, for example, when funds are borrowed for the purchase of land, building construction, or where credit is needed for other purposes. Banks will require certain information about your congregation's financial situation before making a loan. Business establishments may require credit ratings. Only adequate and accurate records can provide this required financial information promptly. Thus, your congregation should operate its finances in a very businesslike manner. That is just good stewardship as well as good business practice!

Among other things, good financial records will enable your congregation to project its plans for growth and outreach into the future. For example, on the basis of previous financial records, you can anticipate seasonal fluctuations in offerings. If July has been a low month in the past, then it will likely be a low month in the year to come. Obviously you will need to keep financial commitments to a minimum during that time of year.

Perhaps December is an exceptionally good month. Then some plans might be made for setting aside a portion of these excess funds to meet contingencies or other expenditures in a low month. Seasonal fluctuations occur in every congregation. Proper planning is necessary to meet those problems. Good financial records provide a way for better management and better stewardship of resources during the peaks and valleys of a year's offerings.

That same kind of planning holds true with expenditures. Insurance premium payments, for instance, may be due and payable annually, but a congregation can save money by paying those premiums once every two or three years instead. Yet, unless the congregation has made plans for doing so, it may be unable to meet the larger payment when it comes due.

It is certainly desirable for your congregation to anticipate receipts and expenditures over the years carefully, to plan for them, and then to adhere to adopted procedures in meeting obligations. "Seat of the pants" planning and spending is neither successful nor wise, nor good stewardship!

The profit principles of business are not appropriate for church accounting. This is especially true when church leaders attempt to maintain large cash balances in the congregational treasury. Some congregations even try to make a cash profit to prove they are in business to make money. But the church is not in business to declare a 20 percent dividend each year! Church offerings are contributed for a specific purpose, and they should be put to work to accomplish that aim as soon as possible.

To be sure, a contingency fund for emergencies is a necessary part of any congregation's financial recordkeeping process. But having large amounts of cash constantly on hand seems unnecessary. Proper planning with the use of "cash forecasts" and other accounting tools can suggest anticipated cash needs far in advance of any requirements to pay.

This means that if a congregation is fully aware of its responsibilities, it will develop some plan, some goal, some system for using its resources in the best way. It means that a definite program will be outlined, that the *what* and *why* of projected goals will be thoroughly discussed, and that a businesslike order will be maintained.

Internal Control

Internal control is a plan of control, not only to detect error or fraud, but to safeguard assets; to check the dependability of financial records; to encourage operating efficiency and adherence to the rules, regulations, and policies set by management: An accounting system for a church is essentially based upon the principles of internal control accepted by that congregation.

Thus, a good system of internal control will help prevent theft. It will keep honest members honest by removing the temptation to dishonesty. And, it will help to defend officials against unjustified claims of incompetence in the management of contributions made by the membership.

The assets of the congregation must be safeguarded from unauthorized use so that dollars are available when needed for programs. For not only would the loss of a large sum be a crime, but it might seriously jeopardize the programs of the church, as well. Appropriate internal control features minimize those risks of loss.

There are, of course, many checks and balances that a congregation might develop to be certain that there is no intentional or unintentional misstatement of any transaction or account balance. And

165

any system of internal control must account for that. But handling cash often proves to be a temptation to steal. And it is that physical asset of cash that is the thrust of the principles listed below. Receivables, inventories, securities, and other assets are not of as much concern as cash, although proper controls must be maintained for those assets as well.

In developing any accounting system so that internal controls are adequate, just plain, good, common sense is important. So any listing of controls includes rather obvious and elementary procedures. Nevertheless, listing them is important. You can check off your own procedures by comparing what you do with what you "ought to do."

1. Don't assign the same person responsibility for more than one of the following tasks: counting the offering, writing checks, recording individual contributions, and reconciling the bank statement with the financial record books.

That separation is important in order to reduce the opportunity for any misappropriation. When one individual has responsibility for more than one function involving cash, the ease of misappropriation is greatly increased. For example, if the same person that counted the offering also kept the individual contribution records, false entries could easily be made to the member's account and the cash pocketed. A verification request to the member would reveal nothing amiss since the record would be accurate. Only an audit of all contributions and a determination that all contributions had not been properly deposited and recorded would reveal the discrepancy. But, that would be time-consuming and would only be done upon suspicion of an irregularity.

Or, if the same person counts the offering and writes the checks, one set of records could be falsified to cover up a discrepancy in the other set. Bank statements reconciled by the person who writes the checks can be used effectively to cover up checks inappropriately written to the embezzler or a fake payee.

2. Make certain that at least two people are in custody of the offering until it has been safely deposited in the bank or placed in a night depository or safe.

It doesn't take much imagination to figure out what could happen to the loose coins and bills in an offering place if only one person has access to them. Since receipts have not nor will not be given for those gifts, there is no way to tell how much money should be in that offering. The temptation is there to slip a few coins or bills out of the pile with no one the wiser for it.

When at least two people must be around that cash all the time until it is safely deposited, the chance of cash going into the wrong pocket is minimized. The two people may not watch each other, but the likelihood of two people entering into a collusion to defraud the church is less likely than for one person.

Not only does this procedure protect the congregation's money, but it also prevents unjustified accusation against an individual suspected of taking the money. No one should agree to handle the cash unless a second person is also assigned the task.

And the rule is important from beginning to end. It is not enough to have several people counting the offering (just because that gets the job done more quickly), but two people need to take the offering plates off the altar, go together to the counting room, count together, and together take the bag to the bank. Such togetherness is an essential element of internal control.

3. Promptly deposit all money—cash or checks—received on Sunday or during the week. A list of checks received should be compared regularly with the bank statement. Those responsible for recordkeeping should not have access to the mail.

The purpose of this control is to prevent any misappropriation of money after it has been received. Midweek mail is not likely to include any cash, but it may include a substantial number of checks. While it is supposed to be relatively difficult to endorse a check made out to someone else, with care it can be. Thus, checks received in midweek, or even those received on Sunday, should be promptly endorsed for deposit and payable to the bank.

Safeguards for protecting such midweek contributions include mail opening by someone not responsible in any way for recordkeeping. Checks should be promptly endorsed by that person and a list made of checks received. A copy of that list may be given to the treasurer and the financial secretary, the latter to make the deposit. The point of that activity is to prevent those responsible for recordkeeping from converting a check to their own use and marking the records as though it had been received.

A comparison of that list with the amount deposited as shown on the bank statement will confirm that the deposit and all the checks listed were received. That comparison may well be made by the person reconciling the bank statement. When confirmation of contributions recorded are sent out to members, it will quickly be evident if the person opening the mail has misappropriated any checks.

The purpose of depositing the Sunday offering promptly is to have a record of all receipts and disbursements. No payment for services should be made from that offering. Checks should be written to pay for any bills. Such a control will not prevent a person from claiming and getting an illegal payment from the church, but at least a check request will have to be made. All bills should be paid by check and all cash received deposited.

4. Encourage all members to use offering envelopes. The purpose of this control is to make certain that each member's contributions are actually received by the congregation as intended. It is obvious that loose cash can easily be removed for personal benefit without anyone else being aware of the loss. An envelope offering means a record will be made of the gift and a confirmation requested from the member. Members should contact the church secretary if they fail to receive a report of their offerings. When adequate procedures are followed, the use of offering envelopes can be an effective internal control feature.

Another purpose for using offering envelopes is to provide the member with a record of gifts to the church for income tax purposes. Offerings made by envelope and verified by the congregation are acceptable to the Internal Revenue Service.

Some pastors prefer to know what each member has given. The use of envelopes makes that possible. And, statistical information about giving patterns, as needed for reporting or projecting, is easily available from offering envelope records.

Offering envelopes are especially useful when members insist on giving cash rather than writing checks. But, either way, the envelope is useful. For their own record and protection of the gift made, all members should be encouraged, where possible, to make their contribution to the church by check.

5. Don't let just anyone have access to the offerings and to the checking account. Just as the same person should not have access to receipts and to the checkbook, access to cash should be carefully defined and limited to only certain persons. Perhaps many people do assist with the counting of the Sunday offering, but if there is any confusion in the procedure, proper controls may be lacking. A selected group of people, thoroughly familiar with the controls and the procedures can count efficiently and accurately. Controlling cash receipts involves careful screening of those who count the cash.

It is also better to limit the number of those authorized to sign checks. There may be lack of control when only one person signs the checks, as well as when the same person counts money and signs checks, too. But six authorized signers is generally unnecessary. Since any two of these could presumably be authorized to sign, the other four, and notably the treasurer, may be unaware of checks written by the other two. Three authorized signers should be sufficient, with the treasurer always in charge of the checkbook.

6. Insist that all payments be by check. Adequate supporting documentation should accompany each check. The purpose of this control is to be certain that a record of all disbursements is kept and

that only those authorized to make payments have done so. A check is a permanent record of a payment. It verifies that a payment has been made, when it was made, to whom it was paid, the amount paid, and even the purpose of the payment.

The only payments made by cash are those from the petty cash fund. Everything else should be paid by check. The supporting voucher designates the authority for the payment. The check signer verifies that authority by writing the check.

7. Require two signatures on every check. Since the treasurers of many congregations generally keep the financial record books and prepare and sign the checks, too, a second signature should be required. Anyone signing a check should examine carefully the support documentation and ascertain that the check is properly authorized.

This control also prevents the treasurer from writing a fraudulent check, absconding with the proceeds, and covering up the act by necessary entries in the records. The second signer must verify the authority. Invoices are marked paid when signed to avoid a duplicate payment and another chance to misappropriate funds. Obviously, blank checks should not be signed in advance by anyone. A check protector machine and the use of prenumbered, imprinted personalized checks are desirable control features.

8. Assign someone other than those who handle cash or keep the financial records the responsibility for receiving and reconciling the bank statement. The purpose of this control is to prevent the treasurer from writing a fraudulent check, covering up the fraud in the books and destroying the cancelled check when it is returned by the bank. Another person designated by the finance committee should have the statement mailed directly from the bank and immediately reconcile that bank balance with the checkbook and journals of the congregation. It means securing the records from the treasurer, verifying all checks cancelled as those authorized, accounting for outstanding checks, and verifying all deposit slips with deposits shown on the bank statement.

The treasurer of a congregation should insist on this procedure, as inconvenient as it may be, if for no other reason than to prevent suspicion of wrongdoing.

9. Use a church budget effectively! The church budget can well be one of the most effective internal controls available to a congregation. By comparing budgeted amounts with actual expenditures, church officers can detect whether funds are being spent as authorized. Any deviations can be immediately investigated.

This kind of regular review is very important. Every member of the official board should examine the financial statements and be prepared to question any serious deviations. Frequent and constant probing often uncovers potentially serious problems.

Of course, the effectiveness of this control depends upon timely financial statements, monthly and as soon as possible.

This control also presumes that reports will be prepared in such a manner that comparisons can be made and marked deviations quickly noted, questioned, and explained.

10. Do not let any financial officers write off any unpaid pledges. If a congregation records pledges as receivables, none should be written off without the explicit approval of the official board. To permit such receivable write-off at will allows those with access to the records to cover up offerings received and not recorded. The write-off quite conveniently obscures the perpetration of that kind of fraud.

11. Keep marketable securities, notes, valuable personal property, cash (coins, bills, or checks) in a safe place. If a congregation has securities, notes, valuable jewels, coins, or other objects, they should be kept in a safe deposit box. Keep cash in a check or savings account.

The purpose of this control is to protect those assets from theft, fire, or improper appropriation. For greatest protection these should not be kept in a safe on the premises but in the custody of a bank. A bank safe-deposit box requiring two signatures for entry is recommended, thus preventing any one person from making an unauthorized entry.

12. Maintain an inventory of assets. This control is necessary to be certain that the congregation knows at all times precisely what assets it has and where they are located. A periodic count to verify the location of all items will determine which, if any, are missing.

Such a record should include a description of the item, cost, date of purchase, location, intended use, and eventual disposition and sale. Such information is not only valuable in keeping track of the assets but, in case of fire, will provide replacement cost information quickly. Such a record is also important in a congregation because employees and volunteers using that equipment come and go. A written record helps to verify what is available.

13. Make sure an annual audit is conducted. The purpose of this control is to have disinterested persons (persons not involved in the financial record keeping procedures) attest to the accuracy of the records and adherence to authorized and generally accepted procedures in the recordkeeping process.

14. Put all of your cash handling procedures into writing. The purpose of this control is to assure continuity in recordkeeping procedures and to provide an explanation to those assigned responsibility. Consistency in recordkeeping and reporting is important in order to note and examine deviation. Control is maintained best by persistently using those procedures approved by the official board.

15. Get a fidelity bond for all cash handlers! The purpose of this control is to make certain that the congregation will, in fact, be reimbursed if an embezzlement does occur. The insurance may also act as a deterrent to misuse because employees will be aware that an insurance company may press more severely for recovery of its loss than may the congregation.

Don't be lolled into an unrealistic dependence on this type of insurance, however. Good records are essential to prove a loss did occur. A suspicion of loss is insufficient for recovery.

Finally, let me assure you that I do not have deep-seated suspicions of church members, as may appear from my previous comments. I have no more suspicion of fraud among church members than I would of anyone else who handles cash in any other organization. The purpose of this discussion is not to arouse doubts about the moral integrity of church members, but to (1) recommend those procedures that are most likely to remove the temptation for fraud or embezzlement, (2) eliminate mere suspicions of dishonesty, (3) protect those responsible for financial records, and (4) maximize the likelihood of discovering a theft.

I have not expressed a lack of confidence but have merely outlined reasonable procedures for the proper care and control of the financial records of a congregation. The larger the congregation, the more descriptive and lengthy such a list would be. Nothing here is new. Any accountant would confirm these procedures as appropriate for any congregation.

Spending Authorizations

Strict control of the congregation's funds also requires proper authorization for spending. All disbursements should be supported by the proper authority and appropriate documentary evidence. Checks should be prepared only on the basis of a properly authorized written document such as invoices, vouchers, payrolls, contracts, etc.

Invoices, statements, and other papers signed by properly authorized individuals can be the basis for payment by the treasurer, providing such disbursements were also previously authorized by the budget or board.

Contracts for salaries, utility bills, and other fixed monthly expenditures are authorized by the congregation when the budget is adopted.

Usually the pastor will be responsible for more purchases than anyone else, but that spending must also be controlled by the budget and the board. As a safeguard to the pastor and the treasurer, every congregation should adopt a definite policy for purchasing goods and authorizing spending.

As you well know, congregations don't always have funds available to meet all obligations. In order that proper consideration be given to paying all congregational obligations, a specific policy ought to be established by the board to designate priorities of payments.

Accounting principles, of course, only specify that payments should be properly authorized, disbursed, and recorded, but Christian principles of stewardship insist on a different order of priority. The Bible teaches that upon the first day of the week a person should lay aside a portion of what has been earned accordingly as God has blessed them. It also promotes regular, proportionate giving—week by week, a definite percentage. It encourages giving to God of the first fruits, not the leftovers! It emphasizes that the mission of the church is to help others.

In establishing an order of priority for making payments, therefore, even the congregation should first determine a definite, proportionate amount of its offering to be used for benevolences each month.

Next should be the pastor's salary. Since the pastor has been called by God and the congregation to serve as the leader of this particular congregation, those costs should be met promptly to help the pastor serve effectively in the community.

Only then should other legal contractual obligations be met, such as mortgage payments, notes, utilities, etc. Other bills would be prioritized according to due date, discounts, credit ratings, etc.

There are no theological grounds for church accounting procedures. There are no biblical references to validate any specific accounting procedures. God's people are to be honest in all things. Principles of good accounting should determine a church accounting procedure.

Modern, tested, and proven methods of keeping account of the church's finances should be used in today's churches. To do so is simply good stewardship!

Basic Accounting System Principles*

Church accounting systems are as numerous and as varied as are congregations. There simply has been no successful effort made to develop a standardized church accounting system. Congregations have been free to develop their own procedures and with each new treasurer, the system often has been changed.

Systems have been suggested, of course, and many books on church finance have proposed a variety of systems.

Generally, most church accounting systems have been developed on a pattern similar to that used by a for-profit enterprise. Thus they are not entirely appropriate for a congregation. Since a congregation is not in the business of generating a profit or accumulating a surplus, church financial statements that reveal net earnings or changes in net worth are not particularly helpful in understanding what has happened to a congregation's cash.

The most successful attempt at a standardized system is that which has been developed by the American Institute of Certified Public Accountants in their guide for accounting methods for nonprofit organizations.

There are certain concepts basic to any church accounting system, as follows:

1. It should be a double entry bookkeeping system.

Single entry systems are not uncommon, but the double entry system of debits and credits provides a check on mathematical accuracy and a certain compatibility with other systems that makes it superior to the single entry system.

In double entry bookkeeping every entry is made twice. Thus, when cash is received, the amount is debited to the cash account (because asset accounts normally have a debit balance) and credited to the income account. Money spent is credited to the cash account (the normal debit balance is reduced) and

---

*Reprinted and adapted by permission from *Cash Management* by Manfred Holck, Jr., copyright 1978, Augsburg Publishing House, Minneapolis, Minn., pages 16-17.

debited to the expense account. In every transaction a debit equals a credit. And the sum of all the debit entries during a period equals the sum of all the credit entries.

Mistakes can still be made, of course, because entries can be debited or credited to the wrong accounts and the debits will still equal the credits. But the chance of mathematical error is reduced significantly over that for a single entry system.

Readers who are not familiar with double entry bookkeeping should study a basic text on accounting in order to understand the difference between debits and credits and how they are used in recording financial transactions.

2. It should be a cash accounting system or a modified cash accrual system.

Sophisticated business accounting systems are all generally accrual basis systems. A family's checkbook accounting system or tax recordkeeping system is generally always a cash system.

In a cash system the only entries ever made are recorded when cash is received or spent. Financial statements reflect only those transactions that have occurred through the receipt or payment of cash.

In an accrual system not only are the cash transactions recorded but any commitments incurred which have not yet been paid, or income promised but not yet received, are recorded and reflected in the financial statements. In addition, certain assets paid for in advance or payments on account received in advance are adjusted to reflect that which has been actually used or earned. Depreciation may also be recorded.

For most congregations, the cash system is generally sufficient to report accurately the financial status of the congregation. However, some congregational treasurers will, in fact, adjust their records on a monthly and or annual basis to reflect certain commitments not yet evidenced by a cash transaction.

Thus, bills that are due but not yet paid, such as for utilities, are recorded as an expense and as a liability of the congregation before being paid. Sometimes pledges, which have been made to the congregation but not yet received, are recorded as income and as a receivable. Again, for further clarification on how accruals are entered into the records, interested readers should refer to a standard accounting textbook.

3. It should be a fund accounting system.

Nonprofit organizations and governmental units generally use what is called a fund accounting approach to recordkeeping. Fund accounting differs from other types of accounting systems in that it separates into specific funds various aspects of the congregation's finances. A business corporation's system is intended to reflect a profit or loss in the operations. It is a one-fund operation.

But nonprofit groups, such as congregations, generally receive and use cash contributions for current operations (current unrestricted fund), for buildings (building fund), to accumulate capital (capital funds), the income to be used for designated purposes (endowment fund), and for special purposes (restricted current funds). Better control over cash, more intelligible reporting, and a better stewardship of the congregation's cash resources are all advantages in using fund accounting.

However, a fund accounting system can be complicated bookkeeping even in the smallest operation. Many more entries are generally required if there are transfers between funds. Financial statement preparation may be more difficult and, in general, the system is difficult to maintain for inexperienced church bookkeepers.

But fund accounting is proper for congregations and should be the system used. The new AICPA accounting principles guide for nonprofit organizations suggests only fund accounting financial statements. A text on fund accounting should be referred to for more information on the mechanics of using fund accounting for congregations.

Just as certain concepts are basic to any church accounting system, certain accounting procedures are basic to any type of accounting system, whether fund accounting or something else. And congregational treasurers need to know the basic mechanics for keeping a set of church financial records. After all, church cash can be controlled only as leaders know how much cash there is or may be expected.

Counting the Cash*

As soon as the worship service concludes on a Sunday morning, two persons assigned the task should remove the offering plates from the altar. The official board should insist that two people go to the altar together to get the money. For right here is the first place where money can be lost unless proper controls are followed.

---

*Reprinted and adapted from *Cash Management* by Manfred Holck, Jr., copyright 1978, Augsburg Publishing House, Minneapolis, Minn., pages 12-13.

Both persons carry the money to the counting place. There, in a quiet, safe, well-lighted room with ample tables, pencils, forms, and an adding machine, the counting can begin promptly.

Some congregations, however, take the offering immediately to the bank and deposit it, uncounted, in the night depository. That's all right providing that on the next day, or soon thereafter, at least two people go to the bank, retrieve the bag, unlock it, and count the money there and then.

Control is thrown away if the money is put into the bank without counting and then the church secretary goes over on Monday morning to count it in a private, locked room at the bank! One person with an uncounted amount of money is in a situation full of potential trouble. And a friendly bank teller should not count the money either, alone, until a deposit slip has been prepared, against which a count can be compared by that teller.

But the best place and the best time to count the Sunday morning offering (or any other offering for that matter) is immediately *after the service and at the church*, not during church, since counting money does not replace worship.

The counting process can be facilitated by using appropriate forms and keeping the procedures as simple as possible. Some suggested steps are these:

1. Separate all loose coins, bills, and checks from the offering envelopes. Prepare recording slips for checks not in envelopes to indicate donor, amount, and purpose.

2. Remove all coins, bills, and checks from the offering envelopes. Be certain the amount removed is correctly marked on the outside of each envelope. If discrepancies appear, mark amount enclosed on the envelope and request the assistant financial secretary to notify the donor.

3. Prepare adding machine tapes to verify the total of coins, bills, and checks removed from envelopes with totals marked on the envelopes.

4. Record various sources of coins, bills, and checks on a counting form.

5. Prepare deposit slip and verify total deposit with total coins, bills, and checks received. Distribute copies of deposit slip and counting form to treasurer and assistant financial secretary. Give all empty envelopes with supporting total tape to assistant financial secretary for recording to individual contributors' records.

6. At least two persons take the deposit bag with appropriate deposit slip to the bank for deposit.

An Accounting System

Sample chart of accounts

Each congregation should adapt this listing to their own situation in order to provide the least complicated procedure for reporting financial transactions to the official board and congregation.

100	ASSETS
110	Cash in bank—checking
120	Cash in bank—savings
130	Petty cash
140	Invested (securities)
150	Church:
	151 Building
	152 Furniture and equipment
	153 Land
160	Parsonage:
	161 Buildings
	162 Furnishings
	163 Land
200	LIABILITIES
210	Special gifts and offerings payable
220	Payroll deductions and withholdings

250	FUND BALANCES
250	General funds
260	Special funds
280	PROPERTY EQUITY
280	Buildings, furniture and equipment, land
300	INCOME BUDGETED
310	Envelope, pledge, and tithe
320	Loose plate offering
330	Church school
340	Interest income
350	Other income
	INCOME UNBUDGETED
380	Designated gifts and offerings
390	Other income
	EXPENSES
400	CAPITAL
410	Debt retirement
420	Capital improvements
500	PROGRAM
510	Nurture and membership care
515	Outreach
520	Christian unity and interreligious concerns
525	Church and society
530	Education/church school
535	Evangelism
540	Higher education and campus ministry
545	Missions
550	Religion and race
555	Stewardship
560	Worship
565	Other program expense
600	OPERATING EXPENSE
610	Finance committee
620	Lay employee benefits
630	Office expense
	631 Postage
	632 Supplies
	633 Telephone
	634 Miscellaneous
640	Property maintenance
	641 Church
	642 Parsonage
	643 Equipment
	644 Pianos and organ
	645 Supplies
650	Insurance

660	Real estate assessments/taxes
670	Church heat, electricity, and water
680	Other operating expense

| 700 | PASTORAL SUPPORT |
| 710 | Pastoral support local church |

    711   Pastor's salary
    712   Pastor's travel expense
    713   Pastor's utilities
    714   Pastor's other allowances and benefits

| 720 | Pastoral support other than local church |

    721   Pension and benefits fund
    722   District Superintendents' fund
    723   Episcopal fund
    724   Equitable salary fund
    725   Temporary general aid fund

| 800 | CONNECTIONAL ADMINISTRATION |
| 810 | Connectional administration fund |

    811   Interdenominational cooperation fund
    812   General administration fund
    813   Jurisdictional administration fund
    814   Area and conference administration funds

| 820 | District administration fund |

900	BENEVOLENCES
910	World service and conference benevolences
915	Ministerial education fund
920	Black College fund
925	Missional priority fund
930	General advance specials
935	World service special gifts
940	General church offerings
945	Conference advance specials
	OTHER BENEVOLENCES
960	Paid to Conference treasurer
970	Paid direct

Forms that may be used for a simplified cash only accounting system may include (as illustrated):

     1. Cash receipts voucher
     2. Monthly report of giving
     3. Cash receipts journal
     4. Cash disbursements journal
     5. Treasurer's report
     6. Chart of accounts

Counting and recording the offering

The appointed tellers (at least two, as previously described) will count the offering and prepare the cash receipts voucher report form. A copy of that report will be forwarded to the treasurer who will record the proper information in the cash receipts journal. Each counting and deposit of offerings must be properly recorded on this form and in this journal. Columnar headings are identical with the listing of possible income designations. Careful attention to the explanation and detail on both forms will enhance accurate recordkeeping. Be sure all entries show proper account numbers or code numbers.

Recording cash disbursements

Information recorded on check stubs can be transferred to the cash disbursements journal and listed in the proper columns. Be sure to identify all entries with the proper account number or code numbers.

The amount of the check is recorded in the first column. The distribution of the check amount is recorded in the proper account column. Individual contributions record forms are completed regularly on the basis of offering envelopes or a special "Advice of Fund Received" form where no envelope is used by the donor.

Treasurer's Report

Total all columns in both the cash receipts journal and the cash disbursements journal. The total of debits must equal the total of all credits on each page.

Summarize all account numbers, in order, along with total amounts to each account number; add the list to verify all amounts have been included.

Copy the information from the prepared summary of both cash receipts and cash disbursements journals to the treasurer's report. To ease the recordkeeping burden, posting to a general ledger is not necessary in this system. The treasurer's report serves as the final report.

All forms are coordinated to simplify the ease of recording and transferring amounts.

Note that year-to-date amounts from the previous treasurer's report must be transferred to the cash receipts and cash disbursements journal each month. This procedure avoids the use of a general ledger and provides the necessary information to continue year-to-date data at the end of the next month. The chart of accounts is an easy way to keep track of what is going on.

This simplified church accounting system can be used by any church to record their offerings and expenses on a timely basis.

The use of a general ledger is possible if a more elaborate system is desired. For a more complete explanation of the use of this system, please see the *Handbook for Local Church Finance Record System* by John C. Espie (Nashville: United Methodist Publishing House, 1976).

INSTRUCTIONS

Treasurer's Report*

These instructions will assist you in preparing the Treasurer's Report form included in the Financial Record System. The form is to be used for any and all of the persons and groups in the local church to whom the treasurer reports—for example, the Committee on Finance, the Administrative Board/Council, the Charge Conference, and the pastor.

The Treasurer's Report should be prepared monthly. It is a summary of all the church's financial transactions for a specified period of time. This means that if a church has more than one treasurer (for example, a separate treasurer for benevolences or for a building fund), each treasurer will need either to

*Taken from the "Treasurer's Report," prepared and edited by The General Council on Finance and Administration. Copyright © 1976 by The United Methodist Publishing House.

CASH RECEIPTS VOUCHER   No. _____

Date _____

To: Treasurer _____ Financial Secretary _____ Pastor _____

Deposited to _____ Account: $_____
Deposited to _____ Account: $_____
Deposited to _____ Account: $_____

SUMMARY OF RECEIPTS

	CREDIT TO CONTRIBUTOR'S ACCOUNT	OTHER	TOTAL
BUDGETED			
Envelope, Pledge, Tithe Income:			
Current Expense	$_____		$_____
Benevolence	$_____		$_____
Building Fund	$_____		$_____
_____	$_____		$_____
Loose Plate Offering		$_____	$_____
Church School Offering		$_____	$_____
Other (Specify)	$_____	$_____	$_____
_____	$_____	$_____	$_____
_____	$_____	$_____	$_____
_____	$_____	$_____	$_____
_____	$_____	$_____	$_____
UNBUDGETED			
Designated Gifts and Special Offerings (Specify)			
_____	$_____	$_____	$_____
_____	$_____	$_____	$_____
_____	$_____	$_____	$_____
_____	$_____	$_____	$_____
Total	$_____	$_____	$_____ *

*Total must equal the amount of the deposit to the bank.

_____

_____

_____

Counting Committee Signatures

_____

All forms reproduced are from the *Handbook for Local Church Finance Record System* by John Espie. Forms prepared and edited by The General Council on Finance and Administration. Copyright © 1976 by The United Methodist Publishing House. Used by permission.

ENV NO.

MONTHLY REPORT OF GIVING

		1	2	3	1	2	3	1	2	3	1	2	3	SUN.
COL. 1	CURRENT EXPENSES OR UNIFIED BUDGET													1
														2
COL. 2	BENEVOLENCES OR													3
														4
COL. 3	BUILDING FUND OR													5
														TOTAL PAID
														PLEDGE DATE
														PAID DATE
		9th MONTH			10th MONTH			11th MONTH			12th MONTH			BAL.

COL. 1 CURRENT EXPENSES OR UNIFIED BUDGET $ $
COL. 2 BENEVOLENCES OR $ $
COL. 3 BUILDING FUND OR $ $

COMMITMENT:
☐ WEEKLY
☐ MONTHLY
☐

DATE	DESIGNATED GIFTS & SPECIAL OFFERINGS	AMOUNT
	TOTAL ▶	

WE ACKNOWLEDGE WITH APPRECIATION YOUR GIFTS AS RECORDED. REGULAR CONTRIBUTIONS ENABLE US TO MEET OUR FINANCIAL OBLIGATIONS PROMPTLY. CONTACT THE FINANCIAL OFFICER IF YOU HAVE QUESTIONS REGARDING THIS REPORT.

CHURCH:
This is 9 months' contribution

PLEASE RETAIN FOR INCOME TAX REFERENCE

OFFICER'S INITIALS   DATE

YR.
MO.

↰FOLD HERE

ENV. NO.

MONTHLY REPORT OF GIVING

		1	2	3	1	2	3	1	2	3	1	2	3	SUN.
COL. 1	CURRENT EXPENSES OR UNIFIED BUDGET													1
														2
COL. 2	BENEVOLENCES OR													3
														4
COL. 3	BUILDING FUND OR													5
														TOTAL PAID
														PLEDGE DATE
														PAID DATE
		5th MONTH			6th MONTH			7th MONTH			8th MONTH			BAL.

COL. 1 CURRENT EXPENSES OR UNIFIED BUDGET $ $
COL. 2 BENEVOLENCES OR $ $
COL. 3 BUILDING FUND OR $ $

COMMITMENT:
☐ WEEKLY
☐ MONTHLY
☐

DATE	DESIGNATED GIFTS & SPECIAL OFFERINGS	AMOUNT
	TOTAL ▶	

WE ACKNOWLEDGE WITH APPRECIATION YOUR GIFTS AS RECORDED. REGULAR CONTRIBUTIONS ENABLE US TO MEET OUR FINANCIAL OBLIGATIONS PROMPTLY. CONTACT THE FINANCIAL OFFICER IF YOU HAVE QUESTIONS REGARDING THIS REPORT

CHURCH:
This is 5 months' contribution

PLEASE RETAIN FOR INCOME TAX REFERENCE

OFFICER'S INITIALS   DATE

YR.
MO.

↰FOLD HERE

ENV. NO.

MONTHLY REPORT OF GIVING

		1	2	3	1	2	3	1	2	3	1	2	3	SUN.
COL. 1	CURRENT EXPENSES OR UNIFIED BUDGET													1
														2
COL. 2	BENEVOLENCES OR													3
														4
COL. 3	BUILDING FUND OR													5
														TOTAL PAID
														PLEDGE DATE
														PAID DATE
		1st MONTH			2nd MONTH			3rd MONTH			4th MONTH			BAL.

COL. 1 CURRENT EXPENSES OR UNIFIED BUDGET $ $
COL. 2 BENEVOLENCES OR $ $
COL. 3 BUILDING FUND OR $ $

COMMITMENT:
☐ WEEKLY
☐ MONTHLY
☐

DATE	DESIGNATED GIFTS & SPECIAL OFFERINGS	AMOUNT
	TOTAL ▶	

WE ACKNOWLEDGE WITH APPRECIATION YOUR GIFTS AS RECORDED. REGULAR CONTRIBUTIONS ENABLE US TO MEET OUR FINANCIAL OBLIGATIONS PROMPTLY. CONTACT THE FINANCIAL OFFICER IF YOU HAVE QUESTIONS REGARDING THIS REPORT.

CHURCH:
This is 1 months' contribution

OFFICER'S INITIALS   DATE

YR.
MO.

PLEASE RETAIN FOR INCOME TAX REFERENCE

↰FOLD HERE

CASH RECEIPTS JOURNAL

CHURCH_____

MONTH/YEAR_____

	DATE	CASH RECEIPTS VOUCHER NO.	DEPOSITED IN BANK	ENVELOPES, PLEDGES, & TITHES	LOOSE PLATE OFFERING	CHURCH SCHOOL	OTHER INCOME	
							DESCRIPTION	AM
1								
2								
3								
4								
5								
6								
7								
8								
9								
10								
11								
12								
13								
14								
15								
16								
17								
18								
19								
20								
21								
22								
23								
24								
25								
26								
27								
28								
29								
30								
31								
32								
33								
34								
35								

DESIGNATED GIFTS AND SPECIAL OFFERINGS								
DESCRIPTION	AMOUNT							
								1
								2
								3
								4
								5
								6
								7
								8
								9
								10
								11
								12
								13
								14
								15
								16
								17
								18
								19
								20
								21
								22
								23
								24
								25
								26
								27
								28
								29
								30
								31
								32
								33
								34
								35

CASH DISBURSEMENTS JOURNAL

CHURCH_____

MONTH/YEAR_____

	DATE		PAYEE	CHECK NO.	(1) CASH CREDIT AMOUNT	(2) PAYROLL TAXES WITHHELD CREDIT (DEBIT)* CODE	AMOUNT	(3) OTHER PAYROLL DEDUCTIONS CREDIT (DEBIT)* CODE	AMOUNT	(4) CAPITOL EXPENSES DEBIT CODE	AMOUNT	(5) PROGRA EXPENS DEBIT CODE	AMO
1													
2													
3													
4													
5													
6													
7													
8													
9													
10													
11													
12													
13													
14													
15													
16													
17													
18													
19													
20													
21													
22													
23													
24													
25													
26													
27													
28													
29													
30													
31													
32													
33													
34													
35													

*PAYMENT OF TAXES WITHHELD AND OTHER PAYROLL DEDUCTIONS TO BE SHOWN IN BRACKETS ( ) IN THESE COLUMNS. WHEN TOTALING, SUBTRACT AMOUNTS IN BRACKETS.

NO. 430437

(6)	(7)		(8)		(9)		(10)		(11)		(12)		(13)		(14)		
RATING PENSE	MINISTERIAL SUPPORT		CONNECTIONAL ADMINISTRATION		BENEVOLENCES		DESIGNATED GIFTS AND SPECIAL OFFERINGS										
EBIT	DEBIT		DEBIT		DEBIT		DEBIT		DEBIT		DEBIT						
AMOUNT	CODE	AMOUNT	CODE	AMOUNT	CODE	AMOUNT	CODE	AMOUNT	CODE	AMOUNT	CODE	AMOUNT	CODE	AMOUNT	CODE	AMOUNT	
																	1
																	2
																	3
																	4
																	5
																	6
																	7
																	8
																	9
																	10
																	11
																	12
																	13
																	14
																	15
																	16
																	17
																	18
																	19
																	20
																	21
																	22
																	23
																	24
																	25
																	26
																	27
																	28
																	29
																	30
																	31
																	32
																	33
																	34
																	35

THE UNITED METHODIST CHURCH

COMMITTEE ON FINANCE
ADMINISTRATIVE BOARD/COUNCIL
and CHARGE CONFERENCE

Treasurer's Report

For the period from _____ , 19____ to_____ , 19____

Church_____

This report form is intended for use as the Treasurer's Report to the Committee on Finance, the Administrative Board/ Council, and when requested, to the Charge Conference. When submitted to the Charge Conference, copies should be prepared for the Recording Secretary, the Pastor, the District Superintendent, and the Treasurer.

CODE	ACCOUNT	ANNUAL APPROVED BUDGET	THIS MONTH	YEAR-TO-DATE	Y-T-D% of BUDGET or BUDGET BALANCE
	CASH BALANCE—Beginning of Period		____	____	
	RECEIPTS				
	Budgeted:				
	Envelopes, Pledges, Tithes	____	____	____	____
	Loose Plate Offering	____	____	____	____
	Church School	____	____	____	____
	Other:				
	_____	____	____	____	____
	_____	____	____	____	____
	_____	____	____	____	____
	_____	____	____	____	____
	_____	____	____	____	____
	_____	____	____	____	____
	Total Budgeted	____	____	____	____
	Unbudgeted:				
	Designated Gifts and				
	Special Offerings:				
	_____	XXXXXX	____	____	XXXXX
	_____	XXXXXX	____	____	XXXXX
	_____	XXXXXX	____	____	XXXXX
	_____	XXXXXX	____	____	XXXXX
	_____	XXXXXX	____	____	XXXXX
	_____	XXXXXX	____	____	XXXXX
	_____	XXXXXX	____	____	XXXXX
	Total Designated Gifts and Special Offerings	XXXXXX	____	____	XXXXX
	TOTAL RECEIPTS	XXXXXX	____	____	XXXXX
	TOTAL AVAILABLE FUNDS	XXXXXX	____	____	XXXXX
	DISBURSEMENTS				
	Budgeted:				
	Debt Retirement	____	____	____	____
	Capital Improvements				
	(See Instructions)	____	____	____	____
	Program Expense:				
	Nurture and Membership Care	____	____	____	____
	Outreach	____	____	____	____

C O D E	ACCOUNT	ANNUAL APPROVED BUDGET	THIS MONTH	YEAR-TO-DATE	Y-T-D% of BUDGET or BUDGET BALANCE
	(Budgeted Disbursements, Cont'd.)				
	Christian Unity & Interreligious Concerns	‗‗‗	‗‗‗	‗‗‗	‗‗‗
	Church and Society	‗‗‗	‗‗‗	‗‗‗	‗‗‗
	Education/Church School	‗‗‗	‗‗‗	‗‗‗	‗‗‗
	Evangelism	‗‗‗	‗‗‗	‗‗‗	‗‗‗
	Higher Education & Campus Ministry	‗‗‗	‗‗‗	‗‗‗	‗‗‗
	Missions	‗‗‗	‗‗‗	‗‗‗	‗‗‗
	Religion and Race	‗‗‗	‗‗‗	‗‗‗	‗‗‗
	Stewardship	‗‗‗	‗‗‗	‗‗‗	‗‗‗
	Worship	‗‗‗	‗‗‗	‗‗‗	‗‗‗
	Other Program:				
	‗‗‗‗‗‗‗‗‗	‗‗‗	‗‗‗	‗‗‗	‗‗‗
	Total Program Expense	‗‗‗	‗‗‗	‗‗‗	
	Operating Expense:				
	Finance Committee	‗‗‗	‗‗‗	‗‗‗	‗‗‗
	Lay Employee Benefits	‗‗‗	‗‗‗	‗‗‗	‗‗‗
	Office Expenses:				
	‗‗‗‗‗‗‗‗‗	‗‗‗	‗‗‗	‗‗‗	‗‗‗
	‗‗‗‗‗‗‗‗‗	‗‗‗	‗‗‗	‗‗‗	‗‗‗
	‗‗‗‗‗‗‗‗‗	‗‗‗	‗‗‗	‗‗‗	‗‗‗
	Property Maintenance:				
	‗‗‗‗‗‗‗‗‗	‗‗‗	‗‗‗	‗‗‗	‗‗‗
	‗‗‗‗‗‗‗‗‗	‗‗‗	‗‗‗	‗‗‗	‗‗‗
	‗‗‗‗‗‗‗‗‗	‗‗‗	‗‗‗	‗‗‗	‗‗‗
	‗‗‗‗‗‗‗‗‗	‗‗‗	‗‗‗	‗‗‗	‗‗‗
	Insurance—Property & Liability	‗‗‗	‗‗‗	‗‗‗	‗‗‗
	Real Estate Taxes/ Assessments	‗‗‗	‗‗‗	‗‗‗	‗‗‗
	Church Electricity, Heat, and Water	‗‗‗	‗‗‗	‗‗‗	‗‗‗
	Other Operating Expense:				
	‗‗‗‗‗‗‗‗‗	‗‗‗	‗‗‗	‗‗‗	‗‗‗
	‗‗‗‗‗‗‗‗‗	‗‗‗	‗‗‗	‗‗‗	‗‗‗
	Total Operating Expense	‗‗‗	‗‗‗	‗‗‗	
	Pastoral Support:				
	Pastoral Support-Local Church:				
	Pastor's Salary	‗‗‗	‗‗‗	‗‗‗	‗‗‗
	Associate's(s') Salary	‗‗‗	‗‗‗	‗‗‗	‗‗‗
	Utilities and Other Cash Allowances:				
	Pastor	‗‗‗	‗‗‗	‗‗‗	‗‗‗
	Associate(s)	‗‗‗	‗‗‗	‗‗‗	‗‗‗
	Travel:				
	Pastor	‗‗‗	‗‗‗	‗‗‗	‗‗‗
	Associate(s)	‗‗‗	‗‗‗	‗‗‗	‗‗‗

CODE	ACCOUNT	ANNUAL APPROVED BUDGET	THIS MONTH	YEAR-TO-DATE	Y-T-D% of BUDGET or BUDGET BALANCE
	(Budgeted Disbursements, Cont'd.) Pastoral Support— Other Than Local Church:				
	Total Pastoral Support				
	Connectional Administration Fund(s): _____				
	Total Connectional Administration				
	Benevolences:				
	World Service and Conference Benevolences				
	Ministerial Education Fund				
	Black College Fund				
	Missional Priority Fund				
	General Advance Specials				
	World Service Special Gifts				
	General Church Offerings				
	Conference Advance Specials				
	Other Benevolences:				
	Total Benevolences				
	Total Budgeted Disbursements				
	Net of Payroll Taxes (Withheld)/Paid		(_____)	(_____)	
	Net Budgeted Disbursements				
	Unbudgeted:				
	Designated Gifts and Special Offerings:				
		XXXXXX			XXXXX
		XXXXXX			XXXXX
		XXXXXX			XXXXX
		XXXXXX			XXXXX
		XXXXXX			XXXXX
		XXXXXX			XXXXX
		XXXXXX			XXXXX
		XXXXXX			XXXXX
	Total Designated Gifts and Special Offerings				XXXXX
	TOTAL DISBURSEMENTS	XXXXXX			XXXXX

C O D E	ACCOUNT	ANNUAL APPROVED BUDGET	THIS MONTH	YEAR-TO-DATE	Y-T-D% of BUDGET or BUDGET BALANCE
	TOTAL CASH BALANCE, END OF PERIOD (Total Available Funds, less Total Disbursements)	XXXXXX	————	————	XXXXX
	Less:				
	Designated Gifts and Special Offerings Rec'd. but not Disbursed—This Month	XXXXXX		————	XXXXX
	Designated Gifts and Special Offerings Previous Month(s)— Still on Hand	XXXXXX		————	XXXXX
	Total Designated Gifts and Special Offerings on Hand	XXXXXX		(————)	XXXXX
	NET AVAILABLE CASH	XXXXXX		————	XXXXX

Worksheet

Worksheet

_____

_____

_____

_____

_____

_____

_____

_____

_____

_____

_____

_____

_____

_____

_____

_____

_____

_____

prepare a separate report or to work with the other treasurers in preparing a joint report. If separate reports are prepared by various treasurers, they should work together to prepare a consolidated report, at least at the end of each year.

Since the report is a summary of financial transactions for a particular month and for the year to date, it can double as a general ledger for many churches; that is, the function usually served by a general ledger in a financial record system will be served by a file of monthly treasurer's reports prepared with this form. For churches that have a complex account structure, a separate general ledger probably will be required, but many churches should find the extra step of maintaining a general ledger unnecessary.

Very small and very large churches may wish to prepare for their own use either a simplified or expanded version of this form. If this approach is taken, it is recommended that the basic outline of this report form be followed, with a smaller or larger number of account titles being entered as appropriate for your church.

Instructions for Using Treasurer's Report

Preparation: To prepare this report form you will need copies of the following: your church's approved budget for the year, your chart of accounts, the cash receipts journal, and the cash disbursements journal for the month.

If this is not the report for the first month of the year, you will also need a copy of your Treasurer's Report from the previous month. Before the Year-to-Date column can be completed, you will need to see that the account classifications used on the previous report are similar to those used on the present form.

First, examine your budget and chart of accounts. Compare them to the account listing on the report form. Your church may not have as many accounts as are included on the report form, or it may have more, but the accounts it has should be comparable to the list on the form. If they are not, you should try to revise your chart of accounts to make it as close to the form as possible. This will make your work easier at the end of the year, since the account classifications on the Treasurer's Report form are designed to feed easily into the Local Church Report to the Annual Conference.

Enter the amount from your church's approved budget in the appropriate spaces in the column headed Annual Approved Budget.

Enter the account numbers you use to designate your various accounts in the Code column.

Enter the appropriate amounts in the line Cash Balance, Beginning of Period. In the This Month column, the figure entered should be the same as the Total Cash Balance, End of Period from your previous report. It should also be the same as the balance from your checkbook (plus any savings account or investment balances) at the beginning of the month. In the Year-to-Date column, the beginning cash balance is the balance at the beginning of your church's fiscal year—usually January 1. *This figure remains the same throughout the year.*

Recording This Month Transactions: Reconcile the bank statement with your checkbook. Prepare the monthly recapitulation on your Cash Receipts Journal and your Cash Disbursements Journal.

Enter the amounts from these recapitulations in the appropriate spaces in the This Month column.

Add the figures entered in the This Month column of the report form to obtain the various subtotals and totals indicated on the form (Total Budgeted Receipts, Total Designated Gifts and Special Offerings Receipts, Total Receipts, Total Program Expenses, Total Operating Expenses, Total Ministerial Support, etc.). Compare these with the corresponding subtotals and totals on the Cash Receipts and Cash Disbursements Journal forms. This serves as a check to make sure no errors have been made in transferring figures from one form to the other. Note that the position of the lines as printed in the column helps to indicate what amounts should be added together for each of the subtotals and totals. To obtain the Total Available Funds figure, add the Cash Balance, Beginning of Period to the Total Receipts.

If your church has employees and deducts certain amounts from their salaries for taxes or other purposes, study the instructions before completing the Budgeted Disbursements section of your report. You may also find it helpful to refer to the instructions for reporting Capital Improvements disbursements and for payments on apportionments.

Subtract the amount of Total Disbursements from the Total Available Funds figure, and enter the difference in the Total Cash Balance, End of Period line. This figure should agree with your checkbook balance, plus savings and other investment balances reflected in this report, at the end of the reporting period.

Under the heading Disbursements Budgeted, the space provided for reporting capital improvements includes the cost of new property and buildings, major purchases of new equipment or furnishings (organs or other musical instruments, heating and cooling equipment, kitchen equipment, audiovisual equipment, furniture), and major renovation. If money for such expenditures is raised separately from the regular budget, that is, if contributors are asked to give money specifically earmarked for those purposes, both the receipts and the expenditures should be reported in the unbudgeted sections of the report form.

Beginning with Pastoral Support—Other Than Local Church and continuing through part of the Benevolences section, much of what you report will be payments on apportionments. The number of accounts you use and their titles will depend on your Annual Conference. You should show a separate line on the report for each separate apportionment in your Annual Conference. If your Annual Conference combines two or more funds listed here into one apportionment, simply disregard the lines you do not need.

If you church withholds amounts for taxes or other purposes from any salaries it pays, and if the amounts withheld have already been disbursed to the Internal Revenue Service, state or city revenue agencies, or other agencies, no special reporting is required on this form. If, however, there is an amount that has been withheld but not yet disbursed, that amount should be entered on the line which reads Net of Payroll Taxes (Withheld)/Paid. This amount should then be subtracted from the Total Budgeted Disbursements figure, and the difference should be entered as the Net Budgeted Disbursements. It is this net figure that should be added to the Total Designated Gifts and Special Offerings Disbursements to yield the amount of Total Disbursements.

It may be worthwhile to examine the reason for this procedure. When a salary is paid, the total amount of that salary for the pay period is charged against a budget expense account. However, the check written to the employee is for a smaller amount, the salary less deductions. Unless this difference is taken into account, the checkbook balance and the Total Cash Balance, End of Period line on the Treasurer's Report form will not agree.

Recording Year-to-Date Totals: In the first month of any year, the This Month and Year-to-Date figures will be identical.

For subsequent months, add the This Month figures to the Year-to-Date figures which appear on the previous month's report. This will yield the new Year-to-Date amounts. (Remember that the Cash Balance, Beginning of Period stays the same in the Year-to-Date column for the entire year.)

Be sure all Year-to-Date amounts from the previous report are reflected in the new report; carry forward Year-to-Date figures from the previous month's report for any accounts which had no This Month amounts.

Add the figures in the Year-to-Date column to determine subtotals and totals, following the same procedures used in the This Month column.

The Cash Balance, End of Period amount should be the same in both columns.

The last column on the report (Year-to-Date Percent of Budget or Budgeted Balance) allows you to show how actual expenditures compare with the approved budget. This can be done in either of two ways: (1) calculate the percentage of the annual approved budget represented by the Year-to-Date amount for each budgeted item, and enter that percentage in this column, or (2) subtract the Year-to-Date amount from the annual approved budget, and enter the difference in this column.

Following the Total Cash Balance, End of Period line is a section of the form which will enable you to determine and report how much of the cash balance is available for use—that is, not designated for some specific purpose. From time to time churches receive special offerings or gifts designated by their donor for a specific purpose. As a matter of principle, these monies should be disbursed for the purpose for which they were intended as quickly as possible. There will be occasions, however, when a reporting period will close with such monies still on hand. Enter the total of such special offerings and designated gifts received but not yet disbursed in the two spaces provided. Subtract the Total Designated Gifts and Special Offerings On Hand from the Total Cash Balance, End of Period. The resulting difference should be entered as Net Available Cash.

The Budget Process

Two basic functions of a church budget are (1) to set realistic goals and objectives for the coming year or years, and (2) to monitor the financial activities of the congregation during the term of the budget. The first function is as important as the second, for without realistic goals a budget may be ineffective for monitoring costs.

A budget should not be prepared by only one person. The process should be a joint effort, actually involving as many people as is practically possible. If the budget is to be a plan of action by which the congregation's program and outreach during the next year is determined, then it must involve the membership all the way from its inception to its final outline as well. Of course, that may not be the easiest way to put a budget together, but it certainly is a necessary procedure if the budget is to represent what your congregation wants.

Listing objectives: Thus, a list of objectives and goals must be agreed upon. Before any dollars are attached to the costs of any programs, your congregation must agree on where it wants to go, what it intends to do, and whether or not existing programs should be continued, expanded, or discarded. Maybe you will only reevaluate what you already have. Maybe you will toss something out which no longer serves a useful purpose although it may have done so in the past. Maybe you will keep the things that are working well and attempt to develop new ideas to replace what hasn't turned out so well in the past.

One way to develop that scheme of goals is to form a large budget planning committee, a committee that can dream dreams they never thought possible to achieve in your congregation (and maybe they still aren't possible). A good cross section of the membership can be called together for one or two meetings just to brainstorm where the congregation should be going. Perhaps as many as forty could attend.

But, prior to that first meeting, someone should prepare an accurate fact sheet about where the congregation has been and what it is doing now. That's so the entire committee will have the same basic information and assumptions about what has been going on.

Knowing what resources are possible and what the congregation's financial history has been can be most helpful to your budget planning committee as it attempts to make its decisions about next year's program.

A planning resource worksheet: At the first meeting of that larger committee, but before any of these facts are made available to the whole membership, the members should be given an opportunity to fill in their individual copies of a planning resource worksheet. This is a listing of all those things those members think their congregation should be doing now or sometime with respect to program.

You can make your own listing of items and questions. Or let the group come up with their own questions. Then, on the worksheet, have columns that can be checked: "O.K., Needs attention, No need, Don't know." Using each one of the program areas, review what you are doing and what you would like to do.

Money is not a consideration at the moment, although it obviously will be for implementing any new programs. However, at the meetings the membership should be encouraged to be creative, freely expressing their attitudes about what they think is and should be happening in their congregation irrespective of the costs.

You will quickly learn that such an activity will use up at least a full evening's meeting. But it can be an exciting time just to dream!

Another meeting might be needed to review the decisions reached or opinions registered at the initial gathering and to draw up a summary statement.

Then the committee will need to attach some dollars to the dreams. Again, unencumbered by any total anticipated income from offerings, the committee can calculate, as accurately as possible, the basic costs for all the programs thought most desirable by a majority of the group. Dollar costs for every program mentioned could be determined, but a realistic appraisal of available resources will quickly show that only a small number of programs can be implemented. Thus, concentration on the more popular suggestions may be the most useful.

It may also be useful to try to agree on some priority listing for all of those suggestions. Sometime someone is going to have to list a proposal of programs and costs that fits into anticipated resources. At this session, therefore, dollar amounts and some consensus on priority can be determined.

And yet one more session of this initial planning group may be necessary to develop a formal proposal or series of proposals to be used to challenge your congregation to a generous response in giving. Because only as your congregation is willing to support the program with money will it be able to implement any of these ideas. Proposals to challenge the membership can be put together as a "must" program, a "needed" program, and a "challenge" program.

The membership is challenged by proposals, not by budgets. The final budget is not adopted generally, therefore, until the congregation has expressed its giving intentions. On that basis a budget is finally developed out of all the good ideas pulled together by this initial planning committee.

What kind of budget? *

There are a variety of budgets and approaches to developing the actual budget document, such as program budgets, line budgets, zero-based budgets, unified budgets, capital budgets, debt retirement budgets, and perhaps others.

1. *Line Item Budget*

The budget probably most frequently used in congregations is the line item budget. That's a budget that lists in line after line the dollars to be spent on salaries, utilities, benevolences, evangelism, Sunday church school, insurance, mortgage payments, nursery care, repairs, etc. Each line item is carefully defined, costs estimated, and amounts budgeted.

2. *Program Budget*

A program budget offers a significant opportunity for creative planning and spending. Such budgets are organized to reflect the costs of programs rather than items of expense. All costs required for a particular program are identified with that program. As with a cost accounting system, the program budget attempts to identify every possible cost of the specific programs proposed.

When using such a budget, the cost of a specific program can be measured to determine its effectiveness by asking what has been accomplished. The pastor's salary, for example, is divided proportionately among those programs in which pastoral leadership is involved. The cost of office supplies is allocated to those programs requiring such supplies.

Program budgets begin by establishing a need and by setting goals. Then programs are described that will fulfill those needs and achieve those goals. The form of the budget becomes important as a tool for planning and decision making, for evaluation and for communication. While costs are still clearly shown and detailed for all expenditures, the focus is on fulfilling the life and mission of the congregation in programs.

3. *Zero-based Budget*

A zero-based budget may be either a line or program budget. The concept of zero-based budgeting is to begin the budget-planning process at zero dollars without regard to past experience. The customary process does not begin with the current budget and necessary adjustments.

Zero-based budgeting ignores any existing budget and starts from "scratch." Obviously, programs already in existence are considered, but to be placed on the new budget an item must again be justified as if it were a "new" program, and new costs are estimated. It is not sufficient to agree on continuing a program. Its costs should be fully justified. Zero-based budgeting ignores the principle of adding an inflation rate to last year's cost to arrive at next year's expected cost. Every cost is assumed to be zero unless the amount requested is justified.

4. *Unified Budget*

The most frequent definition of a unified budget is a budget in which all parts of the congregation's receipts and disbursements are listed. It's a budget that includes funds for every program and organization of the congregation.

Thus, with one document, the entire financial activity of the congregation is planned and reviewed. Total resources and planned use of those funds are clearly described and determined. A unified budget eliminates an outgrowth of separate funds and separate goals, special group fund-raising campaigns, competing organizations, and a multiplicity of bank accounts.

With a unified budget, any organization within the congregation may still retain complete control over the use and disbursement of its monies. Yet that organization's resources and its use of funds is appropriately considered as part of the total activity of the congregation. A unified budget presents a total view of the activities of the congregation in contrast to the often partial statement of resource use and allocation represented by separate church budgets. The unified budget includes and presents restricted funds without removing the restrictions under which the funds are placed.

---

*Reprinted and adapted by permission from *Annual Budgeting* by Manfred Holck, Jr., copyright 1977, Augsburg Publishing House, Minneapolis, Minn.

Congregations using a unified budget will maintain a church treasurer as well as treasurers for each organization, if desired. As funds are received, they are deposited in the congregation's bank account and credited to the organization's appropriate account in the congregation's financial records. Disbursements are authorized by voucher from the organization's treasurer but are paid by the church treasurer or other authorized person.

One checking account within the congregation rather than several (1) provides more effective control over cash since only one treasurer is involved, (2) eliminates the possibility of numerous bank service charges on smaller congregational account balances, (3) avoids the potential loss of funds due to treasurers moving or organizations being discontinued, (4) facilitates preparation of bank reconciliations, (5) simplifies financial statement presentations, and (6) assists in providing a more reliable audit report.

The mechanics of setting up a unified budget are much the same as for developing any church budget. However, with a unified budget each organization and each group specifies its own anticipated receipts and disbursements which are then added to the total congregational budget.

A unified budget is relatively simple to develop. Procedures for accounting for the funds of all of the groups in the congregation may be more difficult.

5. *Capital Budget*

A capital budget specifies sources and uses of funds for a certain building project or major repair project. It carefully describes how the project will be financed. In Luke 14:28 Jesus said, "For which of you, desiring to build a tower, does not first sit down and count the cost, whether he has enough to complete it?"

Capital budgets tend to be line item budgets because they list, item by item, how the funds are going to be spent for land, construction, landscaping, fees, furniture, interest, and other costs. Accounting procedures—releasing these funds under controlled appropriations—prevent overspending, avoid multiple authorizations, and assure the congregation of careful trusteeship of funds.

Budgets for major capital projects are kept separate from benevolence or current operating budgets of the congregation. The life of the capital budget extends until the project is completed and the costs are paid.

6. *Debt Retirement Budget*

A debt retirement budget specifies the way in which the congregation expects to meet its debt commitments on a building or other major project. Such budgets are created for the life of the loans involved.

Initial funds for a capital project may be secured through special fund-raising programs, the sale of land, a bequest, special gifts, or other sources. Budgeting for the use of funds from all sources is the purpose of a debt retirement budget. And even though those same funds may appear in a capital project budget, their inclusion as a source of funds in the debt retirement budget is important, too.

Funds are often accumulated before they are needed for a specific capital project. Thus, a fund-raising campaign for a building project may be undertaken several years before construction is begun. In the meantime, money accumulates in the fund.

It is important that those funds earn as much interest as possible during the interim, since interest income will add to the total funds available. But the way in which those funds are invested is important. Investment objectives will be to seek the highest possible return, necessary liquidity, and the least amount of risk. Certainly, the principal amount of the fund cannot be jeopardized.

When the money will not be needed for some time, government securities and certificates of deposit at federally insured savings and loan institutions may provide maximum return and safety. For less than ninety-day investments a passbook savings account used to suffice, now interest-bearing checking accounts or money market deposit accounts ought to be used. Congregational leaders should explore various investment alternatives. At no time, however, should capital project funds be placed in common stocks or other speculative securities where there is a possibility for loss in value and no guarantee of income.

Congregations may be required to establish a sinking fund in conjunction with a debt retirement program. Such funds are for the purpose of accumulating the money needed to meet irregular or bond redemption requirements. Sinking fund requirements are budgeted so that sufficient money is available each year to deposit into the fund. The appropriate place for such budgeting is a debt retirement budget, although current operating budgets may frequently be used to show sinking fund appropriations. Normally, sinking fund requirements are set by the bond indenture document and administered by a bank trust officer.

The amortization of indebtedness involves payment on a mortgage. Obviously, that periodic cost must be budgeted.

LINE ITEM BUDGET AND PROGRAM BUDGET COMPARED

The Line Item Budget

The Budget of Our Church

For Outreach—

Worldwide	$ 3,000	
National	5,000	
Local	2,000	$ 10,000

For Program—

Christian education	$ 1,000	
Worship and music	800	
Service ministry	500	
Stewardship	500	
Evangelism	300	3,100

For Administration—

Travel allowances	$ 2,500	
Office supplies	1,000	
Building maintenance	1,000	
Utilities	3,000	
Insurance	1,000	8,500

For Debt Retirement—

Church building	$ 6,000	
Parsonage	2,500	8,500

Staff salaries—	29,000
Employee benefits—	6,000
Total budget	$ 65,100

The Program Budget

The Budget for Our Church

Mission to the World—

Worldwide	$ 3,000	
National	5,000	
Local	2,000	$ 10,000

Mission to the Community—

Among the people (Evangelism)	$ 8,350	
In the community (Ecumenical)	1,250	
For the needs of others (Service)	5,750	15,350

Mission to Ourselves—

Education & youth	$ 8,800	
Worship & music	11,950	
Pastoral concerns (visitation)	8,000	
Property maintenance	5,000	
Debt management	6,000	39,750

Total budget	$ 65,100

193

Specific cost allocations:

1. Costs for pastor

Salary		$ 17,000
Employee benefits		3,000
Travel allowance		2,500
Parsonage debt		2,500
		$ 25,000

2. Time allocation for pastor

Evangelism	25%	$ 6,250
Ecumenical	5%	1,250
Service	15%	3,750
Teaching	10%	2,500
Worship	25%	6,250
Visitation	20%	5,000
		$ 25,000

3. Costs for staff

Salaries		$ 12,000
Benefits		3,000
		$ 15,000

4. Time allocation

Evangelism	10%	$ 1,500
Service	10%	1,500
Teaching	30%	4,500
Worship	30%	4,500
Visitation	20%	3,000
		$ 15,000

5. Evangelism

Pastor	$ 6,250
Staff	1,500
Office supplies	300
Program	300
	$ 8,350

6. Ecumenical

Pastor	$ 1,250

7. Service

Pastor	$ 3,750
Staff	1,500
Program	500
	$ 5,750

8. Education

Pastor	$ 2,500
Staff	4,500
Stewardship	500
Office supplies	300
Program	1,000
	$ 8,800

9. Worship

Pastor	$ 6,250
Staff	4,500
Program	800
Office supplies	400
	$ 11,950

10. Pastoral concerns

Pastor	$ 5,000
Staff	3,000
	$8,000

11. Property

Maintenance	$ 1,000
Utilities	3,000
Insurance	1,000
	$ 5,000

12. Debt retirement

Building mortgage	$ 6,000

Budget Worksheet Columnar Headings

Item	Actual 11 mos.	This year est. 1 mo.	Total	This year	Budget	Next-year Budget		
						Minimum	Proposed	Final

Cash Flow Worksheet Columnar Headings

Items from Budget	Total	J	F	M	A	M	J	J	A	S	O	N	D	Total

The Church Audit

Whether your congregation insists on an annual audit or not is the choice you have to make. Audits may cost money. They do take time when done right. The value derived weighed against costs incurred must be carefully considered. Not every congregation has an annual audit. Some *never* do, unfortunately.

Generally, an audit is a series of procedures that test, on a predetermined selective basis, the various transactions occurring in the last year—verifying internal control methods and generally forming an opinion about the financial statements presented. An audit does not guarantee that every transaction was accurately recorded. It is no proof that all funds were handled appropriately.

An audit is an opinion. Through a series of tests, inquiries, and probing investigations, the auditor or auditing committee decides if, based on the information given to them, the financial reports do fairly represent the financial condition of the congregation. Based on a testing of selected transactions—checks written and deposits made—and on their own experiences of similar institutions, the auditors state as precisely as they can if things seem to be in order.

The typical audit may be thought of as one conducted by an independent outside auditor, for a fee, similar to that used by business enterprises. Called an external audit, the examination of the financial records is done by someone hired for that purpose, usually a Certified Public Accountant. The auditor has no relationship to the organization and can review the records and procedures without any interest in the outcome.

An internal audit, on the other hand, is generally performed by a committee of members selected for that purpose. The audit committee's function generally is to make certain, as best they can, that all receipts have been properly deposited in the bank and recorded and that all disbursements have been properly approved. The intensity of such an audit is much less than an external audit. In addition, an internal audit may be an ongoing process of periodic checks and reviews of procedures by the audit committee.

A program audit reviews the attainment of program goals, variances from scheduled objectives. It attempts to evaluate program growth rather than only financial growth. When a master plan has been developed, progress toward those goals can be measured. A program audit checks it out. It monitors progress.

Procedures for an audit committee

Under the direction of the finance committee, the audit committee will have responsibility for examining and reviewing all records and accounts, all insurance policies, records of securities, real estate records, inventories and records of other investments; preparing schedules and reports; and recommending changes and suggestions for improvements to the finance committee. Specific auditing procedures include the following steps:

1. *Cash receipts*

Your committee will need to review the methods for handling monies received from worship service offerings as well as in the mails, trace the amounts so received to the cash receipts journal, compare the entries in the journal with the duplicate deposit slips, and examine the transaction record for proper account classification.

The audit committee will also trace the deposits from the counter's reports to the journal and compare these entries with the deposits actually recorded by the bank. At the same time, it will check the timeliness of the deposit, check the account distribution in the cash receipts journal and check the use of the money received for specific purposes to make certain it got into the proper fund.

2. *Cash expenditures*

All cash disbursements (checks or cash) must be recorded in the cash disbursements journal showing the date, check number, the name of the payee, the amount of the check, and the distribution to the proper account classification.

Then, the audit committee must test-check the bookkeeping entries in the journal for proper recording in the appropriate class of expenditure.

The committee will also foot (add) the journal for mathematical accuracy; examine the authority for writing a check, the authority for approving the payment of invoices, the records of a minister's call, including the current salary and housing arrangements, the adequacy of contract agreements, the action of the official board in their minutes; and verify that the checks written for expenses were actually paid to the proper parties.

If prenumbered checks are used (as they should be), the committee must account for all checks used. If the treasurer has not already done so, the committee should prepare a statement of expenditures for comparison with the adopted budget for the year, as well as analyze expenditures for major improvements, refurbishings, and new equipment for additions to asset accounts.

3. *Bank statement reconciliation*

The audit committee, rather than some other group or individual, should prepare the year-ending reconciliation between the bank balance and the balance shown on the books.

The reconciliation begins with the bank balance, to which is added deposits shown on the books but not yet credited on the bank statement. Outstanding checks are then subtracted to prove the book balance.

In the process of preparing the reconciliation, the committee must also verify on a test-check basis that proper endorsements are on the cancelled checks.

Furthermore, a request to the bank to confirm by direct written confirmation the balances held in the commercial and/or savings accounts is a normal and important procedure. An inspection of bank signature cards for approved signatures will make certain the proper people are writing the checks.

4. *Petty cash funds*

Petty cash funds are difficult to control. Thus proper checks by the committee are important. The committee must determine that disbursement vouchers have proper approval, that reimbursements to the fund are made properly, that maximum figures for individual payments have been established and that there is adequate approval for advances to employees and for IOU's.

5. *Individual member contributions records*

The committee should compare pledge amounts with signed pledges, if any. A test-check of the financial secretary's posting of contributions to the members' records will verify accuracy.

6. *Insurance policies*

A check of all church insurance in force should be made. A schedule of coverages can be completed by the committee to show effective and expiration dates, kind and classification of coverages, maximum amounts of each coverage, premium amounts, and terms of payment. If there is an insurance appraisal, it should be compared with actual insurance coverage.

7. *Amortization of debt*

The committee must verify balances owing to all lenders by a direct confirmation, in writing. It must also review the terms of the loans and prepare a schedule of delinquencies, if any.

8. *Securities and other investments*

The committee must count all securities by the identifying number of certificates or accounts, and then prepare a schedule listing the numbers and amounts for each security. The committee must also make certain that all securities are in the name of the church. It will set forth the pertinent facts concerning other investments such as notes, mortgages, and real estate.

9. *Finally*

The committee should write a letter to the official board outlining their findings and their recommendations for any changes.

CHAPTER 10

FUND-RAISING AND STEWARDSHIP DEVELOPMENT

by Ashley Hale

By FUND-RAISING we mean securing capital funds, or at least funds outside the annual operating budget. Fund-raising and stewardship development have an area of overlap. But a stewardship campaign for building funds would be an anomaly and a building fund-raising campaign that aimed principally to improve the members' understanding of Christian giving would be mighty poor fund-raising.

Fund-raising seeks specific, dollar-amount, usually short-term contributions—gifts and pledges; whereas, stewardship development seeks to upgrade an understanding of giving performance. Fund-raising commitments always have an ending date; whereas, ideally, stewardship commitments are open-ended. Fund-raising tends to distribute the organization's time and energy according to the dollar amounts anticipated (hence, its characteristic emphasis upon the size, rather than the number of gifts); whereas, stewardship development distributes its time and attention more according to the number of gifts.

Fund-raising is especially concerned about gifts from capital to capital; whereas, stewardship development is concerned mostly with gifts from income, and the operations of the church are financed principally by contributions from the members' income. But take building funds for instance: the great church structures of the world were built mostly by gifts from capital. In cases where they were not, the fund-raising usually went on for centuries.

Income to income and capital to capital isn't an ironbound rule, but it's an important distinction that we should keep in mind when considering capital fund-raising.

Yet, these two areas of the church's concern are not mutually exclusive; in fact, they support each other. Good fund-raising promotes better stewardship understanding and performance through the experience of better giving. Better stewardship understanding promotes better fund-raising.

This second statement, that better stewardship promotes better fund-raising, has a solid statistical base. Analysis of many church building-fund campaigns shows that two churches otherwise identical, but one has a higher standard of giving to its budget—the higher budget-giving church can raise more for a building fund.

One might think that the more the members were giving to operations, the less of their money would be available for a capital-fund campaign. But the reverse is true.

Ashley Hale is managing partner of the Church Development Center, San Jacinto, California.

Fund-raising

Your fund-raising potential

The ability of your congregation to contribute to a capital fund over a period of a few years is at least equal to its accustomed budget giving over the same period of time. To make a rough estimate of your short-term capital-fund potential, jot down the dollar amount that your members are now giving, undesignated, to annual operations. Don't include special appeals, earned income, endowment yield, loose plate, or contributions from organizations of the church. Multiply that figure by three and jot that figure down.

You now have a rough, a very rough, estimate of what your congregation could give in a capital-fund campaign—for instance, a building fund—over a period of three years. In other words, your members could give about as much to a building fund over the next three years as they will give, undesignated, to the budget.

Two-thirds of the churches in the United States and Canada can do that well. One sixth can do more. Another sixth can do much more—as much as two or three times more.

These statements about your church's capital fund-raising potential are based on computerized analysis of 5,500 professionally managed church building-fund campaigns for three-year pledges.

So you are probably safe to project that, in any period of three to five years, your capital fund-raising potential is at least the equal of what undesignated contributions to operations will be over the same period. Even that amount, however, does not reveal your full capital fund-raising capability because there is also the matter of your long-range potential.

The largest gifts are seldom produced by campaigns. Instead, they are the result of long-range, patient, highly-individualized cultivation. These mega-gifts are always made principally from capital.

Americans left bequests totaling $5.45 billion to nonprofit organizations in 1982. Thirty-seven of these were for more than a million dollars; they totaled $1.5 billion. We do not know how much of the total $5.45 billion went to churches but we do know how many of the thirty-seven largest did. None. Not one of these $1 million-plus bequests went to religion on any level—national, regional, or local.*

The pastor concerned with balancing this year's operating budget may not be seeking a million-dollar gift or bequest. But there is no reason why most churches should not occasionally receive a gift or bequest to its permanent endowment fund of about the amount of its annual operating budget. The only reason that gifts and bequests of this size are not more common among the churches is that nobody is being asked seriously to consider making them.

The potential is there. One out of every four hundred and twenty-six of your members is probably a millionnaire (the national average).

Seven elements of fund-raising power

One reason that your fund-raising potential may be larger than you think is that your members have more money than you may think. A second reason is that they like to give and do give more than you may know. Americans gave $60 billion to nonprofit organizations in 1982. It is a sobering experience to read in the paper one morning that a family giving $10 a week to the church has given $1 million to his alma mater or to her pet charity.

There is a third reason for your large potential: that you have laity of considerable fund-raising ability, even though neither you nor they know it. This latent power is revealed only when you do the seven things that use it. They are:

---

*Statistics from "Giving, USA," 1983 edition, published by the American Association of Fund-raising Counsel, Inc.

a. *Full goal.* Publish and seek the full amount that you need or want. Don't compromise the goal for fear of failure. The idea isn't to win but to achieve. Only a big goal will call out the best abilities of your most capable laity. Only a big goal will command the respectful attention of the members. Easily achieved goals have no value other than for pleasant retrospective contemplation. To paraphrase, don't make little plans. They have no magic to stir the blood of men or women.

b. *Resolve.* Strong resolve is everything. "And for the support of this declaration, with a firm Reliance on the Protection of divine Providence, we mutually pledge to each other our lives, our Fortunes, and our sacred Honor." Two centuries ago that proved a good way to start a new country. Today it is a good spirit in which to start a significant fund-raising campaign.

c. *Selected lay leadership.* Fund-raising is basically a lay responsibility. Select for each individual position of leadership in fund-raising the one person in the congregation who is best qualified for it. Don't run with any other than first-choice leadership. You don't have to. You are the church.

d. *Pledge.* Raising cash is no test of a church's fund-raising capability, nor of the giving potential of any of its families. In reaching for a high goal, use three-year pledges. For less than all-out goals, reduce the pledge payment period. But, except for minor fund-raising programs, always emphasize pledges, not cash gifts.

e. *Personal conversations.* "Great gifts," said Bishop William Lawrence, the foremost turn-of-the-century personal fund-raiser, "are the result of great conversations." In a major church building-fund campaign, the typical family will make the largest gift that it has ever made to anything. Decisions of this magnitude are not made lightly. Indeed, they are usually made only after much thought, discussion, prayer, and even agony.

The seriousness of the families' decisions merit the personal, individual attention of the church. Preaching, letters, booklets—these are necessarily addressed "to whom it may concern." It is as though all families faced the same situation and wrestled with the same problems in deciding how much to give. But this obviously is not so. Each individual situation is different—even unique.

Therefore provide for each family to make its giving decision in its own home with the advice and guidance of a member whom they respect and who has already made his own exemplary gift. There are various ways to organize these conversations, but what is important is that they happen.

f. *Suggested askings.* It is not sufficiently helpful to suggest that the family should give generously, or sacrificially, or "as the Lord has blessed you." The family decision cannot be an adverb; it must be a dollar amount. Therefore work out specific dollar-amount suggestions for the individual families. These can be developed through general guidelines but should be made as specific as possible. These amounts are never presented as more than helpful suggestions, in the spirit of, "perhaps you may want to consider . . . ."

g. *Advance gifts.* Before the campaign officially opens, secure the pledges of those families who can make the largest gifts and of some others who can be expected to respond generously. These can serve as important, helpful guides and models for the balance of the congregation. It is especially encouraging if, as the campaign opens, you can report that 10 percent or 15 percent of the families have already contributed half of the total goal. This can more often be accomplished than you might think. Be aware, again, of the difference between the every-member canvass and a capital-funds campaign.

Those who make the early, exemplary gifts should constitute the nucleus of your campaign organization.

Five levels of aspiration

You can raise a small capital fund by passing the plate one more time or sending a congregational mailing or two. It is not worthwhile to organize for such modest objectives. At the other extreme, in building a new church or relocating, even a professionally managed campaign for three-year pledges will not alone suffice because the total requirement is more than the members can give within three years.

In computing the potential of a church or, as they say in gymnastics, "degree of difficulty," we use the established giving habit of the congregation as a base. This is the amount that the members are giving, undesignated, to the annual operating budget. It does not include special appeals, earned income, endowment fund yield, gifts of church organizations, or anything other than just plain, direct giving of resident members. Whatever that amount for your church (you jotted it down at the beginning of this chapter), let's call that "the budget" even though that isn't accurate. Now, all goals can be expressed in "times the budget." You may remember that we said earlier that a professionally managed building-fund campaign should raise at least three times the budget.

Of the five levels, let's start with the most modest. For this you need not organize at all. A simple offering will probably do. To organize and visit in the homes would be like using a sledge hammer to drive a carpet tack. Pledges are not necessary.

Between level 1 on the table (Offering) and level 4 (Campaign) you have two options: reduce the pledge-payment period or the number of home visits for pledges. Use whatever pledge-payment period you think appropriate to the goal. Taking your three-year (thirty-six months) potential as 100 percent, the amount that you can raise, as a percentage of your full potential, looks like this:

Pledge-payment period (months)	% of potential
36	100. %
24	72.5
12	40.
6	25.

The other alternative, to reduce the number of home visits, should be conducted the opposite of the way you probably conduct your annual every-member canvass. In the conventional EMC, the church mails the pledge cards and then organizes for home visits to those families that do not respond. You thus spend 85 percent of your time and effort collecting the last 15 percent of the money.

Much better is to select carefully that 10 percent or 15 percent of the families who will best repay a personal visit. Then announce what this small number of families has contributed and mail the pledge cards to the balance of the congregation.

An intermediate between a personal visit and a mailed pledge card is a telephone call. Although we do not have a sufficient data base to establish the relative power of visit, phone, and mailing, we believe that a telephone call is three times as productive as a letter and a home visit three times as productive as a telephone call. The statistical problem is that we know that the relative power of the visit increases as the size of the proposed or actual gift increases, but we don't know by how much. Obviously, if you seek a million-dollar gift, a letter is useless, a telephone call is inappropriate enough to be ill-received, and only personal conversations will do.

At the top of the table, you have a fund-raising program, which is our name for achieving a goal that cannot be attained through a single campaign. On this level, the most common and probably the best practice is a two-stepper: (1) a campaign for three-year pledges, followed immediately by (2) a campaign for two-year pledges.

An interesting variation on this plan is to use "combined fund" pledges for the second campaign. In this style, the pledge is for the total amount of the families' contribution to the capital fund *and* operating fund. Never, never do this in the first campaign but in the second it is all right.

Following the completion of the two-year pledge-payment period, you can conduct the greatest annual every-member canvass in the history of the church. You have (1) temporarily doubled or even tripled the total amount that the members contribute to the church by securing separate, three-year, building-fund pledges. Then you (2) blended the two commitments into a single figure but retained the temporary nature of the pledge by specifying an ending date. Now, (3) you can remove the ending date. Churches have been known to triple their regular budget giving through this five-year, three-step process.

Obviously, this highest level, a fund-raising program, requires long-range vision, patience, tenacity, and lots of good, hard work.

The decision to campaign

The campaign that raises only 75 percent of its goal is not the loser. The campaign that never got started is the loser. Seventy-five percent beats zero percent any time. Sometimes the decision to campaign is difficult to secure, sometimes even impossible. Thorough preparation is always advisable. Before submitting the suggestion of a campaign for official decision, somebody must do these things:

a. *Comprehensive costs*. Secure rough estimates of *all* that is proposed: land purchase, site improvement, new construction, furniture and fixtures, fees, short-term construction loans, and fund-raising. Do not eliminate anything. Do not, for instance, plan to get the costs of furniture after the campaign. Do not fragment the goal in any way.

b. *Interest costs*. Calculate the cost of borrowing. This includes selling bonds to the congregation, for that is only borrowing and nothing more. Get a copy of *Comprehensive Mortgage Payment Tables* from your banker or from Financial Publishing Company, 82 Brookline Avenue, Boston, Massachusetts 12215 and compute the various possibilities.

c. *Fund-raising potential and costs*. Secure an estimate of your fund-raising potential and an estimate of total fund-raising costs (fees and expenses) from a reliable firm of fund-raising consultants.* You will be surprised at how much less it will cost to raise than to borrow the funds you need.

d. *A committee of the board*. Place such information as you have gathered in the hands of a committee of the board that is charged with responsibility to make a recommendation to the board. (Usually, it is even better if the committee conducts these preliminary investigations, but you may have to start the ball rolling yourself.)

e. *Home meetings*. Take a draft of the *tentatively* approved resolution to conduct the campaign to the congregation through a series of small meetings in the homes of the members. Little sessions of six or eight couples will discuss the plan more intelligently, and come up with more good ideas, than any big congregational meeting. Following these five steps the board takes official action.

Many a pastor has told me, "We don't have to go through all those preliminary steps. The congregation has never voted me down on anything." But if you don't take the time and the trouble to prepare carefully, this could be the first time that the congregation does vote you down.

A fund-raising policy committee

It is a good idea to have a committee of the board responsible for the preparations just discussed, rather than for the minister to do them. This can be a standing finance or stewardship committee, but an ad hoc committee selected exclusively for the purpose is even better.

This policy committee, by whatever name, should also recommend to the board whether you will have a do-it-yourself or a professionally managed campaign. (If you are really going for your full potential, you had better bring in the pros.) The question here is not who will actually raise the funds—the campaign organization will do that. The question is whether the leaders of the campaign organization will plan and manage the operation or whether they will hire a firm to do this for them.

---

*My own firm does this without cost—the Church Development Center, 2885 East Aurora Avenue #17, Boulder, Co. 80303. Or write the American Association of Fund-raising Counsel, 25 West 43rd Street, New York, N.Y. 10036.

The policy committee should also secure an appropriation from the board for total campaign expenses.

The policy committee is not the fund-raising organization. It selects and secures the campaign chair and then retires into the background while the campaign is organized and conducted, emerging only to make a full campaign report to the board, whereupon it is dismissed with thanks. However, a recent development is to keep this committee for the pledge-payment period, to see that the postcampaign program is properly organized and conducted. This involves monitoring pledge payments, seeing that families not visited during the campaign or unable to make up their minds during the campaign period are visited, and that new members are visited upon their joining the church.

The pledge card

Except for small projects, you will want to have your own pledge card printed. Use good printing on good stock. Have the name and address of the family individually entered as shown on the sample. Don't distribute any blank pledge cards.

Aside from any introductory statement that you might want, the only text you need is: "I will try to give $_____ a week for 150 weeks (assuming that you are using a three-year pledge-payment period) for a total gift of $_____ beginning _____."
Also provide space for back credits if you are using them and for the names of other members of the family (other than the signer). The visitor (solicitor) should also sign the card and date it.

The specimen shown has two tabs. When a member of the campaign organization selects the card, he signs the outside tab and gives it to his chair or team leader. That tab goes to the campaign office, which always has a record of where every pledge card is. The inside tab provides essential information about the family for the visitor; this information will vary from campaign to campaign, church to church, and family to family.

When the tabs have been removed, the pledge card is 4" × 6". Avoid loading the 4" × 6" main section of the pledge card with anything other than that shown on the specimen. For instance, don't have boxes to check off whether the pledge will be paid weekly, monthly, annually, etc. The pledge should be expressed in only weekly and total amounts. How it will actually be paid is another matter that need not concern the visitor nor the construction of the pledge card.

Extensive experimentation has shown that the collections experience on "I will try to give" is every bit as good as more formal, binding statements.

Back credits

If your church has already conducted some fund-raising for the same goal that you now propose, the decent and effective thing to do is to give full credit for all identifiable gifts that have already been made. The natural, human tendency is to wipe the slate clean, to start fresh as though there had been no previous giving. But this is neither fair nor productive.

Interpret and publicize the new campaign as the continuation of a total fund-raising program. Publish the goal as, for instance, "$500,000, of which we already have $100,000." On each pledge card these three lines should appear:

$_____ previously paid
$_____ new pledge
$_____ TOTAL GIFT

Note that the back credit (the first line) is for the amount previously *paid*. Outstanding amounts pledged but not paid are automatically cancelled with the signing of a new pledge.

Building Fund

Green Mountain United Methodist Church

12755 W. Cedar, Lakewood, Colorado 80228

To pay for our church building, the gathering place for our congregation to study, to share and to serve in the name of Jesus Christ,

I/We will try to give $ _____ a week for 150 weeks for a total contribution of $ _____ to the Green Mountain United Methodist Church BUILDING FUND beginning the _____ of _____ 1984.

Signed: _____

Others sharing in this gift: _____

Previously Paid $ _____

New pledge $ _____

Total gift $ _____

Received by: _____ Date _____

Eval _____

Congreg. Dinner (H) (W) (Y) (S)

S/A $ _____

Occupation:

H: _____

W: _____

THIS CARD TAKEN BY

_____ A/G C/O _____

Print visitor's name here   (circle)   Date

HAND THIS TAB TO TEAM LEADER BEFORE LEAVING ROOM

When there is any question about what a family has previously paid, unquestioningly accept their recollection of the amount.

Admittedly, back credits complicate campaign scoreboarding and gift records. But the extra work is a small price to pay for the powerful benefits—both financial and spiritual—of full recognition and continuity. As one pastor said, "The Lord doesn't care how many decisions you had to make; what does count is your total gift." And you may be certain that that is the way previous givers figure it, no matter how the church does.

Building fund plus budget campaigns

If you want to conduct a capital fund campaign at the usual time of your every-member canvass, or if for any reason you want to protect your budget pledging, you can conduct a two-pledge card campaign. If you do it right, you can increase your budget pledging modestly without decreasing in the slightest the amount raised for the capital fund.

In a BF + B campaign, each family is asked first to sign a budget pledge and *then* a capital-fund pledge. Both pledges can be secured on the same visit but the budget pledge must be signed first. In fact, it is good practice to staple the budget card on top of the building-fund card.

Never, *never*, NEVER use one pledge card for both funds. It confuses the issue, and you'll end up with less money.

Provide space to specify the beginning payment date of the budget pledge but not an ending date. The family indicates only how much a week it will try to give starting when. There is no reason ever to specify an ending date of a budget pledge.

In this two-pledge card campaign, do not set a budget goal. You will secure a modest increase in budget pledging. But when seeking an important capital fund, don't try simultaneously for a spectacular increase in budget pledging.

If you have not been securing your budget pledges through home visits for the past few years, you will experience a substantial increase in the *number* of budget pledges. You will also increase the percentage of your income that is derived from pledge payments—possibly the most valuable source of income that you can have. But, please, do not increase the budget goal.

Organization

A full campaign, calculated to deliver a personal visit to each member family in its home, will require a total organization of about 20 percent of the family count. It works out about like this for every hundred families:

- 100 families
- 10 Advance Gifts families (10% of the total)
- 90 families, net, in the Campaign Division
- 18 members in the Campaign Division, themselves*
- 72 families to be visited by the Campaign Division
- 12 team members required (72 ÷ average of 6)
- 2 teams (12 team members ÷ average of 6)

---

*The campaign chair secures the pledges of team leaders. The team leaders secure the pledges of their team members (visitors). If you require more than six or eight teams, you will have to insert one or more section leaders or campaign vice-chairs between the campaign chair and the team leaders.

CAMPAIGN ORGANIZATION
for a church of 350 to 400 families
This is an actual chart from a real campaign.

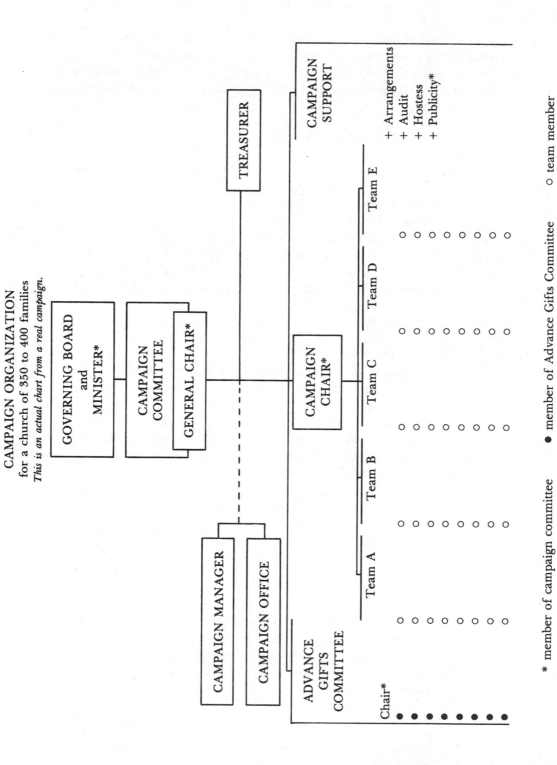

This specimen shows five teams averaging eight team members each. But variations—such as eight teams averaging 5 team members each—will not affect performance.

* member of campaign committee   ● member of Advance Gifts Committee   ○ team member

Using this table as a guide, you can easily create a good table of organization for your church. Just don't worry about symmetry and precise arithmetic ratios. A manager (for instance, a team leader) can lead from four to eight persons doing identical work. A visitor will average between five and eight completed assignments (pledges).

	per 100 families	per your family count
Families	100	_____
Advance Gifts (10%)	10	_____
Net to Campaign Division (90%)	90	_____
Campaign division itself (÷5)	18	_____
Net to Campaign Division	72	_____
Team members required (÷6)	12	_____
Teams required (÷6)	2	_____
Sections required (÷6)	0	_____

The Team:
Building Block of the Campaign Organization

You will note that the campaign organization chart shows (about) eight members of the Advance Gifts Committee and (about) forty team members in the Campaign Division. Now, what is a team?

A team is a group of four to eight visitors (or canvassers, solicitors, or team members). These names all mean the same thing—a person who makes an exemplary pledge and then selects and visits other families of the church to help them make their pledges.

Members of a team visit their prospects individually for the most part, but they sit together at team tables at all meetings. They report—and are graded—as a team, and they help each other in many ways. They often exchange selected pledge cards, or one person "goes with" a fellow team member upon request. They exchange experiences and ideas. They encourage and support each other. *"And ever after, those so involved, despite the grumbling and groaning at the time, will fondly reminisce together over those intense and painful moments when they were really alive"* (Dean M. Kelley).

The team leader (sometimes, team captain) selects prospective team members, secures their pledges, and is responsible for the team's attendance at report meetings. The team leader also selects the families that he or she will personally visit, just as the team members do. Team leaders are the pivot people in any campaign.

Only good givers

There is a general law, and there is a special law in fund-raising that are perhaps as important as any whole book ever written on the subject.

The general law: Only good givers are able to convince other people to be good givers, too.

The special law: only good givers to this particular project make good givers to this particular project.

Nongivers make nongivers. Poor givers make poor givers. Middling givers make middling givers. Good givers make good givers. Great givers make great givers.

Nongivers to this particular project make nongivers to this particular project. Poor givers to this particular project make poor givers to this particular project. Middling givers to this particular project make middling givers to this particular project. Good givers to this project make good givers to this project. Great givers to this project make great givers to this project.

Good giving has two dimensions: the size and the generosity of the gift. It is unusual for a member of the campaign organization to bring in a gift larger or more generous than his or her own. It happens, but not often enough to constitute good fund-raising practice.

Moral: Don't let any middling, poor, or nongivers into the fund-raising organization.

The minister's role in fund-raising

Fund-raising is essentially a lay responsibility. The minister should accept no specific position in the campaign organization. However, the minister is the most important person in the campaign.

As spiritual adviser, the minister should guide, assist, encourage, and support each of the campaign leaders. The minister is not a fund-raiser, but his or her spirit should permeate the entire fund-raising organization.

It is usually best if the minister neither asks anyone to serve in the campaign nor asks anyone for money. Rather, the minister will be asked by various campaign leaders, from time to time, to go with them—to assist in securing an important agreement to serve or to give.

No member of the church is going to accept a position of campaign leadership without the minister's specific endorsement. Nor will any family make a gift of towering importance to the campaign without discussing it with the minister. But in these all-important conversations, it is usually best if the minister goes with a lay leader.

The minister's own gift is the most important that will be made in the entire campaign. This gift should be made early (but not before the campaign) and should be personally witnessed. A well-established formula is for the minister (or, in larger churches, the ministerial staff) to give 1 percent of the goal.

The minister is, ex-officio, a member of all campaign committees and should attend all meetings possible, but not chair any of them.

At every important campaign meeting the minister should be the last speaker on the program. After the minister's remarks and benediction, adjournment should follow immediately.

The campaign calendar

You must set up a schedule, a calendar for the campaign. But don't worship it. Professional campaign managers publish only tentative calendars. The object of the campaign is to win, not to stay on schedule.

The accompanying table of campaign weeks and the sample calendar can be helpful but should not be followed rigidly. In a recent campaign for $3 million that I supervised, when I met with the minister about the middle of the campaign period his first question was: "Are we on schedule?" I gave him the only possible honest answer: "No, but we are winning." (The campaign raised $5 million, but not on schedule.)

After a period of preparation, your campaign committee begins its meetings to approve the campaign plan, select leadership, and develop the suggested askings. The advance gifts committee is organized as soon as possible and, as the chart shows, continues right up to the congregational dinner.

The campaign division organizes while the advance gifts committee is operating and should, by the time of the congregational dinner, have achieved a full and fully pledged organization.

The pivotal point of the calendar is a congregational dinner to which all members are invited. It is

HIGHLIGHTS OF THE CAMPAIGN CALENDAR

WEEK	one	two	three	four	five	six	seven
DAY	S M T W T F S	S M T W T F S	S M T W T F S	S M T W T F S	S M T W T F S	S M T W T F S	S M T W T F S
Preparation		C C	C				
Advance gifts		A	A A	A A	A		
Campaign organization			C TL	TL T	T		
Congregational dinner					■		
Campaign report meetings					●	R R	R R V

Legend:

C   Campaign committee
A   Advance gifts committee
TL Team leaders
T   Teams
■   Congregational dinner
●   Opening dinner
R   Report meeting
V   Victory report

This is a simplified version of the campaign calendar for an actual campaign. Only the details and less important meetings have been eliminated. The church family count was 400. Week one involved only a professional campaign office manager doing advance set-up work.

best held off the church property. No charge for the dinner. The program that night is to explain the need for the campaign, the goal, and the campaign methods, and to introduce the campaign leaders, announce a few pace-setting pledges and the amount raised to date. There must be no solicitation at the dinner.

Two days after the congregational dinner, the campaign officially opens. Thereafter, the campaign division holds three report meetings a week—9:00 p.m. Mondays, Wednesdays, and Fridays—with a final victory report meeting on a Sunday or Monday night. On the specimen calendar, we show an opening dinner for the campaign division, six report meetings over the next two weeks, and a final, victory report meeting the following Sunday.

You will need a mop-up operation. No campaign can deliver a visit in the home of *every* member-family on schedule. But do not use your full campaign organization for this: set up a cadre of your team leaders and a few visitors who performed well in the campaign, and let them mop up. This is preferred to extending the meetings of the full campaign organization that, past a certain point, can become boring.

Revise your campaign calendar as may be found necessary as the campaign proceeds. Naturally, it is better if you can stay with your original schedule, but it is not vital.

LENGTH OF CAMPAIGN
according to the size of the congregation

Number of member-families	Campaign period (weeks)	Number of report meetings
to 80	4	4
to 130	5	5
to 210	6	6
to 880	7	7
to 1,440	9	8
to 2,330	11	9
+2,330	12	10

Use this table of campaign length as a guide only. You may require more time for preparation than we have provided here. But be slow to extend the active solicitation (of the campaign division) or to increase the number of report meetings.

Guidelines to giving

You seek not equal but proportionate gifts—proportionate to the individual family's financial capability. This takes some doing. Your members need guidance in resolving the all-important question: How much should we give? Most of your families will sincerely struggle with this question. And, in that struggle, they need all the help that the church can give.

The more specific that help—in terms of dollars, not percentages, formulas, or generalities—the better. If you can, have the campaign committee work out presumably equitable dollar-amount suggestions for all families. This is a long and difficult task, and it can never be done to anybody's complete satisfaction, but it is the most helpful of all the alternatives.

I have also had very good responses—although not so good as specific dollar amounts—with "one dollar a week for every thousand dollars annual income." In small churches striving mightily

210

to build a proper church plant, or in churches that have already achieved a very high level of budget giving, we do frequently go to "two dollars a week for every thousand dollars of annual income."

Strangely, if you suggest that a family give 5 percent of its income, or any other percentage, what you mostly get is an argument: "Before or after taxes? . . . ," etc. But the $1 per $1,000 does not produce arguments. That doesn't mean that all families will give it, but it does mean that they accept it as a guideline.

Don't use the tithe as a guideline because that is more applicable to budget-giving than to capital fund-giving. It is interesting to note that the Muslim tithe is on capital rather than income. But that idea is seldom acceptable in Christian churches.

Distribution of gifts by size and number

You have often heard it said, that "15 percent of the gifts should produce half of the total goal, and 85 percent the other half." There is a good bit of truth in this cliche but, like most time-honored maxims, it is simplistic.

Professional campaign managers recognize three kinds of churches according to the distribution of assets and income among the families:
1. METRO, wherein there is a considerable distance between the most financially capable families and how much most families have to give.
2. COMMUNITY, wherein there is less distance between the most capable and how much most families have to give.
3. TRACT, wherein there is very little distance between the top and how much families have.

The bromide, "50 percent from 15 percent" applies in only a very general way and actually is more applicable to tract churches than to the other two kinds. The three formulae are:

DOLLARS	METRO	COMM.	TRACT
first 25%	1%	3%	5%
second 25%	10	10	10
third 25%	20	20	20
fourth 25%	69	67	65

You can quickly see that the difference among the three kinds of churches is the percentage of the goal that the largest gifts can account for. On the Metro scale, a mere 1 percent of the families can produce 25 percent of the goal. On the tract, it will require 5 percent of the families to produce the first 25 percent of the goal.

In actual practice, there is a fourth type, wherein more than 5 percent of the gifts are required to produce the first 25 percent of the dollars. However, a shared characteristic of churches of this type is that the total giving, or average giving per family, is low.

Where is your church among these four types? Wherever you think it is, move it up one notch. That is, if you think yours is a tract church, it is much more probably a community; if you think it is a community, it is much more probably a metro.

In setting guidelines—or, preferably, specific, dollar-amount suggestions for individual families—check yourself (or your committee) to see that the suggested amounts are distributed among the families according to the kind of church that you have. That is, if you are a metro church, the campaign must be prepared to ask 1 percent of the families to give the first 25 percent of the goal.

CLERGY DESK BOOK

If all of this strikes you as though we are asking too much of your financially most capable families, consider: almost nobody ever gives more than they are asked to give. John Rockefeller said that he always asked his solicitors how much they thought that he, Rockefeller, should give, and that it was frequently less than Rockefeller already had in mind.

The amount that the churches of the United States and Canada lose each year by asking too little of their financially most capable families certainly runs into the hundreds of millions of dollars, and more probably into the billions—what we call "the uninvited billions."

To ask that a member or family think about giving a certain amount need not be crude, pushy, or high pressure. In Rockefeller's own phrase, "Perhaps you might be willing to consider. . . ."

Home visits: solo or duet?

The popular custom is to make the home visits in pairs. The origins of this practice are obscure, but the results are clear: (1) A member of the duet visit takes more time coordinating schedules with a partner than in actually visiting. (2) In the actual conversation in the home, the members of the duet mostly stumble over each other's feet. (3) The advice, guidance, and help that the family needs is seldom provided by two persons simultaneously.

However, a good team will discuss each visiting assignment individually and make individual decisions. The best way to resolve this old, knotty problem is simply to leave it up to the team member who takes the pledge card of a particular family. If the team member wants help, then ask another member of the team for it. If the visitor would rather go alone, then do that. Let nobody try to legislate the matter.

The most frequent situation in which two visitors are indicated is when one of the team members knows the family to be visited, but makes a gift less than the family should be asked to consider. In that case, the visitor might well ask a larger giver on the team to go along. It is difficult to advise anyone to make a larger gift than the visitor has given.

But, in almost all cases, one evangelist will do better than two or three or any other number, although exceptions to this rule are often encountered in advance gifts.

Perhaps the most crushing observation about the duet system is that it means you must either build a campaign organization twice the size that the professionals use, or the average team member will have to make twice as many visits.

Reporting campaign progress

The conventional thermometer that shows what percentage of the goal has been achieved to date is not only useless, it can be downright misleading. Consider that if, in a campaign for $500,000, you had planned that the ten largest gifts would account for $200,000 but, in fact, they disappointingly accounted for only $100,000.

Your conventional thermometer would show that 5 percent of your families had contributed 20 percent of the goal—and there would be great rejoicing and even dancing in the streets—whereas you have probably lost your campaign. Those families should have accounted for 40 percent of the goal, not 20 percent, and there is no way you can make up the difference.

The best way to report progress visually is on what we call a hollow-bar chart. The hollow bars show the size and number of the gifts that you seek. As gifts are secured, you fill in the bars. About one-third of the way through a campaign, with two-thirds of the goal reported, your successor to the old thermometer might look like this:

212

HOLLOW-BAR CHART

At Campaign Start

| THE GIFTS WE SEEK ☐ | OUR GOAL $750,000 |
| THE GIFTS WE HAVE ☐ | RAISED TO DATE 0 |

#	$	$20,000	$40,000	$60,000	$80,000	$100,000
1	$100,000					
2	50,000					
4	25,000					
10	10,000					
20	5,000					
100	1,000					
200	500					
163	other					
500						

At One-Third of the Way Through

| THE GIFTS WE SEEK ☐ | OUR GOAL $750,000 |
| THE GIFTS WE HAVE ▓ | RAISED TO DATE 475,000 |

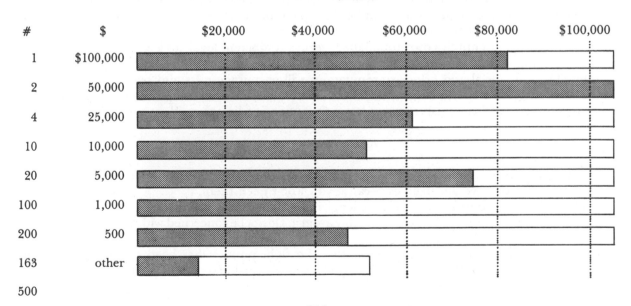

#	$	$20,000	$40,000	$60,000	$80,000	$100,000
1	$100,000					
2	50,000					
4	25,000					
10	10,000					
20	5,000					
100	1,000					
200	500					
163	other					
500						

Post campaign: a possible 30 percent swing

What percentage of the total amount shown on the campaign scoreboard at the victory report meeting will actually be collected? If you follow the common practice of doing very little about it, the probability is about 85 percent or maybe 90 percent. But if you will take some pains, the actual amount collected can be 115 percent of the scoreboard total. That is a swing of as much as 30 percent. That is worth quite a bit of effort, isn't it?

To insure good payments on amounts pledged, set up a monitoring committee. This group meets monthly and reviews all delinquent pledges. It finds what the problem is in each individual case, then decides what to do about it, and then does it or sees that it is done.

The monitoring committee must have authority to reduce or even cancel a pledge, or to set up a new schedule of delayed or reduced payments. Families experiencing temporary financial hardships are often encouraged, by such a committee, to reduce or suspend payments for a while and then extend their payment schedule beyond the formal 150-week (or whatever) period.

To increase the total amount pledged, another group visits the new families as they join the church and secures their pledges for the remainder of the pledge-payment period. For instance, a family joining one year following the campaign will be invited to pledge for a hundred weeks.

This committee is also alert for opportunities to secure pledges from those who were not contacted in the campaign or could not make up their minds how much to give, or who asked to be seen later.

The church should send quarterly reminder notices of the status of individual pledge payments.

Nonmoney gifts

When we talk of fund-raising we think of money-raising—too often. What part of a family's assets or estate consists of cash in the bank? Very little. In 1982, somewhere between seventy-five and one-hundred gifts of $1 million or more were made to nonprofit organizations. How many of these were cash gifts? My personal estimate: none.

Most estates consist of homes, other real estate, personal property, stocks, bonds, and notes. All of these can be given to the church just as well as cash. In fact, often the tax advantages to the givers can far exceed the advantages of cash.

Your church should have a foundation; that is, a nonprofit organization controlled by, but separate from, the church. This organization can be a recipient of both cash and noncash gifts, especially noncash, and especially bequests.

In setting up your church's own foundation, secure competent legal advice. Select and secure as trustees persons known for their experience and success in handling very, very large amounts of money. Their financial and fiduciary reputations will encourage gifts and bequests.

One warning: do not allow the foundation to subsidize the annual operating budget. Budget subsidies of any kind diminish the regular contributions of living, resident members.

Reasons versus excuses

In all fund-raising organization, select the best qualified person for an individual position of leadership. Do not have alternatives because you won't need them.

In all solicitation, invite the family to consider giving a gift of a specific amount. Do not suggest a range of amounts or even a formula if you can possibly avoid it. Do not be concerned with the consequences of a refusal, or of a smaller gift than you anticipate, because neither one is going to happen.

When the person asked to serve knows that the right position has been selected for him or her—when he or she understands that he or she is the best qualified person in the congregation for that position—that person will serve.

214

When the family knows that it is asked to give an amount that is right for it and for the campaign, the family will give that amount.

Occasionally you will encounter a reason for not serving or not giving that you had not anticipated because there is something about the person or family that you did not know. There are, now and then, reasons for refusals. But nine times out of the ten that you experience a negative response, what is given as a reason is not a reason at all—it is an excuse. There is a world of difference.

A legitimate reason must be accepted. ("I cannot serve as chair because I am leaving tomorrow morning on a round the world trip to be gone for four months" or "We cannot give what you ask because we are bankrupt and asking for protection under chapter 11.") But excuses are something different.

The important thing is not to answer excuses. Don't hear them. Pay no attention to them. If you do, you are sunk.

An excuse cannot be answered because it is not valid; it is not real. The person who will offer excuses can think them up faster than you can respond to them. When you try to answer an excuse, you are playing the other person's ball game, and you have already lost the game.

Sam called on Al for his pledge to the building fund. Al refused to give. "Why?" asked Sam.

Al looked annoyed. "Well, if you must know, I don't like the pastor."

"What don't you like about the pastor?" asked an astonished Sam.

Al looked even more uncomfortable and finally blurted out, "He wears those yellow shoes."

"Now Al," said Sam, "What in the world does the pastor wearing yellow shoes have to do with your giving to the building fund?"

Now Al was downright angry. "Sam," he spluttered, "you know as well as I do that when you're not going to give, one excuse is as good as another."

And you know, he was right.

Stewardship Development
The Church Is Not a Charity

On your income tax return, you list what you give to your church as a charitable contribution only because there is no other place to list it. But giving to the church is not charity, and the church is not a charitable institution. Charity is mostly almsgiving, and the church does not seek alms. The *Random House Dictionary* defines *alms* as "money, food, or other donations given to the poor or needy; anything given as charity." The *Oxford English Dictionary* defines *alms* as "charitable relief of the poor; charity, especially as a religious duty."

No matter how desperate the church's needs may seem to be, the church must never beg. Never! In the first place, it is demeaning. The church that thinks of itself as a charity diminishes its ability to fulfill its proper role of counsellor, guide, and adviser. One does not take advice from beggars. If the church adopts the begging role by pleading its needs, it comes dangerously close to the stance of the commission salesman who may call himself a consultant but is paid only if his advice is taken.

What sets the church apart from all other nonprofit institutions in this regard is that it alone has a responsibility to teach its members about giving. No secular institution can do this; none has either the authority or the responsibility.

The beginning of wisdom in stewardship development is to take the focus off the need of the church to receive and put it on the need of its members to give. The takeoff point is not that the church needs money but that it is better to give than to receive —better for the giver.

Some call this good news the *gospel of good giving*. And so shall we.

Church stewardship policies

The church's attitudes toward giving, fund-raising, and stewardship more profoundly affect the giving of its members than all the annual every-member canvasses that it will ever conduct. If the leaders of the church rely upon pleading, or if they think of an every-member canvass as essentially a promotion, or if they think that negative appeals raise the most money, they might just as well not have an every-member canvass. Certainly nothing great is going to happen.

Here are eight areas in which the tacit premises—the mostly unspoken acceptances—of the church can immensely help or terribly hurt all stewardship development efforts.

a. *Giving to others.* The church should set its members a good example. If it wants the members to "give off the top," the church should, itself, give off the top. Lewis G. Wells defined a great church as one that gives away at least as much as it spends on its own adequate budget. (The national average is about 20 percent.) George Regas said, "The world will judge us not on what we spend on ourselves but what we give to others."

b. *EMC before budget.* Just so long as we prepare the annual operating budget and then go to the congregation to raise it, that long we will have to endure financial strains and tensions. A better policy is to cut the umbilical cord that has tied our stewardship development efforts to the needs of the church. Secure the pledges first; then draw up the budget.

c. *Pledges.* In an ideal world we could conduct stewardship development programs and EMC's without pledges. But we are living in a fallen world. A family needs to confront the matter of what part giving is playing in its life and to make a decision about what it will now try to do. This means what priority its giving will have in the family budget.

Don't ever say that the reason for having pledges is so that the church can plan next year's operations. The comfort of the finance committee does not provide a strong motive for a family to move its giving from near bottom on the priority list up to the top.

d. *Weekly offering envelopes.* Do not scorn the humble offering envelope. It is good policy to send offering envelopes to every family of the church, not just those who request them. For one thing, this policy emphasizes weekly pledging and giving. For another, the idea is to *bring* one's offering to the church every week, not just to send it only occasionally. Offering envelopes could cost much more than they do and still be well worth the money.

e. *Minimize special appeals and offerings.* By focusing too much attention on special offerings, we unwittingly train our people to give designated gifts rather than undesignated. Even if this were good fund-raising, it still would not be good stewardship. But it isn't even good fund-raising because those who live by special appeals soon have to have a special appeal just to pay the utilities. You will never get entirely away from designated giving. But do your best.

f. *New member orientation.* The denominations with the highest giving average fully inform, and discuss with new members, "How we think about giving around here" and, to one degree or another, secure a commitment before the person joins—or at least as part of the process of joining. We should all do that.

Or, if the church leaders just can't bring themselves to this policy, you can secure a commitment—or statement of intention—as soon after the joining as can possibly be arranged. Waiting until the next every-member canvass is folly. Waiting also tends, unfortunately, to reveal the low priority that the church places on stewardship understanding and performance.

g. *Nongift income.* It is best for the church to operate on the undesignated giving of its living, resident members. Earned income, endowment yield, sales, events—even bequests—should not subsidize the annual operating budget; they should go to outreach, missions, and causes other than services to the congregation.

There is a strange phenomenon here. The more the budget is subsidized by nongift income, the less the members will give. Thus, you end up subsidizing not the church but the members. This is most clearly illustrated by churches that are subsidized by governments or large endowments.

h. *Your own philanthropic foundation.* When we talk of giving, we usually think, too narrowly, about money, and mostly of money here and now. But the subject of stewardship covers the entire range of the giver's assets. The Islamic tithe, just to illustrate, is on capital.

The very biggest gifts are seldom made from a person's bank account; rather, they come from real or personal property, securities, insurance policies, bequests—and quite often from some combination of several of these.

The best way to prepare your church for these kinds of noncash gifts is to set up a foundation that, although controlled by the church, is an independent financial entity. Secure good legal and professional advice on gifts and taxes before moving on this, but do go ahead. Create a convenient means by which people can give very big gifts.

The stewardship committee

You do want a year-round stewardship committee. Stewardship is a fifty-two-week activity. The successful secular nonprofit organizations work at fund-raising all year. Most churches too readily relegate stewardship to a two-week EMC once a year.

Members of the stewardship committee should be selected exclusively from among the best and biggest givers. You want some of the biggest givers because they alone will be influential with prospective big givers. You want some of the best (i.e., most generous) givers because only generous givers understand stewardship.

If you are going to stay close to one committee, let it be this one. They are the teachers, but you are the teachers' teacher.

A circular process goes on here. As members experience the gospel of good giving, their interest in their spiritual lives increases, and thus their involvement and participation in the life of the church. For where your treasure is, there will your heart be also. And, of course, all of these consequences tend to make the members better stewards, thus closing the circle.

Membership on the committee should not be limited to members of the board.

Opinions differ as to the size of a stewardship committee. My advice is to avoid extremes. Too few (three or four) loads too much responsibility on each member; too many (a dozen) puts too much of a load on you because you will want to maintain a deep personal relationship with each member.

The suggestion will surely be put forward for you to chair this committee. Don't do it. Don't do it for two reasons. First, because stewardship development is essentially a lay responsibility. Second because leading a good stewardship committee can be a life-changing experience that you covet for lay leaders.

All matters concerning stewardship and fund-raising that come before the board should come through the stewardship committee. In all matters concerning stewardship and fund-raising the board should decide only after hearing what the stewardship committee has to say.

The budget allocation for the stewardship committee is not a good place to try to save money.

A good early project for the committee is to draft a comprehensive policy statement touching on the points just discussed under the heading "Church Stewardship Policies." This is neither a simple nor an easy task. The committee might want to keep the statement in draft form, to be used only for its own guidance, for some time before presenting it to the board. Even after its official acceptance, it will probably require occasional revisions.

Operations

What the stewardship committee does will be influenced by denominational customs, tradition, size, and nature of the church, present levels of stewardship understanding and performance and individual leadership personalities. But there are seven areas of concern for all stewardship committees, in addition to establishing policies.

a. *Guidelines.* The members of the church need guidelines—suggestions from the church about what constitutes good giving. Generalizations such as "generous," "sacrificial," or "as the Lord has blessed you" are not helpful. The decision of how much to give will have to be made in dollars or portion of income; therefore, the more specific the guidelines can be, the better.

If the guideline in your church is simply the tithe, I suppose the subject is closed. But it might be wise periodically to calculate what percentage of the church families are tithing. If it isn't a high percentage, you might want to consider additional guidelines, or new ways of presenting or interpreting the tithe.

I have found that $1 a week for every $1,000 annual income is a useful guide in most churches, and $2 a week where the tithe is the standard or where the giving is already high.

Another guideline that is used in all professionally managed fund-raising campaigns (usually, but not always, these are for building funds or some other capital fund) is to divide the member-families into nine levels according to presumed giving capability—just *ability*, not generosity or interest in the church—and then assign a suggested asking amount to each level.

b. *Open-end or closed-end pledges?* The kind of pledge that you recommend to the congregation is important. Most church pledges specify a starting and ending date, which is almost always the next fiscal year. But this ties pledging to the annual operating budget, and that means tying stewardship to the church's needs, which is bad stewardship development, as already noted.

There is a trend toward open-end pledges. These specify a starting, but not an ending date. Closed-end pledges call for a new pledge every year and thus require an every-member canvass of one kind or another annually. Open-end pledges may come up for reconsideration by either the pledging family or the church at any time.

The open-end pledge sets up a requirement for a year-round program of home visits rather than one big, simultaneous EMC. Not all churches can handle that because they don't have a strong enough stewardship committee. However, a few selected home visits each month, instead of everybody all at once, is a much better way to go.

c. *Home visits.* What holds down giving perhaps more than anything else is the churches' tendency to wholesale its stewardship teaching and appeals. Letters and printed materials are addressed "to whom it may concern." Even sermons do not get down to where the problems and the opportunities are. Most stewardship development is wholesaled—generalized as though each family's income, expenses, spiritual maturity, and understanding of stewardship were the same.

I don't suppose that any church with a $100,000 annual budget would try to raise a $500,000 building fund by mailing letters to the congregation. The importance of the decision that each individual family in that church would have to make about how much to give obviously merits more attention and respect than a form letter.

I doubt that anyone would seek a million-dollar gift by writing the prospective donor a letter—much less sending a form letter, or merely preaching to that person on a Sunday morning.

And yet, the decision that you want the family to make—the decision to move its giving up from the bottom of its present position in the family's budget right up to the top—is at least as big and difficult as a decision to make a large building-fund gift.

A thoughtful, earnest conversation in the home with a fellow member who has personally experienced the life-changing dynamics of the gospel of good giving and has requested that he or she be the one to visit that particular family—this is the most helpful and productive instrument of stewardship development.

d. *Annual every-member canvass.* The common practice in the every-member canvass is to mail the pledge cards and then organize a clean-up squad to go get the cards back from those families who did not sign and return them. This system is the reluctant calling on the unconvinced. It uses 85 percent of expended time and energy producing the last 15 percent or less of the money. Further, it contributes nothing to anybody's stewardship education.

Far better is to reverse the process: visit a selected 15 percent of the families first and *then* mail the pledge cards to the remaining 85 percent.

Between the two steps, announce what the 15 percent have done. They probably have increased their giving 30 percent over last year. These families to be visited may be selected on any of several bases, or a combination of them: financial ability to make a large pledge; probability of making a substantially increased pledge; much in need of a personal visit, etc.

e. *Witnessing*. The principal power of the home visit is the personal witnessing of the visitor (canvasser, team member, solicitor, etc.). Be constantly aware that in stewardship development you are changing lives, and the personal testimony of those whose lives have been changed is the root power to change other lives.

All those who make life-changing stewardship decisions should be asked for permission to make their gifts known (but never in print) and to join whatever ad hoc organization is currently conducting a stewardship program. Even stronger than permission to announce is for the giver (especially a husband and wife jointly) to testify personally to (1) how they came to their decision—and especially how difficult it was, (2) how much they have decided to try to give, and (3) how they now feel about their decision.

f. *Monitoring*. The pledge card is a statement of present intention only. Sometimes a family will falter in its payments, or even stop. When that happens it is a danger signal: "Trouble! Problem!" A red flag should go up and a cannon go off. "One of our families is in trouble."

It is my experience that better than 99 percent of all pledges to the church are made in good faith. But some families will experience severe financial reverses, unprecedented medical bills, death, divorce, or unemployment. Others will move or become angry at something that the minister said in a sermon. For these or any other reasons somebody should: (1) know that pledge payments have faltered or stopped, (2) find out why, and (3) do something about it.

In smaller churches, the stewardship committee may want to do this. In larger churches, it is usually more practicable to set up a separate pledge-payment monitoring committee—"monitoring" for short.

Each member of the monitoring committee must have authority to cancel delinquent payments, temporarily suspend payments, or reduce the amount of the pledge. Sooner or later most families will catch up, but the church should not press.

g. *Children and youths*. All churches recognize the importance of beginning stewardship education at the youngest practicable level. But few agree about how this should be done. Denominational principles and practices vary so much that it would probably serve no good purpose to feature any one style in this short article.

But every stewardship committee must take responsibility for seeing that this important element of the church's total stewardship program receives important attention.

Seven stewardship development sins

a. *Low goals*. Expect too little of the congregation, and you will get what you expect. People today are reacting well to great ideas, new visions, bold programs. Don't fear failure. The goal isn't success but achievement. If you never fail, how will you ever know what your church could really do?

b. *Insufficient allocation of leadership time* and attention, and of money for administration. Want to know how to double what your members now give? Pay twice as much attention to the subject.

c. *Begging*. If you must worry about balancing the annual budget, don't do it during the EMC. You won't add a cubit to your stature anyway. The church must never beg. NEVER! Please, no alms.

d. *Negative appeals*. It is false psychology, philosophy, and theology to think that your members will respond better to negative appeals than to positive. Money today is flowing to dazzling goals boldly conceived, dramatically presented, made possible by dynamic, upbeat leadership. Accentuate the positive.

e. *Sealed pledges.* Going to a lot of trouble to absolutely insure the superconfidentiality of a pledge is not only a waste of time, but it is downright foolish. Those who want a veil of secrecy drawn over every pledge are the token givers in thrall to Mammon. They are more concerned about what their fellow members think of them than of what God does. (They say, "What I give is between God and me" and they figure God won't tell.) Don't play their game. Good givers should be asked for permission to announce their gifts. But only with their permission and never in print.

f. *Calling for volunteers.* In stewardship work, the church should be very selective. For a particular position in this field, figure exactly who in the whole congregation is best qualified. That's the person you want. Never issue a general call for volunteers.

g. *The pastor as solicitor.* Resolve here and now that you will never ask any member of your congregation for money. That is a lay responsibility, regardless of what they taught you in seminary.

The gospel of good giving

The dilemma of most church members in the quest for security is real: which comes first: God or Mammon? The church teaches one, but all practical experience and the world seem to teach the other.

"You have to look out for number one."

"A dollar is your best friend."

"Take the cash, and let the credit go."

"It's a rat race."

"Everybody has his hand out."

"Don't do me any favors."

Thorstein Veblen called it "the sickness of an acquisitive society." Kahlil Gibran asked, "What is fear of need but need itself?" Haggai likened it to putting your money in a bag full of holes. Jesus said, "No servant can serve two masters. . . . You cannot serve God and Mammon. . . . For where your treasure is, there will your heart be also."

The pressures of society on every side are to get all that we can and to keep all that we can. But Christianity is a religion of giving. Both the Old and the New Testaments praise giving as a spiritually energizing act. "It is better to give than to receive."

In whom shall we place our trust for security? The church says God. But the arguments in favor of Mammon have considerable appeal and are generally accepted almost everywhere. Mammon may be a false god, but false does not mean powerless. What Mark Twain said of the devil is even more appropriate of Mammon: "To become the spiritual leader of two-thirds of the human race shows uncommon administrative ability."

Jesus said that we should not be anxious about our material needs. But financial anxiety is the most pervasive malady of our time. Like other neuroses, it debilitates without killing, at least physically. But financial anxiety kills spiritually. If we put our first trust for security in Mammon, we wake up one day to find that, although we have gained much, we have lost something, and we suspect that it may be our souls.

Then is when we discover that, although Mammon makes a good servant, he is a terrible master. In anxiety neurosis the proper roles are reversed. We thought we had him working for us. He knew better.

Jesus said that our Father knows that we have need of material things. So, we need not be anxious. He has given us a bountiful planet and the abilities to live full and happy lives on it. He has repeatedly promised us that if we seek first his values, all else will be given to us.

That is a big promise. If it is true, it is surely good news. If it is true, we need not be anxious about money. If it is true, we have no cause for anxiety.

It is true.

And that is the gospel—the good news—of good giving. It is God's promise.

Our need to be givers is more imperative than the need of anyone or anything to receive from us. Everyone must be a giver. It is essential to life to be a giver. The most hopeless bum on skid row will share his insufficient rations with a pet.

We give not because there are needs, nor even for hope of reward. We give because to give is to live and not to give is to perish. It may be a slow death, but it is sure.

For giving is living, and living is loving, and loving is giving. Living is giving and giving is loving and loving is living. That is the gospel of good giving—that it really *is* better to give than to receive—better for the giver. We give that we may have life, and that more abundantly.

COMPUTERS
IN THE CHURCH

IF YOU HAVEN'T already noticed, you will soon: computers are all over the place, including in the church. Many church offices already use computers in place of typewriters, adding machines, addressing equipment, and financial recordkeeping books. Soon you may, too.

The new look in the church office may mean smaller staffs—administrative and support—but the staff will be more specialized. A decade from now, in five years maybe, perhaps even as soon as next year, the impact of automation and computerization will be clearly visible in the efficient, modern church office—small or large church. Eventually the modern church office may have a computer, just as it now has an offset duplicator, a copier, or a new telephone system.

Thus, computers are only one of a new group of highly technical machines many offices are already using. And while computers may seem more complicated than other equipment used in the typical church office, other equipment may be just as complicated. High speed photo copiers, for example, require expertise to operate. And they certainly do more work at less cost than the old mimeograph—less mess, more operator time for other tasks. Telephone systems, also, are much different than just two years ago. And sophisticated printing equipment in the church office can do for churches now what only a commercial printer could do a few years ago.

An explosion is taking place and the church had better join up, or it will be left behind with its antiquated equipment, inefficient management techniques, and more staff than would otherwise be required. The question is how do churches decide when they need a computer to take advantage of all the ways a computer can help to meet the demands of a highly mobile and complex membership. When most church members have a computer in their household, the church without that equipment will simply be in the "dark ages."

So—
—Why does your church need a computer?
—When will your church get its own computer?
—How will your church use the computer?

The answers to those questions are not always easy, but a carefully developed plan will assist the congregation in finding the answers. The place to begin is by appointing a computer selection committee. That small group of members will ask the questions "why," determine the needs, recommend the action, and implement any system purchased. Qualifications and responsibilities of committee members should be approved by the official board before appointment.

COMPUTERS IN THE CHURCH

A Computer Selection Committee

Purpose: To review current and future needs for a computer facility and recommend appropriate action.

Responsible to: The official board.

Size: Eight members of varying experience.

Qualifications:
1. Committed church members
2. Knowledgeable about the church's programs
3. Experienced computer user (two members)
4. No computer experience (two members)
5. Potential staff user (two members)
6. Professional executives or business people (two members)
7. Intense desire to make church procedures more efficient and less costly
8. No computer sales persons or employees of a computer company should be selected for membership (to avoid potential bias or conflict of interest)

Responsibilities:
1. To evaluate the current need for office modernization
2. To determine how the church might use a computer
3. To recommend changes in office equipment and procedures as seen to be needed
4. If a computer is deemed desirable, then:
   a. Determine what the computer will be used for
   b. Recommend necessary software and equipment (after interviewing suppliers)
   c. Prepare a written plan of implementation
   d. Develop a budget for initial purchase and subsequent two-year use
   e. Prepare a formal report

The idea for selecting a computer often comes from those members most familiar with computers where they are employed. Clergy, largely unfamiliar with electronics and uncomfortable around computers, tend to be slow, generally, in recognizing the need for a computer. Too busy to spend a lot of time learning, they continue to go about their parish duties in much the same way as they always have. Only when they suddenly discover from someone else, another clergy person perhaps, all the good things the computer could do for them, do they get interested in the possibilities.

Thus, the appointed committee must explore needs, resources, equipment, programs, and expected uses. The pastor's cooperation in such a study is essential since it is in the church office that the computer will be used most often.

There are many articles that point out why you may need a computer in your church. (There is even a *Christian Computing* magazine!) Articles describe the varieties of hardware and software available. Bookstores have never had so many different volumes about computers.

Technical information on the variety of software programs and hardware equipment is beyond the scope of this publication. Besides, anything specified here would probably be outdated by the time you read the text. Thus, interested congregations and clergy should find available literature about the use of computers, especially in the church, make decisions based on that information. Some of the best resources will not be in books, but in magazine articles.

Certain planning processes and certain principles remain unchanged, even as the technology does change. This chapter is devoted to those principles, not to the specifics of that technology.

The place to begin in your computer selection process is not with the hardware (the equipment) or the software (the programs), but with a search that demonstrates a specific affordable need. Once need and cost are determined, equipment and programs are sought, and training of users is begun.

Consider first the kind of reports and information you are already receiving from various staff. How much time does it take, and how much does it cost for the staff to put those reports together? Can the data be generated more efficiently and more economically with a computer? What additional information can we get from a computer that we don't get now that will help us manage the church more efficiently? Is the information we need gathered more easily and cheaply manually or by computer? How often do we use new reports and will that use be increased when a computer produces any statement or report routinely? How will the computer fit into our long-range needs, and what changes in recordkeeping should be made? What are the primary benefits to be gained from computer use?

Second, consider what it is you expect to gain from the use of a computer. What do you want to do? What do you expect to accomplish? Do you want to gather facts more quickly? Are you eager to cut staff? Generally a computer will permit you to manage your organization more efficiently, gather more information, and do it more accurately, while maintaining a better control over the whole operation than otherwise might be possible. Computers are used to secure facts more rapidly, to get more facts than ever before, and to make computations and sort information almost instantaneously. The computer is a tool, not a substitute, toward increasing your ability to make better decisions based on the information so gained.

And you can't ignore the cost. Computers do still cost a lot of money although far less than only a couple of years ago. Remember when calculators were five hundred dollars and now they are less than ten dollars?

A number of different elements go into the total price for a computer. What another church has is not necessarily what you need or what you will pay.

The cost of the hardware is one thing. But you must also consider the cost of the software, insurance, maintenance, supplies, training, furniture, and the cost of converting your files. Even money used to pay for the system is a cost to be added in. Project your costs carefully. Base your estimates on information gathered from salespersons, catalogs, and those who know what you should have. You will need to shop around to find the best deals.

Unfortunately, the system you select today will probably be outdated in a few years. Many churches have delayed making a purchase intending to wait for something better. That is not good planning, at least not with computers. Because there will probably always be a better time as something new is developed next year. The computer industry is fast moving, and new products are constantly being put on the market.

However, what's there now is good and will be good for a number of years. And it will probably serve your needs very well for a long time, even though something else next year will do it better. Find out what meets your needs now and what is likely to meet your needs in the future. Buy now, and plan to buy again later.

People who have never operated a computer can be intimidated by the mere presence of the keyboard and console. Yet, the same persons when carefully introduced to the computer quickly lose that fear and become hooked on computers. You can learn!

As you search for equipment, consider: how available and reliable is the equipment you're looking at? Is it really suitable for your situation? (Don't know? Get a consultant to help you.) Is the system expandable? Is it easy to operate? What kind of technical support can you expect with programming and operator training? Will the company be around in a few years so you can get replacement parts and maintenance? Are there enough software programs around for you to use on this equipment?

So, when you know this:

What needs will the computer satisfy?
What uses will be made of the computer?
What will a system cost?

When the congregation has committed itself to buy, you are ready to choose the systems that will meet your needs.

Again, keep in mind the total picture. Your computer system, any computer system, is designed to process data in four specific steps:

1. Input—putting data into the system
2. Memory—storing the data entered
3. Processing—using the data
4. Output—producing the information requested

All of these steps are performed by software (the instructions) and hardware (the equipment). The keyboard is used to enter new data, just as a typewriter is used to type information on a sheet of paper. The central processor is used to store the information entered and to make necessary calculations. The CRT (Cathode Ray Tube) is a TV-like display terminal that shows you the data you are entering or the data you requested. The printer prints out the information in "hard copy."

The software is the program that tells the hardware what to do. So first you find the software you need, and then you locate the equipment that will handle the software.

Software programs for churches are now in abundant supply. Their abundance is at once an advantage and yet can be disastrous for the careless shopper. Before you buy anything, watch a demonstration of the package. Will it do what you want? Is it more than you need? Is it enough? Is it a complete church system—membership, accounting, contributions records? Or is it only a partial system? The parts of the program should all fit together so that the directory, for example, can be used to prepare headings for the individual contributions records reports, for mailing labels, or a new directory.

You don't have to write a program from scratch, although you can, of course. But that is expensive and time-consuming. Check with your own church supply store for a listing of programs available. If possible, use something developed just for your denomination.

When purchasing any software programs, check on its reliability. How long has it been in use? Will the writer provide updates? What about technical support? Is the program adequately documented? Can the program be modified easily for your special needs?

Avoid well-meaning members who want to program a system for your church. You'll only be frustrated. Buy something proven from a company that will respond to your needs for technical assistance. In the long run, that will be less costly, less frustrating, and more efficient.

Hardware is the second choice. Consider how much you want to do, how much data will be stored, the way you want to use the data, the speed of the processor, and what peripheral equipment you may want to add later.

Generally, you'll buy the keyboard, processor, and CRT all in one package. The printer may be selected separately. And the kind of printer you select depends on your needs. Do you need a letter-quality printer for correspondence, manuscripts, sermons? They're slower than a dot matrix printer, for example, but have a much better appearance. The fast printers are for a lot of data in a hurry, like a mailing list, a long report, or financial statements. Will you want a wide 15″ carriage or the standard letter-size printer? You must choose.

I use an IBM-AT personal computer with hard disk attached to an Okidata 93 microline dot matrix wide carriage printer. This book manuscript was prepared on that equipment. All of my correspondence, sermons, manuscripts, and even some typesetting for booklets is done on this equipment. I also maintain on this equipment a listing of 27,000 names and addresses of subscribers to my magazine, *The Clergy Journal*.

You decide your need and then match that need to the right system. Need help? Check it out with your computer selection committee. Or hire a consultant.

Preparing Your Church for a New Computer

Selection of a computer and installation of the equipment is only the first step in the process of having a usable, effective computer program at your church. Unless you have personnel who can operate that equipment, all the equipment in the world won't do you much good. So you must carefully train your church employees (including the pastor), to get all the benefits possible out of the computer. You paid a lot of money for improved efficiency. Now you must put it to use.

The obvious place to begin preparing your church for its computer is with the users by (1) seeking their ideas on how a computer should be used in the church, (2) making them feel that they are part of the process, (3) inviting your staff users to the vendor's demonstration of the equipment, and (4) encouraging staff to learn as much as they can about computers.

It is important that your people and your staff have realistic expectations about the computer before it is put to use at the church. For example:

1. You cannot expect to have all the applications up and running within the first month after the system is installed. There is too much for the staff to learn and absorb in such a short time.

2. You cannot expect instant output from the computer. Nothing can be produced—no reports, no letters, no statements—until some pertinent data is first entered into the system, and that can be a tedious task. It may take several months to get everything entered.

3. You cannot expect that all the data that is entered will be 100 percent accurate. The process of verification and correction never ends.

4. You cannot expect the data to be completely always up to date—that requires continuous updating and then entering the information to reflect any changes. For example, the only way to know who has not attended worship services for several months is to record the names of those people who do attend church.

5. You cannot expect that it will be easy to make the computer do what you want it to do. You'll fuss and fret and get irritated because the computer won't react, behave, or produce. Seek help. Look in the documentation; ask experts within the congregation (those who recommended this computer in the first place!). Get help from the vendor. Usually, for most computer problems, there are simple and obvious answers the experts help you with.

6. You cannot expect to learn everything you need to know about your computer in one day. Computer systems are usually complex, involving a wide range of operations. You must be persistent and open to continued learning.

7. You cannot expect the computer to operate without a breakdown, sometime. Be prepared for the occasional breakdown and interruption. Either have a full-service maintenance contract or know where you can go to get repairs done.

8. You cannot expect that you will never lose any data. Expect that your computer will break down at any time and that you will simply lose your data. Regularly make duplicate copies of every file and record, particularly after changes are made.

Someone has to be responsible for the computer operations in your church. Usually several groups of people are involved, with (1) the technicians being those who understand how the computer works and will be used, (2) the administrators supervising the use of the computers, and (3) the operators putting data into the computer.

The technicians know and understand the technical aspects of the computer. Selected from your congregation to help select the computer and to help set up and develop the system you use, the technicians are available as support personnel to answer questions posed by the users.

To be most helpful, the technicians used for your computer system should have a knowledge of microcomputers. Often, people who are familiar with large frame computers won't be too helpful for personal computer technical data. It may be best not to include such persons on the support group since their work experience environment is so much different from the church's computer users.

The primary users and administrators of the computer program will be those who direct the activities for which the computers were obtained. Often an administrator is selected to install the system and train all the people who expect to use it. This individual will need to be able to relate well to clergy and to other staff.

The chief computer administrator will ultimately be the person responsible for being certain the program works the way everyone wants it to work. Thus, the individual must be especially sensitive to changes in office procedures and personnel.

The operators are the persons who have hands-on experience in putting data into the computer, for updating existing data and for making all corrections. Often the operators will be putting in data and extracting reports at the request of staff persons.

Operators need both the ability and the desire to learn to use the computer system effectively. They should have a healthy and realistic attitude toward machines, have an excitement about this new dimension for the church, and be willing to stick with it through periods of frustration, especially at first. Under the supervision of the administrator, the operators will probably train and direct the activities of others who have hands-on use of the system, too.

It is important that proper training be given to any operator or hands-on user of the equipment prior to implementation of the system. Training at the vendor site is desirable, but more personal training can certainly be provided at the church. Creating an air of excitement for those who will use the equipment helps stimulate a positive attitude among users who are not sure about what they will be learning or doing.

Objectives of a carefully developed training program for computer users include:

1. To eliminate any fears of those using the computer system; to make users comfortable with the machine, familiar with the equipment.

2. To help users become familiar with the physical operation of the equipment and the keyboard—how to turn on the machine, how to use diskettes, how to copy files, etc., and then how to know what to do when it doesn't seem to work right!

3. To have users become familiar with the basic commands, know what they are used for, when they should be used, and how to use them.

4. To help users become familiar with existing documentation, know how to read and use it, and how to find answers to their own questions.

5. To encourage users to take existing software programs and use them for the intended purpose.

Anyone using the computer in the church will learn best by having carefully supervised hands-on operating experience. Familiarity with the system comes with using it, not just by reading about it.

Careful planning in the selection, training, and use of the computer in the church will make it one of the most useful tools the church can obtain. It then becomes a valuable and useful asset for more efficient and effective ministry management.

Computers in the Small Church

One young pastor, the Reverend Ronald C. Yergy, pastor of the Lutheran Church of the Holy Spirit in Philadelphia, says this about the use of a computer in his small church:*

Many people assume that only a large congregation can use a computer. Those same people are convinced that the size of a congregation, its resources, and the complexities of its management are the major reasons for considering a computer. However, a small congregation, where the pastor alone represents the staff, can also discover great benefits from computer use.

---

*Reprinted from *The Clergy Journal,* November/December 1983. © Copyright 1983 by Church Management, Inc. Used with permission.

When the pastor serves as the chief recordkeeper, the producer of most written material, the editor and publisher of the newsletter and Sunday bulletin, he/she is covering the same ground that larger congregations sometimes delegate to several paid staff members. These tasks are necessary, but they do consume a great deal of time, time which the pastor could be spending in other areas of ministry. When volunteers are used to help out with typing and recordkeeping, the pastor must still prepare rough copies, oversee the process, and approve the final work. This too is time consuming.

A small computer

It is in this situation, a one-person office, that a small personal computer can be a great benefit. I use a TRS-80 Model III, 48K disk system with a Smith Corona TP1 printer for *all* of my office work. The total investment in this equipment by my congregation and myself was under $2500, and the cost continues to come down.

I maintain the entire parish register on the computer, with printed copies of all records. The program also produces an index for almost instant access to any listing. I keep an updated membership profile on every member, and with this profile and the computer's ability to search through a great number of records rapidly, I can print mailing lists to any combination of members, telephone directories, and listings of almost any nature. With an automatic letter writing program, the computer reduces my memorial acknowledgement letter writing time by well over 75 percent, and compiles a total listing for the financial secretary as well.

Other uses

Other time and energy saving uses for this computer involve keeping all the financial records of the congregation in twenty-three different categories. A young woman in our congregation learned to operate the computer and this program in less than one hour, and has been using it successfully for more than two years. And of course, there is the great benefit of word processing. With an inexpensive, yet powerful program, any type of printed material can be produced easily and completely corrected before it ever appears on your paper. Just the freedom to format the pages of a newsletter, and to do it before it is typed, saves countless hours of re-typing.

A tool

The computer, like any other tool, is only as effective as its user. It will not replace a good secretary, or make an otherwise poor writer a good writer. It will save time on routine tasks. It will make recordkeeping easier and more efficient. It will increase significantly the ease by which written documents are produced. But it does need someone to operate it. The pastor, the occupant of that one-person office, stands to benefit along with the congregation, but he/she needs to be willing to use the computer as a tool. Small personal computers will not use themselves.

Personally, as the pastor of a congregation with only one hundred thirty-eight members, my computer is a tool that cannot be beat. Any small congregation can benefit as well as the big congregations.

A Personal Computer for the Minister

John William Zehring, vice-president for development at Bangor Theological seminary in Bangor, Maine, describes the many ways in which clergy could use a computer even if their church decided against it.*

Let's face it, haven't you caught yourself saying, "If only I could justify . . . ." The lure of the microchip is striking everywhere and the pastorate is no exception. Perhaps you have been attracted by the daily barrage of newspaper and television advertising for home computers. You believe, on faith, that the computer is a powerful machine. Yet isn't it essentially for people who know computer programming or

*From "Ten Excuses to Buy Yourself a Computer" by John William Zehring, *The Clergy Journal*, August 1983. © Copyright 1983 by Church Management, Inc. Used with permission.

for kids who love arcade games or for executives with money to manage and invest? Well, yes, they all use it. But it is so much more.

Maybe you've seen articles on churches using computers. All well and good. But . . . what about one for yourself?

Pastors will likely find that one of the computer's greatest assets is with words and word processing. Few people work with words and ideas more than ministers. So consider it a tool, one that increases both quantity and quality of work rather than a sophisticated toy to simulate the destruction of aliens while resting from your meditations on God's love, forgiveness, and peace.

You deserve it. There are masses of people with a terminal on their desk with no greater mission than rearranging numbers or shooting down flying saucers. But you, servant of God, with a great mission to accomplish and a vision to pursue . . . . You need good tools to enhance your effectiveness and your primary medium: words.

Now, humble as we all are, isn't there a tinge of guilt at this magnetic attraction to an expensive gadget? Can something be fun and so very useful at the same time?

The right tools

A carpenter can certainly justify a power saw. A doctor has no difficulty replacing the old physician's bag of instruments with the latest in medical technology. The right tools are important to have.

The difference between the typewriter and a computer word-processing system is like the difference between a quill tip pen and an electric typewriter. Why?

Speed is one reason. Imagine being able to knock off large percentages of time in the process of writing sermons or articles or correspondence. Some users claim to type about 40 percent faster on the terminal than on an electric typewriter, partly because the keys go faster and partly because of automatic "wrap," which means not having to hit the return key—the words automatically wrap around to the next line. Another factor in speed is the lightning fast ability to make corrections by simply deleting or typing over mistakes . . . no correcting paper or paint and no typos on the final print-out.

Then there is quality. While speed alone may not justify the cost, quality does. Many writers (and pulpiteers) have attested to the importance of rewriting. Hemingway rewrote *A Farewell to Arms* thirty-nine times. With a computer, you can put away the scissors and tape; for a few keys here and there and you have moved words, sentences, paragraphs, or pages wherever you want them. You can insert new text and delete what you don't need. Any rewriting is much easier on the computer and THAT justifies its cost. Then, at the push of another key, the perfect page comes out of your printer.

Is word processing hard to learn? Anyone who has made it through Systematic Theology should have little difficulty following the "user friendly" manuals (called "documentation") for the word-processing programs. Beware of the myth that you must be a computer whiz: You do not need to know computer programming to use word-processing. It's all been done for you on the "program" which you purchase for your computer.

If you're becoming hooked but feel you need a few more good excuses (to buy one for yourself, not the church—that's another case, but a good one), consider some of the following:

Ten reasons why

1. Outlining

If you are the sort of person who begins any writing or speaking project with an outline, you can throw away those pages and pages of revised outlines and notes on scratch paper. With the computer, it's a simple matter to write out your thoughts as quickly as they come and then organize them once they are entered on the screen.

2. Sermons

Whether you are an ardent believer in spending an hour in the study for each minute in the pulpit or if you need to whip out a meditation in only a few hours, your fifty-two annual sermons probably amount to around seven to eight hundred pages of finished, double-spaced copy each year. That doesn't include weddings, funerals, special services, or all your outlining and rough drafts.

Need another copy? It's a simple matter to print another since you have the sermon stored.

One additional advantage of editing sermons from the computer terminal: It doesn't hurt so much when you cut your words, since they went up so easy in the first place. Good preaching and writing is usually concise. But once the sermon manuscript is finished, it can be painful to cut here and there for the sake of a tight message. Text editing by the tube facilitates simpler and tighter writing.

3. *Newsletters*

Whether your church produces a dozen or fifty-two newsletters each year, that's an additional project easily managed with word-processing. Jot ideas down, store them in the memory, and recall them when it's time for the pastor's message in the newsletter.

4. *Correspondence*

Even a klutz at the keyboard can turn out professional looking letters and even "individualized" form letters on a computer. If you find yourself using certain phrases or paragraphs over and over, you can store them and recall them with a button—no need to retype; it appears instantly.

5. *Files*

Storing your files and records on the computer saves space and time. Depending on the format, you can store about one hundred to one hundred fifty pages of text on a 5¼-inch "floppy diskette" (which runs about four dollars). Ten diskettes fit into a case or box about the size of a small Bible.

Suppose you wanted to include two paragraphs from your newsletter notes in a short article for your denominational publication. No problem. Simply recall the file on the newsletter note, block off the section you need and delete the rest. That creates a new file, leaving the original untouched, and you can print out the two paragraphs or include them as a part of the short article.

Good organization suggests having a disk for sermons, another for correspondence, another for miscellaneous records, and so on. But you can move your files around from disk to disk.

6. *Spelling*

By simply typing a word like *spell* or *check*, a program with a dictionary automatically checks all of your words. It asks you to look at and skip or correct any words it doesn't recognize (e.g. names, places, technical terms, etc.). Then, it automatically corrects your original document for you. The computer, of course, can't proofread for syntax or grammar. It wouldn't, for example, know the difference between "their" and "there." Both are spelled correctly—you have to proofread for context (it can't, after all, walk on water!) Another advantage of the spelling program: You can type as fast as humanly possible, let the spelling program catch your mistakes, and then proofread for context and syntax.

7. *Writing for Publication*

Clergy who work everyday with ideas and words often have a wealth of experiences and insights which might be valuable for publication. Have you ever caught yourself saying that you had an idea for an article or book . . . if you only had time? Here is a tool that not only buys you time, but makes the process of writing for publication more enjoyable. If you like to get the most miles for your money, swap blocks of text back and forth between sermons, newsletters, and articles without retyping them. After all, if it was a good, original, and creative idea in the first place, why not use it for more than one audience?

8. *Recordkeeping*

In addition to word-processing, there are programs for creating records and files which make it easy to manage your information and even cross-index it in many ways.

One great advantage of using word processing for recordkeeping is known as "global search." This means that typing a word like "Find" and then a string of letters or words (called, what else: a "string"), you are instantly transported to those words. For example, if the file of this article were loaded on the screen and the "Find: 'on the screen' " was typed, this sentence would immediately appear. No hunting for it through pages and pages of text.

Imagine the advantages of this for quickly finding records of sermons, weddings hymns, or baptisms!

9. *Illustrations, Quotes, Stories, Sermon Ideas, and Anecdotes*

Many pastors probably have files of stories, anecdotes, ideas, illustrations, and sermons materials. Perhaps you have found yourself saying . . . "Now where did I put . . . ?"

With these entered into a computer file, simply use the global search to recall them—even if you can only remember a word or two. And once you have recalled them, block them off, delete the rest (the original stays in the file on the disk), and instantly insert them into your text. Or, simply keep a computer record of where you have filed a clipping or the page number from a book.

10. *Everything Else*

There are, of course, more than ten excuses, but by now you probably have a head filled with rationalizations for buying yourself such a handy tool. A few other ideas, if you still need more. . . .

Put your *Resume* or *Profile* on computer when searching for a new job and easily tailor each application.

Financial and Tax Records, with many specialized programs, are easily kept on computer.

Keep abreast of *Technology.*

It is possible to purchase the Bible on diskette. Throw away the concordance, for just think how easy it would be to find any verse with the global search feature by just remembering a few words.

Finally, it's downright addicting! That's good news for you, bad news for your family. You'll find that fear of staring at a blank page replaced by an eagerness to write and fill up the screen, knowing that you can edit on the screen once your ideas and words are behind the blinking cursor.

What about a Computer for Your Church?

Is it hard to learn?

How can anyone who has studied Hebrew or Greek even ask such a question?

It takes a short while to discover how computers think and to become accustomed to some jargon (just like theology has its jargon). But don't make the mistake of thinking you need to take a computer course to use a home computer. The programs or "software" you use (word processing is software) are explained in accompanying manuals (documentation), and as more people buy computers, the instructions are becoming easier to understand.

Some of the computer magazines available on newsstands (e.g., *Creative Computing, Popular Computing*) give you a good sense of the products, although it's possible to be overcome with jargon and technical information. Sales representatives at the many new computer stores are more than happy to explain how home computers work, and the best sales people won't try to show off their own specialized knowledge to impress you. Within your congregation, chances are good that some member has a home computer who would love to explain its many capacities.

No, it's not terribly hard to learn, especially if you are adept at teaching yourself new things. But the sources of information come at you from many directions, and there is rarely one source that puts them all together.

Is it all peaches and cream?

No. The word *glitch* was invented for people who use computers. So was "bug" and "#%$&*#"! Figure on something always going wrong, at least at first. *Something* won't work right, you will lose all the information on some disk, a piece of equipment will need repair, or some instruction will appear to be written in Chinese. It happens.

So, why bother? Because, even with glitches and equipment breakdowns, it's a small price to pay for this incredible tool.

Are there tax advantages?

Yes, depending on how you use the computer and your tax bracket. If you purchase the computer, printer, and word-processing program strictly for business, you can depreciate the cost and deduct supply expenses. Check with the IRS or your tax accountant for details.

Should I buy now or later?

It's catch-22. Will prices come down or technology improve even more if I wait six months? Probably. But then, if you buy in six months, six months from then the same thing will happen. How long do you want to postpone the decision? If you're going to buy, get the system that will do what you need now and tell yourself that you will be satisfied with it, even when you see lower prices or different technology in the future. Of course, many computers today are able to be upgraded as new innovations become available.

How much will it cost?

That depends on lots of things, like what model you want, where you buy, extra accessories and programs, and so on. For word processing you will need a computer with a disk drive (make sure it is

231

capable of lower case letters and more than forty character lines). You'll need the software (e.g., word processing, spelling program), some disks, and a printer with a cable to hook it to the computer.

There are many systems available, sometimes sold as word-processing packages with everything you need, for $2,500 to $3,000. In many cases, that would include a daisy-wheel printer (for finished copy, which looks like it is produced by a good electric typewriter) rather than a dot-matrix printer (which is faster, cheaper, and okay if you're not sending it to anyone). On sale or through mail-order discount brokers, the cost can be even less.

Get some advice from an impartial third party on what you need. Don't buy an inferior tool that you will have to upgrade soon, and be careful not to purchase more than you need. And, service (and consultation) on your system is worth its weight in gold.

Software

Data base elements for a complete church computer system are available from most larger denominational publishing houses. One of the most effective is that produced for the Lutheran churches called "Lutheran Computer Information System," available from Fortress Press, 2900 Queen Lane, Philadelphia, Pa. 19129. Similar software systems are "UMIS/plus" and UMIS/300," from The United Methodist Publishing House, Electronic Publishing, 1661 N. Northwest Highway, Park Ridge, Ill. 60068 (312/299-4411).

Several commercially produced software programs for churches are also available such as from BPI in Austin, Texas, or MSI in Ft. Worth, Texas, or TOM in Seattle, Washington. Your local computer store should have information on sources of available church software. Or you can write to your denominational publication house. But be cautious in selecting any software since you must be sure it will provide you with the information you want and is adaptable to your computer hardware.

CHAPTER 12

MEMBERSHIP ENLISTMENT AND CULTIVATION

I DONT UNDERSTAND," complained board member Sam Kohn. "All those strange faces on Sunday morning and yet our membership drops. What's going on?"

"That's right. I noticed the same," chimed in Betty Carlson. "I know who all the members are, and I see all those visitors once, but not again. Why can't the pastor get those people to join?"

"I stand out there in the narthex, and I watch all those new people go in and out, yet they never join our church." Charlene Cox always counted the new faces each Sunday morning at First Church.

Herman Brown, over at Second Church, had the opposite reaction. "Pastor, why don't we see any new faces here on Sunday morning? Surely there are new people out there looking for a church. Why don't they come here?"

"You're absolutely right," responded Sally Sampson. "I know of at least three new families in our neighborhood, and they all went over to First first, but joined Third Church. And they never even came by here. If I had had the time, I could have talked to them."

"All those new members! Wow! That's great, pastor. How you do it I'll never know. But it's sure good to see all those people joining up." That was Gerald Cause exuding over the increase of new members at Third Church.

"Yes, but I don't see our attendance going up, and I don't know any of those new people. They never come back," complained Susan Arndt. "Why don't they stay? Doesn't the pastor keep in touch?"

Some congregations simply cannot get new people to come to their church, or when they do come, have difficulty handling a steady influx of new people or assimilating new people into the congregation. All three of these situations are at the heart of the problems facing many congregations: how to get people to the church in the first place; then once there, how to get a commitment; and once they join, how to keep them coming.

Aggressive leadership can be the key to reversing those trends. Active involvement by other members and staff, not just the pastor, can turn a potentially exciting new member possibility into a reality that strengthens the life and mission of the church.

Common reasons why a few congregations never grow:

1. Too often a congregation's leadership simply waits for the people to come, expecting them to be enticed into a building by its mere presence.

2. Lots of visitors may show, but without follow-up calls to their homes, not many of those people will be repeats. They go where they perceive a friendly welcome waits.

3. Successful programs to sign up new members may add numbers to the rolls, but participation in programs and activities is virtually nonexistent. "We don't push anymore. If they want to share in the

programs, that's their choice. The newsletter lists the programs each week. Anyone can come." Some congregations never personally invite anyone to anything.

4. "When a member needs me, I respond." Some pastors visit only when there are problems, a death, or someone wants to give money. Failure to stay in touch even without problems is a common reason for membership apathy.

So, what do you do?

The purpose of this chapter is to offer helps in (1) getting the people there to begin with, and once there, encouraging them to stay and (2) then involving them actively and aggressively once they are part of the fellowship.

Getting the People to Say Yes

Every congregation has developed its own evangelistic techniques, that is, the procedures for reaching out to people outside the fellowship, inviting them to share the excitement of the gospel in their place. For many it's a rather haphazard process, done as the spirit moves the pastor. Often the lay leadership is not involved and seldom do the members take an active part in recruiting new members.

Yet, the people won't just come, at least not most of them. True, there are some people who want to get involved and they will go looking and they will join and they will get involved. But that's not most people. If you want the church to grow, you and your people must get out and "beat the bushes." Even the best placed and most attractive church building won't automatically guarantee an increase in membership. Of course, a church building back in a corner, old and unkempt, off the main street, will attract even fewer people, probably none. In either case, however, an active program of invitation and assimilation can bring in the people, anyway. But most people don't just come, on their own.

Contacting new residents

In growing communities new people are constantly moving into the area. A large national corporation announces a major decision to employ 2,200 people on a 150-acre tract just outside the city limits. A major new shopping center is planned near your church building. A housing developer gets City Council approval for a 500-home subdivision on vacant land one mile north of your church. And already there may be a high saturation of apartments, condos, and townhouses in the area. People are moving in and out. Mobility is high, yet the net inflow into the community stays more than the outflow.

In the midst of that scenario, most congregations cannot help but grow. But again, it doesn't just happen. It must be planned, and it must be nurtured.

Other places may not be booming, in fact may be declining. Still new people come to some of those places; unchurched people stay in the area; and members still need to be cultivated, nurtured, maybe even coddled some.

Instead of waiting for newcomers to show up on a Sunday morning, aggressive church leaders will locate the names of newcomers and send each a personalized welcome letter (done on the church's word processor). With today's office machines, even computer generated letters can appear to be personally typed and signed.

Sources for names and addresses are available from many places. Try the local bank, real estate agencies, the local Welcome Wagon, or other Newcomer service. Seek their cooperation in locating new people. Encourage members to spot moving vans on their blocks, report the address to the church, and then make a personal visit and invitation.

Check your sources of names more carefully:

—Worship attendance cards. Visitors at worship are often the best prospects. Use a worship attendance list or provide attendance cards. Use a guest book. Use oral announcements to invite visitors to share their intentions. Be certain someone besides the pastor always greets every visitor. Know the names of every person in church on Sunday morning. There are prospective members in the crowd.

—Search the church record books. There are people who have been married at your church who are not members. Families of church members for whom you've held a funeral service may be possibilities for contact. Are there any teenagers not confirmed who should be by now? How about the nonmember spouses of members? Look through the membership records of the church organization to locate nonmember participants.

—Encourage members to participate. Each calendar quarter send every member a 3 × 5 prospect name card and ask for their help in locating the unchurched and inactive. Ask everyone to give at least one name.

PROSPECT MEMBER CARD

Here's a Prospective Member Name

Here's the name _____

Here's why I think this person may be interested in Christ Church:

_____

_____

If someone calls on this person(s), you may say I gave their name _____

You may call me for more information _____

My name: _____

—Ask others for names. As your evangelism committee goes out each week on assigned calls, have them ask about people who should be visited. Use the Shepherd groups to find other people in their community. Don't overlook the hospital as a source for names, especially visits to relatives and friends of members. Knock on the doors of apartments and ask for names. Know the manager. Follow up on leads. Use neighborhood association meetings to ferret out other potentially interested persons.

—Use the community. Welcome Wagon isn't the only place to get names. Try the utility company for names of new people. The newspaper may be willing to give you names of new subscribers. New school enrollees are always new residents.

—Use telephone surveys. Some church groups have developed "telethones" to contact every name in the local telephone book. The survey reveals who goes or does not go where to church. Telephone invitations can be helpful in locating potentially interested people. Follow-up personal visits mean you are serious about your invitation.

—Use a door-to-door census. A community-wide census is a systematic way of finding out who claims to be a church member. Much like a telephone survey, but with person-to-person contact, invitations are easier to make and a person's response to your questions are easier to evaluate.

CHECKLIST FOR A COMMUNITY-WIDE CENSUS

1. Define carefully the area to be surveyed. Use a map.
2. Estimate population; determine volunteer needs.
3. Be specific about the area—streets, house numbers, etc.—each person should cover. Fifty homes is a lot of doorbells!
4. Enlist interested people and arrange for a meeting so everyone knows where they're going and what they're doing. Prepare instruction packets.

5. Follow up on all prospects revealed in the census. Keep a good file on progress of each family and each canvasser.
6. Share with other churches the carefully gathered census information you have collected. The church is a body, each a part of the other. The people you can't touch may be reached by the church next door.

—Use your denomination's membership referral service. You send in names of members who have moved. The central clearing office forwards that information on to the church nearest your member in the new community. Contact is made promptly thanks to your timely referral and the prompt response of the pastor at the new place. Likewise, when you receive names, a prompt visit by phone or in person may be essential in retaining the interest of that family.

A letter of welcome sets the tone for later letters or personal follow-up visits whenever new people move in.

LETTER OF WELCOME TO NEWCOMERS IN COMMUNITY

Mr. and Mrs. _____

Address _____

_____

Dear Mr. and Mrs. _____ ,

Welcome to our community! It is good to know you have arrived. And we hope by now you are well on the way to getting settled, informed, and involved in our community life.

On behalf of the officers and members of Christ Church, we extend a most hearty welcome to you. And we would like to help you make this transition to a new community one that will be fulfilling and satisfying for you and each member of your family.

We cordially invite you to worship with us and to be involved in as many programs and activities as you care to share with us. Our church building at 4th and Brazos is conveniently located to your house. Sunday morning services are at 9:00 A.M. and 11:00 A.M. with Sunday church school for everyone at 10:00 A.M..

Our staff is committed to the idea that every Christian should be involved in a church home near their own home. If you are already a member of another local congregation, this letter is simply our sincere welcome to you to the community. If you are searching for a church home, we invite you here.

If there is anything that we can do to make your move and stay in our community more comfortable, please let us hear from you.

Sincerely,

Pastor _____

Included in that letter should be an appropriate brochure of information about the community and the church.

One congregation developed a "Directory of Information for New Residents," with the basic idea that all new residents in a community, even if moving only from another section of town, need certain information about the new area and the services provided. All new residents need to know about utility hookups, garbage collection days, nearby emergency clinics, where to vote, churches, and even an area map. Moving from another city requires more information: auto registration, driver's license, schools, post office, etc.

Many newcomer services provide a listing of such services, but a directory prepared by the church may be more inclusive and certainly an impressive service by a church. Names, telephone numbers, addresses—even basic information about age requirements for school or driver's license would be helpful.

One congregation's directory index included these items:

INDEX TO COMMUNITY SERVICES

Animal licenses
Area shopping centers
Auto registration, titles, tags
Bridges
Buses
Child services
Churches and synagogues
Counseling
Day care
Dental society
Disabled services
Drivers' licenses
Drug addiction/alcoholism
Electric company
Emergency numbers
Employment
English language classes
Garbage, trash collection days
General information
Health clinic
Homestead exemption
Hospitals/emergency clinics
Hunting/fishing licenses
Legal aid
Medical society
Medicare
Newspapers
Post offices
Recreation
Schools
Social security
Tax collector
Tax information
Telephone installation and service
United Parcel Service
Veterans affairs
Voter registration
Utilities
Water/wastewater service

An attractive brochure is important. With a careful stewardship of available resources, and without being cheap about it, a congregation can make a very appealing and useful booklet.

Congregations could use such a directory in a variety of ways in ministry by:

—including the directory in a letter sent to all new residents.

—sending a copy to worship visitors who indicate they are new residents.

—encouraging members to distribute copies to new residents in their community.

—placing copies in local real estate offices, banks, apartment complexes, and shopping centers.
—providing quantities in bulk to the personnel offices of new corporations locating in the area or other businesses seeking new employees.
—including copies in the resource packets distributed by Welcome Wagon or Newcomers groups to new residents.

Information about the church can be shared with interested residents through an attractive church brochure. The basic elements of a church brochure include:
—church names, address, telephone number, and names and telephone numbers of pastors
—directions on how to get to the church building
—hours of worship, education, organizations
—names of organizations, leaders, purpose, contact telephone numbers, time and dates of meetings, activities.
—music programs of the church including choir time and dates for practice.
—educational opportunities for all members of the family
—frequency of Holy Communion
—greetings (brief) from the pastor.

A New Member Brochure

An active member of one congregation describes how her congregation developed a church brochure:

HOW TO CREATE A NEW MEMBER BROCHURE*
by Mary E. Stoltz

As an outsider moving into Columbus, Wisconsin (pop. 4000), I found myself somewhat lost and unfamiliar with my surroundings. My husband and I knew no one and had to flounder about for some time before friendships and affiliations were formed. Even after two years here, we had joined clubs and church, but we weren't comfortable with the whos and hows and whys of getting things done in our new community.

Years later, as a member of Faith Lutheran Church Council, I found myself in the midst of a discussion on how to make our new members feel more welcome, comfortable, and useful in the congregation. Traditionally a community peopled by retired farmers of the area and their immediate families, the make-up of the community was changing and many younger families were moving in. We realized that we needed to do more to respond to their needs for establishing ties.

New members had always been presented to the congregation during services and welcomed by an evangelism chairman, but that was about it. I recalled how startled I had been as a new member upon being called to work on a committee for a women's group. I didn't even know I was a *member* of this group! As a council, we knew there were many such confusions that new people must be facing. How could we clear out the cobwebs, as well as make people feel truly welcome and important to our group?

The brochure

We decided that a membership brochure explaining the various groups, services, and functions of the congregation would be helpful. After taking stock of our needs, budget, and what we wished to have the brochure explain, we talked to representatives from other congregations to see if any of them might provide us some guidelines on how to proceed. Surprisingly, none of them had ever used the brochure approach. We were on our own. And so, with our experiences as a background, I'd like to explain our brochure development.

The first thing to consider is, of course, budget. We had allocated for evangelism $100 from our general budget, not a huge sum. Larger churches may, of course, have larger or more flexible figures to work with.

*Reprinted from *The Clergy Journal*, April 1984. © Copyright 1984 by Church Management, Inc. Used with permission.

At any rate, before going any further, set a firm figure and stick to it! It will provide you leverage for dealing with printing companies as they bid for your job, and you will also be less tempted to add frills and expansions which they may recommend later.

The next logical step, before any writing or composition takes place, is to consult as many printing companies as possible within your area for quotes and *advice!* Printing companies range from "quick print" operations to newspapers to large publishing firms. We were amazed—you may be also—at how their years of experience with every imaginable kind of printing job can help. Ask about paper selection (there are *many* different weights and qualities), layouts, print size and spacing, colors, drawings, photos, print styles, etc. Each of these items can significantly alter the cost of your particular job, and consideration of different formats and styles can also determine just how much information you can present to your readers.

The most valuable piece of information one local printer gave us was to use a tri-fold layout. We could use just one sheet of heavy-grade paper per brochure, cutting material charges considerably, and yet by printing on both sides for eventual folding, have room for virtually everything we might want to say.

Artwork

Photographs or pictures involving several colors are terribly expensive to reproduce. If you absolutely must have some artwork included, however, try to provide your own sketches or *basic* artwork that can be reproduced in the same color as the text of your brochure. In this way, your printer can use a process like photocopying—he simply "takes a picture of the picture" and imposes it on the face of the brochure or wherever you wish it placed. In our case, we wanted our face page to be a picture of our lovely, modern building. We asked an artist/member to make a pen drawing to scale for the size of our front page, and submitted it to the printer.

Another way to save on costs is to do a work-up of the final layout of the brochure yourself. Type style and column sizes will all be different in the finished product, but you can closely approximate how much can fit onto each page. This not only saves you money in labor, but it should also assure you that the brochure will be laid out exactly as *you* wish it to be, not as the printer sees fit. Always check with the printer though, to make sure you aren't trying to do something that will not work.

One other tip to keep in mind has to do with volume rates. We found that we could have 500 copies printed for only slightly more money than 300 and still stay within our budget. Each printer will have breakdown limits, but essentially dropping the rates beyond certain numbers is standard. To take advantage of this while realizing that this same printing may be used for several years can be a problem. In our case we solved it by inserting blanks wherever a name or phone number was required. In that way we could order in quantity and still work with the natural changes in leadership and personnel that occur with time.

Compilation

Once all the technical arrangements have been made, the real work of compiling something meaningful and useful to your new members can begin. Here again, each church will have a different set of needs and requirements. Let me use ours as an example since it has served us well.

Since our primary goal was to alert people from outside the church and community to the groups and services active in our congregation, the major portion of our brochure was used to detail them. Following the message of welcome and our pastor's name and phone number, each group from the choir to confirmation classes is listed with a space for entering the current head of that group and his or her phone number. Also included here is a two or three line summary of purpose, meeting times, etc. These listings, however, used up only two of the six available "pages" in our tri-fold design. Utilizing the front page cover with the sketched picture of our building left three more pages to be filled.

A brief history of our young congregation filled another page and, more importantly, pointed up the spirit of independence and determination which had gotten us so well established. It also exhibited to newcomers that this church they were joining had been started and supported largely by one-time "outsiders" just like themselves.

With two pages left, we dedicated one of them to a guide to the large, abstract stained-glass windows flanking the side walls of the church since many questions had been received about them. The "back" page was left blank to leave space for anything which the pastor or evangelism committee needed to write in when members were received.

239

But the completed brochure, though providing a welcome bridge to new members, cannot be a welcoming committee in itself. Nor can it provide needed information about housing, organizations in the community, day care, etc. Nor does it even guarantee that new faces will be recognized and welcomed by established members of the congregation. But to try to meet all these needs, our newly formed evangelism committee adopted the following procedures:

1. After services on the day when new members are received, Polaroid pictures are taken and displayed on the church bulletin board for about two months to acquaint "old" members with the faces of "new" members.

2. A member of the committee, along with the pastor, personally greets each family and remains with them after services to introduce them among members.

3. In addition to the membership brochure, each new member is given a pledge card and offering envelopes, a copy of the constitution and bylaws of the church, and literature about community services and groups.

4. Each family is assigned a "liaison" from the evangelism committee to act as their personal guide whenever problems or questions of adjustment arise.

The brochure and program briefly outlined above have been in effect in our small congregation for about four years now, with great success. Every church can provide this basic kind of information to its new members by following these easy steps, thereby helping newcomers through a period of adjustment with as little confusion or embarrassment as possible. The result may be a more cohesive and integrated group of people, eager and happy to be working together.

Evangelism

An astute and successful pastor once commented: "Nothing can replace the personal influence of a call in the home of a prospective member by the pastor." A follow-up call by lay leaders accentuates the positive feelings of the first call.

Visitors who have expressed an interest in sharing in the membership and life of the congregation must be carefully invited to make a commitment and once committed, encouraged to participate as much as they wish. But the key to securing that commitment lies in the strength and organization of the church's evangelism program. Making contact with new residents opens doors. A visitor to the worship services has one foot in the door. How the congregation deals with those prospects will influence their decision to come again or to keep on looking elsewhere.

An ambitious proposal for evangelism is that suggested by Ross W. Marrs of the First United Methodist Church in Bloomington, Indiana. Recently he submitted the following challenge to his already large and growing church membership:

EVANGELISM IS A FOUR-LETTER WORD

In fact, evangelism is three four-letter words: OPEN, CARE, WORK.

1. *OPEN*
An open and accepting spirit must be present in a congregation if it is to be able to assimilate into its life all that variety of persons who give consideration to becoming a part of its life.

Some of the subtle ways in which we give evidence of that open spirit are:

a. Greeting persons on Sunday. Do we say "We are glad to have you with us?" or "Will the visitors please stand?" or "We hope you will make our church your church home." These and other such statements clearly project a host-guest church with a conscious group who understands itself as the church, which will be glad to decide who else to let in. Why not, "All of us are gathered here today in a spirit of worship and joy. It is in that spirit that every person is greeted, etc." or, "Moved by his spirit we gather to hear his word and be made new. As the people of God we greet one another with joy, etc."

b. Giving the shaping and execution of life, program and mission of the congregation into the hands of the laity. The message will soon get around that this is a congregation where people can make decisions and implement them, not a place where they pencil in the visions and dreams of the ministers and staff with their time and energies.

c. Establishing an atmosphere of freedom and choice of involvement. Guilt motivation, pressure, arm twisting, and recruiting are out. Such methods serve only to ensure visions of the church as a corral into which persons are being herded in anxiety for spiritual safety or to be milked for money, talent, and time. If they are left alone, and if periodic offers of some form of membership enquiry without obligation is offered, they will, in their own good time, become members.

d. Making clear information available to all on a constant basis. Communication is the name of the game. Bulletin inserts, posters, newsletters, etc., can be used to be certain that all persons are aware of the places where they can tie into the life of the congregation in service, witness, growth, worship.

e. Offering a broad range of opportunities on all age levels for fellowship with no catches, remedial and catch-up study, service and witness opportunities, and spiritual growth possibilities.

2. CARE

Almost every action, decision, and policy will let people know whether this is a congregation which really cares. Some examples are:

a. Concern for the building. Is it an expendable building which can be dirtied and repainted, or a shrine to be kept unspotted?

b. Relating each newcomer person or family to someone in the congregation so that when need arises the contact is made.

c. The presence of ministers especially designed to speak to unique situations in the parish. For example, does the church in a young adult atmosphere provide paid child care at all events where parents are expected? Is there a weekday care center especially adapted to child needs or elderly needs? Is there a bus for elderly who wish to come but can no longer drive? Elevator?

d. Are there greeters, friendly ushers, and members who understand that they are the congregation and that the perception that people carry away will be the one they give?

e. Take time to create age-sex profiles of the leadership of the congregation, the membership, and those who are at worship. If they do not match what does that say? Does the leadership range need to be broadened in order to ensure that all interests are represented in decision-making? Is there an indication that some parts of the congregation are not attending, and can we isolate the reasons for that?

f. Are the activities of the church limited to traditional times and places, or are they scattered throughout the week and perhaps even in places other than the church?

g. Do we leave the impression that only what goes on at the church building is one's religious life? Or, are we ready to let persons know that we really do accept all the things they do as an extension of their church-life so that there is no perceptible dichotomy between the two? It is possible to make persons who are doing quite well as Christians all over the community feel quite badly about their religious commitment because they are not in the building enough.

These are but a beginning of the areas that can be explored under the topics OPEN and CARE. You can add to the list for yourself. These are enough, however, to remind us all that if these two levels are intact and healthy, the development of a "system" is probably secondary. Such a "system" will, of course, reflect the life and potential of the congregation. Whatever system or method is used the key word is WORK—it will require WORK. If that worship is allied to an OPEN spirit and an atmosphere of CARE, evangelism will cease to be something the church does and will be what the church is.

3. WORK

Here is what takes place at First United Methodist Church in Bloomington, Indiana. It may be that some parts are irrelevant to other congregations. It may also be that some ideas new to you will surface. This is no ideal system; it is the way one church WORKS and indicates that any church can find a way to WORK its evangelism program if it has the will to do so.

a. Prospects may be gained by many methods. But the major way in which new constituents are identified here is by use of the attendance registration sheet. It may sound repetitive to say it every Sunday, but remember, it won't be repetitive for the newcomer. Get that thing passed and ask clearly for the information you seek.

b. An attendance secretary evaluates the attendance sheets on Monday morning, keeps attendance of constituents on the back of 3 × 5 file card (blue for students, white for other residents) and passes on to the minister those sheets containing information important to the leadership.

c. A letter is sent to all new persons who live in town. (Sending letters out of town is nice but expensive and unproductive). The letter is open and informative and contains a brochure on the life of the congregation along with a postage-paid reply card on which persons can indicate their interests.

d. The minister then writes notes where appropriate and calls by phone all new families and interviews them—welcome—get acquainted—invite back—where from—children, ages, schools—job—

241

involvements, etc. This information is noted on a four-part pad which is then broken up and each piece routed to appropriate groups which understand that they, too, are to call and welcome, express interest and invite. The minister keeps a copy for occasional checking to watch progress of persons.

e. If the interview by phone warrants it, the family is put on the minister's list for visitation and forwarded to the appointments secretary. An appointment is then made that is amenable to both the family and the minister. The minister prefers that the entire family be present when the call is made.

f. A preprinted letter form is mailed to persons already members who live near the new constituent advising them of their address and phone number and encouraging a contact for welcoming and getting acquainted.

g. The minister makes the arranged first call just to get acquainted and to respond to questions. Information or perceptions gathered during this visit may prompt phone calls or notes to others in the congregation.

h. If appropriate and helpful, the name of the family may be spun off to the associate pastor for program who will phone or visit and seek to further facilitate communication and involvement. In the case of an elderly couple, referral may be made to the parish visitor for constant contact and care.

i. Everyone concerned keeps the family "in view" until it is clear that they have made a choice to be involved or have dropped away. The minister does this by visual contact, by constant checking of information—interview sheet and by periodically going through the 3×5 card file created by the attendance secretary.

j. Somewhere along the way families will ask about membership and appropriate response can be made at that time.

k. Periodically, usually three times each year, an evening of inquiry is announced by newsletter, bulletin, and verbal word during worship. A letter of invitation is sent to all constituents with appropriate return cards.

l. An evening of inquiry is then arranged which generally lasts 3 to 4 hours and includes:
Dinner.
Introductions.
Greetings from persons already members who have served as hosts and hostesses at small table groups.
Filmstrips on the life of the church.
Presentations by programming groups in the congregation and staff.
Lecture on the development of the faith and the history and nature of the church by the senior pastor.
Question and answer period.
Listing of options.
Reply forms furnished which allow for several responses including none.
Individual follow-up is made to determine specific needs in each case.
Formal reception into membership in a public ceremony.
Further referrals if appropriate.

m. In the case of children:
—Family records and church school records are combed for names of candidates for a confirmation class.
—General publicity is released in all materials of the church.
—A date is set for orientation at which parents and youth attend in order to let all know the purpose and extent of what is about to take place.
—The group decides on days and time in cooperation with staff.
—Two groups are usually formed in order to keep them small and to ensure better attendance since youth can float from one group to another when the need arises.
—Twelve to fifteen weeks of one hour classes begin and end with full two-day retreats. The first is an effort to get the group committed, and the second, to wrap matters up, insure full understanding, and have time for each individual.
—The parents are consulted regarding their evaluation of readiness.
—The youth makes a decision.
—Those who are to become members are received on Confirmation Sunday, which is usually set on a date when all can be present.

Thus, the matter of evangelism is comprehensive in the life of the church. It is no added-on feature, no separate event or activity, but integrated into all that takes place. And true evangelism takes place wherever the spirit of the congregation is OPEN and accepting, where all that is said and done leaves the message that we CARE and where everybody involved is committed to WORK.

Indeed, evangelism is a four-letter word. In fact, three of them!

MEMBERSHIP ENLISTMENT AND CULTIVATION

Church Record Information

When prospective members are committed to sharing in the fellowship, carefully developed materials about the faith expressed in that communion, about responsibilities for participation in the life of the church, and about commitment to living and giving as Christians ought to be given to each new member. It is not enough, if lasting commitments to the life of the church are going to be made, just to welcome people in who happen to be attracted by the pastor or the building or the friendships extended. Active members have a conviction of faith shared with others with whom they worship. Shallow convictions create weak commitments. Better to know and to be involved and to be of service than to place a name on the rolls one Sunday and never see the members again.

Most clergy offer a learning experience for people interested in becoming an active part of the congregation. Whether active elsewhere previously or inactive, where as members of the denomination or not, pastors want to help their members know about the church. Some pastors prefer a one-on-one time of instruction in the home; others prefer a scheduled training session at the church.

A format* developed by one group for an eight-week program of two hours each session was this:

Session 1: What Christians Believe.
   About the Creeds, the Trinity, Christology
Session 2: Lutheran Teachings and Practices.
   About the church year, liturgy, vestments
Session 3: Lutheran Teachings and Practices.
   About Holy Communion and Baptism
Session 4: Fellowship in the Christian Life.
   About the fellowship groups of the parish. Lay readers from each group will speak to the class.
Session 5: Service in the Christian Life.
   About the committees or task groups of the parish. Chairpeople to speak to the class.
Session 6: Christian Stewardship.
   About the goals and budget of the congregation. Hand out commitment sheets and pledge
      cards. Use the stewardship chairperson.
Session 7: The Way We Do Things Here.
   About such things as the annual traditions, how to get a good idea implemented, the pastor's
      office hours, where the flower chart is, etc. Include worship chairperson. Tour building.
Session 8: During the eighth week, set up a personal interview with each person or family. During
      this interview do the following:
      —determine readiness to join;
      —collect commitment sheets & pledge cards
      —get information for parish register;
      —write for transfers;
      —get council approval;
      —review the service of reception into membership
      —give their names to their shepherds
Receive these people into membership within two weeks.

A wealth of information can be secured from each family. Where a church uses a personal computer, that information can be as large a bank of data as may be desired. Most programs already provide space for more information than can ever be collected.

*Adapted from *Witness*—A Handbook for Evangelism Committees, copyright 1982, Parish Life Press, Philadelphia, Pa., page 42. Used by permission.

243

With manual membership records, too much information is never used nor easily kept updated. One simple record of information for church records on new members—the bare minimum—would be the following:

INFORMATION FOR THE CHURCH RECORDS

Name _____

Address _____ Phone _____

Business connection _____

Business address _____ Phone _____

Date of birth _____ Marital status _____

Parents' names in full (if member under age 20) _____

_____

Parents' church affiliation _____

How received into membership in this church:

  Have you been baptized? _____

  Do you come by

    Confession of faith _____

    Reaffirmation of faith _____

    Certificate _____

If you come by reaffirmation or certificate, what is the name of the church with which you were formerly a member, and what is its address?

  Church name _____

  Address _____

  Shall we send for your letter? _____

  Have you previously participated in some form of service in churches and Sunday schools? How?

_____

Another more complete record of commitment, involvement and stewardship of skills and time, would be the Personal Record on pages 245 and 246.

At the same time a member fills in the basic information form or even a personal record of past church involvement, it will be helpful to have an interest form or enlistment form completed also. Asking new members what they like to do and are willing to do gives church leaders an opportunity to know and use those interests in the life of the church.

An interest survey questionnaire and checklist developed as part of The United Methodist Church stewardship program appears on pages 247 and 248.

But people do not respond well to a checklist without some understanding of what each opportunity means. A job/task description for many of these positions can be prepared to assist in recruiting participants. A supply of 3 × 5 cards can be kept in the church office. Whenever the pastor makes calls or people express interest in a particular activity, the appropriate card can be given out. A display rack of "interest cards" will make the opportunity more visible to interested persons.

A written description for each of the tasks believed important in the life of the church is extremely helpful in keeping everyone—new and continuing members both—properly informed. Recruitment for specific tasks is simplified when the responsibilities are carefully explained and described. (See "Service Opportunity Cards" page 249.)

PERSONAL RECORD

Name _____   Telephone: Home_____
Address _____   Work_____
         _____   Date of birth_____
Occupation_____   Agency/firm_____

Educational background: ☐ High school ☐ College ☐ Technical school ☐ Advanced degree ☐ Other_____
Major area of study or training_____
Special interests and hobbies_____
_____

Other family members	Relationship	Date of birth	Date baptized	Church member (What church?)

Marital status ☐ Single ☐ Married ☐ Single parent ☐ Widow

Age Group ☐ Under 12 ☐ 12-18 ☐ 18-25 ☐ 25-35 ☐ 35-45 ☐ 45-65 ☐ Over 65

Group relationship(s) ☐ Church school class ☐ UMW ☐ UMM ☐ UMYF ☐ Choir
                      ☐ Study group ☐ Prayer group ☐ Other_____
Membership: Date joined this church_____
            Means: ☐ Confession of faith ☐ Transfer: name of church_____
            Termination: Date_____ Reason_____

Years

Services and giving record										
Regular contributor										
Regular worship attendance										
Regular church school attendance										
Usher										
Choir										
Teacher										

Service training record (Seminars, worships, leadership schools, etc.)

Photo

Kind of event	Date

Kind of event	Date

Prepared and edited by The General Council on Finance and Administration. Published by The United Methodist Publishing House, Nashville, Tennessee. Used with permission.

NAME:_____

ADDRESS:_____

_____

FAMILY/HOUSEHOLD ROLL

NAME	RELATION-SHIP	DATE OF BIRTH	DATE OF BAPTISM	MEMBERSHIP STATUS (✓)					DATE RECEIVED INTO FULL MEMBERSHIP	MEMBERSHIP TERMINATED		CHANGES/REMARKS
				PM	CR	AF	AS	FM		DATE	HOW	

NAME:_____

INVOLVEMENT IN CONGREGATION:

INTERESTS AND SKILLS:

SPECIAL NEEDS:

PERSONAL INTEREST SURVEY

Name_____

Address_____

Phone_____

1. What are your special abilities? (For example, reading, sewing, cooking, singing, acting, listening, woodwork, crafts, relating to others, etc.)_____

   _____

   _____

   _____

2. What do you most enjoy doing?_____

   _____

3. What are some of the things you have always wanted to do, but have never found the time?_____

   _____

   _____

4. What skills do you have that you would like to improve?_____

   _____

5. Would you be willing to serve on a task force to plan and guide a talent fair?_____

   _____

Return to_____

Church_____

Return by_____ , 19_____ .

INTEREST SURVEY

Name:_____
        (LAST)   (FIRST)   (MIDDLE)

Address:_____
        (CITY)   (ZIP)

Many opportunities are available to serve and participate in the life of our church. Not all opportunities exist at any given time. However, an indication of your personal preferences will be better recognized if you will take time to let our church know what you really enjoy doing. Listed below and on the reverse side are some areas of present needs and possibilities for you. Please indicate (with an X in the appropriate boxes) what you would like to do in the life of our church—not necessarily what you feel you *should* do. Church life survives because of people like you getting satisfaction from involvement and participation.

SUNDAY SERVICES
- ☐ GREETER
- ☐ USHER
- ☐ COFFEE CHAT
- ☐ COMMUNION
- ☐ ACOLYTE SUPERVISOR
- ☐ LAY READER
- ☐ MEMBER RIDES
- ☐ CHURCH VAN
- ☐ INFORMATION BOOTH
- ☐ VISITORS
- ☐ FLOWERS
- ☐ CHOIR
- ☐ SOLOIST
- ☐ ORGANIST
- ☐ PIANIST
- ☐ OTHER...........................
  ....

PASTORAL AID
- ☐ CALLING
- ☐ NEW MEMBERS
- ☐ CONSULTANT—LEGAL
- ☐ CONSULTANT—MEDICAL
- ☐ CONSULTANT—FINANCIAL
- ☐ CONSULTANT—COMPUTER
- ☐ CONSULTANT—DEMOGRAPHICS
- ☐ PUBLIC RELATIONS
- ☐ OTHER...........................
  ....

SOCIAL AND SERVICE
- ☐ MASTER OF CEREMONIES
- ☐ POSTERS AND PUBLICITY
- ☐ ENTERTAINMENT
- ☐ PANCAKE BREAKFASTS
- ☐ HOBBIES
- ☐ SEWING
- ☐ ART
- ☐ WEDDING ASSISTANT
- ☐ BLOOD BANK
- ☐ UNITED METHODIST WOMEN
- ☐ UNITED METHODIST MEN
- ☐ CHURCH HISTORY
- ☐ OTHER...........................
  ....

YOUTH PROGRAMS AND SUNDAY SCHOOL
- ☐ TEACHER
- ☐ HELPER
- ☐ NURSERY
- ☐ TREATS
- ☐ COUNSELOR
- ☐ MUSICIAN
- ☐ TOYS
- ☐ TRANSPORTATION
- ☐ OTHER...........................
  ....

ARTS AND CRAFTS
- ☐ SEWING, STITCHING
- ☐ SHOPPING
- ☐ COOKING/BAKING
- ☐ RECORD/TAPE
- ☐ INTERIOR DECORATION
- ☐ MUSIC—SINGING
- ☐ MUSIC—INSTRUMENTAL
- ☐ DANCING
- ☐ WRITING
- ☐ ACTING
- ☐ PHOTOGRAPHY
- ☐ FURNITURE REPAIR
- ☐ CARPET/DRAPES
- ☐ OTHER...........................
  ....

BUILDINGS AND GROUNDS
- ☐ WEED AND TRIM
- ☐ PAINTING
- ☐ WAX AND POLISH
- ☐ WASH WINDOWS
- ☐ LANDSCAPE AND PLANT
- ☐ HEATING AND AIR COND.
- ☐ BRICK AND CONCRETE
- ☐ STUCCO AND PLASTER
- ☐ ELECTRICAL
- ☐ ELECTRONIC
- ☐ SOUND AND CHIMES
- ☐ PLUMBING
- ☐ WATERING
- ☐ CARPENTRY
- ☐ SECURITY SYSTEMS
- ☐ PARKING LOT
- ☐ SIGNS
- ☐ BULBS AND LAMPS
- ☐ OTHER...........................
  ....

THE WORK OF THE CHURCH
- ☐ ADMINISTRATIVE BOARD
- ☐ COUNCIL ON MINISTRIES
- ☐ FINANCE
- ☐ TRUSTEES
- ☐ PASTOR-PARISH
- ☐ STEWARDSHIP
- ☐ RELIGION AND RACE
- ☐ MISSION TO WORLD
- ☐ EVANGELISM
- ☐ MUSIC AND ARTS
- ☐ EDUCATION
- ☐ WORSHIP
- ☐ CHRISTIAN UNITY
- ☐ CHURCH AND SOCIETY
- ☐ CAMPUS MINISTRIES

SOCIAL
- ☐ PICNICS
- ☐ BBQ'S
- ☐ BAZAAR
- ☐ PARTIES
- ☐ CRAFTS
- ☐ TRAVEL
- ☐ SPORTS
- ☐ THEATRE
- ☐ BOY SCOUTS
- ☐ GIRL SCOUTS
- ☐ OTHER...........................
  ....

ADMINISTRATION
- ☐ TYPING
- ☐ SHORTHAND
- ☐ GENERAL OFFICE
- ☐ TELEPHONE
- ☐ LIBRARY
- ☐ ERRANDS
- ☐ MINUTES—MEETINGS
- ☐ POSTERS
- ☐ COMPUTER PROGRAM
- ☐ BUSINESS MACHINES
- ☐ CULTURAL EVENTS
- ☐ MEMORIALS
- ☐ ESTATE PLANNING
- ☐ MUSIC COMMITTEE

Thank you for your participation. Please return this to the office or mail it to the church.

SERVICE OPPORTUNITY CARD

Worship: Interpretive Dance

Need: Persons to share in the worship experience through interpretation of Scripture and song with body movement.

Goal of service: to provide a new and meaningful expression of worship to those who gather on a Sunday morning by interpreting the message of words with graceful and meaningful dance.

Time: Once a month at the second service.

Training: Practice each Sunday at 4:00 P.M.

Contact: Carol Donnan

Phone: 382-9444

SERVICE OPPORTUNITY CARD

Visitation: with Shut-ins

Need: A person to visit church members in nursing homes and retirement centers.

Goal of service: To maintain a relationship with these members of the congregation so that they may continue to fill a part of the life of their church and experience the love and care of God.

Time: Two afternoons a week (to be arranged), for at least three months.

Training: A training workshop for this service will be held in the church parlor, January 10, from 2:00 to 3:00 P.M.

Contact: Jane Jones

Phone: 849-8904

SERVICE OPPORTUNITY CARD

Transportation: Sunday Church School Students

Need: A person to drive the church van for transporting Sunday church school students without any transportation to and from the church building.

Goal of service: To provide regular transportation for members of the congregation who are unable or unwilling to secure alternate means of getting to SCS; to maintain a continuing relationship with persons who might not otherwise participate in the life of the church.

Time: One Sunday morning a month, 8:00 A.M. to 11:00 A.M.

Training: In service training once each six months, as announced.

Contact: John Garfield

Phone: 812-5422

Getting the People to Stick with It

It is one thing to gather all of that information, yet another to get a commitment, involving the people so that they remain faithful, supportive, interested, and involved. Integrating new members into the life of the church is not an easy task, but is certainly a continuing task.

Many congregations, upon receiving new members, provide a certificate of membership, evidence of an official relationship with the church. The actual order for reception of members is usually specified in the official hymnbook of the denomination, although many pastors develop their own service.

A rosebud or carnation is often pinned to each new member's clothing to help members recognize these people. Nametags are crucial. The newsletter informs the membership of names, addresses, and phone numbers of all new people. And letters are sent, as previously described, to neighbors of new members encouraging them to share the life of the church with these new members. Committee chairpersons are asked to contact those who have expressed an interest in the work of that group. The coordinator of volunteers can make sure that everyone who wants to serve is asked to do so in a meaningful way.

People are sensitive; people want to be accepted. And it is not enough that a person should seek out their own involvement. People want to be asked. No possibility should be overlooked to be certain that each new member is fully acquainted with the church, its programs, the people, and with those individuals with whom they may share similar interests and skills.

Pastors are the key toward developing that close relationship between member and church. The pastor is the spiritual leader as well as motivator, team captain and church administrator. And the way pastors develop relationships with members is through their pastoral calling. Aggressive church leadership requires constant visitation in homes, hospitals, nursing homes, or at a place of business. Constant contact is essential. People expect the pastor to be personally concerned in their lives, and they want that contact where they are—not just in church.

An annual visit on each member by the pastor or other staff member is crucial toward retaining positive relationships. For older members a visit on their birthdays or wedding anniversaries can be especially meaningful and eagerly anticipated. And on any other occasion of significance in the lives of members (such as the anniversary of the death of a spouse), a pastoral call will be much appreciated.

Pastors need to be aware of the importance of this constant contact and exposure. Special groups in the membership need special attention. Men and women in the Armed Services, for example, need to be contacted regularly by letter, even telephone. College students, out-of-town members, those traveling overseas for an extensive time should have special attention—letters, notes, mention in the newsletter.

When appropriate, it is important for the membership to be kept informed of the illnesses and troubles of members who need prayer and support. Not only the pastor, but the congregation also has a ministry to these people. All possible ways should support that ministry. Prayer groups, weekly Bible studies, the Sunday bulletin, the newsletter, and word-of-mouth are all effective means of communicating special needs.

Creative ways of helping members support the pastoral ministry have been developed by many congregations. One congregation prepares a second church directory arranged by street numbers rather than names. Thus, a family at 620 Oak Street could easily identify neighbors who are church members, the Browns at 602 Oak Street, the Nelsons at 615 and so on. Another congregation lists names and addresses by area, so neighbors on other streets can identify nearby church members. And some congregations develop careful plans for a shepherding program or group-block program or Touch-and-Care program—all centered around a small cluster of church members who care about each other, who want to help and support, and who keep the pastor informed of needs.

A Shepherding Plan

An effective shepherding program for membership conservation and caring is usually organized around clusters of groups of approximately ten families. The pastor is the head shepherd for this organization. Each cluster of three shepherding groups has a leader and then each group of ten families has a leader.

The purpose of a neighborhood shepherd group is to offer an easy and comfortable way for neighbors who are church members to get better acquainted. New members, when feeling accepted, can find such a group extremely supportive. By sharing the life of the congregation in this small group, others become informed, involved, and active in the church.

Of course, the group is to help current members, too. When the elderly are part of the group, invitations to go places can be offered. Some offer babysitting services, and regular get-togethers become an important part of the life of that group.

Good leadership is essential to the functioning of shepherd groups. Leaders of groups must:
—know the program of the church
—be aware of who participates in what
—recall the names of most people who attend church
—determine needs of the group
—determine how to meet those needs
—make necessary decisions when required and do so promptly
—expect the ways people react to facing a committed Christian
—recognize techniques of good management and personnel relations
—have a firm sense of their own commitment to the church

A congregation of three hundred families may organize thirty groups, each led by a shepherd with a zone leader for groups of three shepherds. Groups are most often geographic, but they can be from scattered areas as well. Having friends in the same group gives good support. Mixing active and inactive members, executives with blue-collar employees, professionals with homemakers all offer a potentially good mix.

Once organized, the shepherd is responsible for maintaining enthusiasm, spirit, and involvement of all. Frequent contact with the members of the group by phone, visit, or a social gathering in someone's home or at the church stimulates active sharing and participation in the life of the church. It is important that the church office be kept informed of illnesses, deaths, births, special needs, and crises so that pastoral contact can be made promptly.

The pastor cannot do everything, even in the smallest church. Volunteers are required. And the shepherd group leader helps best by being the eyes and ears for the church. This kind of concerned help greatly assists clergy in meeting the needs of people.

Complaints never end. "The pastor never calls." "I was in and out of the hospital before the pastor tried to visit." But, unless a pastor knows, a pastor simply cannot respond. Shepherd leaders provide that constant contact.

Holding the group together becomes a real challenge. Shepherd leaders, therefore, need to be prepared to stay in touch, arrange social events, arrange for transportation, and visit the people. Shepherds become assistant pastors in the congregation.

And on a regular basis, the leaders get together in a retreat setting to discuss progress, frustrations, and improving procedures. The pastor is the key link to that program. Only as the pastor cultivates the leaders will those leaders care about the people assigned to them. Constant contact between pastor and people is important for comfort, encouragement, support, and for developing a closer relationship with this core of trained and dedicated workers.

About your older members

Older church members, whether new or longtime in the church, require special attention. An effective church administrator will have a careful listing of the older members, their status, condition, needs, etc. The use of a computer will help the assimilation and use of that information.

251

Special attention needs to be given to programs for the elderly—a weekly community day-out at the church for games and fun, meals-on-wheels, and other emphases. Daytime use of the church building consists of programs for the elderly; night-time use is limited to the younger groups. A staff member should be responsible for using the voluntary help that able, elderly members are willing to give. A survey of skills and experience of just older persons (but similar to the interest surveys previously illustrated) will uncover many useful ways in which the elderly can use their skills to support others.

Lectures, special programs, tours, and study programs can be developed for the elderly. A senior citizens' center can offer programs on a daily basis to others beyond the membership. A transportation pool can help the elderly who no longer drive to get to the church.

And shut-ins need continuous attention. Regular pastor attention is imperative, even crucial. A committee of volunteers responsible for the shut-in members can be of considerable help in meeting needs. Weekly visits are not too often, and special attention to birthdays dare not be overlooked. Mailing the Sunday bulletins, distributing altar flowers, mailing cards "to remember you by" are all satisfying and useful ministries.

Pastoral recognition of those older members who have served the church faithfully for a long time is always appropriate. While this can be done anytime, the annual meeting offers a good opportunity for special recognition.

Ministering to the sick

All parish pastors visit members who are hurt or ill. It is the heart of ministry. But not all sick visits are helpful visits. The skilled and trained pastor knows when to visit, how long to stay, when to leave. And careful attention to the needs of people in distress is the mark of a caring congregation.

All sick people have some things in common. They feel pain, they have fears, their life-style may have to change, and they have many questions, fears, doubts, and worries. The minister listens to their needs and lets the people share and unload. The sensitive caller knows when to talk and when to listen.

Sick people have a lot of time to think. And the more they think, the more they worry about matters that are important to them. Suggesting prayer, citing Scriptures and offering materials that encourage prayer and trust in God can be helpful.

Sick people lose their privacy and develop a sense of helplessness. Many must depend on others to assist them with basic hygienic needs. But, the ministering pastor should encourage self-reliance whenever appropriate. If during a visit the person needs to adjust the TV or answer the phone or reach for a tissue, let the person do it. If the sick person is supposed to walk—encourage and help. Self-pity becomes the patient's worse enemy.

Worry, self-pity, loneliness, depression, fear, anger—these are all concerns of the sick. Sensitive pastoral visitors will make every positive effort to change those negative attitudes.

The sick person who is lonely and depressed needs to talk. The pastor must take time to listen, and be willing to sit and not hurry off nor appear to be impatient to leave. The pastor can help the lonely person to reach out to help someone else by providing notepaper and pen so the sick person can write notes of appreciation to people who have helped.

Some sick people will complain about everything. They are critical of the doctors and nurses, don't like the food, lose their tempers, and refuse to follow instructions. These people are angry and need to be helped to accept their surroundings and the things they cannot change.

Or sick people may be afraid of the unknown, afraid of what might happen, afraid to face reality. The caring pastor will suggest prayer and not offer a medical explanation or opinion.

The most frequent question sick people ask is "Why?" Why did this happen to me? Often there is no logical explanation and the wise pastor will not try to explain. God's ways are simply beyond our understanding. Accepting that which cannot be explained, understood, or changed is a vital part of the ministry of healing. Explanation may only confuse. And the caring pastor is not threatened with an inability to explain.

For a ministry to the sick is most often a ministry of listening. But that ministry is supported by sharing helpful reading material—bulletins, special helpful tracts, booklets such as Granger Westberg's *Good Grief* (Fortress Press). Many printed aids are available. The best should be shared. Remember that the sick have plenty of time.

Since the pastor cannot possibly visit all the sick every day, a group of caring members (such as a Stephen's Ministry program) can be enlisted to help. Special training is important for this small cadre of visitors, but their ministry (along with that of other staff) can help maintain a regular "caring presence" of the congregation.

Developing Special Congregational Programs

When something is always going on in a church building, people believe a lot of good things are happening, and that this must be a very active, energetic group. Indeed, lots of activity does suggest a lot is going on. It presumes a lot of involvement by a lot of people to a lot of things. An array of special programs and activities for every group in the congregation can be as varied as all the people who make up the church. And while many churches have a lot of things going on, the church that keeps its members is the one that develops the programs in which those people will participate. Many church members might be amazed if they were to see a list of everything that goes on in their church buildings. And it may be helpful to share that listing sometimes in the newsletter.

Of course, having a program available does not automatically mean everyone is involved. Pastoral administration must also develop *appropriate* programs that will get the people involved. Then special invitations, carpools, and neighbor encouragement are necessary to tell people what's happening. Furthermore, recognition of participation assists in retaining that involvement. It is one thing to be sympathetic to the needs of people, but active response and participation in the life of the church can generate a spirit of support and involvement that is bound to enhance every congregational program, activity, or educational endeavor. Effective pastoral ministry is not only one of concern; it also involves frequent involvement of people in program.

List all those programs and activities that go on at your church that involve people in relationships, service, fellowship, outreach and spiritual enrichment. Then examine how the following principles of organization relate to those programs.

1. Every program must fit in with the overall objectives of the church and have the approval of the official board either formally or tacitly.

2. In keeping with the spirit of cooperation and team support, all staff should be enthusiastic supporters of all church-sponsored programs. Disagreement should be expressed in staff meetings only. Thus the agenda for the annual staff meeting should include time for review of all programs.

3. A representative from the official board appointed to the planning group of every organization will facilitate coordination of programs and reduce duplication of effort and wasted movement due to ineffective communication.

4. Volunteers on the communications committee can offer help to program leaders in promoting their ideas and in being certain developing programs are adhering to stated goals and objectives of service.

5. When programs require money, leadership from the finance committee may be required to avoid (1) financial commitments not approved or (2) potential financial disasters due to sloppy management.

6. The success of any congregation is directly related to the active involvement in programs of the greatest number of people. Involved members are active members simply because they are putting

their own efforts into a cause they want to see succeed. Troubled congregations are generally "run" by a handful of the old faithfuls or by some faction. Vibrant congregations probably involve just about every member in something, not only in being there but also in making the decisions that can affect other people.

"Successful congregations" are sensitive to the needs of people. Caring for the membership is done best when it is done by all the people under the caring leadership of the pastor (the manager and administrator).

Keeping Records on the People Who Stay

The pastor is generally responsible for being certain church records are kept accurately and up-to-date. This is especially true of ecclesiastical records, but it is just as true of any other record required—property, finance, attendance, minutes, etc. Accurate membership statistics require accurate recordkeeping by all pastors of all churches. Any deficiency anywhere distorts the official facts.

There are numerous records for which clergy are responsible:

1. Consider historical documents. Usually the minister alone knows the location of documents appropriate for the archives. But the official board should appoint an interested group of members to maintain important church records, keep a current listing, and provide such special handling as may be necessary to preserve old documents. When your church is ready for its one hundredth or two hundredth or more birthday, someone will want to know the history. Someone needs to keep tab on the documents and write the story. The oral history dies when the older members die. A safe deposit box should be maintained for valuable documents, tape recordings, and mementos.

2. Don't ignore current documents. Whatever goes on in your church today will be history tomorrow. Retaining records of current activity and member involvement is as important as dusting off musty records of a century ago. Take lots of photographs of people and activities. Be certain every photo is marked, labeled, and the people correctly identified. News clippings of church events should be filed permanently. All Sunday bulletins, newsletters, and minutes of each board meeting should be filed in order by date. Even the minutes of organizations—as dull and uninformative as most seem—can be filed with historic records for the purpose of maintaining a current activities file (which becomes the historical file of tomorrow.)

3. Keep all minutes. The secretary of the board should maintain a complete set of minutes of the board, congregation, and every committee or organization from whom that record can be obtained. More interesting information may be discovered in old minutes than almost from any other source of church records.

Minutes are a confidential record of the meeting of a group. They must be kept permanently—bound and neatly written and arranged. Corrections should be noted after each official board meeting. Without that group's specific permission, no one should have access to the minutes. Of course, minutes can be shared, but the official board makes the decision about who, when, and how.

4. Use the annual reports. Each year's summary of progress, results, programs, statistics, finances, and activities can easily be summed up in the annual reports record. This record then becomes a basic document of the life and activity of the congregation. It tells people what they need to know; it reports results of programs they approved long ago; and it can be quite interesting reading.

5. Statistical records are an "evil necessity," so say some clergy. But, statistics help us to know what is going on now and what past trends have affected the present. Enrollments in Sunday church school, attendance at worship, membership drops and increases, financial reports, and many other statistics all help church people to know what they are doing and how well the project is going in terms of numbers.

6. Retain copies of some correspondence. The pastor's secretary must have a filing system that will retain important correspondence records written by the pastor. Most correspondence is not worth keeping. A copy is not even necessary. But some letters are important and should be retained in the permanent files of the church. Obsolete materials are destroyed, permanent records deposited with the archivist. Using microfilms or even a computer may be a space-saving way of retaining lots of old records.

7. Keep membership records up-to-date. Whatever data you have elected to keep on each person is useful to you only if kept current.

8. Pay special attention to permanent church records. For historical purposes and often legal requirements as well, records of baptisms, weddings, and official board actions may be extremely important.

In every denomination, congregations maintain a "Parish Register" of some sort. This is the official record of all official acts by the pastor or those other acts authorized by the congregation. It is the legal record of what was done with people. And even though a congregation may have a computer for membership accounting, the official book or register of ecclesiastical acts remains as the basic official statistical record of church membership.

a. List the ministers. A chronological listing of all the pastors who have ever served the congregation is usually the first record in the book. Installation date, service record, previous pastorate, and succeeding pastorates would be shown. Of course, a permanent file of data separate from the official register would be maintained for historical purposes.

b. List the official board members. Promptly, upon election, resignation, or termination of office, the official register should be changed to include new names and necessary notations about changes. In some congregations, the new members of the official board are asked to sign the register publicly when they are installed.

c. List baptisms. The importance of church baptism records has been emphasized as older people without birth certificates have applied for passports and social security benefits. Proof of birth is often secured only by proof of baptism in some musty church record book. In more recent decades, with the issuance of birth certificates to almost all infants, the use of church records for certifying a birth is not as crucial. Nevertheless, recording the date of baptism, parents' and sponsors' names, place, and date of birth is still a useful way to list the child as a new church member.

d. List confirmations. Notations should be made first in the baptismal record regarding a baptism, and then pertinent information listed in the confirmation record as evidence of the "adult" membership of the young person.

e. List the members. A chronological listing of members by date of affiliation with the congregation is the most common procedure. Complete information on name, membership status, type and date of reception, and baptismal record is usually included.

f. List communions. The official parish register can be used for a record of participation in communion celebrations. While a computer record or other procedure may prove more efficient for recording and analyzing, the official register book traditionally has been the source for maintaining this evidence of active church membership.

g. List deaths. Whenever a member dies or the pastor conducts a funeral, the official register should contain pertinent information. The date and place of death should be noted in the listing, and the membership record promptly corrected. The names of any deceased members should be immediately removed from the active membership file, any address label file, or computer file.

h. List transfers, removals, and resignations. In the membership section of the official register, prompt proper notations should be made beside the names of those who have left or otherwise been removed from the membership. Appropriate removal from other active files and mailing lists is desirable.

FAMILY/HOUSEHOLD ROLL

NAME: _____

ADDRESS: _____

NAME	RELATION-SHIP	DATE OF BIRTH	DATE OF BAPTISM	MEMBERSHIP STATUS (✓)					DATE RECEIVED INTO FULL MEMBERSHIP	MEMBERSHIP TERMINATED		CHANGES/REMARKS
				PM	CR	AF	AS	FM		DATE	HOW	

INVOLVEMENT IN CONGREGATION:

INTERESTS AND SKILLS:

SPECIAL NEEDS:

From *Membership Record System Manual* by Robert A. Kramer. Forms prepared and edited by The Council on Finance and Administration. Copyright © 1980 by The United Methodist Publishing House. Used by permission.

RECORD OF BAPTISMS

Baptismal Reference Number	PERSON BAPTIZED		DATE	PLACE CITY, COUNTY, AND STATE	PREPARATORY MEMBER	PARENTS	OFFICIATING MINISTER
	Family	Christian	Birth	Birth			
	Address		Baptism	Baptism			
	Family	Christian	Birth	Birth			
	Address		Baptism	Baptism			
	Family	Christian	Birth	Birth			
	Address		Baptism	Baptism			
	Family	Christian	Birth	Birth			
	Address		Baptism	Baptism			
	Family	Christian	Birth	Birth			
	Address		Baptism	Baptism			
	Family	Christian	Birth	Birth			
	Address		Baptism	Baptism			
	Family	Christian	Birth	Birth			
	Address		Baptism	Baptism			
	Family	Christian	Birth	Birth			
	Address		Baptism	Baptism			
	Family	Christian	Birth	Birth			
	Address		Baptism	Baptism			
	Family	Christian	Birth	Birth			
	Address		Baptism	Baptism			

CONSTITUENCY ROLL

Baptismal Reference Number	NAME	ADDRESS	DATE OF BIRTH	PROSPECT FOR MEMBERSHIP (/)	REMOVED	
					DATE	HOW

RECORD OF MARRIAGES

FULL NAME		ADDRESS	MEMBER OF THIS CHURCH (✓)	OFFICIATING MINISTER, DATE, AND PLACE OF MARRIAGE		LICENSE ISSUED BY		NEW ADDRESS
FAMILY	CHRISTIAN							
Man				Minister		County		
Woman				Date		State		
				Place		License Number		
Man				Minister		County		
Woman				Date		State		
				Place		License Number		
Man				Minister		County		
Woman				Date		State		
				Place		License Number		
Man				Minister		County		
Woman				Date		State		
				Place		License Number		
Man				Minister		County		
Woman				Date		State		
				Place		License Number		
Man				Minister		County		
Woman				Date		State		
				Place		License Number		
Man				Minister		County		
Woman				Date		State		
				Place		License Number		
Man				Minister		County		
Woman				Date		State		
				Place		License Number		
Man				Minister		County		
Woman				Date		State		
				Place		License Number		
Man				Minister		County		
Woman				Date		State		
				Place		License Number		

RECORD OF DEATHS

FULL NAME		MEMBER OF THIS CHURCH (✓)	CHRONO-LOGICAL REFERENCE NUMBER	DATE OF DEATH	DISPOSITION OF BODY		OFFICIATING MINISTER
FAMILY	CHRISTIAN				CEMETERY, CREMATION, OTHER	CITY, COUNTY, AND STATE	

REMOVED BY ACTION OF CHARGE CONFERENCE

Chronological Reference Number	Date of Final Charge Conference Action	NAME	LAST KNOWN ADDRESS	REASON FOR REMOVAL	RESTORED/ TRANSFERRED

HISTORICAL RECORD

Why Some Churches Grow

It's no secret that some churches simply grow more rapidly than others. In fact, some churches don't grow at all.

I am convinced that growing churches are that way in large part because of positive and aggressive leadership attitudes. Yes, location makes a difference, and some churches are doomed to die before they start. Yes, neighborhoods change and only herculean efforts can save a church there, but herculean efforts aren't exerted. Yes, congregations suffer reverses, people get angry, finances take a nose dive. Some churches, many churches, will never grow . . . but some do!

Here is a succinct listing of characteristics for those churches that do grow—why people join those churches and what visitors experience when they come to church.*

This is why some churches are growing

1. Some churches are growing because they want to grow! It's a feeling, an attitude, a desire born of a conviction that God wants them to grow.

2. They plan for growth. This is evident in their priorities, in their programs, in their activities, in the way they staff, in the training they provide for leaders, in every aspect of their ministry.

3. They are willing to pay the price. This is true of both the pastor and the members of the congregation. They are willing to invest time, money, and abilities.

4. They are willing to risk change. Things do not remain the same when growth takes place. Growth is dynamic; it brings changes, challenges, and opportunities.

5. They have high membership standards. Growing churches take mission seriously, and they expect new members to do the same.

6. They offer many new-member classes.

7. They find unmet needs in the community and begin to meet those needs.

8. They advertise.

9. They make sure their buildings and grounds invite people. They can give a positive answer to questions such as: Can visitors find your building? Do you have enough parking? Does your property look like anyone cares? Does your sign give (accurate) worship times?

10. They make sure they welcome visitors.

11. They encourage each other to invite friends and relatives.

12. They emphasize Christian fellowship. They care about one another. Caring for persons means:
    —Sorrowing and rejoicing with them.
    —Calling to say you missed them when they were absent.
    —Praying for them and with them.
    —Helping their families with food, babysitting, and housecleaning when they are in the hospital (and after they come home).
    —Having a fellowship group for all ages.
    —Inviting them to meetings and fellowship events.
    —Visiting them regularly at home.
    —Making available small sharing groups.
    —Etc.

13. They provide the best possible opportunities for Christian education on Sunday and at other times, for all ages.

---

*Adapted from *Witness*—A Handbook for Evangelism Committees, copyright 1982, Parish Life Press, Philadelphia, Pa., pages 17-19. Used by permission.

14. They see the church as one class of people, the whole people of God engaged in a common ministry.

This is why people join the church

Another way to see the signficance of attitudes and how they affect church growth is to ask the question: Why do people join the church? Here are some answers:

1. "Someone invited me." The invitation may have been direct and verbal or it may have been subtle, such as a member's life-style, values, attitudes, or positive statements about their church.

2. "I was looking for something with meaning." The church has a message. God's Word does provide meaning. Where that Word is proclaimed, where there are opportunities to explore one's values and beliefs in light of the Word, where members freely share their faith stories, persons who are struggling with the perplexities of life will be helped.

3. "They care about me." Many persons (most of us) want to be a part of a caring community where there is friendliness, support for one another, and opportunities for giving and receiving.

4. "I was sought out. They found me." A church member showed a gentle concern, a willingness to listen, a willingness to allow time for the development of a relationship, and was willing to make a call in the first place.

5. "I had a problem." Life is full of problems, and people suffer because of them. When one faces a personal crisis, nearly everything is questioned: the meaning of life, goodness, God, work, friends. Whatever the crisis (dissolution of a marriage or a relationship, death of a loved one, severe or terminal illness, loss of a job, feeling of rejection, drug or alcohol addiction), it is a time when a person needs a caring fellowship and an affirmation of God's love.

6. "I felt God's call." God's people are to witness, to plant the seed of the Word. We may be surprised by when and how the seed takes root and grows. Some persons sense that the Holy Spirit is calling them, and they respond. We rejoice!

7. "I felt guilty and afraid." When people feel bad about life or fear the judgment of God or fear death, they need the comfort of God's grace and the fellowship of those who have experienced that grace.

8. "The pastor impressed me. The message, the life-style, the commitment, the attitude were consistent. . . ."

9. "I participated in an event at the church." Weddings, funerals, baptisms, confirmations, special services, seminars, retreats, conferences, marriage encounters, scouts, picnics—there are many events where persons become acquainted with the church and the individuals who are members of that church.

And what do the visitors at our church experience?

One visit can tell much about a congregation and its members. Generally, visitors are very much aware of the climate. Therefore, ask yourself some questions:

1. What is our attitude toward those who visit a worship service? Does our attitude, our lack of welcome, our body language say, "We like things as they are; don't change it"? Are we saying, nonverbally, that they probably won't like it well enough to return? Is our worship atmosphere and environment pleasant? Does it encourage participation in the worship?

2. How can visitors learn about our church? Do we have brochures, newsletters, bulletins, doorknob hangers, circulars, mailings?

Do we advertise in the local newspapers? Do we buy space other than on the church page? Do we provide adequate, accurate information such as name, address, driving instructions, schedule of services, major activities, pastor's name, phone numbers, where to park?

Do we have similar information in the Yellow Pages? In local directories?

Do we provide a twenty-four-hour recorded message on the main church phone number whenever the church office is closed? This message should relay the name of the person to be contacted in case of an emergency, times of worship services, driving and public transportation instructions, parking locations, special activities in the near future, and the time when the church office will reopen.

3. How can visitors find their way? Is our church's name on a sign that is easily seen from the road and easily read? Is the information on the sign accurate? Is the sign lighted at night?

Are there signs that indicate the entrances to the parking lot, sanctuary, Sunday church school classes, and church offices?

Is there someone available to give visitors directions when they enter the building? To answer questions? To extend hospitality?

4. How do we handle visitors' special concerns? Do we help them so they know where to sit? Where classes are located? Where to meet children after classes or after the service?

Do we explain in advance any unique characteristics of the service? Do we make sure they receive a bulletin?

Do members help visitors follow the service if they are not familiar with our worship?

Do our greeters avoid pouncing on visitors?

Do we make it easy for visitors to tell us if they are interested in the church and any of its activities? Are registration forms or cards available in the pews or in the worship books?

Do we have coffee after the worship? Are visitors invited—personally? Are visitors introduced to members by members?

Are brochures available that describe the congregation and its ministry?

Are visitors contacted within twenty-four hours through a personal letter or phone call thanking them for visiting?

Are you able to evaluate your congregation's growth and appeal to visitors through those questions? It is clear that if these are the characteristics of growing churches because this is what people experience, then positive attitudes about your own church and its mission is crucial to gaining the membership and caring for the people.

Sam Kohn, Betty Carlson, Charlene Cox, Herman Brown, and Sally Simpson all had questions about the stunted growth of their congregations. But they never got involved. They expected the people just to come and stay on their own. No wonder their churches never grew!

CHAPTER 13

CHURCHES PAY TAXES

SOME CHURCHES DO pay taxes.

Generally, however, churches are exempt from most taxes, but sometimes some taxes are required. For example:

—Churches pay social security tax on the wages paid to all employees (except on wages paid to ministers).

—Churches may have to pay property taxes on a second parsonage (sometimes even on the first).

—Churches pay income taxes on unrelated business income.

—Churches are usually required to pay workers' compensation taxes or insurance.

But churches do not pay many other taxes:

—Churches do not pay the unemployment compensation tax.

—Churches do not pay state sales taxes (generally).

—Churches do not pay property taxes (in most places).

—Churches do not pay income taxes on their income (except when unrelated to their business purpose).

—Churches do not pay social security taxes on the wages paid to their ordained employees.

Payroll Taxes

Since January 1, 1984, all congregations have been required to withhold social security taxes and pay the employer social security tax on all wages paid to all full-time or part-time employees (except clergy) who earn at least one hundred dollars during the year. An exemption is possible when the church puts in writing that it is opposed to Social Security for religious reasons.

Previously, all churches enjoyed an exemption from this tax (although some congregations did waive their exemption), but the 1983 amendments to the Social Security Act changed all that. Thus, congregations that have any employees in addition to their ministers must withhold social security taxes and pay the required employer tax. Income taxes must also be withheld, but then churches have always been required to withhold income taxes on wages paid to all employees (except clergy).

Under the tax act of 1984, some congregations are not required to withhold social security taxes on wages paid to nonministerial employees. When that congregation has a long history of conscientious opposition to the payment of social security taxes (or any taxes), then under certain circumstances no employer tax is due, but then employees must pay self-employment social security tax on wages received.

CHURCHES PAY TAXES

Income tax withholding

If your congregation has employees to whom wages are paid, such as an organist, custodian, or secretary, whether full-time or part-time, those wages are subject to income tax withholding. Income may be so low, however, and claimed exemptions so high that no withholding is required. But you cannot just assume that earnings are low and exemptions high as to preclude any income tax withholdings. You must determine that from the proper tables. Congregations, the same as any employer, are required to withhold applicable income taxes.

The amount of income taxes to be withheld is determined by reference to the appropriate withholding tables in the Internal Revenue Publication 15, "Circular E." Generally, a person earning less than two hundred dollars a month would not have to have any income taxes withheld. But withholding, like income taxes, depends on the number of exemption allowances claimed, marital status, and the amount of wages paid.

Social security tax withholding

All congregations, except as noted above, are required to withhold appropriate social security taxes from wages paid to employees and to pay the employer social security tax.

It is not sufficient, in order to avoid such withholding and tax payment, to claim that the organist or custodian is an independent contractor, thus exempt from social security tax as employees, when in fact that person is treated as though an employee. The Internal Revenue Service applies the common-law rules with respect to employer-employee relationships and asks if the means and methods by which the work is performed is under the control of the church. If so, the person is an employee no matter what kind of formal contract may be produced to show other intentions.

Nevertheless, contracts may be entered into with individual contractors who are not employees. A janitorial firm or group of custodians could be independent contractors. The definition of who is an employee is indeed carefully monitored by IRS.

Who is an employee?

There are no clear-cut guidelines to help your congregation determine who is and who is not an employee of your church. Yet it will be important for you to know who are employees because since January 1, 1984, all congregations must pay social security taxes on the wages paid to all employees (except the minister) who earn at least one hundred dollars during the year.

The difference to your budget is worth more than 7 percent of wages paid. Each year the difference is worth even more as the employer tax goes up. Thus, if people can be paid for services without being employees, it could save your church budget a lot of dollars, not to mention the dollars saved by the employees.

Prior to 1984 many congregations had never withheld anything from anyone's pay. Now, though, they are doing so for anyone considered an employee.

In order to avoid the tax, some congregations have considered making all of their employees simply self-employed independent contractors. They expect to do that by just calling those persons independent contractors. They may draw up a formal contract, but many congregations will assume it to be so anyway just because they say so.

That would be the easy way. Unfortunately, the IRS will probably not go along with that idea no matter what you call those people. Even a formal written contract may not suffice if, in fact, you treat those persons as employees.

In some situations a contract arrangement might be possible. For example, if you use a custodial service, that would be an independent contract arrangement and no payroll taxes would have to be withheld. You might also use a secretarial agency to secure the services of a secretary—the church pays the agency a fee for the use of an individual, while the agency pays the employee's wages and benefits. An independent organist, for example, might be a teacher of individual pupils, play the organ for other groups and generally do all of his or her work for other people under contract.

Nevertheless, if upon audit IRS suspects that the person is really being treated like an employee—especially if you continue to provide pension, health or other benefits—, the person will be considered an employee and the wages taxed accordingly.

How, then, does IRS determine who is an employee and who is not? The clearest explanation is found in the Regulations to the Internal Revenue Code, Section 31.3401(c)-1(b). The section reads as follows:

> Generally the relationship of employer and employee exists when the person for whom services are performed has the right to control and direct the individual who performs the services, not only as to the result to be accomplished by the work but also as to the details and means by which that result is accomplished. That is, an employee is subject to the will and control of the employer not only as to what shall be done but how it shall be done. In this connection, it is not necessary that the employer actually direct or control the manner in which the services are performed; it is sufficient if he has the right to do so. The right to discharge is also an important factor indicating that the person possessing that right is an employer. Other factors characteristic of an employer, but not necessarily present in every case, are the furnishing of tools and the furnishing of a place to work to the individual who performs the services. In general, if an individual is subject to the control or direction of another merely as to the result to be accomplished by the work and not as to the means and methods of accomplishing the result, that person is not an employee.

In applying this common-law definition to employees, one must ask whether the means and methods by which the person does the assigned job are subject to the right of control of the church that is paying the compensation. If the answer is yes, then that person will be considered an employee.

When a church hires a specific individual to do a specific job rather than contracting with an organization or business to do that job with whatever personnel may be assigned, that individual is probably an employee. According to IRS, when an employing organization "provides a place for the employees to work and has the right to, and does in fact, control and direct the details and means by which they accomplish the desired results of such work," those persons are employees.

The following guidelines can help determine who is an employee and who may be an independent contractor.

Employees are those who are:
—required to comply with instructions
—enjoy a continuous relationship with the employer
—do their work personally
—work full-time for the employer (could be part-time, too)
—are subject to dismissal
—can quit without incurring liability
—are reimbursed for expenses
—must submit reports
—are given training
—do work that is integrated into the business

Independent contractors would:
—be permitted to employ assistants
—set their own order and sequence of work
—set their own hours of work
—be able to work for someone else at the same time
—be paid by the job (not hourly, daily, weekly, or monthly)
—be able to provide services to the public
—have the opportunity to make a profit or loss
—furnish their own tools
—be permitted to work on someone else's business premises
—have a substantial financial investment in the work

Thus, to use a yard service or janitorial service in caring for the yard and church building, an independent contract arrangement could exist, presumably, if the service used provides their own equipment (their own "means") and is free to use whatever procedure (their own "methods") they desire in order to do the required job. Any control by the church over the kind of equipment used or the method by which the organization goes about doing the job required, could make the persons doing the job employees.

It is difficult to see how an organist can be other than an employee under this definition even if that person is self-employed otherwise and teaches individual pupils. After all, the "means" for doing the job are provided by the church—the organ. And the "method" for doing the job is to play the organ in the way in which the pastor, choir director, or worship and music committee desires.

As for the church secretary, the only way that person would not be an employee would be if she or he were secured from a secretarial agency or pool. An individual secretary hired by the church to use the church's typewriter and office equipment is an employee whose methods of getting the job done are generally well described by church office procedures. And the person is certainly subject to dismissal by the employing organization.

Still, the issue is not always going to be clear to all church treasurers. But, keep in mind that failure to withhold social security taxes can obligate the church to paying the taxes personally—both employee and employer taxes—plus interest and late payment penalties.

SOCIAL SECURITY TAX RATE TABLE

Year	Employee		Self-employed			
	Old Rate	New Rate	Old Rate	New Rate	Tax Credit	Effective Rate
1984	6.7%	6.7%	9.35%	14.00%	2.7%	11.3%
1985	7.05	7.05	9.90%	14.10%	2.3%	11.8%
1986	7.15	7.15	10.00%	14.30%	2.0%	12.3%
1987	7.15	7.15	10.00%	14.30%	2.0%	12.3%
1988	7.15	7.51	10.00%	15.02%	2.0%	13.02%
1989	7.15	7.51	10.00%	15.02%	2.0%	13.02%
1990	7.65	7.65	10.75%	15.30%	-0-	**

**The 1990 effective rate cannot be determined now because the rate is applicable to a lower amount (usually) and because of the business-expense credit then applicable.

In one situation a congregation that withheld social security taxes for a few years under rules that were in effect prior to January 1, 1984, and then discontinued doing so because they thought they were exempt, was assessed the employee and employer taxes, plus interest, plus late payment penalties. They were liable because they had waived their exemption once they began withholding. After January 1, 1984, congregations that fail to withhold because they believe their people are independent contractors had better be sure of their situation. A wrong decision could become a costly matter when the person retires and claims social security benefits for wages paid during employment with that church.

Even though the guidelines are not always clear, it is important that congregations recognize their responsibilities as employers. All other employers are required to pay such taxes. Is there any reason why congregations should not provide the same employee benefits for their employees? In the past, wages earned from a nonprofit organization were not subject to any social security tax—self-employment or employee. Now, finally employees of nonprofit organizations, including churches, will have the same retirement, survivor, disability, and health benefits available from social security as are available to employees of for-profit organizations.

The new law is fair and equitable, even if it does put a new bite into a church budget already burdened with more demands than available resources. Churches have been off the hook for a long time. The time ended January 1, 1984.

Employer
identification number (EIN)

Since your congregation is now required to report employment taxes (income taxes and social security taxes withheld and due) and give out tax statements to employees (W-2 forms to employees, including the pastor, and information regarding taxes withheld), your congregation will need an Employer Identification Number.

If you don't have that number, you can ask the IRS for Form SS-4 "Application for Employer Identification Number." Then your congregation must use that EIN on all items sent to IRS, including the W-2 wage statement given to all employees.

Upon receipt of your EIN, you will receive a copy of IRS Publication 15, "Circular E" with complete instructions on withholding, remitting, and reporting employment taxes withheld and payable.

W-4 form: employee's
withholding allowance certificate

All employees, whether part-time or full-time, must complete a W-4 form. That form reports the number of withholding allowances requested by the employee and is the basis upon which the amount of income tax to be withheld is determined. A W-4 remains valid until a new one is furnished. Except as noted, all W-4 forms are retained by the employer.

If any employee, other than the minister, reports no tax to be withheld and expected wages will be more than two hundred dollars a week, or claims more than fourteen withholding allowances, copies of those W-4 forms are to be sent to IRS.

The minister should note on a W-4 that no income taxes are to be withheld pursuant to Sec. 3401(a)(9) of the Internal Revenue Code. That code section specifically exempts a minister's wages from income tax withholding. Of course, if the minister wants income taxes withheld, then the W-4 will indicate the correct number of withholding allowances requested and any additional income taxes to be withheld.

Employees who actually paid no income taxes in the previous year nor expect to pay any tax in the current year, such as college students, should request that no taxes be withheld in the current year by completing the appropriate lines on the W-4. Employees who claim exempt status under this

19**89**   Form W-4

Department of the Treasury
Internal Revenue Service

Purpose. Complete Form W-4 so that your employer can withhold the correct amount of Federal income tax from your pay.

Exemption From Withholding. Read line 6 of the certificate below to see if you can claim exempt status. If exempt, only complete the certificate; but do not complete lines 4 and 5. No Federal income tax will be withheld from your pay.

Basic Instructions. Employees who are not exempt should complete the Personal Allowances Worksheet. Additional worksheets are provided on page 2 for employees to adjust their withholding allowances based on itemized deductions, adjustments to income, or two-earner/two-job situations. Complete all worksheets that apply to your situation. The worksheets will help you figure the number of withholding allowances you are

entitled to claim. However, you may claim fewer allowances than this.

Head of Household. Generally, you may claim head of household filing status on your tax return only if you are unmarried and pay more than 50% of the costs of keeping up a home for yourself and your dependent(s) or other qualifying individuals.

Nonwage Income. If you have a large amount of nonwage income, such as interest or dividends, you should consider making estimated tax payments using Form 1040-ES. Otherwise, you may find that you owe additional tax at the end of the year.

Two-Earner/Two-Jobs. If you have a working spouse or more than one job, figure the total number of allowances you are entitled to claim on all jobs using worksheets from only one Form

W-4. This total should be divided among all jobs. Your withholding will usually be most accurate when all allowances are claimed on the W-4 filed for the highest paying job and zero allowances are claimed for the others.

Advance Earned Income Credit. If you are eligible for this credit, you can receive it added to your paycheck throughout the year. For details, obtain Form W-5 from your employer.

Check Your Withholding. After your W-4 takes effect, you can use **Publication 919**, Is My Withholding Correct for 1989?, to see how the dollar amount you are having withheld compares to your estimated total annual tax. Call 1-800-424-3676 (in Hawaii and Alaska, check your local telephone directory) to obtain this publication.

Personal Allowances Worksheet

A Enter "1" for **yourself** if no one else can claim you as a dependent . . . . **A** _____

B Enter "1" if: {
1. You are single and have only one job; or
2. You are married, have only one job, and your spouse does not work; or
3. Your wages from a second job or your spouse's wages (or the total of both) are $2,500 or less.
} . . . . **B** _____

C Enter "1" for your **spouse.** But, you may choose to enter "0" if you are married and have either a working spouse or more than one job (this may help you avoid having too little tax withheld) . . . . **C** _____

D Enter number of **dependents** (other than your spouse or yourself) whom you will claim on your tax return . . . . . . **D** _____

E Enter "1" if you will file as a **head of household** on your tax return (see conditions under "Head of Household," above) . . **E** _____

F Enter "1" if you have at least $1,500 of **child or dependent care expenses** for which you plan to claim a credit . . . . **F** _____

G Add lines A through F and enter total here . . . . ▶ **G** _____

For accuracy, do all worksheets that apply. {
- If you plan to **itemize or claim adjustments to income** and want to reduce your withholding, turn to the Deductions and Adjustments Worksheet on page 2.
- If you are **single** and have **more than one job** and your combined earnings from all jobs exceed $25,000 OR if you are **married** and have a **working spouse or more than one job**, and the combined earnings from all jobs exceed $40,000, then turn to the Two-Earner/Two-Job Worksheet on page 2 if you want to avoid having too little tax withheld.
- If **neither** of the above situations applies to you, **stop here** and enter the number from line G on line 4 of Form W-4 below.
}

------------------- **Cut here and give the certificate to your employer. Keep the top portion for your records.** -------------------

Form **W-4**
Department of the Treasury
Internal Revenue Service

Employee's Withholding Allowance Certificate
▶ **For Privacy Act and Paperwork Reduction Act Notice, see reverse.**

OMB No. 1545-0010
19**89**

1 Type or print your first name and middle initial	Last name	2 Your social security number

Home address (number and street or rural route) City or town, state, and ZIP code	3 Marital Status	☐ Single ☐ Married ☐ Married, but withhold at higher Single rate. **Note:** If married, but legally separated, or spouse is a nonresident alien, check the Single box.

4 Total number of allowances you are claiming (from line G above or from the Worksheets on back if they apply) . . . | **4** |

5 Additional amount, if any, you want deducted from each pay . . . . | **5** $ |

6 I claim exemption from withholding and I certify that I meet **ALL** of the following conditions for exemption:
- Last year I had a right to a refund of **ALL** Federal income tax withheld because I had **NO** tax liability; **AND**
- This year I expect a refund of **ALL** Federal income tax withheld because I expect to have **NO** tax liability; **AND**
- This year if my income exceeds $500 and includes nonwage income, another person cannot claim me as a dependent.

If you meet all of the above conditions, enter the year effective and "EXEMPT" here . . . . . ▶ | **6** | 19

7 Are you a full-time student? (**Note:** *Full-time students are not automatically exempt.*) . . . . | **7** ☐ Yes ☐ No

Under penalties of perjury, I certify that I am entitled to the number of withholding allowances claimed on this certificate or entitled to claim exempt status.

Employee's signature ▶ _____ **Date** ▶ _____ , 198___

8 Employer's name and address (**Employer:** Complete 8 and 10 **only if sending to IRS**)	9 Office code (optional)	10 Employer identification number

271

Deductions and Adjustments Worksheet

Note: *Use this worksheet only if you plan to itemize deductions or claim adjustments to income on your 1989 tax return.*

1. Enter an estimate of your 1989 itemized deductions. These include: qualifying home mortgage interest, 20% of personal interest, charitable contributions, state and local taxes (but not sales taxes), medical expenses in excess of 7.5% of your income, and miscellaneous deductions (most miscellaneous deductions are now deductible only in excess of 2% of your income) . . . . 1 $ _____

2. Enter: { $5,200 if married filing jointly or qualifying widow(er)
          $4,550 if head of household
          $3,100 if single
          $2,600 if married filing separately } . . . . 2 $ _____

3. **Subtract** line 2 from line 1. If line 2 is greater than line 1, enter zero . . . . 3 $ _____
4. Enter an estimate of your 1989 adjustments to income. These include alimony paid and deductible IRA contributions . . 4 $ _____
5. **Add** lines 3 and 4 and enter the total . . . . 5 $ _____
6. Enter an estimate of your 1989 nonwage income (such as dividends or interest income) . . . . . 6 $ _____
7. **Subtract** line 6 from line 5. Enter the result, but not less than zero . . . . 7 $ _____
8. **Divide** the amount on line 7 by $2,000 and enter the result here. Drop any fraction . . . . 8 _____
9. Enter the number from Personal Allowances Worksheet, line G, on page 1 . . . . 9 _____
10. **Add** lines 8 and 9 and enter the total here. If you plan to use the Two-Earner/Two-Job Worksheet, also enter the total on line 1, below. Otherwise, **stop here** and enter this total on Form W-4, line 4 on page 1 . . . . . 10 _____

Two-Earner/Two-Job Worksheet

Note: *Use this worksheet only if the instructions at line G on page 1 direct you here.*

1. Enter the number from line G on page 1 (or from line 10 above if you used the Deductions and Adjustments Worksheet) . 1 _____
2. Find the number in **Table 1** below that applies to the **LOWEST** paying job and enter it here . . . . . . 2 _____
3. If line 1 is **GREATER THAN OR EQUAL TO** line 2, subtract line 2 from line 1. Enter the result here (if zero, enter "0") and on Form W-4, line 4, on page 1. **DO NOT** use the rest of this worksheet. . . . . 3 _____

Note: *If line 1 is **LESS THAN** line 2, enter "0" on Form W-4, line 4, on page 1. Complete lines 4–9 to calculate the additional dollar withholding necessary to avoid a year-end tax bill.*

4. Enter the number from line 2 of this worksheet . . . . 4 _____
5. Enter the number from line 1 of this worksheet . . . . 5 _____
6. **Subtract** line 5 from line 4 . . . . 6 _____
7. Find the amount in **Table 2** below that applies to the **HIGHEST** paying job and enter it here . . . . . . 7 $ _____
8. **Multiply** line 7 by line 6 and enter the result here. This is the additional annual withholding amount needed 8 $ _____
9. Divide line 8 by the number of pay periods each year. (For example, divide by 26 if you are paid every other week.) Enter the result here and on Form W-4, line 5, page 1. This is the additional amount to be withheld from each paycheck . . . 9 $ _____

Table 1: Two-Earner/Two-Job Worksheet

Married Filing Jointly		All Others	
If wages from **LOWEST** paying job are—	Enter on line 2 above	If wages from **LOWEST** paying job are—	Enter on line 2 above
0 - $4,000	0	0 - $4,000	0
4,001 - 8,000	1	4,001 - 8,000	1
8,001 - 18,000	2	8,001 - 13,000	2
18,001 - 21,000	3	13,001 - 15,000	3
21,001 - 23,000	4	15,001 - 19,000	4
23,001 - 25,000	5	19,001 and over	5
25,001 - 27,000	6		
27,001 - 32,000	7		
32,001 - 38,000	8		
38,001 - 42,000	9		
42,001 and over	10		

Table 2: Two-Earner/Two-Job Worksheet

Married Filing Jointly		All Others	
If wages from **HIGHEST** paying job are—	Enter on line 7 above	If wages from **HIGHEST** paying job are—	Enter on line 7 above
0 - $40,000	$300	0 - $23,000	$300
40,001 - 84,000	560	23,001 - 50,000	560
84,001 and over	660	50,001 and over	660

Privacy Act and Paperwork Reduction Act Notice.—We ask for this information to carry out the Internal Revenue laws of the United States. We may give the information to the Department of Justice for civil or criminal litigation and to cities, states, and the District of Columbia for use in administering their tax laws. You are required to give this information to your employer.

The time needed to complete this form will vary depending on individual circumstances. The estimated average time is: **Recordkeeping** 46 mins., **Learning about the law or the form** 10 mins., **Preparing the form** 70 mins. If you have comments concerning the accuracy of these time estimates or suggestions for making this form more simple, we would be happy to hear from you. You can write to the **Internal Revenue Service,** Washington, DC 20224, Attention: IRS Reports Clearance Officer, TR:FP; or the **Office of Management and Budget,** Paperwork Reduction Project, Washington, DC 20503.

★U.S.GPO:1988-0-205-055

provision must renew their status by filing a new W-4 form by February 15 to continue that exemption.

You must file a new form with your employer within ten days from the time you expect to have income tax liability for the year and begin having tax withheld. If you are not having income tax withheld this year, but you expect to have income tax liability next year, you must file a new W-4 by December 1.

On the appropriate line of the W-4, employees may request additional income tax withheld. Ministers who elect to have their income taxes withheld need to list the amount of additional money to be withheld to cover expected self-employment social security taxes or other income.

Form 941: employer's
quarterly federal tax return

Once a congregation has received an employer identification number from the IRS, the congregation will automatically begin to receive form 941 each calendar quarter. (See form on pages 274 and 275.) These forms are to be used to report wages paid and taxes that the congregation has withheld and that are now owed for the quarter.

By the last day of the month following the end of each quarter, form 941 must be filed and all withholdings and taxes paid.

In general, as soon as the congregation owes more than five hundred dollars for employment taxes (withholding of income and social security taxes, plus the employer's share of social security taxes), the congregation must deposit that money in an authorized bank depository, probably the bank where the congregation has its checking account. A coupon booklet with tax forms for purposes of identifying various tax deposits will be sent by the IRS. The payment and properly marked coupon must be deposited promptly. In any event, form 941 is filed quarterly, and any balance due on taxes withheld is paid at that time—no balance due should exceed five hundred dollars.

On form 941 the following information is to be reported: Line 2: Total wages paid subject to withholding plus other compensation, including the taxable wages paid to the minister.

Line 3: Total income tax withheld from all wages.

Line 6: Total social security wages paid (this may not be the same amount of wages as reported on line 2) and the amount of tax due on those wages (employee and employer tax combined).

Line 11: Total payment due to IRS is the sum of income taxes withheld, social security taxes withheld, and social security taxes due from the employer.

Line 14: You must also report on form 941 any deposits made for accumulated withholdings and taxes due.

Line 15: Upon filing form 941, any taxes still due must be paid.

W-2 form
wage and tax statement

At the end of the calendar year, employers receive a quantity of employment tax forms from IRS. By January 31, each employee must be given a W-2 form showing any income taxes or social security taxes withheld. On the W-2 form will be the employer's name, address, zip code, and EIN; the employee's name, address, zip code, and social security number (SSN). Federal income taxes withheld are reported in box 9. All wages paid are reported in box 10. Social security taxes withheld are reported on box 11 (none for ministers). Social security wages paid (none for ministers) are reported in box 13.

On the minister's W-2 form, report salary paid (including any social security allowance and car allowance) in box 10. If federal income taxes are withheld, fill in box 9; otherwise leave it blank. Since

Form 941
(Rev. January 1989)
Department of the Treasury
Internal Revenue Service

Employer's Quarterly Federal Tax Return

4141   ▶ **For Paperwork Reduction Act Notice, see page 2.**
Please type or print.

Your name,
address,
employer
identification
number, and
calendar
quarter of
return.
(If not
correct,
please
change.)

Name (as distinguished from trade name)	Date quarter ended
Trade name, if any	Employer identification number
Address and ZIP code	

OMB No. 1545-0029
Expires: 5-31-91

| T |
| FF |
| FD |
| FP |
| I |
| T |

If address is
different from
prior return,
check here ▶ ☐

IRS Use

1 1 1 1 1 1 1 1 1 1 1   2   3 3 3 3 3 3   4 4 4

5 5 5   6   7   8 8 8 8 8   9 9 9   10 10 10 10 10 10 10 10 10 10

If you do not have to file returns in the future, check here . . . ▶ ☐   Date final wages paid . . . . ▶

If you are a seasonal employer, see **Seasonal employer** on page 2 and check here . . . ▶ ☐

1a Number of employees (except household) employed in the pay period that includes March 12th ▶	1a	
b If you are a subsidiary corporation AND your parent corporation files a consolidated Form 1120, enter parent corporation employer identification number (EIN) . . ▶ 1b –		
2 Total wages and tips subject to withholding, plus other compensation . . . . ▶	2	
3 Total income tax withheld from wages, tips, pensions, annuities, sick pay, gambling, etc. . . . ▶	3	
4 Adjustment of withheld income tax for preceding quarters of calendar year (see instructions) . . ▶	4	
5 Adjusted total of income tax withheld (see instructions)	5	
6 Taxable social security wages paid . . . . . $ _____ × 15.02% (.1502) .	6	
7a Taxable tips reported . . . . $ _____ × 15.02% (.1502) .	7a	
b Taxable hospital insurance wages paid . . . . $ _____ × 2.9% (.029). . .	7b	
8 Total social security taxes (add lines 6, 7a, and 7b)	8	
9 Adjustment of social security taxes (see instructions for required explanation)	9	
10 Adjusted total of social security taxes (see instructions) . . . . ▶	10	
11 Backup withholding (see instructions)	11	
12 Adjustment of backup withholding tax for preceding quarters of calendar year . . . . . ▶	12	
13 Adjusted total of backup withholding	13	
14 Total taxes (add lines 5, 10, and 13)	14	
15 Advance earned income credit (EIC) payments, if any . . . . ▶	15	
16 Net taxes (subtract line 15 from line 14). **This must equal line IV below** (plus line IV of Schedule A (Form 941) if you have treated backup withholding as a separate liability) . . . . . . ▶	16	
17 Total deposits for quarter, including overpayment applied from a prior quarter, from your records . ▶	17	
18 Balance due (subtract line 17 from line 16). This should be less than $500. Pay to IRS . . . ▶	18	
19 If line 17 is more than line 16, enter overpayment here ▶ $ _____ and check if to be:		

☐ Applied to next return   **OR**   ☐ Refunded.

Record of Federal Tax Liability (Complete if line 16 is $500 or more.) See the instructions on page 4 for details before checking these boxes.

Check only if you made eighth-monthly deposits using the 95% rule ▶ ☐   Check only if you are a first time 3-banking-day depositor ▶ ☐

Date wages paid	Show tax liability here, **not deposits.** IRS gets deposit data from FTD coupons.					
	First month of quarter		Second month of quarter		Third month of quarter	
▶ 1st through 3rd	A		I		Q	
4th through 7th	B		J		R	
8th through 11th	C		K		S	
12th through 15th	D		L		T	
16th through 19th	E		M		U	
20th through 22nd	F		N		V	
23rd through 25th	G		O		W	
26th through the last	H		P		X	
Total liability for month	I		II		III	

Do NOT Show Federal Tax Deposits Here

IV Total for quarter (add lines **I, II,** and **III**). **This must equal line 16 above** . . . . ▶

Sign Here

Under penalties of perjury, I declare that I have examined this return, including accompanying schedules and statements, and to the best of my knowledge and belief, it is true, correct, and complete.

Signature ▶   Title ▶   Date ▶

the congregation cannot withhold social security taxes from the minister's pay, boxes 11 and 13 for the minister are left blank on the W-2. Any state income tax withheld should be reported in the appropriate boxes.

Generally, the housing allowance is not reported on the W-2 form since it is excludable from taxable income. (Although some tax advisors suggest showing the housing allowance as a footnote on the W-2 in one of the empty boxes at the bottom. The note would indicate that the taxpayer is a minister and that the housing allowance is not subject to income tax.)

In box 16, report on the W-2 any congregational contributions to a pension plan for the minister that is classified as a 403(b) type plan. Contributions to an Individual Retirement Account made by the minister must be shown on the W-2 as part of gross income. And if an equity allowance is paid (for clergy in parsonages, for example), that, too, must appear on the Form W-2 if it is considered currently subject to income tax. If the equity allowance contribution is to be a tax-sheltered plan of some sort, then it would appear in box 16 on the W-2. The minister's W-2 form should also show any other taxable income paid to the minister by the church, such as a taxable Christmas gift or other bonus.

W-2 form: wage and tax statement

W-3 form transmittal of income and tax statements

The congregation must file the W-3 form to transmit all its W-2 forms to IRS. The annual Federal Employment Tax Forms packet sent to all employers includes the necessary W-3 forms.

The purpose of the W-3 form is to summarize for the IRS the number of W-2's being transmitted. Required information includes the name, address, zip code, and EIN of the employer; the number of W-2's being transmitted; total amount of federal income tax, wages, and social security tax withheld; and social security wages reported on all of the W-2's.

A W-3 form and all attached W-2's must be submitted to your nearest Social Security Administration Center by February 28. No money is sent with the W-3.

275

DO NOT STAPLE

1 Control number	33333	For Official Use Only ▶ OMB No. 1545-0008			

☐ Kind of Payer ▶	2 941/941E ☐ Military ☐ 943 ☐ CT-1 ☐ 942 ☐ Medicare gov't. emp. ☐	3	4	5 Total number of statements

6 Allocated tips	7 Advance EIC payments	8 Establishment number
9 Federal income tax withheld	10 Wages, tips, and other compensation	11 Social security tax withheld
12 Employer's state I.D. number	13 Social security wages	14 Social security tips
15 Employer's identification number		16 Other EIN used this year
17 Employer's name		18 Gross annuity, pension, etc. (Form W-2P)
		20 Taxable amount (Form W-2P)
		21 Income tax withheld by third-party payer
19 Employer's address and ZIP code (If available, place label over boxes 15, 17, and 19.)		

Under penalties of perjury, I declare that I have examined this return and accompanying documents, and to the best of my knowledge and belief they are true, correct, and complete.

Signature ▶ _____   Title ▶ _____   Date ▶ _____

Telephone number (optional)_____

Form W-3 Transmittal of Income and Tax Statements 1989

Department of the Treasury
Internal Revenue Service

Please return this entire page with the accompanying Forms W-2 or W-2P to the Social Security Administration address for your state as listed below. **Household employers filing Forms W-2 for household employees should send the forms to the Albuquerque Data Operations Center.** Note: Extra postage may be necessary if the report you send contains more than a few pages or if the envelope is larger than letter size. Do NOT order forms from the addresses listed below. You may order forms by calling 1-800-424-FORM (3676).

If your legal residence, principal place of business, office or agency is located in ▼	Use this address ▼
Alaska, Arizona, California, Colorado, Hawaii, Idaho, Iowa, Minnesota, Missouri, Montana, Nebraska, Nevada, North Dakota, Oregon, South Dakota, Utah, Washington, Wisconsin, Wyoming	Social Security Administration Salinas Data Operations Center Salinas, CA 93911
Alabama, Arkansas, Florida, Georgia, Illinois, Kansas, Louisiana, Mississippi, New Mexico, Oklahoma, South Carolina, Tennessee, Texas	Social Security Administration Albuquerque Data Operations Center Albuquerque, NM 87180
Connecticut, Delaware, District of Columbia, Indiana, Kentucky, Maine, Maryland, Massachusetts, Michigan, New Hampshire, New Jersey, New York, North Carolina, Ohio, Pennsylvania, Rhode Island, Vermont, Virginia, West Virginia	Social Security Administration Wilkes-Barre Data Operations Center Wilkes-Barre, PA 18769
If you have no legal residence or principal place of business in any state	Social Security Administration Wilkes-Barre Data Operations Center Wilkes-Barre, PA 18769

Paperwork Reduction Act Notice.—We ask for this information to carry out the Internal Revenue laws of the United States. We need it to ensure that taxpayers are complying with these laws and to allow us to figure and collect the right amount of tax. You are required to give us this information.

The time needed to complete and file this form will vary depending on individual circumstances.

The estimated average time is 25 minutes. If you have comments concerning the accuracy of this time estimate or suggestions for making this form more simple, we would be happy to hear from you. You can write to the **Internal Revenue Service,** Washington, DC 20224, Attention: IRS Reports Clearance Officer TR:FP; or the **Office of Management and Budget,** Paperwork Reduction Project (1545-0008), Washington, DC 20503.

276

PAYROLL RECORD   *Employee's payroll record*

Employee's name _____

Social Security Number _____

Address _____

Date of W-4 Form _____ Exemption allowances ____

Additional income tax to be withheld $_____

Is employee exempt from income tax withholding? _____

Rates: Hourly $_____ Weekly $_____ Monthly $_____

	Gross Pay	Income Tax Withheld	FICA Tax Withheld	Other Withholding	Check Amount
Jan.					
Feb.					
Mar.					
First Qrt.					
Apr.					
May					
June					
Second Qrt.					
July					
Aug.					
Sept.					
Third Qrt.					
Oct.					
Nov.					
Dec.					
Fourth Qrt					
Total					

Form 1099 and form 1096

If more than six hundred dollars is paid to any independent contractor, then Form 1099-MISC, "Statement for Recipients of Miscellaneous Income," must be completed. So, for example, if the custodian is an independent contractor, form 1099 is appropriate. Ministers who claim to be self-employed for income tax purposes also receive form 1099. The organist, yard person, or anyone else to whom at least six hundred dollars is paid (and who is not an employee for whom income and social security taxes are withheld), must receive form 1099.

Then, form 1096 (shown on page 280), "Annual Summary and Transmittal of U.S. Information Returns" must also be filed. Copy B of all 1099's that have been issued are to be transmitted with 1096.

Form 1099: statement
for recipients of miscellaneous income

9595 ☐ VOID ☐ CORRECTED	For Official Use Only	
Type or machine print PAYER'S name, street address, city, state, and ZIP code	1 Rents $	OMB No. 1545-0115 **1989** Statement for Recipients of	**Miscellaneous Income**
	2 Royalties $		
PAYER'S Federal identification number / RECIPIENT'S identification number	3 Prizes and awards $	4 Federal income tax withheld $	**Copy A For Internal Revenue Service Center**
Type or machine print RECIPIENT'S name (first, middle, last)	5 Fishing boat proceeds $	6 Medical and health care payments $	For Paperwork Reduction Act Notice and instructions for completing this form, see Instructions for Forms 1099, 1098, 5498, 1096, and W-2G.
Street address	7 Nonemployee compensation $	8 Substitute payments in lieu of dividends or interest $	
City, state, and ZIP code	9 Payer made direct sales of $5,000 or more of consumer products to a buyer (recipient) for resale . . . . ▶ ☐		
Account number (optional)	10 Crop insurance proceeds $		

Form **1099-MISC**   Do NOT Cut or Separate Forms on This Page   Department of the Treasury - Internal Revenue Service

Tax on Unrelated Business Income

Until 1976, churches did not pay any taxes on any of their income, no matter what the source. But in tax legislation of 1970, it was voted to tax the income churches earned in certain circumstances. Such tax was called an income tax on the unrelated business income of the church.

Generally, the income of a church is taxable under only two conditions: (1) when income is derived from a business that is regularly carried on and the conduct of which does not have a substantial causal relationship—other than the mere production of income—to the achievements of the purpose for which the church was granted its tax exemption in the first place; and (2) when income is produced by debt-financed property.

The rules are complicated and there are exceptions to many of them. However, most churches need not be concerned about this matter since few churches would have unrelated business income under the definitions set forth in the law. Furthermore, churches are exempt from filing a 990 form to report their income unless they do have unrelated business income.

Exceptions and exemptions to the general rules:

Passive income is not considered income from the conduct of a business and thus generally not taxable. This would include income from dividends, interest, annuities, royalties, rents from real

278

DO NOT STAPLE   6969   ☐ CORRECTED

| Form **1096**
Department of the Treasury
Internal Revenue Service | **Annual Summary and Transmittal of
U.S. Information Returns** | OMB No. 1545-0108
19**89** |

┌ Type or machine print FILER'S name (or attach label)   ┐

    Street address   **PLACE LABEL HERE**

    City, state, and ZIP code

└   ┘

| If you are not using a preprinted label, enter in Box 1 or 2 below the identification number you used as the filer on the information returns being transmitted. Do not fill in both Boxes 1 and 2. | Name of person to contact if IRS needs more information

Telephone number
( ) | **For Official Use Only**
☐☐☐☐☐☐☐ ☐☐ |

1 Employer identification number	2 Social security number	3 Total number of documents	4 Federal income tax withheld $	5 Total amount reported with this Form 1096 $

Check only one box below to indicate the type of forms being transmitted.   If this is your FINAL return, check here . . . . . ☐

☐	☐	☐	☐	☐	☐	☐	☐	☐	☐	☐	☐	☐
W-2G 32	1098 81	1099-A 80	1099-B 79	1099-DIV 91	1099-G 86	1099-INT 92	1099-MISC 95	1099-OID 96	1099-PATR 97	1099-R 98	1099-S 75	5498 28

Under penalties of perjury, I declare that I have examined this return and accompanying documents and, to the best of my knowledge and belief, they are true, correct, and complete.

Signature ▶ ....   Title ▶ ....   Date ▶ ....

Please return this entire page to the Internal Revenue Service. Photocopies are NOT acceptable.

Instructions

Purpose of Form.—Use this form to transmit Forms W-2G, 1098, 1099, and 5498 to the Internal Revenue Service.

Completing Form 1096.—If you received a preprinted label from IRS with Package 1099, place the label in the name and address area of this form inside the brackets. Make any necessary corrections to your name and address on the label. However, do not use the label if the taxpayer identification number (TIN) shown is incorrect. If you are not using a preprinted label, enter the filer's name, address, and TIN in the spaces provided on the form. **The name, address, and TIN you enter on this form must be the same as those you enter in the upper left area of Form 1099, 1098, 5498, or W-2G.** A filer includes a payer, a recipient of mortgage interest payments, a broker, a barter exchange, a person reporting real estate transactions, a trustee or issuer of an individual retirement arrangement (including an IRA or SEP), and a lender who acquires an interest in secured property or who has reason to know that the property has been abandoned. Individuals not in a trade or business should enter their social security number in Box 2; sole proprietors and all others should enter their employer identification number in Box 1. However, sole proprietors who are not required to have an employer identification number should enter their social security number in Box 2.

Group the forms by form number and submit each group with a separate Form 1096. For example, if you must file both Forms 1098 and Forms 1099-A, complete one Form 1096 to transmit your Forms 1098 and another Form 1096 to transmit your Forms 1099-A.

In Box 3, enter the number of forms you are transmitting with this Form 1096. Do not include blank or voided forms in your total. Enter the number of correctly completed forms, not the number of pages, being transmitted. For example, if you send one page of three-to-a-page Forms 5498 with a Form 1096 and you have correctly completed two Forms 5498 on that page, enter 2 in Box 3 of Form 1096. Check the appropriate box to indicate the type of form you are transmitting.

No entry is required in Box 5 if you are filing Form 1099-A or 1099-G. For all other forms, enter in Box 5 of Form 1096 the total of the amounts from the specific boxes of the forms listed below:

Form W-2G	Box 1
Form 1098	Box 1
Form 1099-B	Boxes 2, 3, and 6
Form 1099-DIV	Boxes 1a, 5, and 6
Form 1099-INT	Boxes 1 and 3
Form 1099-MISC	Boxes 1, 2, 3, 5, 6, 7, 8, and 10
Form 1099-OID	Boxes 1 and 2
Form 1099-PATR	Boxes 1, 2, 3, and 5
Form 1099-R	Boxes 1 and 8
Form 1099-S	Box 2
Form 5498	Boxes 1 and 2

If you will not be filing Forms 1099, 1098, 5498, or W-2G in the future, either on paper or on magnetic media, please check the "FINAL return" box.

If you are filing a Form 1096 for corrected information returns, enter an "X" in the CORRECTED box at the top of this form.

For more information about filing, see the separate Instructions for Forms 1099, 1098, 5498, 1096, and W-2G.

For Paperwork Reduction Act Notice, see separate Instructions for Forms 1099, 1098, 5498, 1096, and W-2G.   Form **1096** (1989)

property, and gains on the sale of property—provided none of that property is being held for sale to customers who are in business. Nevertheless, any of this kind of income received from debt-financed property (you borrowed money to secure the asset) would be taxable (but read on for some exceptions).

Furthermore, if the income previously described comes from a corporation controlled by the church and that corporation is not tax exempt, the income would probably be taxable. This rule prevents a church from setting up a corporation for the purpose of running a business and paying no tax on the profits.

Substantially related business activities that are highly successful commercial enterprises (the income of which contributes substantially to the tax exempt purposes of the church) is not taxable income, generally. This would include the (1) sale of religious mementos and all printed religious materials; (2) sponsorship of religious tours to the Holy Land; (3) operation of an exempt gift shop in a hospital; and (4) the operation of a parking lot for use by patients of a hospital, or churchgoers.

Volunteer labor that produces income does not subject the church to tax on that income. When all of the work on a project, bazaar, activity, or products for sale is done substantially by volunteers, the resulting income is exempt from tax.

However, some volunteers may be paid anyway by being reimbursed for expenses, and by receiving room and board, etc. Such reimbursements, says the IRS, could constitute compensation and thus remove such persons from the volunteer status. Too many nonvolunteers involved in a money-making project will change the status of that income from excludable to taxable.

Donated merchandise when sold by the church does not generally create taxable income. If nearly all of that sold has been donated, then no tax is due on any of the sales.

Business for convenience of members does not produce taxable income, generally. Examples would be the thrift shop in a hospital or a parking lot for the benefit of churchgoers, even if a fee is charged. If the general public is urged to use the facilities, the business becomes taxable.

Infrequent fund-raising activities can produce nontaxable income. The income tax on unrelated business income refers to profits from a commercial activity regularly carried on by the church. Here are three kinds of infrequent activities:

1. Infrequent activities are not regular business activities, such as an annual bazaar, carnival, or dinner-dance. The Tax Reform Act of 1984 exempted games of chance (such as bingo) from the unrelated business income tax even though such games may be carried on on a regular basis.

2. Some regular activities considered irregular are the food stand at the local fair for two weeks. But a summer conference grounds available to the public is a regular business, making its income taxable.

3. Some regular activities do not produce taxable income because they are conducted without competitive and promotional efforts that an identical commercial firm might use. Thus, the sale of a tract of real estate long ago secured through a gift or otherwise (but not debt-financed) is sold off in parcels without promotion and without the assistance of a real estate person or advertising. Such sales are not taxable income.

Other exemptions include the income derived from the operation of a cemetery used exclusively for members, a sale of trinkets to raise funds, etc. Thus, income derived from a commercial activity not specifically exempt under the considerations listed above would be taxable as follows.

Some common taxable income producing activities

Advertising in church bulletins, newsletters, and annual reports is a business activity that is subject to income tax. Sometimes the income may not be taxable if it is not a regular activity, or if all the work performed is by volunteers, or if the activity is substantially related to the exempt status of the church. Furthermore, a tax is imposed when these exemptions do not apply but only if the advertising and the publication that the advertising appears in are profitable.

Crop-sharing arrangements on leased farm land where crops are shared rather than cash rent paid, will be taxable, depending on the degree of involvement in the decision-making on farming procedures by the congregation. The less involvement in management, the more likely no tax is due.

Mineral income would be taxable if the church has a working interest, rather than just a royalty interest in production.

Parking lot/garage income is, as previously stated, probably taxable income if the facility is not staffed by volunteers and is not used exclusively for the convenience of the church members. Regular operation creates taxable income.

Rental income from personal property income is taxable unless the rental income contributes strongly to the tax exempt purpose of the church.

Rental income from real estate is taxable if the property (1) is purchased with borrowed money; (2) is obtained by leasing property to a controlled corporation, and (3) rent is determined by some percentage of net income or profits of the person leasing the property. Income from the rental of a residence is income from real estate rental, but income from the use of space where a service is also provided (garages, warehouse, hotels) is not income from real property and will be considered as taxable income from compensation paid.

Keep in mind that any net profit derived from the use of the borrowed funds to purchase an investment is generally fully taxable income.

Congregations who owe the unrelated business tax should complete a form 990.

Other Taxes

Unemployment compensation tax

Federal and state laws impose unemployment taxes on most employers in order to finance the costs of unemployment benefits. However, The Federal Unemployment Tax Act (FUTA) generally exempts services performed for a religious organization. Thus churches do not pay this tax nor are church employees eligible for unemployment compensation payments.

Worker's compensation

Most states require that all employers provide a worker's compensation insurance plan (unless the plan is supported with a state tax). In some states, churches are exempt from such coverage. Nevertheless, it is important that churches consider worker's compensation insurance, especially if the law so requires, but also to provide payment to any employee injured while on the church's business.

State sales tax

In most states, religious organizations are exempt from paying any sales tax on merchandise purchased for use by the church in its program. Often, however, a state does require that an exemption number be secured.

Property taxes

The local property tax assessor/collector will determine, based on state law, whether the church's property should be exempt from the real estate taxes. In most states the majority of church buildings are exempt. In some states the parsonage is also exempt. But in many states, real estate property owned by the church is taxable unless it is used specifically for worship or the residence of the minister. An empty lot held for the purposes of building a new church building may indeed require the payment of a property tax.

Ditzen, Lowell Russell. *Handbook of Church Administration.* New York: Macmillan, 1962.

Espie, John C. *Handbook for Local Church Financial Record System.* Nashville: Abingdon Press, 1977.

Gray, Robert N. *Managing the Church: Business Methods and Church Administration.* Austin, Tex.: Church Management, Inc., 1971.

Gross, Malvern J., Jr. and William Warshauer. *Financial and Accounting Guide for Nonprofit Organizations,* 3rd ed. New York: Ronald Press, 1983.

Hammar, Richard R. *Pastor, Church and Law.* Springfield, Mo.: Gospel Publishing House, 1983.

Holck, Manfred, Jr. *Accounting Methods for the Small Church.* Minneapolis: Augsburg Publishing House, 1966.

———. *Annual Budgeting.* Minneapolis: Augsburg Publishing House, 1977.

———. *Cash Management.* Minneapolis: Augsburg Publishing House, 1978.

———. *Church Finance in a Complex Economy.* Nashville: Abingdon Press, 1983.

———. *Complete Handbook of Church Accounting.* Englewood Cliffs, N.J.: Prentice-Hall, 1978.

———. *Money and Your Church.* New Cannan, Conn.: Keats Publishing Co., 1974.

Hopkins, Bruce R. *The Law of Tax-Exempt Organizations,* 3rd ed. New York: Ronald Press, 1979.

Leach, William H. *Handbook of Church Management.* Englewood Cliffs, N.J.: Prentice-Hall, 1958.

McCormally, Kevin, ed. *How to Get More for Your Money.* Washington, D.C.: The Kiplinger Washington Editors, Inc., 1981.

Montana, Patrick J. and Diane Borst, eds. *Managing Non-profit Organizations.* New York: American Management Association, 1979.

Myers, Marvin. *Managing the Business Affairs of the Church.* Nashville: The Sunday School Board of the Southern Baptist Convention, 1981.

Olenick, Arnold J. and Phil Olenick, eds. *Making the Non-Profit Organization Work.* Englewood Cliffs, N.J.: Institute for Business Planning, 1983.

Rieke, Thomas C. and John C. Espie. *Opportunities in Stewardship.* Nashville: Discipleship Resources-Tidings, 1975.

Rudge, Peter F. *Management in the Church.* New York: McGraw-Hill, 1976.